*Charles Bronson*

# Charles Bronson

## *The 95 Films and the 156 Television Appearances*

*by* Michael R. Pitts

McFarland & Company, Inc., Publishers
*Jefferson, North Carolina, and London*

## ALSO BY MICHAEL R. PITTS

*Poverty Row Studios, 1929–1940: An Illustrated History of 55 Independent Film Companies, with a Filmography for Each*
(McFarland, 1997)

*Western Movies: A TV and Video Guide to 4200 Genre Films*
(McFarland, 1986; paperback, 1997)

*Hollywood and American History: A Filmography of Over 250 Motion Pictures Depicting U.S. History*
(McFarland, 1984)

*Horror Film Stars*
(McFarland, 1981; second edition, 1991)

**Frontispiece: Charles Bronson in *Death Hunt* (20th Century–Fox, 1981)**

**Library of Congress Cataloguing-in-Publication Data**

Pitts, Michael R.
Charles Bronson : the 95 films and the 156 television appearances / by Michael R. Pitts.
p. cm.
Includes bibliographical references and index.

**ISBN-13: 978-0-7864-1702-5**
(softcover : 50# alkaline paper) ♾

1. Bronson, Charles, 1920– . I. Title.
PN2287.B693P58 2003
791.43'028'092—DC21 99-31430
CIP

British Library Cataloguing-in-Publication data are available



Manufactured in the United States of America

*McFarland & Company, Inc., Publishers*
*Box 611, Jefferson, North Carolina 28640*
*www.mcfarlandpub.com*

For Carolyn and Angela

# Acknowledgments

I would like to thank the following for their help in the preparation of this volume: Bertil Lundgren, Jim Meyer, Ray White, James Robert Parish, Bob Reed, Gary Kramer, Richard Bojarski, The Library of Congress Motion Picture, Broadcasting and Recorded Sound Division (Madeline F. Matz, Edwin M. Matthais), the Carnegie Library of Pittsburgh (Paula Kepich, Mary W. Remmel), Buck Rainey, David Rothel, Mrs. Tim (Berdee) Holt, Laura Gwaltney, Andreas Hoppe, Peggy Stewart, and Vincent Terrace.

# Contents

# Introduction

Charles Bronson is a very private man. This book does not involve itself with his private life but instead takes a detailed look at the public Charles Bronson, the actor beloved by millions worldwide for his motion picture and television appearances. Anyone looking for biographical material should read some of the unauthorized biographies listed in this book's bibliography or the volumes written by his late wife, Jill Ireland, *Life Wish* and *Life Lines*.

For the record: The actor was born Charles Dennis Buchinsky in Ehrenfeld, Pennsylvania, on November 3, 1921. Ehrenfeld, also called Scooptown, is located in a coal mining area in Cambria County, Croyle Township. Charles was the fifth son in 15 children born to Walter and Mary (Valinsky) Buchinsky. Walter Buchinsky, a Lithuanian who had been in the Russian Czar's army, migrated to the United States in 1906. Unable to read or write (although his wife could do both), he worked in the coal mines, dying in 1933.

Charles graduated from high school in 1939, the first member of his family to do so. He worked in the coal mine office and later in the mines before being drafted into World War II in 1943. After the war he went East and became involved in theatre work, eventually appearing in the play *The Night of January 16* in Manhattan in 1948. It is possible he may have appeared also in early live television in Gotham, although no record of such work exists. He married Harriet Tendler on September 30, 1949, in Atlantic City, New Jersey, and they moved to California, where he enrolled in the Pasadena Playhouse. Less than a year later he won a part in the feature film *U.S.S. Teakettle (You're in the Navy Now)*, released late in 1951, and the next year he began working in network television dramas. He may also have done radio work, but the Library of Congress does not have any listings of him in this medium.

Bronson's innate talent is readily apparent even in his earliest screen and television work. Unlike other performers whose early work sometimes shows unsteady foundations for their later success, Charles Bronson appears to have always had the talent and ability that eventually made him an international favorite. Veterans Administration aptitude tests taken after his Army discharge in 1946 had shown that Bronson rated high in the field of creative arts, and no doubt his ability translated into his ease in becoming an actor. One only has to look at one of his early television roles, such as the sympathetic doctor in the "My Brother Joe" episode of *Medic* in 1954, to see that the talent was always there, not an affectation but the true ability to translate a character to film.

As the 1950s progressed, Charles Bronson—who used the name Charles Buchinsky or Buchinski until 1954—worked in movies and television, slowly but steadily climbing the ladder of success. He soon became known as a reliable and talented actor and there were few lulls in his career. He actually became a star in 1958 with a quartet of "B" movies (*Machine Gun Kelly, Gang War, Showdown at Boot Hill, When Hell Broke Loose*) and the next year he headlined his first television series, *Man with a Camera*. By the early 1960s he was considered one of Hollywood's most solid character actors. No less an authority on acting than Charles Laughton noted of Bronson that he "has the strongest face in the business, and he is also one of its best actors."

For most of the 1960s Charles Bronson's career was in the pattern of co-starring in films, some blockbusters like *The Magnificent Seven* (1960), *The Great Escape* (1963) and *The Dirty Dozen* (1967); being called in to try to save television series (*Empire* [1963] and *The Travels of Jaimie McPheeters* [1963–64]); and performing diverse guest roles in television programs. A series of events, however, led the change from character actor to international star by the end of the decade. In 1962 Paul Kohner became his agent, and he began to have a cult following in France following the belated release there of *Machine Gun Kelly* (1958) plus showings of *Guns of Diablo* (1964) and *This Rugged Land* (1965), which had come from U.S. television programs. In 1965 his first marriage ended; he married actress Jill Ireland three years later. By that time he had scored a sensation in France co-starring with Alain Delon in *Adieu l'Ami* (1968), and the next year he was even bigger in Sergio Leone's *C'Era una Volta il West (Once Upon a Time in the West)*. Sporting a mustache and modish clothes, Charles Bronson became an international star in *La Passager de la Pluie* in 1969, and two years later he was voted the most popular film star in the world.

In the past three decades, Charles Bronson has headlined over forty feature films which made hundreds of millions of dollars worldwide. During that time he grew from an international film star to a cultural icon. Perhaps no other actor has known such worldwide popularity as Bronson. Whether in the Orient, South America (where he was voted the world's sexiest man), Europe, Australia or the United States, Charles Bronson became a larger-than-life character. In his homeland in particular, where stardom did not come until the early 1970s, he has taken on major heroic status through his *Death Wish* movies. Watching the character of Paul Kersey, the sidewalk vigilante, in action, Americans found cathartic release from their fears of moral disintegration and international setbacks. In Charles Bronson, and the characters he played, Americans had a hero who could overcome society's adversities and yet retain his self-respect. The extent to which he has become a part of our cultural heritage is reflected in the way his name crops up in various contexts, such as the book title *Charles Bronson, Samurai, and Other Feminine Images: A Transitive Response to the Left Hand of Darkness* by Marleen S. Barr (Bowling Green State University Popular Press, 1981), and the 1995 Columbia feature film *Un Día en Bogotá con Charles Bronson* (A Day in Bogota with Charles Bronson), in which a young actor tries to emulate Bronson's macho image.

Perhaps no actor has been more demeaned by the critics and loved by the public than Charles Bronson. Critics, especially the effete clique so horrified by his vigilante characterizations, have long lambasted Bronson for the violence in his features and for being "the great stone face." Violence, of course, is a reflection of the times, not a product of Charles Bronson and his movies, and as an actor Bronson has a long and very successful history of underplaying his roles. Anyone can roll his eyes, mumble a few words and stare off into space. It takes real talent to convey emotion economically, and this is something at which Charles Bronson has always excelled.

Today Charles Bronson has reached a career pinnacle few others have attained. Well into his seventies, he continues to make the type of action films which have endeared him to millions the world over. The image of the great film hero still lives in the characterizations popularized by Bronson. In France he was *Le Sacre Monstre* (The Holy Monster) and in Italy *Il Brutto* (The Ugly One), but whatever the moniker he remains one of the most enigmatic yet universally endearing of all film stars.

While one may view a Charles Bronson movie for thrills and action, it is also clearly evident that along with his immense popularity, he is truly a very fine actor.

Michael R. Pitts
*Spring 1999*

# The Films

The following text abbreviations are used in the film credits—**P:** Producer; **EP:** Executive Producer; **AP:** Associate Producer; **D:** Director; **Sc:** Script; **St:** Story; **Ph:** Photography; **Ed:** Editor; **Mus:** Music; **AD:** Art Director; **Asst Dir:** Assistant Director; **Sd:** Sound; **Sp Eff:** Special Effects; **Asst:** Assistant; **Supv:** Supervisor; **Prod:** Production; **Mgr:** Manager.

## *Act of Vengeance* (Lorimar/Telepictures, 1986) 96 minutes Color

*P:* Jack Clements & Iris Sawyer. *EP:* Frank Konigsberg & Larry Sanitsky. *AP:* Barry Jossen & Jules Schwerin. *D:* Jack Mackenzie. *Sc:* Scott Spencer, from the book by Trevor Armbrister. *Ph:* Phil Meheux. *Ed:* Stephen Singleton & Michael Cooke. *Mus:* Frankie Miller. *AD:* Dave Davis. *Prod Design:* Phil Jeffries. *Costume Design:* Linda Kemp. *Casting:* Mary Colquhoun. *Canada Casting:* Stuart Aikins. *Makeup:* Suzanne Benoit. *Hairstylist:* James D. Brown. *Asst Dir:* Ian Madden, Louise Casselman & Andrew Shea. *Camera Operator:* Andy Chmura. *Prod Mgr:* David Coatsworth. *Prod Coordinator:* Debbie Cooke. *Set Decorators:* Anthony Greco & Gustave Meunier. *Prod Sd Mixer:* Bryan Day. *Mus Ed:* Dan Garde. *Re-recording Mixers:* John "Doc" Wilkinson, Grover B. Helsley & Richard D. Rogers. *Supv Sd Ed:* Marvin Walowitz & Karen Wilson. *Sc Supv:* Penelope Hynam. *Transportation Coordinator:* Fred Ionson. *Boom Operator:* Michael La Croix. *Sp Eff:* Martin Malivoire. *Stunt Coordinator:* Dwayne McLean. *Stunts:* Shane Cordell, Rick Forsaythe, Terry McGaverin, Dwayne McLean, Bill Myers & John Stoneham. *Property Master:* Don Miloyevich. *Asst Property Master:* Vic Rigler. *Key Grip:* Andrew Mulkani. *Location Mgr:* Howard Rothschild. *Gaffer:* Jim Wright. *Wardrobe Mistress:* Madeline Stewart. *Asst Wardrobe:* D. Graham Doherty. *Prod Accountant:* Joanne Jackson. *Extra Casting:* Allsorts. *Titles:* Howard A. Anderson Company. *Prod Secretary:* Janet Damp. *Film Clips:* Ken Cramer. *Additional Music:* John Altman. *Asst Ed—United Kingdom:* Anthony Morris. *Asst Ed—U.S.:* Paul Anderson. *Asst Ed—Toronto:* Lee Searles. *ADR Ed:* Becky Sullivan. *ADR Casting:* Barbara Harris. *Sd Re-recording:* Ryder Sound Service.

**CAST:** Charles Bronson (Jock Yablonski), Ellen Burstyn (Margaret "Peg" Yablonski), Wilford Brimley (Tony Boyle), Hoyt Axton (Silous Huddleston), Robert Schenkkan (Paul Gilly), Ellen Barkin (Annette Gilly), Joseph Kell (Chip Yablonski), Alf (Humphries) Humphreys (Ken Yablonski), Maury Chaykin (Claude Vealey), Caroline Kava

(Charlotte Yablonski), Peg Murray (Ellen Rogers), William Newman (Ezra Morgan), Alan North (Albert Pass), Raynor Scheine (Terrance Madden), Tom Harvey (Warren Alexander), Ken Pogue (Earl Skidmore), Keanu Reeves (Buddy Martin), Marc Strange (Pete), Chuck Shamata (Millard Atler), Gordon Allen (Voice in Crowd), Jan Austin (Shirley #1), James Bearden (William Prater), Christopher Benson (Poll Watcher), Peter Colvey (Young Miner), Don Daynard (Newscaster), Ferne Downey (Reporter), Erin Flannery (Erin Skidmore), Angie Gei (Jean Green), Pam Hyatt (Gloria Fischer), Robyn Jaffe (Wanda), Jack Jessop (Thomas Peterson), Gordon Jocelyn (Bartender), Audrei Kairen (Singer), Derek Keurvorst, John MacMaster, Phil Rash, Stephen Walsh (Reporters), Elena Kudaba (Martha), Arlene Mazerolle (Young Woman), Paul McCallum (Billy), Danny Pawlick (Gary Skidmore), Jan Schoettle (Shirley #2), Scott Spencer (Minister), Karen Woolridge (Melanie), Gordon Woolvett (Bobby).

The 1969 Yuletide murders of United Mine Workers labor leader Joseph (Jock) Yablonski, his wife and daughter made headlines and the ensuing investigation brought down Tony Boyle, the man who had just defeated Yablonski for another four year term as the union's president. Subsequently it was proved that Boyle had hired three men to kill Yablonski and his family with the trio and Boyle being convicted of first degree murder. Boyle died in prison in 1985. This original Home Box Office (HBO) film recreated the events leading up to the murders and their aftermath. It zeroed in on the rivalry between Boyle and Yablonski, union corruption and the trio hired to kill Yablonski. Unfortunately too much screen time was given to the killers instead of other far more historically interesting aspects of the drama. Made

**Charles Bronson and Ellen Burstyn in *Act of Vengeance* (Lorimar/Telepictures, 1986).**

on a $4 million budget, *Act of Vengeance* was Charles Bronson's first TV movie since *Raid on Entebbe* in 1978. It premiered on HBO on April 20, 1986, and then was issued theatrically abroad.

Filmed in Toronto, Canada, and Pittsburgh, Pennsylvania, the drama is billed as "A True Story." It opens in Clarksville, Pennsylvania, in 1968 at a family birthday celebration for Jock Yablonski (Charles Bronson) and then switches to a small coal mining town in West Virginia where 80 men die after being trapped in a mine explosion. Yablonski, an executive with the United Mine Workers Union of America, becomes upset with union president Tony Boyle (Wilford Brimley) when the latter fails to blame the mine owners for the tragedy. He also does not like it when Boyle asks him to lie about missing money from the union's pension fund. Upon the urging of his wife Margaret (Ellen Burstyn), and after a showdown with Boyle, Yablonski announces he will oppose Boyle for the presidency of the union in the upcoming election. When he hears the news of Yablonski's opposition, Boyle is told by ally Albert Pass (Alan North) that if Jock wins they will all go to jail. Starting his campaign, Yablonski goes to the rank and file miners for support while Boyle caters to the higher echelon of the union. When he hears Yablonski promise to put him in jail for crimes against the union, Boyle calls Pass and orders a hit on his opponent. Pass goes to local union leader Silous Huddleston (Hoyt Axton) who hires out the job to Paul Gilly (Robert Schenkkan), who is married to Silous' promiscuous daughter Annette (Ellen Barkin), who uses sex to convince her husband to carry out the hit. During the campaign, tactics get dirty and Jock is physically attacked while greeting miners but with the aid of his sons Chip (Joseph Kell) and Ken (Alf Humphries) vows to continue the fight although his longtime aid Ezra Morgan (William Newman) drops out of the campaign. One of Gilly's cohorts, Claude Vealey (Maury Chaykin), attempts to kill Yablonski but gets cold feet and runs away. Just before the election Yablonski's daughter Charlotte (Caroline Kava) tells her mother she is scared for the family's safety. The night of the election Yablonski learns that Boyle has fixed the race but vows to continue the fight. When Boyle learns Yablonski intends to contest the election he re-orders the hit on his opponent. Meanwhile Ezra comes to Yablonski with proof that Boyle fixed the election returns in his district. That night Gilly, Vealey and a third man, Buddy Martin (Keanu Reeves), sneak into the Yablonski house and murder Jock, Margaret and Charlotte in their sleep. Following the murders, the Yablonski sons enlist the aid of union members in getting justice and bringing back honesty to the United Mine Workers.

Working without his mustache for the first time since *Hard Times* (1975), Charles Bronson gave a fine performance as Jock Yablonski, deftly bringing out the integrity and dignity of the character, who was loyal to his family and his beliefs. Ellen Burstyn brings strength to the role of Margaret

Yablonski and Wilford Brimley, who had appeared in such Bronson features as *Borderline* (1980) and *10 to Midnight* (1983), was excellent as the foul-mouthed, corrupt and evil Tony Boyle, the man to whom John L. Lewis gave control of the United Mine Workers. Country singer Hoyt Axton had only a small role as the union man who set up the murders; in real life this character died of black lung disease. Ellen Barkin was good as Axton's slut daughter, as was Maury Chaykin as the neurotic hired killer. Future star Keanu Reeves played the third killer, the character believing he was a man of destiny.

Critical reaction to *Act of Vengeance* was mixed although most found it historically sound. *Variety* noted, "Powerful, suspenseful, even obscene, *Act of Vengeance* shows how strong a telefilm based on fact can be; it's compelling." Regarding the star, the same reviewer said, "Bronson's strengths are manifest throughout the vidpick.... Bronson's effective command, Burstyn's strong, supportive wife, and Brimley's deadly Boyle are powerful statements." On the other hand, John J. O'Connor wrote in the *New York Times*, "The Yablonski story is, or at least should be, a moving chronicle of conscience rising up in opposition to unquestioned power and the inescapable lesson that absolute arrogance corrupts absolutely. This HBO presentation makes perfunctory gestures in that direction but the movie is clearly more fascinated with the violence and kinky sex habits of the misfits hired to kill the Yablonskis." As for the lead he adds "the leaden Mr. Bronson is about as interesting as a sack of bituminous coal, which becomes painfully evident as, without mustache, he goes through the noble-victim motions...." Judith Crist said in *TV Guide* that Bronson, Burstyn and Brimley were "impressive," adding, "We could do without the explicit detail of the killer's sex life; this excellent real-life melodrama carries sufficient in-cold-blood passion of its own." *Mark Satern's Illustrated Guide to Video's Best* (1994) called it an "excellent drama ... Bronson, Burstyn and Brimley all excel in their roles." Alvin H. Marrill wrote in *Movies Made for Television* (1989) that the telefilm "showed Bronson in a strikingly different light from his lengthy string of vigilante roles on the big screen," while *Leonard Maltin's 1998 Movie & Video Guide* (1997) thought it "passionless." Steven H. Scheuer in *Movies on TV and Videocassette* (1990) claimed "this dramatization still manages to come across like fiction." Several reviewers noted Charles Bronson's family's mining background in discussing *Act of Vengeance*. Bill Steigerwald in the *Los Angeles Times* complained that this "Hollywood version of Yablonski's crusade gives the viewer virtually no hint of how his death effected sweeping changes within the UMW (United Mine Workers)." He also noted that neither the Yablonski family or current UMW leadership were overly pleased with the telefilm. Richard David Story wrote in *USA Today*, "Despite the title, this dour and sour HBO movie isn't another Charles Bronson *Death Wish Fantasy*.... This is a disturbing look at the 1969 murders.... Frank in depicting violence and sex in the underworld, it would get an R rating in theaters." He added, "As the gregarious Yablonski, Bronson is cast against type. He's verbal. And effective."

## *Adieu l'Ami (Farewell, Friend)* (Greenwich Film Productions/ Medusa Distribuzione, 1968) 95 minutes Color

*P:* Serge Silberman. *AP:* Ulrich Picard. *D:* Jean Herman. *Sc:* Sebastien Japrisot & Jean Herman. *Ph:* Jean-Jacques Tarbes. *Ed:* Helene Plemiannikov. *AD:* Jacques Dugied. *Sets:* Tanine Autre. *Mus:* Francoise de Roubaix. *Asst Dir:* Pierre Lary & Pierre Grunstein. *Sd:* Jean Labussiere. *Sd Ed:* Dominique Amy. *Props:* Eric Simon. *Makeup:* Fernande Hugi. *Prod Mgr:* V. Pickard.

**CAST:** Alain Delon (Dr. Dino Barran), Charles Bronson (Franz Propp), Olga Georges-Picot (Isabelle Manue), Brigitte Fossey (Dominique "Waterloo" Austerlitz), Bernard Fresson (Inspector Antoine Meloutis), Michel Barcet (Inspector Muratti), Guy Delmore (Man from Neuilly), Ellen Bahl (Martha), Andre Dumas (Personnel Director), Steve Eckardt (Big Man), Lisette Lebon (Gilberte), Marianna Falk (Catherine), Catherine Sola (Nurse); Jean-Claude Ballard, Stephane Buoy, Marie-Noelle Gresset, Sandrine Schmidt.

If any one feature film can be pinpointed as the launching pad for Charles Bronson's international stardom it is *Adieu l'Ami.* The feature proved to be the most successful financially in France in 1968 and it also did well the next year when issued in Italy as *Due Sporche Carogne—Tecnica di una Rapina.* At first reluctant to do the feature, Bronson finally accepted the role at the urging of his agent, Paul Kohner, and for a fee of $100,000, twice the amount he usually received for a film role. Alain Delon, who was next only to perennial favorite Jean Gabin in French film popularity, personally recommended Bronson for the co-starring role after seeing his performance in *Machine Gun Kelly* (1958). Jill Ireland was mentioned for one of the female leads but the part went to former French child star Brigitte Fossey, best known for *Forbidden Games* (1951). Despite its European success, *Adieu l'Ami*, although shot in both French and English language versions, was never shown in the United States, despite the fact Paramount bought it for U.S. and Canadian distribution. Under the translated title of *Farewell, Friend*, it was finally screened in Great Britain in 1976. The film is best known in America via video under the title *Honor Among Thieves*, running 90 minutes, five minutes shy of its original running time.

Returning to Marseilles after their tour of duty in the Algerian War, French soldiers Dr. Dino Barran (Alain Delon) and Franz Propp (Charles Bronson), a transplanted American, share an uneasy alliance. Propp wants Barran to join him and a band of mercenaries fighting in the Congo but the doctor refuses. Barran gets mixed up with Isabelle (Olga Georges-Picot), a beautiful young woman who was the lover of Barran's wartime pal Mozart, who the doctor accidentally shot thinking he was an enemy soldier. The girl wants Barran to take a job as a physician in a large office building so he can return bearer bonds to the corporation safe, the bonds having been stolen by Mozart. When Isabelle comes up with a way to photograph the combination to the safe, Barran agrees, not knowing the safe will contain over two million francs deposited there over the Christmas holidays. Meanwhile Franz is on the run from the law for having procured a beautiful prostitute for several depraved businessmen and then having robbed and beaten up the clients.

While looking for Barran at his place of work, Franz realizes the doctor is up to something and the two get locked in the building. When Franz learns that Barran plans to open the safe he wants half the loot. Since only three of the seven letters opening the safe were revealed by the photographs, the two men take turns trying the various combinations between checks by the building guards. After over 3,600 tries, they get the safe open only to find it is empty. The two fight and accidentally get locked in the vault with Barran realizing that Isabelle used him as a patsy. Eventually the two break through a wall and escape only to find a guard has been murdered.

When the building opens Barran and Franz go separately to Orly Airport, planning to rendezvous in Marseilles. When Franz sees the police after Barran, he causes a disturbance and is captured while Barran makes a getaway to the home of his nurse, Dominique (Brigitte Fossey). Under interrogation by police Inspector Meloutis (Bernard Fresson), Franz does not reveal his working with Barran. The doctor and Dominique go to the office building for Dominique's work card so he can prove her existence to the police, who are following him. There Isabelle arrives planning to kill Barran since she and Dominique are lovers; they planned and executed the robbery with the nurse killing the guard. The police overhear the women's confession to Barran and in a shootout Isabelle kills Inspector Muratti (Michel Barcet) and in turn the officers gun down both girls. As Franz is being taken to jail for his involvement in bilking the prostitute's clients, he and Barran meet but do not acknowledge each other.

The character of Franz Propp delighted European audiences and solidified Charles Bronson as a Continental star. His Propp is a cool, calculating, amoral scoundrel, who is still quite likable. He realizes he is a born loser but does his best to make the most of it. Early in the film he tells Dr. Barran, "When I pick a side you can bet the other side will win. Well, there are lots of wars to be lost." To Propp, winning or losing is not important but profit is what counts. Still the characters of Barran and Propp learn to respect each other and the finale finds neither willing to turn in the other. Propp even gets himself arrested on an old charge in order to avoid implicating Barran in their vault break-in.

*Variety* thought *Adieu l'Ami* a "Fairly slickly made film" and the *Monthly*

*Film Bulletin* felt it was "a stylish thriller, marred by a glib and overly busy plot which, like others in the genre, appears to have been worked out backwards." The French publication *Le Figaro* said Delon and Bronson "form a remarkable pair—as worthy of praise as the most famous Hollywood duo." Even more to the point was H. Talvat in *Cine-Club Mediterranée*, "Delon is crushed by Charles Bronson, the superb beast of the Hollywood forests. Everything Delon portrays by force, Bronson plays with suppleness."

Alain Delon and Charles Bronson, who shared a mutual interest in art, would team again four years later in *Soleil Rouge (Red Sun)* (1971) but this time first billing went to Bronson.

A couple of *Adieu l'Ami*'s plot ploys are of some interest. Early in the film Propp wins Barran's revolver (the one later used to shoot the guard; Barran has bought it back from Propp) by dropping five heavy coins into a full cup of liquid without spilling it. Later in a mental showdown with the cops, Propp again tries the trick and loses, thus forcing him to reveal his activities with the prostitute, which sends him to jail at the film's finale. Also of interest is the nickname of Barran's nurse, Dominique. She is called "Waterloo" because she always fails her medical exams; she has been a first year medical student for three years. The actual date of the Battle of Waterloo provides the numbers for the combination of the safe containing two million francs.

Following the completion of *Adieu l'Ami*, CCC-Film of West Germany, in cooperation with C.C.I. of Rome and Corona-Film Paris, announced that Charles Bronson would play the title role in *Michael Strogoff*, under the direction of George Lautner, and co-starring Martin Held and Werner Peters. The production did not materialize and Bronson went to work for director Sergio Leone in *C'Era una Volta il West* (1969).

## *Apache* (United Artists, 1954) 91 minutes Color

*P:* Harold Hecht. *D:* Robert Aldrich. *Sc:* James R. Webb, from the novel *Bronco Apache* by Paul I. Wellman. *Ph:* Ernest Laszlo. *Ed:* Alan Crosland Jr. *Mus:* David Raksin. *Sets:* Joseph Kish. *AD:* Nicolai Remisoff. *Asst Dir:* Sid Sidman.

**CAST:** Burt Lancaster (Massai), Jean Peters (Nalinle), John McIntire (Al Seiber), Charles Buchinsky (Hondo), John Dehner (Weddle), Paul Guilfoyle (Santos), Ian MacDonald (Glagg), Walter Sande (Lieutenant Colonel Beck), Morris Ankrum (Dawson), Monte Blue (Geronimo).

A dying Geronimo (Monte Blue) surrenders and his tribe is sent on a march to imprisonment at St. Augustine, but one warrior, Massai (Burt Lancaster), escapes and vows to continue fighting the white man's army. In hiding he finds pretty Nalinle (Jean Peters) who joins his cause but prefers living in peace. The army hires scout Al Seiber (John McIntire) to bring in Massai and he is assisted by Apache soldier Hondo (Charles Buchinsky). Massai is captured twice and

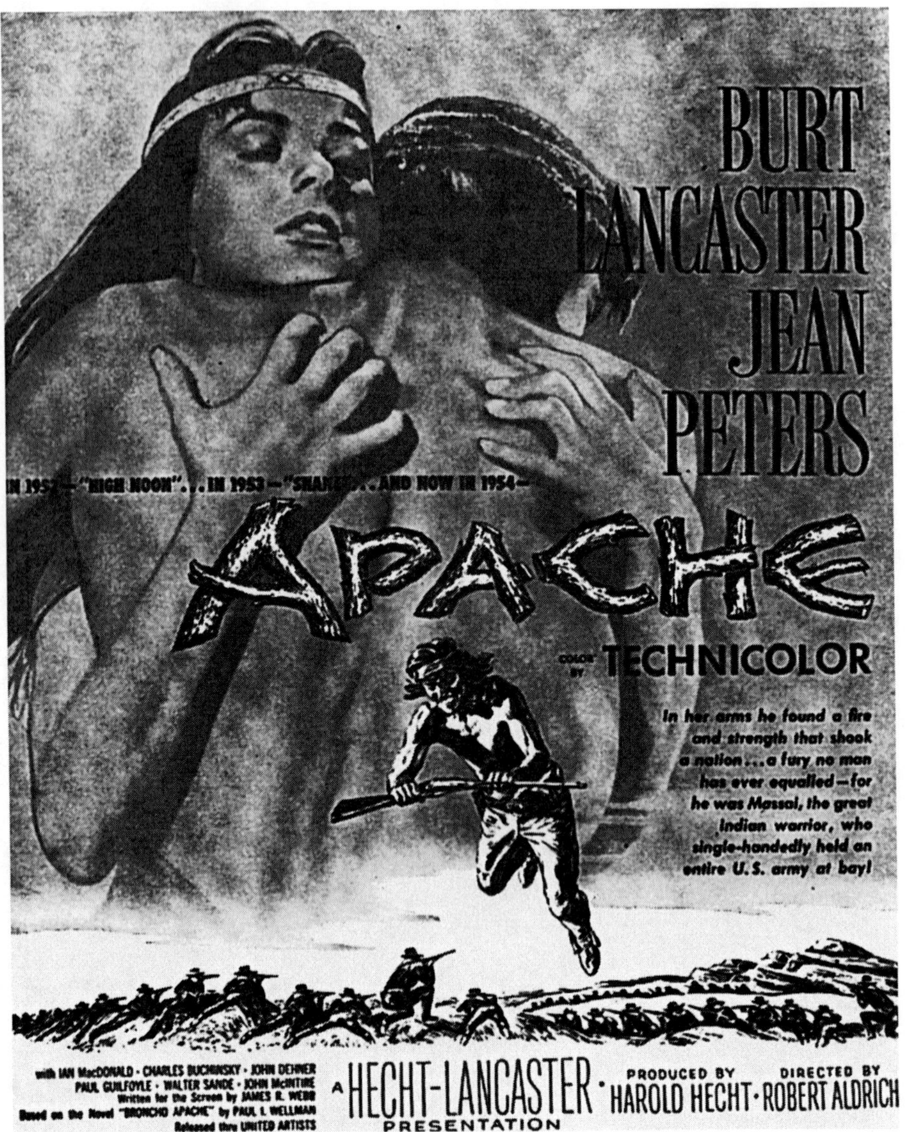


**Poster for *Apache* (United Artists, 1954).**

chained but he escapes both times into the mountains with Nalinle to continue his one-man war against the army and the oppressors of his people, like crooked Indian agent Weddle (John Dehner), only to be betrayed by Santos (Paul Guilfoyle), the girl's Apache father. After a lengthy struggle Massai and Nalinle make a home for themselves in the mountains away from the white man.

Filmed near Sonora, California, *Apache* was the initial feature of Hecht-Lancaster Productions and was made for slightly under one million dollars with another $350,000 spent to publicize the movie. Thanks to having worked previously with Robert Aldrich in television, Charles Bronson landed the showy role of Apache scout Hondo and obtained fourth billing in his first outing as a Native American. He handled the part with finesse and received good reviews in a feature dominated by star and co-producer Burt Lancaster. Thanks to his good work in the film Bronson was hired by Hecht-Lancaster for their next feature with director Robert Aldrich, *Vera Cruz*, released the same year.

*Apache*, while popular with the public, garnered mixed reviews. *Variety* called it "a rugged action saga in best Burt Lancaster style of muscle-flexing" noting "Main plot switch is viewing Indian from sympathetic angle, even though his knife, arrows, bullets often find their marks among white soldiers." The same reviewer included Bronson among the supporting cast of "excellent assists." The Lansing, Michigan, *State-Journal* included him with "other characterizations capably handled" adding the film itself contained "the glint of authentic history." The *New York Times*, however, called it a "real disappointment" adding "the picture is strangely slow and even dull—a rather half-hearted dramatic embroidery of history that seems mainly concerned with foisting the gritty muscularity of Burt Lancaster, who is perfectly cast physically." In *The Western* (1983), Phil Hardy called *Apache* a "hard-hitting Indian western ... Aldrich's direction, with its fluid traveling shots, is marvelously assured." He noted, however, that United Artists forced Hecht-Lancaster to end the feature on a happy note. In its original conception Massai was to be shot by the army after finally settling down peacefully with Nalinle. The filmed finale had hostilities cease between Massai and the army as the brave and his squaw go to the mountains in peace.

*Apache* was the final theatrical film of silent film star Monte Blue, who gives a poignant performance at the beginning of the feature as the dying Geronimo.

## *Assassination* (Cannon Group, 1987) 88 minutes Color

*P:* Pancho Kohner. *EP:* Menahem Golan & Yoram Globus. *D:* Peter Hunt. *Sc:* Richard Sale, from his novel *My Affair with the President's Wife*. *Ph:* Hanania Baer. *Ed:* James Heckert. *Mus:* Robert Ragland & Valentine McCallum. *Prod Design:* William Cruse. *Stunt Coordinator:* Jack Gill. *AD:* James S. Culp. *Prod Mgr:* George Van Hoy & Barbara Michaels. *Asst Dir:* Craig Huston, Terence D. Buchinsky & Robert C. Ortwin Jr. *Prod Executive:* Ronny Yacov. *Casting:* Perry Bullington. *Sd:* Thomas Brandau. *Set Decorator:* Patricia Hall. *Costumes:* Shelley Kamarov. *Prod Coordinator:* Jeanne M. O'Brien. *Sp Eff:* Pioneer FX. *Sp Eff Crew:* Melbourne A. Arnold, John Hixson Jr. & David H. Lott Jr.

*Mus Supv:* Paula Erickson. *Stunts:* John F. Alden, Al Jones, Rick Avery, John F. MacCarthy, Christine Bauer, Matt McColm, Simon Bossierre, Spike Silver, Debbie Evans, Donna Evans, Charlie Skeen, Steve Striklin, Andy Gill, Michael Tillman & Ed Hamilton. *Camera Operator:* Bernard Aroux. *Asst Camera Operators:* Dan Elsaseer & Dave Rudd. *Second Asst Ph:* Randy Sanofsky. *Additional Second Asst Ph:* Michael E. Little & Tommy Frimmerman. *Cable Man:* Tom Russo. *Helicopter Camera Operator:* Jack Cooperman. *Boom Operator:* Jerome R. Vitucci. *Art Department Coordinator:* Christine Schlessinger. *Construction Consultant:* John C. Keasey Jr. *Lead Foreman:* Bob Trojan. *Set Decorators:* Rodger M. Pitts, Sharon Vijoen & W. Brooke Wheeler. *Property Master:* Edwin Brewer. *Asst Property Master:* Mark Heiner. *Lead Man:* Mark A. Haskins. *Key Grips:* John Sayka & Jonathan Wolf. *Best Grip Boy:* Joseph A. Presson. *Grips:* John Bruin & Levon Beshelman. *Gaffer:* James Rosenthall. *Best Boy Electrician:* Mark Buckalew. *Electrician:* Richard E. Beeman. *Costume Designer:* Heidi Freudlich Giles. *Set Costumer:* Marcie Olivi. *Male Costumer:* Michael Abbott. *Makeup Artist & Hair Supv:* Claudia Thompson. *Makeup & Hair Asst:* Ron Peaker. *Producer's Asst:* Patricia G. Payro. *Sc Supv:* Brenda Weissman. *Director's Asst:* Nicholas Kourtis. *Location Mgr:* Larry Pearson. *Still Photographer:* Gale M. Adler. *Unit Publicist:* Karin Joret. *Prod Asst:* Amy L. Grandrath, Judith R. Strow, Joseph Benn & Dawn-Leslie Allen. *Aerial Coordinator:* Mischa Hausserman. *Boat Coordinator:* Ransom Walrod. *Post Prod Supv:* Michael R. Sloan. *First Asst Ed:* Andrew Silver & Dennis Brandt. *Recording:* Todd A-O & Glen Glenn. *Second Asst Ed:* Julie Hall. *Supv Sd Ed:* Mike Le Maire. *Dialogue Ed:* Tony Palk. *Foley Ed:* Karola Storr. *Second Asst Sd Ed:* Michael Murphy & Steve Schwalbe. *Re-recording Mixers:* Gary Burgoise, Chris Carpenter & Dean Okrand. *Title Design:* Walter K. Baldwin & Helene Henderson. *Main Titles & Opticals:* Westheimer Company. *Color Timer:* Angelo Russo. *Negative Cutting:* Ron Vitello & Ann-Marie Vitello. *Color:* TVC. *Mus Ed:* Ken Johnson & Steve Livingston. *Second Unit Crew, Washington D.C.—Location Mgr:* Carol Flaisher. *Wardrobe Asst:* Kate Adair-Cowart. *Makeup Artist:* Terri Trupp. *Property Asst:* Susan Weiss. *Second Asst Cameraman:* William J. Gray. *Dolly Grip:* Steve Seitz. *Second Grip:* Joshua W. Spring. *Grip:* John R. Dunkin. *Best Boy Electrician:* Robert Waybright. *Transportation Coordinators:* Jimmy Jones & Udel Renfro. *Transportation Captain:* Mitchell J. Masoner. *Transportation Co-Captain:* Kevin Haynes. *Extra Casting:* Dennis Hansen. *Stand-Ins:* John F. MacCarthy, Susan J. Thompson & Mikoto Tokoro.

**CAST:** Charles Bronson (Jay "Killey" Killion), Jill Ireland (Laramie "Lara" Royce Craig), Stephen Elliott (Fitzroy), Jan Gan Boyd (Charlotte "Charlie" Chong), Randy Brooks (Tyler Loudermilk), Erik Stern (Reno Bracken), Michael Ansara (Senator Hector Bunsen), James Staley (Briggs), Kathryn Leigh Scott (Polly Sims), James Acheson (Osborne Weems), Jim McMullan (The Zipper), William Hayes (Pritchard Young), William Prince (Harry H. Royce), Charles Howerton (President Calvin Craig), Chris Alcaide (Chief Justice), Jack Gill (Kerry Fane), Mischa Hausserman (Danzig), Robert Axelrod (Derek Finney), Peter Lupus (TV Announcer), Beverly Thompson (June Merkel), Natalie Alexander (Claire Thompson), Linda Harwood (Sally Moore), Mikoko Tokoro (Bartender), Susan J. Thompson (Journalist), Arthur Hansel (Barstow), John Salvi (Platt), Frank Zagarino (Secret Service Driver), Tony Borgia (Bomb Squad Man), Paul

**Opposite: Advertisement for *Assassination* (Cannon Group, 1987).**

BRONSON

ASSASSINATION

THE CANNON GROUP, INC. CHARLES BRONSON
GOLAN-GLOBUS PETER HUNT ASSASSINATION
JILL IRELAND · STEPHEN ELLIOTT · JAN GAN BOYD · RANDY BROOKS
MICHAEL ANSARA · WILLIAM PRINCE ROBERT O. RAGLAND VALENTINE McCALLUM
HANANIA BAER MENAHEM GOLAN YORAM GLOBUS RICHARD SALE
CANNON PANCHO KOHNER PETER HUNT

McCallum (Sandy Ott), Robert Dowdell (Captain "Cappy" Ogilvy), Jason Scura (Captain Hammond), Larry Sellers (Indian Joe), Lucille Bliss (Older Lady), John Hawker (Porter), James Frank Clark (Locomotive Engineer), Michael Weldon, Ed Levitt (FBI Agents), Vivian Tyus (Maid), David L. Bilson (Willy Maine), Elizabeth Lauren (Moonbeam), J. Michael Patterson (Conductor), Clayton D. Wright (Helicopter Pilot).

"You're going to miss the hell out of Nancy Reagan" is one of the best remembered lines in *Assassination*, a fast-paced, taut thriller starring Charles Bronson as a Secret Service agent protecting Jill Ireland as the president's wife from a hired assassin. With much location filming in Washington, D.C., the film has an authentic look although outside the capitol one tends to see mountain peaks throughout the country, and in Kokomo, Indiana, there are glimpses of palm trees and mountains, neither of which are in central Indiana. The film, which grossed over $6 million domestically, was the last time Charles Bronson and Jill Ireland worked together before her death in 1990. It also reunited Bronson with director Peter Hunt from *Death Hunt* (1981) and for the second time Richard Sale adapted one of his novels to the screen as a Bronson vehicle, the first being *The White Buffalo* in 1977.

Upon returning to work following surgery, Secret Service agent Jay Killion (Charles Bronson) is informed by his boss, Fitzroy (Stephen Elliott), that he is to be in charge of security for the new first lady, Lara Royce Craig (Jill Ireland), beginning with the inauguration parade. Killion finds Lara very difficult and strong-minded and he ends up causing her to have a black eye by pulling her onto their car's floorboard when a motorcycle explodes near them during the inauguration parade. Killion suspects terrorist Reno Bracken (Erik Stern) is behind the explosion although officially it was an accident. When Lara leaves the White House without security clearance she is held at Andrews Air Force Base until the president (Charles Howerton) gives his go-ahead for her trip to California. Killion goes along on the trip as do agents Charlotte "Charlie" Chong (Jan Gan Boyd), who is in love with Killion, and Tyler Loudermilk (Randy Brooks). As they are awaiting the arrival of Lara's father's yacht at Newport the craft explodes and Killion suspects someone is trying to kill the First Lady. When she plans a speaking engagement, Killion forces Lara to go by car instead of a planned helicopter which is fired at by a sniper who makes a successful getaway. The president, who thinks terrorists are after Killion, takes him off guarding his wife but while tailing her secretary Killion sees Lara leaving an event in the guise of a hippie. He follows her and she asks him to help her get away from those who are trying to kill her. They stop at a motel and there Killion spots Pritchard Young (William Hayes), Bracken's right-hand man. Young opens fire on their room but Lara makes an escape and Killion kills him. At Gettysburg they get on a bus which takes them to Indiana and from there they head west on motor bikes. Lara tells Killion the president is impotent and he tells her she is being stalked by a killer because if she gives the president a divorce he will lose the next election, but if he runs as a widower he will be a hero. They are attacked by a man in a truck but he is killed by drowning and the duo take a train to Wyoming. There they are stalked by Bracken but they elude him and Lara tells Killion she has been in touch with her husband. Taking a dune buggy, Killion and Lara head to Lake Tahoe where her wealthy father (William Prince) has a lakeside home. Killion sends for Charlie and Loudermilk to join them there and when Bracken attacks from the lake Killion pursues him. The two have a final showdown in a nearby woods with Killion killing Bracken who before dying admits that he was hired by Senator Hector Bunsen (Michael Ansara), the president's chief-of-staff. Later when FBI agents (Michael Weldon, Ed Levitt) try to take Bunsen into custody he falls from a glass elevator to his death. It is announced that Bunsen died from ill health as Killion leaves his job to go to work for Lara's father. He also faces probable wedlock with Charlie.

The body count in *Assassination* is high and so are the explosions, which include a barn, yacht, car, truck and boat. Charles Bronson and Jill Ireland work well together as the frustrated agent and strong-willed First Lady. Jan Gan Boyd is quite sexy as the young woman in love with the recently divorced Killion and Michael Ansara is justly villainous as is Erik Stern as the hitman Bracken.

Like many entertaining Charles Bronson thrillers, *Assassination* did not appeal to critics. *People Weekly* said, "Maybe this sorry Charles Bronson vehicle won't hurt his future as a box office draw, but it won't help.... There is plenty of character nondevelopment." Vincent Canby wrote in the *New York Times*, "In spite of the noisy explosion with which the film is scored, *Assassination* has a majestic, slightly arthritic pace that's almost soothing.... The story makes no sense whatsoever and most of the performances are awful, but that's not important in a Charles Bronson vehicle. His is an implacable movie presence, quite unlike any other. It's good to know that he's still in there, squinting at the bad guys and occasionally dispatching them with as little effort as possible." Gannett News Service writer William Wolf thought, "*Assassination* is filled with customary Bronson heroics, but the script by Richard Sale leaves any semblance of White House dignity in a shambles.... There are the requisite chases, explosions, killings, near misses, and use of heavy-duty artillery. At least the movie, directed by Peter Hunt, holds one's attention. But oh, that plot." In the *Los Angeles Times*, Michael Wilmington said the film "is a floundering enterprise, almost like a hit squad that's lost its bullets." Regarding the star, however, he wrote, "As the slightly gone-to-seed but battle-hardened Jay Killion, he (Bronson) remains, as always, cool, adroitly understated, the very picture of no-nonsense professionalism. Bronson clips off his lines with the battle-weary disgust of a tough-shell veteran. He strikes the right sparks with his wife and co-star Jill Ireland." Deborah

J. Kunk wrote in the *Los Angeles Herald Examiner* that the film was a "harmless yarn.... Despite the heavy artillery trotted out—including automatic weapons and heat-seeking missiles—*Assassination* isn't a shoot-'em-up. It's a travelogue." Some reviewers, however, liked the film. *Variety* called it a "fun Bronson vehicle" adding, "What makes the film watchable anyway is Bronson's self-assured charm. No matter that he's reaching retirement age for a Secret Service man and has no business chasing young hippies, Bronson has by now mastered a low-key but menacing presence that's simply fun to watch and rarely has he been better." Richard Freedman in the Newark, New Jersey, *Star-Ledger* agreed, saying it was "by far the blithest and best movie of his career ... Bronson never looked better on screen."

The movie's working titles were *The President's Wife* and *Assassin*.

## *Battle of the Bulge* (Warner Bros., 1965) 167 minutes Color

*P:* Milton Sperling & Philip Yordan. *D:* Ken Annakin. *Sc:* Philip Yordan, Milton Sperling & John Melson. *Ph:* John Hilyard. *Ed:* Derek Parsons. *Mus:* Benjamin Frankel. *Sp Eff:* Alex Weldon. *Second Unit Photographer:* John Cabrera. *Aerial Photographer:* Jack Willoughby. *Asst Dir:* Jose Lopez Rodero, Martin Sacristan & Luis Garcia. *AD:* Eugene Lourie. *Sd Ed:* Kurt Herrnfeld. *Sd:* David Hilyard & Gordon McCallum. *Costume Design:* Laure De Zarate. *Dialogue Coach:* Janet Brandt. *Prod Supv:* Bernard Glasser. *Unit Manager:* Leon Chooluck. *Prod Mgr:* Tibor Reeves & Gregorio Sacristan. *Post-Prod Executive:* L.A. Sansom. *Prod Coordinator:* Lou Brandt. *Sc Supvs:* Joy Mercer & Marie Wachsman. *Wardrobe:* Charles Simminger. *Makeup:* Trevor Crole-Rees. *Sp Eff Asst:* Richard Parker, Kit West & Basilio Cortijo. *Co-Unit Mgrs:* Miguel Perez & Juan Estelrich. *Advisors:* Major General Meinard von Lauchert, Lieutenant Colonel Luis Martin Pozuelo, Lieutenant Colonel Sherman Joff, Edward King. *Miniatures:* Henri Assola.

**CAST:** Henry Fonda (Lieutenant Colonel Kiley), Robert Shaw (Colonel Hessler), Robert Ryan (General Grey), Dana Andrews (Colonel Pritchard), George Montgomery (Sergeant Duquesne), Ty Hardin (Schumacher), Pier Angeli (Louise), Barbara Werle (Elena), Charles Bronson (Major Wolenski), Werner Peters (General Kohler), Hans Christian (Conrad), James MacArthur (Lieutenant Weaver), Telly Savalas (Guffy), William Conrad (Narrator), Karl Otto Alberty (Von Diepel); Steve Rowland, Robert Woods, Axel Anderson, Victor Brandt, Robert Royal, Russ Stoddard, Charles Stalnaker, David Thomson, Sebastian Cavalieri, Raoul Perez, Jack Gaskins, Janet Brandt, Max Slaten, Carl Rapp, Donald Pickering, Bud Strait, Peter Herendeen, Ben Tatar, Paul Eshelman, Richard Zeidman, John Schereschewsky, Richard Baxter, William Boone, John Clarke, Ward Maule, Paul Polansky, Freddie Toehl, Leland Wyler, Quinn Donoghue, John Friess, Reginald Gillam, Peter Grzcegorczyk, Richard Laver, Harry Van Der Linden, Derek Robertson, Martin Rolin.

Director Ken Annakin had previously co-directed the box office blockbuster *The Longest Day* (1962) about the Normandy invasion. For Sidney Harmon and United States Pictures he directed this look at the Nazi's last big attempt to thwart the Allies advance into Germany in 1944, filmed in Spain in Ultra-Panavision Cinerama and Technicolor. The result was an overlong action fest which was historically inaccurate. Charles Bronson was featured as a Polish-American officer, Wolenski, who shows up about one-half hour into the proceedings and is killed off not long after the halfway point as his character is sacrificed for the sake of battle strategy. As usual he tended to get far better reviews than the film but overall *Battle of the Bulge* is one of his least remembered roles of the 1960s, sandwiched between *The Great Escape* (1963) and *The Dirty Dozen* (1967), both superior, and far more successful, World War II action melodramas.

Late in 1944, the Allies feel a quick victory over Germany is in the offing. Lieutenant Colonel Kiley (Henry Fonda), a U.S. intelligence officer, believes, however, the Nazis will mount a major offensive in Belgium's Ardennes Forest. He reports his feelings to his commanding officers, Colonel Pritchard (Dana Andrews) and Colonel Grey (Robert Ryan), but they think he is wrong since the enemy is too battle weary to carry out such an offensive. Unknown to them, German hero Colonel Hessler (Robert Shaw) has returned from the Russian front to carry out just such an offensive using ground troops backed by new Tiger tanks. When poor weather conditions ground the Allies' airplanes, Hessler makes his move and the Allies are further confused by German spies dressed as Allied military police causing havoc behind the lines. The assault is so strong the Allied forces retreat but Kiley feels the Germans will soon run out of petrol to run their tanks. With the aid of Lieutenant Weaver (James MacArthur), the wounded Kiley and his squad are able to recapture several large fuel dumps from the saboteurs, although another officer, Major Wolenski (Charles Bronson), loses his life for the Allied cause. The Allied soldiers set fire to the fuel dumps and when the Germans arrive they find they can proceed no further due to the lack of fuel, thus ending the historic assault.

Large scale World War II films were very popular in the 1960s and 1970s and *Battle of the Bulge*, while one of the lesser of these, was roadshown in the United States, projected in two parts with an intermission. Its domestic take was $5.1 million at the box office. When released to the general trade, the movie was cut from 167 to 140 minutes.

*Variety* called the film "a rousing, commercial battlefield action-drama of the emotions and activities of U.S. and German forces" while the *New York Times* noted "this picture, as a sober, factual, stirring reenactment of history and an honest contemplation of a key crisis of World War II, is best suited to youngsters who go for bombastic spectacles." Judith Crist complained in the *New York Herald Tribune* that the film "will do little but irritate World War II veterans or buffs by what the producers politely term the 'synthesizing' of details of this one phase of the war." F. Maurice Speed in *Film Review 1966–68* (1967) called the feature "Spectacularly successful, sweeping

Cinerama reconstruction...." James Robert Parish wrote in *The Great Combat Pictures* (1990) that "the film was a conglomerate fabrication more concerned with cashing in on the cycle of epic war films than in presenting true or dramatic reality." Jay Robert Nash and Stanley Ralph Ross said in *The Motion Picture Guide* (1985), "The movie is very inaccurate and any veteran of the real battle laughs at the idea of the climax taking place on a butte with squadrons of tanks facing each other down in a mechanized *High Noon*." *The Family Guide to Movies on Video* (1988), edited by Henry Herx and Tony Zaza, opined, "In an ambitious, wide-ranging epic, director Ken Annakin tries to turn one of the most brutal battles of World War II into star-studded international entertainment." *Newsweek* said, "*Battle of the Bulge* is an uncommonly convincing carnival of carnage. When soldiers died in Cinerama and Ultra-Panavision they die it up big."

## *Big House, U.S.A.* (United Artists, 1955) 82 minutes B/W

*P:* Aubrey Schenk. *D:* Howard D. Koch. *Sc:* John C. Higgins. *Ph:* Gordon Avil. *Ed:* John F. Schreyer. *Mus:* Paul Dunlap. *Asst Dir:* Harold Klein. *Prod Design:* Charles D. Hall. *Ph Sp Eff:* Howard Anderson Co. *Casting Supv:* John G. Stephens. *Property Master:* Tom Coleman. *First Asst Camera:* William Margulies. *Lighting Technician:* Robert S. Comer. *Wardrobe:* Tommy Thompson. *Sd Mixer:* Frank Webster. *Sd Ed:* John A. Bushelman. *Mus Ed:* Lester Morris.

CAST: Broderick Crawford (Rollo Lamar), Ralph Meeker (Jerry Barker), Reed Hadley (FBI Agent James Madden), Randy Farr (Emily Evans), William Talman (Machine Gun Mason), Lon Chaney (Alamo Smith), Charles Bronson (Benny Kelly), Peter Votrain (Danny Lambert), Roy Roberts (Chief Ranger Erickson), Willis Bouchey (Robertson Lambert), Bart Burns (Warden), Jan Merlin (Boat Captain), Robert Bray (Ranger McCormick).

At a boy's camp at the Royal Gorge Park, young Danny Lambert (Peter Votrain) suffers an asthma attack and runs away when nurse Emily Evans (Randy Farr) attempts to give him a shot. He is found by Jerry Barker (Ralph Meeker) who takes him to an abandoned lookout post where he leaves the boy and then tries to extort $200,000 in ransom from his wealthy father (Willis Bouchey). Mr. Lambert pays the ransom then informs the local ranger chief (Roy Roberts) who calls in FBI agent James Madden (Reed Hadley). Trying to escape, the boy falls from the lookout post and is killed. Barker hides his body. Later Barker is stopped for possessing a gun and is found to have some of the ransom money. Since the boy is never found, Barker is convicted only on an extortion charge and sent to Cascabel Island Prison. Known as "The Ice Man" because of his demeanor, Barker is assigned to a cell in the "Lion's Den" with bankrobber, killer and heist planner Rollo Lamar (Broderick Crawford), gunman Machine Gun Mason (William Talman), mad dog killer

Benny Kelly (Charles Bronson) and murderer, narcotics runner and wetback smuggler Alamo Smith (Lon Chaney). Because he is believed to be a child killer, the other prisoners shun Barker but when he sees another prisoner die in a steam boiler as he worked on an escape plan, Barker keeps quiet and Rollo realizes he is no squealer. Rollo plans to take the unwilling Barker along on the planned escape since he wants to get the rest of the ransom money Barker has hidden. Meanwhile Agent Madden is able to connect Emily Evans with Barker and proves they set up the kidnapping of the Lambert boy. Rollo, Mason, Benny and Alamo, forcing Barker to go with them, escape from prison via a boiler which they had connected to a tunnel. From the tunnel they swim to a waiting boat but Rollo nearly dies and is saved by Benny. On board Rollo orders Mason to kill Benny whose face and fingers are burned beyond recognition. They want the authorities to believe the body belongs to Barker so the hunt for the ransom will be stopped. When he finds out Benny has been killed Alamo goes after Rollo, who shoots him. Madden and the FBI realize that Barker is not dead and they go to the park to await his trying to recover the ransom money he buried there. Rollo and Mason force Barker to take them to the money and when they find it

**William Talman, Broderick Crawford, Lon Chaney, Ralph Meeker and Charles Bronson in *Big House, U.S.A.* (United Artists, 1955).**

they plan to throw Barker off a cliff, but the park rangers begin shooting and Mason is killed. Rollo turns coward and surrenders. Later both Rollo and Barker die in the gas chamber for their crimes.

With on-location filming in Canon City, Colorado, and at Royal Gorge Park, *Big House, U.S.A.* was told in the semidocumentary fashion so popular in the 1950s. Allegedly based on a true case, the film was made by Bel-Air Productions, owned by producer Aubrey Schenk and director Howard W. Koch. Its chief interest lay with the expert performances from its lead players and filming in the scenic Colorado Mountains and at the Cascabel Island Prison facility. *New York Times* reviewer Howard Thompson felt the film was "a good crime melodrama gone wrong" and that the scenario "kept the sleuthing methodical and on the sidelines. They clear the decks for some graphic but standard bloodiness on the part of Mr. Meeker and his snarling kind." On the latter topic, *Variety* noted, "Plenty of violence is featured throughout in some rather chilling scenes, but fits the tough character in which the story deals ... melodrama provides a fair amount of entertainment." *The Monthly Film Bulletin*, however, disliked the movie: "The characters here depicted are so brutal as to anaesthetize all sympathy, and their savagery is minutely explored by the director, Howard W. Koch, in a manner that leaves one shocked yet disinterested. The playing is indifferent, and the film as a whole singularly distasteful." *National Parent-Teacher* called the movie, "A brutal, well-produced crime melodrama...." Particularly brutal were the scenes of a convict being scalded to death in a boiler and the use of a blowtorch on Benny Kelly.

Bronson was certainly in good acting company in *Big House, U.S.A.*, which allowed him equal footing with such top-flight thespians as Broderick Crawford (with whom he worked in a bit part in *The Mob* four years earlier), Ralph Meeker, Lon Chaney, and William Talman. For him to hold his own with such distinguished players certainly proved that Bronson had learned his craft well and that he had developed into a screen presence of considerable depth and strength. In some ways the part of Benny Kelly was similar to that of Ben Hastings in *Crime Wave* (1953). Both are brutal, murderous men seething with emotions more physical than verbal. For Charles Bronson to be able to project such characterizations at this stage of his career shows the foundation for the screen persona that would elevate him to worldwide stardom within the next fifteen years.

*Big House, U.S.A.* got U.S. and British showings in 1955 and in France and West Germany the next year but it was not released in Denmark until 1958.

After *Big House, U.S.A.*, Bel-Air Productions turned out two 1956 horror films with Lon Chaney, *The Indestructible Man* and *The Black Sleep*.

## *Bloodhounds of Broadway* (20th Century–Fox, October 1952)

90 minutes Color

*P:* George Jessel. *D:* Harmon Jones. *Sc:* Sy Gomberg. *St:* Damon Runyon. *Adaptation:* Albert Mannheimer. *Ph:* Edward Cronjager. *Ed:* George A. Gittens. *AD:* Lyle Wheeler & J. Russell Spencer. *Songs:* Eliot Daniel, Ben Oakland & Paul Webster. *Musical Settings:* Joseph C. Wright. *Musical Numbers D:* Robert Sidney. *Asst Dir:* Stanley Hough.

**CAST:** Mitzi Gaynor (Emily Ann Stackerlee), Scott Brady (Robert "Numbers" Foster), Mitzi Green (Tessi Sammis), Marguerite Chapman (Yvonne), Michael O'Shea (Inspector McNamara), Wally Vernon (Poorly Sammis), Henry Slade (Dave the Dude), George E. Stone (Ropes McGonigle), Edwin Max (Lookout Louie), Richard Allan (Curtaintime Charlie), Sharon Baird (Little Elida), Ralph Volkie (Frankie Ferraccio), Charles Buchinski (Pittsburgh Philo), Timothy Carey (Crockett Pace), William [Bill] Walker (Uncle Old Fella), Paul Wexler (Theo Pace), Alfred Mizner (Foy Pace), Emile Meyer (Skipper), Joe McTurk (Process Server), Mary Wickes (Mother), Mabel Paige (Madame Moana), Dayton Lummis (Chairman), Gregg Martell (Sergeant Moran), Phil Tully (Lieutenant Moran), Al Green (Drunk), Bee Humphries (Apple Annie), Harry Corden (Selly Bennett), Van Des Autels (Senator), David Wolfe (Counsel), Robert Long (Presiding Senator), Charles Tannen, Al Hill, Ed McNally (Men).

In order to avoid state prosecution and to get away from his lawman nemesis Inspector McNamara (Michael O'Shea), notorious bookie Robert "Numbers" Foster (Scott Brady) and his hypochondriac pal Poorly Sammis (Wally Vernon) flee Gotham and end up in the Georgia backwoods where they meet aspiring stage actress Emily Ann Stackerlee (Mitzi Gaynor) who winds up saving Numbers' life. Not only does Numbers fall for Emily Ann but he brings her to Broadway where she headlines Dave the Dude's (Henry Slade) nightclub, becoming a big success. When all is settled with the law, Numbers and Emily Ann find happiness together.

George Jessel produced this spritely musical comedy populated with Damon Runyon characters (i.e., Dave the Dude, Apple Annie, Lookout Louie, Ropes McGonigle) and lots of dance numbers and songs, including a couple of brand new numbers, "Bye Low" and "Jack of Diamonds." Thanks to the comedy emphasis, the film was pleasantly entertaining and nicely showcased stars Mitzi Gaynor, Scott Brady and former child star Mitzi Green. For Charles Bronson it offered the supporting role of Pittsburgh Philo, a crony of Numbers Foster, and it gave the actor the opportunity to deliver a few good comedy lines while playing a humorous thug, as he did in *Pat and Mike* (1952).

*Variety* called the Technicolor musical "a pleasant 89 [sic] minutes of screen diversion" while the *New York Times* opined the feature "is obviously not calculated to preserve the late writer's (Runyon) racy style." *Time* thought it "a good-humored cinemusical" but *Newsweek* found it to be "a blithe Technicolor foolishment ... the plot and characters are strictly sub–Lardner, and the music only so-so...."

*Bloodhounds of Broadway* refers to two small dogs belonging to heroine Mitzi Gaynor and they proved to be the musical's best scene-stealers.

## *Borderline* (ITC Film Distributors/ITC Entertainment/Associated Film Distribution, 1980) 105 minutes Color

*P:* James Nelson. *EP:* Martin Starger. *D:* Gerrold Freedman. *Sc:* Steve Kline & Gerrold Freedman. *Ph:* Tak Fujimoto. *Ed:* John F. Link II. *Mus:* Gil Melle. *AD:* Michel Lavesque. *In Charge of Prod:* Richard L. O'Connor. *Executive Prod Mgr:* Howard Alston. *Post Prod Supv:* James Potter. *Prod Mgr:* Christopher A. Seiter. *Asst Dir:* Charles A. Myers & Mary Ellen Canniff. *Technical Advisor:* Albert S. (Ab) Taylor. *Set Decorator:* Richard Spero. *Costumes:* Ron Archer. *Gaffer:* Mel Maxwell. *Stunt Coordinator:* John Moio. *Stuntmen:* Mike Adams, Bob K. Cummings, John Escobar, Mike Johnson, Charles Picerni Jr., Thomas Rosales, David Candiente, Larry Durant, Eddie Hice, Victor Paul & Sorin S. Punscopie. *Casting:* Tom Kibbee & Camille Taylor. *Sc Supv:* Mini Leder & Sandy Nelson. *Camera Operator:* Ray de la Motte. *Asst Camera Operators:* Horace Jordan & Michael Chavez. *Sd Prod Mixer:* Gene Cantamese. *Producer's Asst:* Susan Becon. *Transportation Coordinator:* Bob Hendrix. *Transportation Captain:* Edward A. Wirth. *Prod Coordinator:* Shirley Snyder. *Associate Ed:* Mary McGlone. *Sd Eff:* William Wistrom. *Vocal Effects:* Allison Caine. *Re-recording:* Ray West, Dick Tyler & Bob Minkler. *Titles & Optics:* CFI. *Location Auditor:* Penny McCarthy. *Mexico AP:* Octavio E. Elias. *Music Casting:* Robert Badami. *Construction Coordinator:* Robert E. Krume. *Sp Eff:* Wayne Beauchamp. *Publicist:* Joan Eisenberger. *Boom Man:* Paul A. Bruce. *Property Master:* Sol Sommatino. *Set Designer:* Beverli Egan. *Model Builder:* John Curtis. *Still Photographer:* John Monte. *Makeup:* Mark Reedall. *Key Grip:* Tom Ramsey. *Craft Service:* Fred Borchers. *Prod Assistants:* David Arntzen & Scott Chestnut. *Location Mgr:* Maxwell Mendes. *Glen Glenn P.A.P. System:* William A. Thiederman. *Atmosphere:* Extracast.

**CAST:** Charles Bronson (Jeb Maynard), Bruno Kirby (Jimmy Fante), Bert Remsen (Carl J. Richards), Michael Lerner (Henry Lydell), Kenneth McMillan (Malcolm Wallace), Ed Harris (Hotchkiss, The Marine), Karmin Murcelo (Elena Morales), Enrique Castillo (Arturo), A. Wilford Brimley (Scooter Jackson), Norman Alden (Willie Lambert), James Victor (Mirandez), Panchito Gomez (Benito Morales), John Ashton (Charlie Monroe), Lawrence P. Casey (Andy Davis), Charles Cyphers (Ski), John Roselius, Murray MacLeod (FBI Agents), Jerry De Wilde (Police Photographer), Katherine Pass (Mrs. Stine), Virgil Frye (Bandit Leader), Luis Contreras (Bandit), Eduardo Ricard (Mexican Policeman), John O'Banion (Morgue Attendant), Rodger La Rue (Reporter), Tanya Russell (Alien Girl), Virginia Bingham (Kathy Landry), Anthony Munoz (Guatemalan), Ray Ochoa (Bartender), Ab Taylor, Frank Deatsch, Juan DeLira (Border Patrolmen), Tammy Wilson (Border Patrolwoman), Chris Coronado, Tony Alvarenga, Ferdinand Pina, Arnold Diaz (Alien Guides), Sy Fuentes, Carlos Munoz (Drivers), Norberto Hernandez (Shantytown Woman), Ross Reynolds (Helicopter Pilot).

*Borderline* was Charles Bronson's first U.S. release of the 1980s, given theatrical showings in the summer of 1980. Although *Caboblanco* was released in Europe earlier in the year, it would not play the states until early the next year. *Borderline* was also Bronson's second film for Lew Grade, now billed simply as Lord Grade, the presenter of the production. Over the years a number of features such as *Border Incident* (1949) and *Wetbacks* (1956) have looked at the problem of alien smuggling along the U.S.–Mexican border. By 1979, however, more than a million aliens were being smuggled across the border annually and the situation was not only an important political issue but also hot news. *Borderline* takes a no-nonsense look at the problem, giving equal doses of coverage to the duty of the Border Patrol to control the smuggling, the plight of the people being smuggled into the U.S. and the crooks who took their money and sold them into bondage.

The story begins in December 1979, with news that four busloads of wetbacks will be smuggled across the Mexican border north of Nogales. The Border Patrol in that sector, led by Jeb Maynard (Charles Bronson), sets out to capture the illegal aliens. They are successful in cornering one group while another near San Diego is pulled over by patrolman Scooter Jackson (A. Wilford Brimley) for a routine check. When he discovers the aliens in the truck he is killed by the supervisor of the smuggling operation, Hotchkiss (Ed Harris), an ex–Marine. Also killed is a young boy (Panchito Gomez) who was among the aliens. When he learns of the killings, Maynard vows revenge although the FBI claims it was a drug killing. Some of the aliens are taken to the ranch of Carl Richards (Bert Remsen), Hotchkiss' employer. Richards, in turn, works for San Diego businessman Henry Lydell (Michael Lerner) who masterminds the alien smuggling operation by selling the wetbacks to customers in large East Coast and Midwest cities, grossing over two million dollars a month. Meanwhile, Maynard traces the dead boy to his mother, Elena Morales (Karmin Murcelo), who works as a domestic for a family in La Jolla. After telling her of her son's death he asks her help in catching the killers. Together the two go into Mexico and then buy (through a corrupt Mexican policeman [Eduardo Ricard]) their way back into the U.S. joining a group of aliens being smuggled into the country. That night the group is attacked by bandits and while Maynard and Elena make a successful getaway, so does their guide Arturo (Enrique Castillo). Maynard promises Elena he will work to get her permanent residence status but feels he has failed in trying to find the killer, whose footprint he identified at the murder scene by a deep cut mark in the boot heel. Thanks to work by rookie patrolman Jimmy Fante (Bruno Kirby), Maynard is able to trace a pesticide found on tomatoes near Jackson's body to Richards' ranch and there finds a group of squatters. At the ranch Maynard also finds more footprints like those at the murder scene. Feeling the heat from the Border Patrol, Lydell tells Richards to run two thousand wetbacks across the border over Christmas Eve. Maynard tracks down Arturo and forces him to admit that it was Hotchkiss who killed Scooter. He also finds

**Charles Bronson in *Borderline* (Associated Film Distribution, 1980).**

out about the planned alien run and has his men at the ranch where they arrest Richards and detain the aliens as they arrive. When Hotchkiss comes in the final convoy he spots Maynard and tries to escape but Jeb pursues him, first by car and then on foot, and kills him in a shootout. Later Richards gets a fine and a light jail sentence for alien smuggling but Lydell is found innocent due to lack of evidence.

Jeb Maynard is one of the sparest of Charles Bronson's screen characters. He is shown to be a man who lives for his job, loyal to friends and allies and one who has a spartan lifestyle with his dumpy apartment and beat up old convertible being examples. When telling his men to find the killer of their co-worker he orders, "I don't want any of that crap about probable cause." Overall the feature takes a downbeat approach to its subject of alien smuggling. "Sleep tight America. Your tax dollars are hard at work," Scooter Jackson proclaims as the patrolmen set out to bring in a group of aliens. Later in the film, rancher Richards and his bloated capitalist boss Lydell confer about their operation. Lydell kids that someday they may be listed on the stock exchange. Richards retorts with a crack about "wetback futures" and Lydell counters, "Wetbacks don't have a future."

Filmed on location in southern California and northern Mexico, including Tijuana, *Borderline* has an arid atmosphere, both in its terrain and pessimistic outlook. Border patrolmen are pictured as overworked, underpaid and understaffed in their endless efforts to stem the tide of alien smuggling. There are the stories of aliens who are caught and recaught several times in the same week, of a group left to starve to death by their guides and of an old man who sold his tailor shop in Mexico only to have all his money taken from him by those bringing him into the United States.

For once critics took some favorable notice of one of Charles Bronson's features with *Borderline*. It is interesting to note that his earlier film *Mr. Majestyk* (1974) also touched on the problem of alien smuggling but critics turned up their noses at it because it developed into a traditional action thriller. Since *Borderline* stuck to the business of an accepted social issue, the critics tended to be more favorable. *Variety* said, "It tackles a serious subject ... with workmanlike dramatic skill and a notable preference for realism over hokum." Regarding Bronson's role, the same reviewer stated, "Bronson is hunched and hated virtually throughout ... (his) deep-lined face is mostly masked by heavy shadow. That hardly damages his enduring charisma, however, and the actor's apparent commitment to conveying the reality of the role is a definite plus." The *San Francisco Voice* said, "*Borderline* raises the consciousness for the plight of aliens, but more importantly, it's a well-crafted film that sustains interest and suspense." The same writer noted, "Bronson gives a nice low-key performance with overtones of compassion and warmth when allowed...." The *Los Angeles Herald-Examiner* called the film "tired action-adventure that looks more like an episode of a television series than a film." In the *Los Angeles Times*, Frank de Olmo wrote, "It is the propaganda film that the Border Patrol has always wanted to help it convince the public that it needs more money and manpower to beat back the alien hordes." In a later article, however, the same newspaper noted *Borderline* was doing "above-average business in its Spanish subtitled form in theatres along the border states." Made on a budget of $8.5 million and employing some 2,000 extras to portray illegal aliens, the movie grossed around $3 million in three weeks in five states: Arizona, California, New Mexico, Oklahoma and Texas.

*Borderline* was released in England in 1982 and West Germany in 1985. By this time several other features were also issued dealing with the same subject, including *The Border* (1982), which cast Jack Nicholson as a border patrolman on the take from alien smugglers. An earlier feature, *Alambrista!* (1977) told the plight of a Mexican boy smuggled across the border and exploited in his new homeland.

## *Breach of Faith: A Family of Cops II* (CBS-TV, 1997)

95 minutes Color

*P:* John Ryan. *EP:* Douglas S. Cramer. *D:* David Greene. *Sc-Executive Consultant:* Joel Blasberg. *Ph:* Ronald Oriuex, *Ed:* Michael Pacek. *Mus:* Peter Manning Robinson. *Prod Mgr:* Seamus Flannery. *Stunt Coordinator:* Roderick Lodescu. *Stunts:* Paul Ravovski, Dwayne Downer, Danny Lima, Marco Bianco, Real Andrews, Robert Racki, Mirielle Dumond, Brian Jakersky, Danny Belley, Matt Birman, Water Masko, Steve Lodescu & Nick Nolan. *Prod Supv:* Michael Brownstone. *Asst Dir:* Karen Pike & Howard Rothchild. *Costume Design:* Marty Partridge-Raynor. *Location Mgr:* Erik K.Snyder. *Camera Operator:* Peter Luxford. *Sd Mixer:* Erv Copestake. *Gaffer:* Robert Davidson. *First Asst Ph:* Colleen Norcross. *Hair Stylist:* Lucy Orton. *Key Grip:* Rick Fester. *Boom Operator:* Kelly Wright. *Asst AD:* Roderick Mayne. *Sc Supv:* Mary Canty. *Transportation Coordinator:* Tom Osmond. *Property Master:* Steve Levitt. *Set Decorator:* Anne Chester. *Makeup:* Maribeth Knezen. *Sp Eff:* Brock Jollifee. *Unit Publicist:* Betty Michaelsmyth. *Transportation Captain:* Elsa "Dee Dee" Scruton. *Russian Translator:* Olly Jasen. *Extra Casting:* Nancy Botting. *First Asst Ed:* John Cameron. *Project Mgr:* Tracey Doddkin. *Post Prod Supv:* Gregor Hutchison. *Post Prod Coordinator:* Ann Henhoffer. *Foley Artist:* Sid Lieberman. *Sp Eff Ed:* Scott Thiesen. *Prod Secretary:* Sherri McGrath. *Producers' Asst:* Tessa Abdull. *Post Prod Coordinator:* James Chima. *Dialogue/ADR Director:* Tim Roberts. *Re-Recording Mixers:* Mike Baskerville & Jamie Sulek.

**CAST:** Charles Bronson (Inspector Paul Fein), Joe Penny (Detective Ben Fein), Diane Ladd (Shelly Fein), Angela Featherstone (Jackie Fein), Barbara Williams (Kate Fein), Sebastian Spence (Officer Eddie Fein), Kim Weeks (Amy Myers), Andrew Jackson (Boris), Mimi Kuzyk (Mrs. Ivanov), David Hemblen (Mr. Ivanov), Cynthia Belliveau (Melanie Fein), Mark Humphrey (Matthew), John Evans (Allen), Heather Gordon (Tali), Ruby Smith-Merovitz (Maya), Kari Machet (Marina), David Ferry (Victor), Victor Ertmanis (Toni Pietrov), Nathan Carter (Ronnie Grissom), Jodi Page (Female Panel Member), Kathleen Trowell (Miss Woodel), Amy Stewart (Natalie), Jamie Hayden Devlin (Andrew Baskin), Dorothy Gordon (Mrs. Sandoski), Patricia Yeatman (Mrs. Grissom), Peter Kosaka (Japanese Driver), Tom Melisis (Restaurant Owner), Wendy Lyon (Mrs. Baskin), Katya Ladan (Russian Translator), Father Tom Daly (Priest), Tony Perri (Head Waiter).

Following the ratings success of *A Family of Cops* in 1995, Charles Bronson starred in this sequel which was also set in Milwaukee, Wisconsin, although the majority of the lensing was done in Canada. Like the initial outing, the film centered around the family of Jewish law enforcers as they try to solve a crime, this time the murder of a priest. While the first movie had younger daughter Jackie as the family rebel, this time out she has settled down and opts to join her father and two brothers on the police force. Also adding to the family flavor is the appearance of Diane Ladd as Paul Fein's sister, Aunt Shelly, a psychologist with lots of sage advice. This time out the villains take direct aim at Fein and his family, hoping to discourage them from solving the heinous crime. As *Daily Variety* succinctly

Advertisement for *Breach of Faith: A Family of Cops II* (CBS-TV, 1997).

put it, "Don't mess with Charles Bronson. Not even if you're the Russian Mafia."

When a Milwaukee priest is killed in the confessional of his church, police Inspector Paul Fein (Charles Bronson) and his son, Detective Ben Fein (Joe Penny), are placed in charge of the investigation. Meanwhile Fein's oldest daughter, attorney Kate Fein (Barbara Williams), works to get a parole for a 12-year-old boy (Nathan Carter) convicted of aiding in the murder of an old man. Younger daughter Jackie Fein (Angela Featherstone) is frustrated in trying to find a job and fit into conventional society. Inspector Fein comes to believe the priest was killed by the Russian Mafia as his youngest son, Eddie Fein (Sebastian Spence), is involved in a shoot-out with robbers. Eddie's partner Philo is killed as Eddie mortally wounds the robbers, one of whom is the boy his oldest sister got out on parole. The same night three masked men attack Inspector Fein outside his house and warn him to look elsewhere for the priest killer. Jackie announces plans to join the policy academy, much to her family's dismay. One of the suspects in the priest killing, Pietrov (Victor Ertmanis), is found dead in a park and the church altar boy, Andrew (Jamie Hayden Devlin), is afraid to talk. Eddie is beaten by thugs in his apartment and Kate is attacked by a masked intruder in her home but he is run off by a neighbor. The attackers, Boris (Andrew Jackson) and Illyah, tell Inspector Fein to close the case of the priest's killing or his family will be in further danger. A plainclothes policeman puts plants on Boris and Illyah during a restaurant scuffle and Inspector Fein and his men trail them to a strip club where Ben interrogates Marina (Kari Machet), a waitress and Boris' girlfriend. Afraid of her lover, the young woman reveals that Boris and Illyah killed the priest on orders from the boss because the priest learned the identity of the Russian Mafia leader through a confession from a fence, Polasky, who was also murdered. When the police take Marina into custody, Boris threatens Fein's family and the next day gunmen shoot up Ben's home but no one is injured. Clandestinely, Inspector Fein calls the thugs and tells them he wants to make a deal. They drive him to a vacant house where he overpowers his opponents and forces Boris to reveal his boss' name. Fein then goes to the leader's house and makes an arrest. The family, joined by Inspector Fein's new girlfriend, Ben's partner, is left in peace.

"Take them away, read them their rights and then shoot them," Inspector Paul Fein tells the police officers upon their first arresting Boris and Illyah. Only a fair sequel to *A Family of Cops* (1995), the telefeature contained too many subplots and a rather slow-moving first half. The film stresses Jewish family unity more than the first entry and also provides Paul Fein with a romantic interest in Ben's pretty, mature partner. At the finale Bronson really goes into action, beating up three thugs and shooting two others as he wraps up the case.

*TV Guide* reported the telefeature was "a tale much harder to swallow than the brew that made the town famous. Bronson does a fine job, adding a grandfatherly dimension to his usual stoic tough guy." Michael Farkash wrote in the *Hollywood Reporter*, "There are few suspenseful moments in this serviceable but somewhat predictable, well-photographed thriller.... Bronson's portrayal is understated but effective."

*Breach of Faith: A Family of Cops II* was telecast on February 2, 1997, and proved to be a ratings success as the sixteenth most viewed program the week it was shown.

## *Breakheart Pass* (United Artists, 1976) 95 minutes Color

*P:* Jerry Gershwin. *EP:* Elliott Kastner. *D:* Tom Gries. *Sc:* Alistair McLean, from his novel. *Ph:* Lucien Ballard. *Ed:* Byron Brandt. *Mus:* Jerry Goldsmith. *AD:* Herbert S. Deverill & Richard Gilbert Clayton. *Second Unit Director:* Yakima Canutt. *Asst Dir:* Ronald L. Schwary, Ron Wright, Peter Gries, Lorin Salob & Tony Brand. *Second Unit Ph:* Robert McBride. *Prod Design:* Johannes Larson. *Sets:* Darrell Silvera. *Sp Eff:* A.D. Flowers, Gerald Endler & Logan Frazee Jr. *Prod Mgr:* Don Guest. *Sc Supv:* Michael Preece. *First Asst Cameraman:* Harry Young. *Second Asst Cameraman:* Michael Dennis Weldon. *Camera Operator:* Ralph Gerling. *Second Camera Operator:* Ron Vargas. *Asst Set Decorators:* Nigel Boucher & M. Garcia. *Rear Process Coordinator:* Bill Hansard. *Prop Master:* Sam Gordon. *Asst Prop Master:* David Coleman. *Key Grip:* Clyde Hart. *Grip Best Boy:* Kenneth Adams. *Dolly Grip:* Fred Richter. *Gaffer:* Dick Hart. *Gaffer Best Boy:* Randolph Glass. *Wardrobe:* Thomas Dawson, T. Costich & Paula Kaatz. *Asst AD:* Kim Swados. *Sd Mixer:* Gene Cantamese. *Boom Operator:* Don Merritt. *Makeup:* Phillip Rhodes & Joe Di Bella. *Hairdressers:* Vivienne Walker & Josephine Turner. *Asst Ed:* George Villasenor. *Casting:* Lou Di Giaimo. *Generator Operator:* Lee Smith. *Special Lamp Operators:* J. Marlett & P. Marlett. *Transportation:* Jerry Molen. *Prod Accountant:* Stanley Mark. *Location Accountant:* Selma Brown. *Paymaster:* Dori Miles. *Prod Asst:* Susan Landau. *Prod Secretary:* Joanie Laine. *Wrangler Boss:* Rudy Ugland. *Helicopter Pilot:* James Gavin. *Still Photographer:* Kenny Bell. *Press Agent:* Ernie Anderson. *Title Design:* Phil Norman. *Consultant Foreman:* Victor Clay Johnson. *Stuntmen:* Joe Canutt, Howard Curtis, Mickey Gilbert, Terry Leonard & Tony Brubaker. *Mus Ed:* Kenneth J. Hall. *Transportation Asst:* Thomas Marshall. *UA Representative:* Lionel Lober. *Asst Eff Ed:* Samuel Gemmett. *Costumer:* Thomas Dawson. *Hair Stylists:* Evelyn Freece & Alma Johnson. *Asst Second Unit Ph:* Ray De La Motte. *First Aid:* David Miller. *Dubbing Mixer:* Donald Mitchell. *Grips:* George Ressler, Allan Maylander. Richard Borchar, James Ball, Bob Sordell & Guy Pozell.

CAST: Charles Bronson (John Deakin/John Murray), Ben Johnson (Marshal Nathan Pearce), Jill Ireland (Marcia Solville), Richard Crenna (Governor Richard Fairchild), Charles Durning (Frank O'Brien), Ed Lauter (Major Claremount), David Huddleston (Dr. Edward Molyneux), William McKinney (Rev. Theodore Peabody), Robert Tessier (Levi Calhoun), Roy Jenson (Chris Banlon), Archie Moore (Carlos), Casey Tibbs (Jackson), Scott Newman (Rafferty), Joe Knapp (Henry), Read Morgan (Captain Oakland), Robert Rothwell (Lieutenant Newell), Rayford Barnes (Ballew), Eldon Burke (Ferguson), Eddie Little Sky

(Chief White Hand), John Mitchum (Red Beard), Keith McConnell (Gabriel), Doug Atkins (Jebbo), Sally Kirkland (Jane-Marie), Sally Kemp (Prostitute), Irv Falling (Colonel Scoville), Bill Klem (Seamon Devlin).

Charles Bronson returned to the Western in 1976 with *Breakheart Pass*, which Alistair McLean adapted to the screen from his best-selling novel. Bronson chose Tom Gries to direct the feature having worked well with him on *Breakout* the previous year. Filming took place in the snow country of the Bitterroot Mountains in Idaho with the locomotive used being an actual wood-burning one and a 19th-century private train car was also employed for authenticity. The movie proved to be a flavorful combination of the action, mystery and Western genres and was not only highly entertaining but also good box office. A highlight of the film was the second unit direction by veteran stuntman Yakima Canutt (his son Joe Canutt was one of the stuntmen on the film) and especially exciting was a fight between Charles Bronson and former light heavyweight boxing champion Archie Moore on top of a moving train. Also the dynamiting sequences, which did not include miniatures, are well-staged and exciting.

Taking place following the Civil War, the film opens with a transport train from Reese City bound for Fort Humboldt, the hub of the gold and silver traffic between California and Nevada, stopping at the town of Myrtle City for water. After a coded message is received for Governor Richard Fairchild (Richard Crenna), who is on the train, two army officers disappear. Major Claremont (Ed Lauter) is in charge of soldiers guarding the governor as well as other passengers, including Marcia Scoville (Jill Ireland), who is going to the fort to be with her father, the commander there; a doctor (David Huddleston), a minister (William McKinney) and Frank O'Brien (Charles Durning), who is in charge of the train. In town lawman Nathan Pearce (Ben Johnson), who is also the local Indian agent, arrests John Deakin, alias John Murray (Charles Bronson), who is wanted for arson and murder. On board the train the group is told that Fort Humboldt is in the grip of a diphtheria epidemic and that the train is carrying needed medical supplies as well as reinforcements since the Paiute Indians under the leadership of Chief White Hand (Eddie Little Sky) are hostile. In reality outlaw Calhoun (Robert Tessier) and his gang, who are allied with White Hand, have taken over the fort although he is supposed to be held in custody there for Pearce. With 20 hours to rendezvous with the garrison at Breakheart Pass, the doctor is found murdered, the fireman is thrown from the train and killed and the cars carrying the soldiers are unlatched from the train and crash, killing all aboard. When the train stops that night so the engineer (Roy Jenson) can sleep, Deakin telegraphs the fort that the soldiers are safe. Calhoun then plans to send White Hand and his men to murder the soldiers when the train arrives at the Pass. Next the preacher disappears and

Deakin finds the medical supplies are actually guns and ammunition and he also finds the dead body of the minister, who was a Secret Service agent. The train's chef Carlos (Archie Moore) finds Deakin in the supply car and tries to kill him but they fight on top of the moving train and Carlos falls overboard to his death. Deakin then confides to Marica that he works for the Secret Service and that he has been tracking the stolen rifles on board the train. He has her go for Major Claremont and in her compartment the three hear Governor Fairchild, who is the woman's lover, tell Pearce to kill both men. When the engineer is shot after attacking a soldier, Deakin runs the train and at Breakheart Pass he and Claremont jump off as the Indians attack. Both men plant dynamite which blows up the tracks and after stealing horses from the Indians, Deakin blows up the supply car. Claremont rides to the fort and sets the men there free and they arrive to defeat the Indians. Calhoun, who tries to abduct Marica, is shot by Fairchild who is killed by Claremont when he tries to escape. When O'Brien tries to start the train to escape, Deakin shoots him and he also kills Pearce in a showdown.

*Breakheart Pass*' plot is interesting in that the characters who seem to be the good guys all turn out to be villains, while Bronson's character masquerades as a coward and a murderer in order to carry out his mission. The acting in the film is top flight.

In the *Los Angeles Herald-Examiner*, Richard Cuskelly called the film "an offbeat Western murder mystery" adding Bronson "plays essentially the same stolid, monosyllabic hero he always plays." *Variety* called it "an entertaining mixture of period western and whodunit." Regarding the star, the trade paper reported, "Bronson's emotional range in this context runs to par, which is of scant consequence. The character is him and he's the character, and it little matters that one could never be in doubt about said character as an upright man all the way." Kevin Thomas in the *Los Angeles Times* wrote that the film "has lots of lively action sequences ... but also lots of gratuitous violence, trite dialogue and shallow characterizations." In the *Palm Beach (Florida) Post-Times*, Jerry Renninger called the film "a rather ho-hum western of negligible incandescence." Richard Schickel in *Time* did not like the film and blamed the author: "The trouble is that writer MacLean, adapting his own novel, is at heart a puzzlemaker, not a picturemaker." Writing in *Video Times* (February 1985), Don Abramson said Bronson "gives one of his best performances in this film. It would have been nice if these performances could have been grafted onto a better screenplay."

## *Breakout* (Columbia, 1975) 96 minutes Color

*P:* Robert Chartoff & Irwin Winkler. *EP:* Ron Buck. *D:* Tom Gries. *Sc:* Howard B. Kreitsek, Marc Norman & Elliott Baker, from the novel *The Ten-*

*Second Jailbreak* by Warren Hinckle, William Turner & Eliot Asinof. *Ph:* Lucien Ballard. *Ed:* Bud Isaacs. *Mus:* Jerry Goldsmith. *AD:* Alfred Sweeney Jr. *Sets:* Ira Bates. *Sp Eff:* Augie Lohman. *Sd:* Al Overton Jr. *Prod Mgr:* Sheldon Schrager. *Asst Dir:* Ronald L. Schwary & Peter Gries. *Sc Supv:* Frank Kowalski. *Camera Operator:* Dick Johnson. *Asst Ph:* Harry Young, Bob McBride, Ralph Guerling & Richard Yruicich. *Asst Ed:* Tony Radecki. *Props:* Sam Gordon. *Asst Props:* David Coleman. *Prod Secretary:* Mary Winters. *Mikeman:* Don Bolger. *Casting Director:* Mike Fenton. *Casting:* Fenton–Feinberg. *Costume Designer:* Bill Thomas. *Men's Wardrobe:* Lambert Marks. *Women's Wardrobe:* Edna Taylor. *Greensman:* Mike Winkelman. *Wind Machine Operator:* Phil Corey. *Helicopter Pilots:* Jim Garvin & Jim Hatton. *Pilots:* Frank Tallman & Frank Pine. *Makeup:* Joe Di Bella. *Hairdresser:* Kay Pownall. *Head Grip:* Clyde V. Hart. *Grips:* Harold Rabusse, Lee Crossover & Gene Mendez. *Best Boys:* Bob Tatson & Ron Tickle. *Crab Dolly:* Lee Kosgrove. *Head Gaffer:* Cliff Hutchinson. *Electricians:* Bob Wooton, Boyd Cordell & Chuck Howard. *Construction Coordinator:* Bill Maldonaldo. *Stunt Coordinator:* Dick Dial. *Auditor:* Vince Martinez. *Producers' Secretaries:* Gloria Gonzalez & Janet Crosby. *Transportation Coordinator:* Jerry Molen. *Drivers:* Jerry Callahan, Mike Connally, Tino Caira, Earl Pierson, Dick Sand, J. Gary, John Rasmussen & J. Miller. *Publicist:* Ernie Anderson. *Still Photographer:* Kenny Bell. *Painter:* John Lattanzio. *Title Design:* Phil Norman. *Spanish–French Units: Asst Dir:* Antonio Tuerella De Lacourt. *Prod Coordinator:* Roberto Robert Tanes. *Prod Mgr:* Jean Pierre Servi-Mercanton. *Set Design:* Julio Juanes. *Chief Grip:* Francisco Sanz. *Asst Dir:* Miguel Cheyo. *Unit Mgr:* Robert Saussier. *Ph:* Manuel Berenguer Serra & Felix Martin. *Chief Electrician:* Ingnatio Rodriguez.

**CAST:** Charles Bronson (Nick Colton), Robert Duvall (Jay Wagner), Jill Ireland (Ann Wagner), John Huston (Harris Wagner), Randy Quaid (Hawk Hawkins), Sheree North (Myrna Spencer), Alejandro Rey (Sanchez), Paul Mantee (Cable), Alan Vint (Harve), Roy Jenson (Spencer), Emilio Fernandez (Warden), Jorge Moreno (Sosa), Will B. White (Second Officer), Sidney Klute (Henderson), Chalo Gonzales (Border Guard), Antonio Tuerella, Don Noriego Frill (Prison Guards).

Charles Bronson followed up *Death Wish* (1974) with two more box office blockbusters, *Breakout* and *Hard Times*, both released in 1975. *Breakout* came first in the spring of 1975 and it was a hugely popular item which failed to register with critics but which made a big hit with the public, both in the U.S. and abroad. Columbia Pictures spent more than $3.5 million to promote the film and the investment paid off handsomely with income of nearly $13 million in the film's first two weeks of statewide showings. The film was a fairly light-hearted romp which gave Charles Bronson the opportunity to play low key comedy and at the same time provide all the action expected by his fans. *Breakout* was based on an actual incident although publicity for the film claimed it was fictional. Although amusing in parts, the film opens and closes with gory scenes: the first shows a man being shot three times with a revolver while at the finale an assassin is ripped apart by an airplane propeller. Another unpleasant scene has Robert Duvall's character attempting to escape from prison by joining a corpse in a coffin and almost being buried alive. An underlying romantic theme had Charles Bronson and Jill Ireland's

**Charles Bronson and Sheree North in *Breakout* (Columbia, 1975).**

characters becoming attracted to each other although her character is married to Duvall's. When discussing the initial escape attempt, Bronson's character tells Ireland's, "A part of me hopes it doesn't work." All of the actors seem to be having fun with their parts, particularly Bronson, Sheree North as his old flame and Randy Quaid as his pal.

A man buying his way out of prison in Mexico in 1971 is murdered and the blame is placed on American businessman Jay Wagner (Robert Duvall), a resident of Chile. The whole scheme has been set up by Wagner's grandfather (John Huston) because his activities are felt detrimental to the family business empire. In Mexico Jay is found guilty and sent to prison for 28 years. The grandfather tells Jay's wife Ann (Jill Ireland) he will help financially to get his grandson out of jail and she and her lawyer (Alejandro Rey), who is really a spy for the grandfather, go to pilot Nick Colton (Charles Bronson), who with his friend Hawk Hawkins (Randy Quaid), operate a fly-by-night air service. She hires Nick without telling him her husband is in prison. Nick and Ann make the trip to Mexico but when they try to set down

**Charles Bronson in *Breakout* (Columbia, 1975).**

on a road where Jay is doing day labor with other prisoners, Nick takes off and returns home. At first Nick is very angry with Ann but he agrees to try again and he has Hawk dress like a hooker to get information to Jay in prison. The guards spot Hawk, however, and beat him up and Nick tells Ann he will get Jay out for $50,000. The woman agrees and Nick works up a plan using helicopter pilot Harve (Alan Vint), his old girlfriend Myrna (Sheree North), who is now married to a policeman (Roy Jenson), and Hawk. When Harve finds out they are to pull a prison break he backs out so Nick flies the chopper, with Hawk and Myrna coming along via auto. At the prison word has been given to Jay as to when to be in the prison courtyard for the pickup, and when Nick sets down the chopper there the ailing Jay arrives and they make a getaway although Jay's friend Sosa (Jorge Moreno), who has murdered the prison's warden (Emilio Fernandez), is shot in the escape attempt. Myrna and Hawk have drawn the prison guards away with Myrna claiming she is being raped. After being chased by the guards they rendezvous with Nick and Jay. Harve flies away in the chopper while Nick, Jay, Myrna and Hawk escape in Nick's plane. Via radio they are ordered to set down in Brownsville, Texas, for inspection and there an agent (Paul Mantee) for Jay's grandfather tries to kill him but is stopped by Nick. Jay is reunited with Ann while Nick, Hawk and Myrna are $50,000 richer.

While Columbia sent out 1,300 prints of *Breakout* in the U.S. alone, claiming "the most spectacular saturation blitz of any motion picture," including 17,000 radio announcements nationally the first week of release, the blitz did not translate into good reviews. *Variety* only gave the film a three paragraph review stating, "*Breakout* is a cheap effort for the fast exploitation playoff." Hunter George in *The Miami Herald* said, "*Breakout* doesn't pretend to be anything great, and it's not. It is a formula film tailored for Charles Bronson, another in the mold that has brought Bronson so much notoriety that audiences cheer when he makes his first appearance. Here is the independent-minded, well-muscled, glowering character that people love." Kevin Thomas in the *Los Angeles Times* wrote, "To put it kindly *Breakout* is one of the poorer Charles Bronson action pictures." Judith Crist noted in *New York* magazine, "Charles Bronson fans will find him as squinting, suntanned, and gung-ho as ever as a free-lance pilot in *Breakout*, which boasts an absolutely incomprehensible and unmotivated plot via its screenplay…" *Cue* magazine said the writers of *Breakout* "haven't created a film worth seeing" while the *Christian Science Monitor* thought the film "begins with a mighty promising plot and fine cast but gets swamped by its own lack of imagination and polish." Bridget Byrne opined in the *Los Angeles Herald-Examiner*, "*Breakout* is a Charles Bronson movie. That generally means (with a notable exception in *Death Wish*) poor dialogue, good action, crummy plot, a great deal of Bronson, his T-shirt cut up to show off his shoulder muscles, and much too much of Jill Ireland (Mrs. Bronson), looking made-up for a sound stage rather than the wind-blown airfields where most of the action occurs."

In reality *Breakout* deserved little of the critical roasting it reccived. Evidently the public paid little attention to the movie reviewers and flocked to the feature in droves, both in this country and overseas. Since the movie was based on an actual incident (the escape of Joel David Kaplan from a Mexican prison in 1971) the government of Mexico would not allow the film to be shot there. Instead California, Spain and France were used to simulate Mexico. Veteran Mexican film actor and director Emilio Fernandez portrayed the sadistic prison warden.

Tim Gries replaced Michael Ritchie as the director of *Breakout* very early in the production and he and Charles Bronson would reteam the next year for another "break" feature, *Breakheart Pass*.

## *Bull of the West* (Universal, 1971) 94 minutes Color

*P:* Harry Tatelman & James Duff McAdams. *AP:* Tony Patino. *D:* Paul Stanley & Jerry Hopper. *Sc:* Richard Fiedler & Don Ingalls. *St:* Borden Chase

& D.D. Beauchamp. *St:* James Duff McAdams, from "Man Without a Star" by Dee Linford. *Ph:* Benjamin H. Kline. *Ed:* Gene Palmer. *AD:* George Patrick. *Mus Supv:* Hal Mooney. *Sd:* James T. Porter & Lyle Cain. *Makeup:* Bud Westmore & Leo Lotito Jr. *Unit Prod Mgr:* Ben Bishop. *Asst Dir:* Len Berke & Ben Bishop. *Hair Stylists:* Larry Germain & Florence Bush. *Color Coordinator:* Robert Brower. *Color Consultant:* Alex Guiroga. *Sets:* John McCarthy.

**CAST:** Lee J. Cobb (Judge Henry Garth), Charles Bronson (Ben Justin), Brian Keith (Johnny Wade), Lois Nettleton (Mary Justin), George Kennedy (Tom "Bear" Suchette), James Drury (The Virginian), Doug McClure (Trampas), Gary Clarke (Steve), Geraldine Brooks (Georgia Bishop), Ben Johnson (Fred Spinner), De Forrest Kelley (Ben Telly), Bob Random (Lummis), Vito Scotti (Gilley), Paul Fix (Narrator).

Like *This Rugged Land* (1965), *Bull of the West* was compiled from U.S. television material and issued in Europe as a feature film to cash in on Charles Bronson's new-found international popularity. Perhaps the telefeature's history is more of interest than its content. It was made up of two episodes of the popular NBC-TV series *The Virginian*, a 60-minute Western based on the 1902 novel by Owen Wister. The series ran from 1962 to 1971 and in its last season was called *The Men from Shiloh*. For *Bull of the West*, two segments, "Duel at Shiloh" (telecast January 2, 1963) and "Nobility of Kings" (shown November 10, 1965), were re-edited into a feature-length production. Charles Bronson guest starred in "Nobility of Kings," which in turn was a loose remake of the 1955 feature film *Man Without a Star* starring Kirk Douglas, which was then remade in 1969 as the feature *A Man Called Gannon*.

The plot of *Bull of the West* is a bit hazy as the action jumps back and forth between the two episodes. Charles Bronson plays rancher Ben Justin, a loner who is distant from his young wife (Lois Nettleton) and his son by a former marriage. Justin resists joining Judge Garth (Lee J. Cobb), the owner of a big Wyoming cattle empire, and other ranchers in their cattlemen's association. With his last savings, Ben buys a prize angus bull (the title character) and increases his herd but he has trouble coming to grips with his son becoming a man and his own past failures. Meanwhile drifters Johnny Wade (Brian Keith) and Steve (Gary Clarke) arrive in the area by riding a freight train and hook up with ambitious ranch owner Georgia Bishop (Geraldine Brooks) who plans to use the open range to become rich. Her plans clash with those of Garth and the other cattlemen and when she tries to run a herd through fenced land, Garth and the others, including Justin (via intercut footage), stop the stampede. In a showdown, Steve is forced to kill Wade. Meanwhile Justin, who is about to send his herd to market with those of other ranchers, finds his cattle are diseased and he shoots them, including the prize bull. The other ranchers, however, rally to his side and agree to give him cattle to restart his herd.

While fairly good small-screen entertainment, the combination of the two episodes of *The Virginian* resulted in very minor big-screen fare. Charles

Bronson was more than capable in projecting the multi-layered facets of his character's complicated personality and he was ably assisted by Lois Nettleton as his loyal, understanding wife. It is Bronson's presence alone, however, which makes this otherwise tawdry telefeature watchable.

*Bull of the West* was released theatrically in Europe in 1972–1973. In Italy it was called *Il Solitario del West*, in France *Le Solitaire de l'Quest*, in Sweden *Tjuren Fran Western*, in Denmark *Tyren Fra Western* and in West Germany *Der Einsame*. In the United States it appears on video under the titles *Bull of the West* and *Hot Lead*.

In 1976 Universal took Charles Bronson's other guest appearance in *The Virginian* (an episode called "The Reckoning," telecast September 13, 1967) and combined it with another with Lee Marvin into yet a second telefeature, *The Meanest Men in the West*, which again saw theatrical release in Europe as a "new" movie.

The West German publication *Medium* (June 1972) said the telefilm was "confused." The translation of the German title *Der Einsame* is *The Lonely One*.

## *Caboblanco* (Avco-Embassy, 1980) 87 minutes Color

*P:* Lance Hool & Paul A. Joseph. *EP:* Martin V. Smith. *AP:* Alan Conrad Hool. *D:* J. Lee Thompson. *Sc:* Mort Fine & Milton Golman. *St:* James Granby Hunter & Lance Pool. *Ph:* Alex Phillips Jr. *Ed:* Michael Anderson. *Mus:* Jerry Goldsmith. *Song:* Jerry Goldsmith & Carol Heather. *Asst Dir:* Jesus Marin. *Costume Design:* Tiarila. *AD:* Jose Rodriguez Granada. *Underwater Eff:* Genaro Hurtado. *Asst Ed:* Peter Lee Thompson, Carol Ann Di Guiseppe & Sergio Ortega. *Property Mgr:* Chico Day & Joe Cavalier. *Unit Prod Mgr:* Alfonso Sanchez Tello. *Asst Unit Prod Mgr:* Aurelio Ortiz & Federico Serano. *Producers' Asst:* Lucinda Smith. *Prod Coordinator:* R.J. Black. *Camera Operator:* Carlos Montano. *Prod Secretary:* Sonia Fritz. *Boom Men:* Jorge Gomez & Efren Flores. *Still Man:* Alfredo Rubocaba. *Wardrobe:* Alfonso Govea. *Asst Wardrobe:* Juanita Oliver & Enrique Villavencio. *Property Master:* Antonio Mata. *Re-recording:* Herbert Litt. *Sp Eff:* Laurencio Cordero & Jess Duran. *Sc Supv:* Jose Luis Ortego. *Set Decorator:* Jorge de la Borbolla. *Accountant:* Saryl Horvitz. *Special Promotional Services:* Manny Zwaaf. *Asst Set Decorators:* Ricardo Arena & Jorge Morales. *Press Coordinator—Mexico:* Marion De Lagos. *Makeup:* Joe Di Bella. *Hairstyles:* Christine George. *Mus Ed:* Len Engel. *Gaffer:* Luis Garcia Paredes. *Head Electrician:* Adolfo Lara. *Stuntman:* Tony Epper. *Publicity:* Rogers & Cowan. *Publicity Coordinator:* Ira Teller. *Location Auditor:* Herbert S. McReynolds. *Assistant Location Auditor:* Darlene McReynolds. *Crane Operator:* Norman Wolke. *Optical Eff:* Westminister Company. *Dialogue Coach:* Joe Kane. *Sd Ed:* Neiman-Teller Associates. *Director's Secretary:* Arlene Harris. *Production Associates:* Guillermo Novarro, David Glazer & Karen Posner. *Second Asst Dir:* Terence Buchinsky. *Aerial Sequences:* Mischa Hausserman. *First Asst Ph:* Manuel Padres Luna. *Vocal Eff Advisor:* Allison Caine. *Orchestrations:* Arthur Morton. *Special Still Photography:* Steve Shapiro. *Cinemobile Driver:* Dalibor Raos. *Stunt Coordinator:* Benny Robbins. *Grips:* Graciano Perez, Jose Campos,

Pasqual Villa, Mario Hernandez Luna, Antonio Ramirez & Salvadore Serrano. *Asst Prod Secretary:* Kiku Cavalier.

**CAST:** Charles Bronson (Giff Hoyt), Jason Robards (Gunther Beckdorff), Dominique Sanda (Marie Allesandri), Fernando Rey (Terredo), Simon MacCorkindale (Lewis Clarkson), Camilla Sparv (Hera), Gilbert Roland (Dr. Ramirez), Denny Miller (Horst), James Booth (John Baker), Jorge Russek (Provincial Minister), Clifton James (Lorrimer), Ernest Esparza (Pepe), Jose Chavez (Bustamante), Carlos Romano (Miguel), Martin LaSalle (Aparicio), Alan Conrad, Stephen Peck (British Crewmen), Manuel Martin (Inquest Clerk), Aldo Sambrell (Policeman), Jose Carlos Ruiz (Hernandez), Carlos Bravo (Sanchez), Ana De Sade (Rosa), Pedro Damian (Eduardo), Gerardo Zepeda (Canero), Lefty (The Parrot).

Principal photography for *Caboblanco* (spelled as two words, *Cabo Blanco,* in prerelease publicity) began in November 1978, in the small town of Barra de Navidad, on the west coast of Mexico. The film, subtitled *Where Legends Are Born,* was not given mass release until the spring of 1981 in the United States, although it debuted in Europe in 1980, except for West Germany where it did not see theatrical release until 1983. A United States–Spanish co-production, the film was made on a $10 million dollar budget and is one of the most visually beautiful of all of Charles Bronson's features thanks to its scenic locales and the photography of Alex Phillips Jr. Unfortunately the movie has been unfairly compared to *Casablanca* (1942) because of their similar titles and a very slight plot similarity. Because of this, critics were unjustly strident about the rather entertaining effort and it did not do well stateside. *Los Angeles Channel Z Magazine* (December 1981) noted, "Prior to shooting, *Caboblanco* had a giant preproduction ad campaign. It was rumored that *Caboblanco* was going to have more than a few elements in common with *Casablanca*.... The budget was enormous. An international cast was signed ... [it] had all the elements of an 'up-front, want-to-see' box office attraction. But the film opened this year in Los Angeles with a slim advertising campaign and almost no fanfare. More publicity surrounded the 'making of the deal' than the release of the picture!"

Set in the remote fishing village of Caboblanco on the coast of Peru in 1948, the film opens with a British survey ship headed by Lewis Clarkson (Simon MacCorkindale) losing a diver (James Booth) in an explosion. At the same time mysterious beauty Marie Allesandri (Dominique Sanda) arrives in the village looking for her lover, Jacques Laceour. She takes a room at the hotel-bar of ex-patriate American Giff Hoyt (Charles Bronson) but has her passport held by the local police chief Terredo (Fernando Rey). Giff knew Laceour and he tells Marie that Jacques left after recovering from being shot, leaving Giff his parrot Lefty. Terredo takes orders from fugitive Nazi Gunther Beckdorff (Jason Robards) who lives in a mansion surrounded by a small hired army. He was the one who ordered Terredo to detain the girl. Giff goes to see Beckdorff and tells him not to let Marie be harmed. He also finds out

Advertisement for *Caboblanco* (Avco-Embassy, 1980).

that his ex-girlfriend Hera (Camilla Sparv), now a lush, is the German's mistress. When the diver's death is ruled an accident by Terredo, Clarkson objects. Later he confesses to Giff that he works for the British Secret Service and his expedition is looking for a sunken treasure ship, the *Brittany*. Giff informs him that Beckdorff is also looking for the ship and was probably responsible for the diver's death. The provincial minister (Jorge Russek), who is in cahoots with Beckdorff in trying to locate the ship, tells Terredo that American authorities are after Hoyt on a murder charge as he wants Giff to pay more protection money. Hera comes to Giff's bar and tells him Beckdorff has thrown her out; Giff gives her a room. After telling Marie about Hera and the fact she will never see Laceour again, Giff and Marie become lovers and she tells him the sunken ship contains $22 million in gold and that Laceour knew the location where it sank. Clarkson takes a boat to Beckdorff's hideout and finds diving equipment and explosives but he is wounded by the Nazi's men. Giff helps him escape and takes him to the local alcoholic physician, Dr. Ramirez (Gilbert Roland). Marie visits Beckdorff who tells her he forged the postcard that brought her to Caboblanco in search of Laceour because he thinks she knows the whereabouts of the ship. She tells him Giff knows the location and that he will tell her and she, Beckdorff and the provincial minister will split the profits. That night a tearful Marie tells Giff she sold him out to Beckdorff as the latter's henchman Horst (Denny Miller) and his men come looking for him. Marie hides Giff but the angry Horst badly beats Hora. Giff comes to her rescue and in the fight Horst is killed. Giff then goes to Terredo and calls Beckdorff, telling him to come to his bar if he wants to find out the location of the ship. Terredo demands that Giff be his prisoner and at the bar Giff confronts Beckdorff who says the ship does not carry gold but precious jewels the Nazis took from countries all over Europe. Giff gets the drop on Beckdorff and Terredo does not come to his aid. The Nazi realizes he is beaten and rather than go back to Germany to hang he takes poison. Terredo retains control of Caboblanco, and Giff and Marie stay together with the code to the treasure revealed by the parrot.

*Caboblanco* nicely captures the flavor of post–World War II Peru and its background music included the songs "Tangerine," "Moonlight Serenade," "I've Got My Love to Keep Me Warm" and Nat (King) Cole's recording of "The Very Thought of You." It also contained a new song written by the film's music composer, Jerry Goldsmith, and Carol Heather called "Heaven Knows." Thanks to the gorgeous locales and appealing cast, *Caboblanco* makes for a nice 87 minute entertainment. Charles Bronson is very good as the American hiding in Peru. He tells Marie at one point he was there because he killed a man but does not elaborate on his situation. "This is my home" he says. Dominique Sanda is statuesque and very sexy as the alluring Marie and Jason Robards nicely handles the role of the cold-blooded Nazi. Fernando Rey is especially good as the local police chief, as are Camilla Sparv as Giff's ex-lover and Simon MacCorkindale as the British Secret Service Agent. Denny Miller has a few good scenes as the sadistic Horst but Gilbert Roland is wasted in the role of Dr. Ramirez.

Nearly all of the critics unfortunately compared *Caboblanco* to *Casablanca* and the results were not kind. *Box Office* reported, "Since no one dared to remake *Casablanca*, the makers of *Caboblanco* have tried to evoke many of the same elements without actually copying. They would have done better to steal." *Variety* called it a "tenuous leftover" adding that it "was perhaps begun as a tongue-in-cheek remake, but lost its way or lacked necessary dash to make it work. Result is particularly muddy, no matter how perceived." Kevin Thomas wrote in the *Los Angeles Times*, "*Caboblanco* is a feeble attempt to resurrect romantic '40s intrigue, but its script is too listless and uninspired to all its people to acquire any individuality or even come to life."

## *C'Era una Volta il West (Once Upon a Time in the West)*

(Paramount, 1969) 165 minutes Color

*EP:* Fulvio Morsella. *AP:* Bino Cicogna. *D:* Sergio Leone. *Sc:* Sergio Donati & Sergio Leone. *St:* Dario Argento, Bernardo Bertolucci & Sergio Leone. *Ph:* Tonino Delli Colli. *Ed:* Nino Baragli. *Mus:* Ennio Morricone. *AD:* Carlo Simi. *Set Decorator:* Carlo Leva. *Makeup:* Alberto De Rossi. *Sd:* Claudio Maielli. *Hairdresser:* Grazia De Rossi. *Unit Manager:* Ugo Tucci. *Prod Mgr:* Claudio Mancini. *Asst Prod Mgr:* Camillo Teti. *Prod Secretary:* George Risi. *Asst Dir:* Giancarlo Santi. *Continuity:* Serena Canevari. *Asst Cameramen:* Franco Di Giacomo & Guiseppe Lanci. *Asst AD:* Tonio Palombi. *Wardrobe:* Marilu Carteny. *Still Photographer:* Angelo Novi.

**CAST:** Claudia Cardinale (Jill McBain), Henry Fonda (Frank), Jason Robards (Cheyenne), Charles Bronson (Harmonica), Gabriele Ferzetti (Mr. Morton), Woody Strode (Stony), Jack Elam (Knuckles), Frank Wolff (Brett McBain), Keenan Wynn (Sheriff), Lionel Stander (Bartender), Marco Zuanelli (Wobbles), Paolo Stoppa (Sam), John Frederick, Michael Harvey (Members of Frank's Gang), Enzio Santianello (Timmy McBain), Aldo Sambrell (Man from Cheyenne), Dino Mele (Young Harmonica), Benito Stefanelli (Station Manager), Marilu Carteny (Maureen McBain), Livio Andronico, Salvo Basile, Luigi Ciavarro, Spartaco Conversi.

In reviewing *Once Upon a Time in the West* in *New Republic*, Stanley Kauffmann said, "The story could have been told, as it often has, in 80 minutes, or so." While many others have called the film Sergio Leone's masterpiece, Kauffmann is right on target. Visually stunning with impressive acting, a haunting musical score and containing the gritty, arid atmosphere of the pioneer West, this $5 million production shot in Arizona, Utah and Spain with interiors lensed at Cinecitta Studios in Rome is nonetheless a great deal of pomp and circumstance built on a banal script. The story is told visually, often reminding one of a silent film with music while choppy dialogue carries along the storyline. Leone's main interest seems to be imagery and at this he excels, although the cast often appears to be reacting rather than acting. Still the feature is not without interest and it must be given credit for giving Charles Bronson another major boost toward international stardom.

The film opens at the remote ranch of Irishman Brett McBain (Frank Wolff), who with his three children is expecting the arrival of his beautiful new bride Jill (Claudia Cardinale). Instead he and his offspring are massacred by gunman Frank (Henry Fonda) and his henchmen. Meanwhile three of Frank's men have been gunned down at a local train station by a mysterious stranger known as Harmonica (Charles Bronson), who they had planned to ambush upon Frank's orders. Jill arrives from New Orleans to find her new husband and stepchildren dead with outlaw Cheyenne (Jason Robards) and his gang blamed for the massacre. Harmonica warns Cheyenne that a posse is after him while Jill searches the ranch house looking for her late husband's supposed wealth. Cheyenne arrives there also with the same goal in mind but neither find what they are seeking. Harmonica trails Frank, with the help of local laundryman Wobbles (Marco Zuanelli), who does not know he is being followed. He finds Frank aboard a private train owned by railroad magnate Mr. Morton (Gabriele Ferzetti), a cripple, and he finds out Morton wants the McBain ranch because the railroad needs the right-of-way as it contains water needed for steam engines. Harmonica is captured by Frank's men but after Frank leaves to kill Jill he is set free by Cheyenne. Frank abducts the girl and takes her to his remote hide-out where he plans to rape and kill her but instead she beds him willingly. Frank sets the girl free on the condition that she sell the ranch to the highest bidder. At an auction conducted by the local sheriff (Keenan Wynn) Frank's men try to control the bidding but are outfoxed by Harmonica who bids $5,000, saying he will pay with the reward money for capturing Cheyenne. Meanwhile Morton doublecrosses Frank and hires the latter's own men to kill him. Harmonica, however, aids Frank because he wants the latter for himself. In a shootout with the rest of Frank's gang Cheyenne is badly wounded and Frank returns to the private car to find Morton dying. He then returns to town for a showdown with Harmonica and is mortally wounded. Before dying he remembers that years earlier he had hung Harmonica's brother and this was the latter's revenge. Both Harmonica and Cheyenne return to Jill but both leave, Cheyenne to die and Harmonica to drift. Jill now welcomes the newcomers to her land, with the changes planned by her late husband making her a wealthy woman.

At a cost of $250,000, Sergio Leone built one of the largest western sets ever constructed, near the village of Guadix in Spain. It consisted of 70 buildings, finished both inside and out, with a saloon, stores, houses and a hotel. Even the area's red soil was used to match that of frontier Arizona. In researching the film Leone spent almost a year in Arizona, Utah and Texas and he used the American Railway Archives to help make his story of the coming of the railroad to the West more authentic.

**Charles Bronson in *C'Era una Volta il West* (Once Upon a Time in the West) (Paramount, 1969).**

For Charles Bronson *Once Upon a Time in the West* proved that the fourth time is the lucky charm. Sergio Leone had previously wanted Bronson for the leads in *Per un Pugno di Dollari* (*A Fistful of Dollars*) (1964), with the part going to Clint Eastwood; *Per Qualche Dollaro in Più* (*For a Few Dollars More*) (1965), that role going to Lee Van Cleef; and *Il Buono, il Brutto, Il Cattivo* (*The Good, the Bad and the Ugly*) (1966), with the role of Mr. Ugly played by Eli Wallach. Finally Bronson was able to accept the role of Harmonica and he played the laconic, but vengeful, stranger so perfectly that it became one of his most popular and best remembered roles. While *Time* magazine thought the film "Tedium in the tumbleweed" it added, "The picture, such as it is, belongs to Charles Bronson. A flinty character actor who has appeared in everything from *The Great Escape* to *The Dirty Dozen*, he plays his first important lead with commendable skill."

Overall critics either loved or disliked the film, there seemed to be no middle ground. In Europe it was a tremendous success and in France it even did better than *Adieu l'Ami*, solidifying Bronson's popularity in that country. In the United States, however, Paramount cut the film by nearly a half hour making the plotline more jumbled than ever. As a result it got a quick playoff, thus depriving Bronson again of a good showcase in his own homeland.

Retrospective reviews of *Once Upon a Time in the West* tend to be more telling than contemporary ones. Phil Hardy wrote in *The Western* (1983), "Leone's classic fairy tale of violence intertwines and gives a mythical edge to two classic Western themes, the revenge story and the arrival of civilization in the West. The result is a bizarre cross between *The Iron Horse* (1924) and *The Big Trail* (1930), a film that examines the impact on the frontier of the Colt .45, the dollar and the railroad's 'beautiful shiny rails.'" In *The Paramount Story* (1985), John Douglas Eames said that "Leone crammed elements of virtually every similar winner ever filmed, not the least the violence of his Clint Eastwood *Dollar* movies. The result fell short of his epic goal, but crowded audiences enjoyed a feast of blood-spattered excitement." "Sergio Leone's most ambitious and most acclaimed film, considered by many critics as the greatest of the Spaghetti Westerns, is certainly memorable for its spectacular cast.... This is a bigger-than-life, sprawling tale," commented Thomas Weisser in his excellent filmography *Spaghetti Westerns—the Good, The Bad and the Violent* (1992). In *Guide for the Film Fanatic* (1986), Danny Perry stated, "Baroque epic western is Sergio Leone's masterpiece. It is also his most pessimistic film: its end signals the death of his 'ancient race' of superwarriors (first seen in his Clint Eastwood *Dollar* films) and the moment when there is no more resistance to advancing civilization...."

The three most striking features of *Once Upon a Time in the West* are Tonino Delli Colli's photography, the music soundtrack by Ennio Morricone and the film's cast of stars. Certainly Charles Bronson's work as Harmonica dominates the proceedings but he is ably assisted by Claudia Cardinale as the beautiful prostitute whose hopes for a better life are suddenly shattered by the killing of her new husband. Jason Robards too is excellent as the good-natured outlaw and much has been made of the casting of usual hero Henry Fonda as the cold-blooded killer. Frank Wolff is effective in his brief scenes as McBain while Gabriele Ferzetti is fine as the corrupt businessman. Sadly Keenan Wynn, Jack Elam, Woody Strode and Lionel Stander have too little to do for effective emoting.

Fortunately the original 165-minute version of the film has been restored for U.S. showings on video and television, thus giving the viewer a complete look at a very important entry in Charles Bronson's filmography.

Viewed at either running time, the film's surprising weak point is its script. This is somewhat puzzling considering the talent involved in developing the movie's storyline. The screenplay is credited to Sergio Donati and Sergio Leone, from a story by Leone, Bernardo Bertolucci and Dario Argento. While *Once Upon a Time in the West* is the only Spaghetti Western in the Bertolucci cannon, he went on to direct such noted features as *Last Tango in Paris* (1973), *1900* (1977) and *The Last Emperor* (1987), writing or co-writing the scripts for all his films. Dario Argento wrote *Oggi a Me ... Domani a te* (Today It's Me ... Tomorrow You) (1968) and *Un Esercito di Cinque Uomini*

(1969), released in the U.S. as *Five Man Army*, before becoming a cult director of thrillers like *The Bird with the Crystal Plummage* 1970), *Deep Red: Hatchet Murders* (1975) and *Suspiria* (1977). Sergio Leone had a hand in writing his trilogy with Clint Eastwood, the three films rejected by Charles Bronson, and he also worked again with Sergio Donati on the script for *Duck You Sucker* in 1971, the last Spaghetti Western he directed. The least known of the group, Sergio Donati wrote several top notch genre efforts, including the classic Lee Van Cleef starrer, *The Big Gundown* (1966), *Navajo Joe* (1966) starring Burt Reynolds, *Face to Face* (1967) and *Dollars for a Fast Gun* (1968).

## *Chato's Land* (United Artists, 1972) 100 minutes Color

*P-D:* Michael Winner. *Sc:* Gerald Wilson. *Ph:* Robert Paynter. *Ed:* Freddie Wilson. *Mus:* Jerry Fielding. *AD:* Manolo Manpaso. *Asst Dir:* Peter Price, Antonio Tarruella & Stefano Capriati. *Second Unit Director:* Raul Perez Cubero. *Sp Eff:* Antonio Parra. *Sd:* Terence Rawlings, Chris Kent & Hugh Strain. *Prod Supv:* Clifton Brandon. *Prod Mgr:* Jose Maria Rodriguez. *Wardrobe:* Ron Beck. *Makeup:* Richard Mills & Mariano Rey. *Asst AD:* Rafael Ablanque. *Dialogue Editor:* Russ Hill. *Camera Operator:* Anthony Throke. *Stunt Coordinators:* Christopher Kent & Paddy Cunningham. *Camera Asst:* Douglas O'Neons. *Hair Dresser:* Antonio Lopez. *Continuity:* Pamela Carlton. *Property Master:* Ray Thaynor. *Chief Wrangler:* Rudy Ugland. *Prod Asst:* Stephen Cory. *Stillsman:* Antonio Luego.

CAST: Charles Bronson (Pardon Chato), Jack Palance (Captain Quincey Whitmore), Richard Basehart (Nye Buell), James Whitmore (Joshua Everette), Simon Oakland (Jubal Hooker), Ralph Waite (Elias Hooker), Richard Jordan (Earl Hooker), Victor French (Martin Hall), William Watson (Harvey Lansing), Roddy McMillan (Gavin Malechie), Paul Young (Brady Logan), Lee Patterson (George Dunn), Rudy Ugland (Will Coop), Raul Castro (Mexican Scout), Sonia Rangan (Chato's Woman), Verna Harvey (Shelby Hooker), Sally Adez (Moira Logan), Clive Endersby (Jacob Meade), Peter Dyneley (Sheriff Ezra Saunders), Hugh McDermott (George the Bartender), Rebecca Wilson (Edna Malechie); Florencio Amarilla, Clestino Gonzalez, Roland Grand, Louis Amarilla.

*Chato's Land* marked Charles Bronson's return to U.S. financed movies with this Scimitar Film Production filmed in Spain by producer-director Michael Winner, whom Bronson would eventually work with on six occasions, half of them *Death Wish* features. Made in eight weeks, *Chato's Land* is a reworking of *The Lost Patrol* (1934) which was later done as a Western, *Bad Lands* (1939). This time out the protagonist is the half-breed Apache title character portrayed by Charles Bronson. It is one of his least vocal parts, his dialogue being made up of only a few words in English and some sentences in Apache. Bronson, however, dominated the film with his strong, forceful performance as the revengeful Chato who goes from the hunted to the hunter. "Bronson is a standout" said *Variety*, and *Films and Filming* said he "dominates

Poster for *Chato's Land* (United Artists, 1972).

the film by a mystic presence." Certainly the script gave the actor opportunities to act without dialogue, proving just how good Bronson is at visuals. Scenes where he toys with the posse find Chato dressed in his regular attire but when he begins to hunt down the men in earnest, after they have raped his wife, he dons the attire of an Apache warrior. The cat-and-mouse game between Chato and the posse keeps the film moving as does the interesting characterizations by the rest of the cast. Particularly good are the Spanish locales for the Old West and Robert Paynter's excellent photography.

In a dusty Western town half-breed Apache Pardon Chato (Charles Bronson) is harassed by a redneck sheriff (Peter Dyneley) who dies when he pulls a gun on Chato. Making a quick getaway, Chato is followed by a posse led by former Confederate Captain Quincey Whitmore (Jack Palance), his old friend Nye Buell (Richard Basehart) and Martin Hall (Victor French), who witnessed the shooting. That night they stay at the ranch of the Hooker brothers and the next day the three, Jubal (Simon Oakland), Elias (Ralph Waite) and Earl (Richard Jordan), join the group as do ranchers Joshua Everette (James Whitmore), Gavin Malechie (Roddy McMillan), his friend George (Lee Patterson) and his Mexican tracker (Raul Castro). One posse member, Will Coop (Rudy Ugland), takes a bad fall and cannot continue and that night Chato sneaks into camp and cuts their water bags. Continuing the chase, the posse finds and burns a deserted Apache village but Chato leads them into the desert and ambushes them. He scatters their horses and they lose three of them before continuing the chase. Chato then returns home to his woman (Sonia Rangan) and son and later goes away with another brave to round up wild horses. The posse stumbles onto his home and the Hooker brothers rape Chato's wife and tie her up as bait. The boy tells Chato what happened and that night he sets fire to the pen holding the posse's horses. When the men go to put out the blaze he rescues his woman but his friend is killed by Jubal. The next morning Earl goes after the woman and is killed by Chato. By now Whitmore realizes Chato is using the land to fight them and as the posse rides Hall is shot off his horse. Although the men go after Chato on foot, they cannot find him and that night he pins them down in their camp. The next day Hall dies and Chato shoots the Mexican scout. When Whitmore and Buell go after Chato on foot the latter kills Buell, while back in camp the captain wants to turn back but Jubal refuses, wanting revenge for Earl's death. At gunpoint he makes Whitmore promise to stay, but two other members, Joshua, who has a broken shoulder from a fall off his horse, and Harvey (William Watson) leave and Elias shoots Joshua while Jubal does the same to Whitmore when he tries to stop his brother. Elias goes after Harvey, who is killed by Chato, and Elias too meets death at the hands of the half-breed. Back in camp Whitmore succumbs, leaving only Jubal and his unwilling saddlemates, Malechie and George. They surprise Jubal when his back is turned and beat him to death with huge rocks. The two then head out into the desert and that night Chato kills Malechie as he stands by their campfire. The next day Chato confronts George, who is now on foot. He does not kill him but leaves him to the justice of the land.

Much of the plot of *Chato's Land* reflects on the arrogance and greed of the white men who conquered the West. Most of the posse are pictured as racists. Early in the film when the Jubal brothers try to get neighbor Jacob Meade (Clive Endersby) to ride with them to hunt Chato he refuses saying he will not ride with the likes of them. Only Malechie and George try to stop the rape of Chato's woman by the Hooker brothers, even the basically decent Captain Whitmore refuses to intercede. Whitmore, who leads the hunt dressed in his Confederate war garb and brandishing a sword, spends much of the time reliving the War of the Rebellion. "Hell, it was a good war," he states, remembering all the battles, the men killed and the lost glory. The film also nicely captures the futility of frontier existence. Even an unredeemed character like the randy Earl Hooker knows his life isn't much. He tells his brother Elias, "What have we got? Hatin', killin', whorin', runnin' scratch cattle."

Although Charles Bronson highlights the film in his portrayal of the stoic Chato, the rest of the cast is superb. Jack Palance shares above the title billing with Bronson and he gives a fine, subdued performance as the old soldier as does Richard Basehart as his whiskey soaked pal. James Whitmore is fine as the rancher who goes along on the quest more out of duty than desire as does the basically decent character of Malechie, played nicely by Roddy McMillan. Victor French is good as the sheriff's friend who instigates the hunt and Simon Oakland, Ralph Waite and Richard Jordan are memorable as the slimy Hooker brothers.

*Chato's Land* was another big Bronson box office moneymaker around the world although it did only minor business in the United States when released here by United Artists. For the first time a Bronson starrer got the notice of the critics in his homeland, but most were not impressed with the feature. *Variety* said the "film carries certain suspense, drive and grim realism but lacks story development that would have made this a real winner." Phil Hardy in *The Western* (1983) noted, "(Michael) Winner's direction, with its over-reliance on the zoom lens and its budget-paring ridiculous day-for-night cinematography, drains the film of any resonance." In *The Family Guide to Movies on Video* (1988), Henry Herx and Tony Zaza called the film a "Failed Western.... Directed by Michael Winner, the problem is that once the movie gets into the groove of steady killing, it becomes both tedious and glaring in its cumulative brutality." Despite the protests of violence, the movie was released with a PG rating.

Charles Bronson apparently enjoyed working with director Michael Winner, who had previously helmed such outings as Burt Lancaster in *Lawman* (1971) and Marlon Brando in *The Nightcomers* (1972), and he requested him for his next feature, *The Mechanic* (1972), which marked Bronson's first work in Hollywood since an episode of the TV series *Dundee and the Culhane* in 1967.

## *Chino* see *Valdez il Mezzosangue*

## *Città Violenta (The Family)* (Fono Roma/Inidis/Universal France, 1970) 109 minutes Color

*P:* Arrigo [Harry] Columbo & Georgio [George] Papi. *AP:* Solly Bianco. *D:* Sergio Sollima. *Sc:* Sauro Scavolini, Gianfranco Galligarich, Lina Wertmuller & Sergio Sollima. *St:* Dino Maiuri & Massimo De Rita. *Ph:* Aldo Tonti. *Ed:* Nino Baragli. *Mus:* Ennio Morricone. *Sd:* Aldo De Martini. *AD:* Franco Fumagalli. *Asst Dir:* Fabrizio Gianni. *Prod Mgr:* Piero Donati. *Racing Supervisor:* Remy Julienne.

CAST: Charles Bronson (Jeff Heston), Telly Savalas (Al Weber), Jill Ireland (Vanessa Shelton), Michel Constantin (Killain), Umberto Orsini (Steve), George Savalas (Shapiro), Ray Sanders, Benjamin Lev (Cellmates), Peter Dane (Tom Shandy), Stirling Moss, Dennis Holmes, John Siefer (Themselves).

Independent hit man Jeff Heston (Charles Bronson) meets and falls in love with beautiful photographer's model Vanessa Shelton (Jill Ireland). After spending time with Vanessa, Jeff is hired by wealthy businessman-race car driver Coogan* to kill his rich uncle, who he shoots while the old man is aboard his yacht. Later Jeff and Vanessa are chased by men in a car and Coogan shoots Jeff but he manages to escape although he is sent to prison for killing one of Coogan's men. Steve (Umberto Orsini), Jeff's lawyer, gets him out of jail and he goes to his mentor Killain (Michel Constantin), now a drug addict, and asks him to locate Coogan and Vanessa, who he realizes are lovers. Coogan participates in the Can-Am auto race in Michigan and Jeff goes there and from ambush shoots out Coogan's tire during the race, causing him to crash through a brick wall and die in a terrible fire. Jeff then finds Vanessa at a social gathering and he takes her to a waterfront warehouse where he plans to rape her but realizes he is still in love with her. As they plan to go away together, Jeff is given photos of his killing Coogan and is then ushered to the estate of Al Weber (Telly Savalas), a Mafia boss trying to go straight. He wants Jeff to work for his organization but the latter will not commit himself, especially when he finds out Weber is married to Vanessa. When Vanessa invites Jeff to her cottage retreat he goes, planning to kill her, but again he cannot because of his love for the beautiful blonde. He does, however, shoot Killain, who Weber hired to kill them both. Vanessa then helps Jeff to set up Weber who he shoots but when he goes to meet the woman at their scheduled rendezvous he finds he has been trailed by the police. Jeff manages to escape as the now widowed Vanessa takes over the Weber empire, reducing her cohort Steve to an underling role in the operation. As Vanessa and Steve ride in a glass-encased elevator to a board

**The actor playing Coogan is not credited on screen or in reviews. The Swedish publication* Screen *lists Michel Constantin as Coogan, but he played the part of Killain.*

"THE GODFATHER"
gave you an offer you couldn't refuse.
"THE FAMILY"
gives you no alternative!

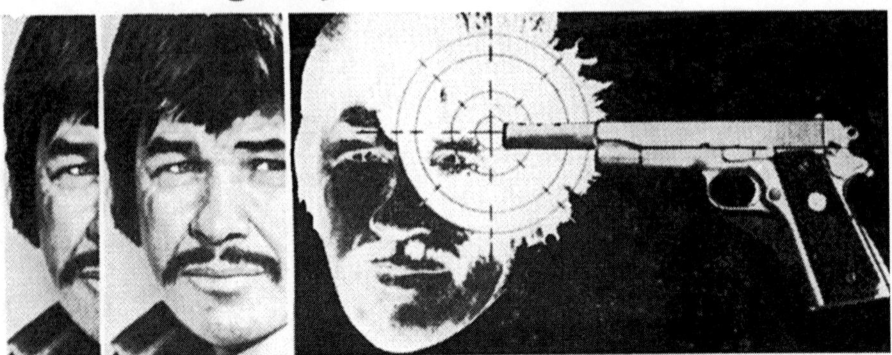

Charles Bronson
Telly Savalas
Jill Ireland

in Technicolor
with Umberto Orsini and Michel Costantin
directed by Sergio Sollima
coproduced by Unidis–Fono Roma–Universal France

Advertisement for *The Family* (Intercontinental Co-Productions, 1974), the U.S. release title of *Città Violenta* (Fono Roma/Inidis/Universal France, 1970).

of directors' meeting in a skyscraper built by Weber, Jeff shoots them from a nearby building. He then waits for the police and baits a rookie cop into killing him.

Beginning with a lengthy car chase and continuing through a myriad of plot twists, *Città Violenta* is a hard to follow, splicy gangster melodrama enhanced by good work from Charles Bronson as the hit man and Jill Ireland as the gorgeous femme fatale. It is the first of the many films in which they co-star after no scenes together in *Villa Rides!* (1968) and only a brief one in *La Passager de la Pluie* (1969). Telly Savalas, who had worked with Bronson in *The Dirty Dozen* (1967), puts in a slick cameo as the Mafia don while his brother George Savalas has a small role as a slimy, double-crossing garage operator. Michel Constantin, who would also be in Bronson's next starrer, *de la Part des Copains* (1971), underplays his scenes as a fellow hit man, while Umberto Orsini is properly oily as the corrupt lawyer. Sergio Sollima's direction is choppy with the film containing too many abrupt cuts to give it proper cohesion. Director-screenwriter Sollima also helmed Spaghetti Westerns like *The Big Gundown* (1966), *Face to Face* (1967), *Run, Man, Run* (1967) and the horror film *Devil in the Brain* (1972). Co-scripter Lina Wertmuller went on to direct movies such as *Seduction of Mimi* (1974), *Blood Feud* (1979) and *Summer Night* (1987).

Despite its drawbacks, *Città Violenta* is not without interest. It is important as Charles Bronson's first solo starring vehicle following his elevation to international stardom and its success proved to investors that the Bronson name meant big box office returns. Bronson and Jill Ireland work quite well together and certain scenes are well staged: Jeff showing no fear of a tarantula in his jail cell, his methodical methods of setting up his hit of Coogan and the finale where he kills Vanessa and Steve. With some location work in New Orleans (the city of the title), the movie also contains some beautiful bayou scenery. There is also pungent dialogue. In one scene Weber invites Jeff to join his organization and Jeff tells him he has always been an "orphan," to which Weber replies, "There is no divorce in our family." When Jeff plans to rape Vanessa in the dockside warehouse, they are interrupted by three men violently beating another. "Why is it when I'm with you I end up in blood and violence," she asks. Jeff replies, "The whole city is full of blood and violence. You only see it when you are with me." The Can-Am racing scenes appear little better than stock footage although several famous race drivers can be glimpsed.

When *Città Violenta* premiered in Rome in October 1970, the reviewer for *Variety* said the movie was "dominated by Charles Bronson in rare form" adding the "Film is more than exciting film entertainment, stylishly conceived and directed." The feature proved to be a big success internationally with release by Rank in Great Britain in 1971 as *Violent City* and in Sweden the same year as *Den Brutala Staden*. Following the pattern of most Bronson features of the time, however, it was not issued in the United States until 1974 by International Co-Productions as *The Family*. That title was used to cash in on the popular gangster film vogue started in the U.S. by *The Godfather* (1972). Another alternate title for the feature is *Final Shot*. It was issued in France in 1971 as *Cité de la Violence*. Steven H. Scheuer wrote in *The Complete Guide to Videocassette Movies* (1987) that it was a "violent, stylish thriller ... Director Sollima tries to get past the cliches in the script by steamrolling over them; he doesn't succeed, but at least the film doesn't stand still long enough for you to be aware of them."

It has been said the *Città Violenta* is an example of how great Charles Bronson's popularity was at the time of its release because he was able to carry such a flimsy vehicle to such successful box office returns. The same can also be said of his next two features, the fairly exciting *De la Part des Copains* (1971) and the not-so-good *Quelqu'un Derrière la Porte* (1971). In fact, Bronson's popularity was so great in Europe at the time and the demand for his films so strong that companies began distributing some of his U.S. television shows as "new" movies. *This Rugged Land* (1965) returned to European big screens as did *Guns of Diablo* (1964). These were followed by *Bull of the West* (1971) and *The Meanest Men in the West* (1976).

## *The Clown* (Metro-Goldwyn-Mayer, 1953) 91 minutes B/W

*P:* William H. Wright. *D:* Robert Z. Leonard. *Sc:* Martin Rackin, from the Screenplay "The Champ" by Leonard Praskins & Frances Marion. *Ph:* Paul C. Vogel. *Ed:* Gene Ruggiero. *Mus:* David Rose. *AD:* Cedric Gibbons & Wade B. Rubottom.

**CAST:** Red Skelton (Dodo Delwyn), Jane Greer (Paula Henderson), Tim Considine (Dink Delwyn), Loring Smith (Goldie), Philip Ober (Ralph K. Henderson), Lou Lubin (Little Julie), Fay Roope (Dr. Strauss), Walter Reed (Joe Hoagley), Edward Marr (TV Director), Jonathan Cott (Floor Director), Don Beddoe (Gallagher), Steve Forrest (Young Man), Ned Glass (Danny Dayler), Steve Carruthers (Maitre d'Hotel), Billy Barty (Midget Clown), Lucille Knoch (Girl), David Saber (Silvio), Sandra Gould (Bunny), Gil Perkins (Dundee), Danny Richards Jr. (Herman), Mickey Little (Lefty), Charles Calvert (Jackson), Karen Steele (Blonde), Jack Heasley, Bob Heasley (Twins), Helene Millard (Miss Batson), Forrest Lewis (Pawnbroker), Charles Buchinsky (Eddie), Robert Ford (Al Zerney), John McKee (Counterman), Jan Wayne, Vicki Raaf (Women), Jesse Kirkpatrick (Sergeant), Martha Wentworth (Neighbor), Inge Jolles (Secretary), Harry Staton (Hogarth), Roger Moore (Man with Hogarth), Linda Bennett (Judy), Wilson Wood (Wardrobe Man), Frank Nelson (Charlie), Thomas Dillon (Clancy), Paul Raymond (Young Man), James Horan, Al Freeman (Men), Tom Urray (Vendor), Mary Foran (Heavy Girl), Sharon Saunders (Girl), David Blair (TV Page Boy), Brick Sullivan (Stagehand), Cy Stevens (Makeup Man), G. Pat Collins (Mr. Christenson), Shirley Mitchell (Mrs. Blotto), Robert R. Stephenson (Counterman), Jimmie Thompson,

Allen O'Locklin, Tony Merrill (Ad-Libbers), Al Hill, Jerry Schumacher, Barry Regan (Dice Players), Lennie Bremen (George), Lee Phelps (Sergeant), Joe Evans, Walter Ridge, George Boyce, Donald Kerr, Mickey Golden (Attendants), Jules Brock, Eve Martel, Neva Martel (Dancers).

Frances Marion's Academy Award–winning story "The Champ," which had starred Wallace Beery and Jackie Cooper in 1931, was refashioned into this maudlin tale with Red Skelton, who was about to give up his movie career for a lengthy stay on television The *Monthly Film Bulletin* complained, "This is the poor man's *Limelight*.... Sentimentality in its sloppiest form abounds. This is not good Skelton." On the other hand *Variety* found it to be "an acceptable family-trade offering."

Instead of playing a boxer, Red Skelton was cast as Dodo Delwyn, a once famous Florenz Ziegfeld comedian whose station has fallen to that of the clown in a third-rate amusement park. Plagued by alcohol, Dodo lives with his young son Dink (Tim Considine) who does his best to care for his father, whom he loves. When Dodo loses his job he shows up drunk at an audition but an old friend (Loring Smith) gets him a club appearance, although he loses his earnings in a poker game. When he is arrested in a raid, Dodo agrees to give Dink back to his ex-wife Paula (Jane Greer), the boy's mother. Realizing Dink is not happy away from his dad, Paula sends him back to Dodo who is about to appear on a television program. The show is a big success and re-establishes Dodo's comic reputation but his years of drinking and poor health lead to his death following the telecast.

*The Clown* gave Charles Bronson another bit part, this time as gambler Eddie, who helps fleece Dodo out of his club date earnings in a poker game. The film, however, would prove to bc Bronson's final small part as afterwards the size of his roles would begin to increase and he would get more attention, both from audiences and critics.

"*The Clown* gives TV comic (Red) Skelton an opportunity to perform one of his specialties: drunk and pratfall routines. But the picture is mostly an unblushing jerker of glycerin tears," said *Time* magazine. *Newsweek* also complained that "nothing alters the fact that the story was maudlin to begin with and remains maudlin in essence."

## *Crime Wave* (Warner Bros., 1954) 74 minutes B/W

*P:* Bryan Foy. *D:* Andre De Toth. *Sc:* Crane Wilbur, Bernard Gordon & Richard Wormser. *St:* John Hawkins & Ward Hawkins. *Ph:* Bert Glennon. *Ed:* Thomas Reilly. *Mus:* David Buttolph. *AD:* Stanley Fleischer. *Asst Dir:* James McMahon. *Sd:* Stanley Jones.

**CAST:** Sterling Hayden (Detective Sergeant Sims), Gene Nelson (Steve Lacey), Phyllis Kirk (Ellen Lacey), Ted De Corsia (Doc Penny), Charles Buchinsky (Ben Hastings), Jay Novello (Otto Hessler), James Bell (Daniel O'Keefe), Dub Taylor (Gus Snider),

Gayle Kellogg (Kelly), Mack Chandler (Sully), Timothy Carey (Johnny Haslett), Richard Benjamin (Mark), Iris Adrian (Hastings' Girlfriend), James Hayward (Zenner), Fritz Feld (Man), Ned Young (Gat Morgan), Sandy Sanders (Officer), John Pickard, John Veitch (Information Officers), Diane Fortier, Mary Alan Hokanson, Ruth Lee, Eileen Elliott (Police Announcers), Shirley O'Hara (Young Woman), Charles Crane, Don Gibson, Bert Moorhouse, Jack Kenney (Detectives), Harry Wilson (Parolee), Jack Woody (Stoolier), Harry Lauter (Uniform Officer), Mary Newton (Mrs. O'Keefe), Hank Worden (Sweeney), Bill Schroff (Delivery Man), Dennis Dengate, Joe Bassett, Fred Coby (Officers), Faith Kruger, Tom Clarke (Salvation Army Singers), Guy Wilkerson, Lyle Latell (Hoodlums), George Ross (Cop), Fred Stevens, Shirley Whitney (Young Couple), Ted Ryan (Janitor), Tommy Jackson (Floor Guard).

Three convicts, Doc Penny (Ted De Corsia), Ben Hastings (Charles Buchinsky) and Johnny Haslett (Timothy Carey), escape from San Quentin and take refuge in the home of former convict and now parolee Steve Lacey (Gene Nelson) and his pretty wife Ellen (Phyllis Kirk). Toothpick-chewing police Detective Sergeant Sims (Sterling Hayden) gets on the trail of the three escapees and learns of their whereabouts from an informer (Jay Novello) who is killed by Hastings. With Haslett killed in a shootout with the law, Doc and Hastings take Steve and Ellen hostage and seek shelter in Chinatown as they plan to rob a bank for getaway money. The two, however, leave behind a clue in the Lacey home and Sims is able to trace them to their robbery site with a battle ensuing in which the gangsters are killed. Steve then is able to prove he was not helping the escapees and he and Ellen resume their normal lives.

Fifth billed as the cold blooded killer Ben Hastings, Charles Bronson was reunited with producer Bryan Foy, director Andre De Toth and scripter Crane Wilbur with whom he had done *House of Wax* released previous in the year. Unlike the mute Igor from that film, Bronson's menace not only talks but also conveys evil by his very presence. He is especially convincing in his unsaid but physically projected lustful feelings for Mrs. Lacey. While issued mainly as a dual biller, *Crime Wave* provided Charles Bronson with a strong character role and one which he played most convincingly.

*Crime Wave* was filmed as *The City Is Dark* and issued under that title in Great Britain. There the *Monthly Film Bulletin* opined, "Average-to-good crime story, which starts excitingly, loses its grip in the middle, but revives at the end with a gripping bank holdup. Los Angeles settings are well used, and the police procedure is unflatteringly realistic." *Time* magazine called the film a "Muscular little thriller that carries more conviction than many more high-toned movie melodramas." *The Hollywood Reporter*, however, complained about the film's attempts at realism by noting, "Tempo also suffers from the attempt at a semi-documentary flavor, the continuous repetition of police routine and the atmospheric scenes, while authentic enough, bring the story to a halt." *Farm Journal* called *Crime Wave* a "Better than the routine gangster melodrama."

For the record, the feature was Gene Nelson's first non-dancing film assignment.

## *Death Hunt* (20th Century–Fox, 1981) 97 minutes Color

*P:* Murray Shostak. *EP:* Albert S. Ruddy & Raymond Chow. *AP:* Robert Baylis. *D:* Peter Hunt. *Sc:* Michael Grais & Mark Victor. *Ph:* James Devis. *Ed:* Allan Jacobs & John F. Burnett. *Mus:* Jerrold Immel. *Prod Designer:* Ted Haworth. *Prod Supv:* Andre Morgan. *Casting:* Reuben Cannon & Associates. *Unit Prod Mgr:* Les Kimber. *Asst Dir:* Frank Ernst & David MacLeod. *Second Unit Ph:* Richard Leiterman. *Camera Operator:* Rod Parkhurst. *Sc Supv:* Pam Carlton. *Set Decorator:* Bob Benton. *Set Designer:* Tom Hoherty. *Costume Designer:* Olga Dimitrov. *Makeup:* Bill Morgan. *Hairstylist:* Paul LeBlanc. *Stunt Coordinator:* Alex Green. *Sp Eff:* Tom Fischer & John Thomas. *Asst Ed:* William Jacobs & Mario Leone. *Apprentice Ed:* Cathy Rose. *Dialogue Ed:* Carl Mahakian. *Sd Design:* New Creative Sound-Ray Alba, Bert Schoenfeld, Paul Hochman & Carolyn Colwell. *Sd:* Richard Lightstone. *Rerecording Mixers:* Robert K. Litt, David J. Kimball & Elliot Tyson. *Mus Ed:* James Henrikson & Michael Tronick. *Casting:* Canadian Casting Associates. *Extra Casting:* Bryan Gliserman. *Producer's Asst:* Margo Baxley. *Post Prod Supv:* Pinetree Post Prod Services-Marlene Rubenstein. *Asst to Executive in Charge of Production* David Chan. *Second Unit Directors:* Bob Lockwood & Paul Baxley. *Camera Operator:* Cam MacDonald. *Focus:* Peter K. Smith. *Wesscam Operators:* Ron Goodman & Margaret Herron. *Key Grip:* Michael Kohne. *Gaffer:* Ron Chegwidden. *Best Boy:* Herb Reischl. *Property Master:* John Berger. *Animal Trainers:* Mark Weiner, Dennis Grisco, Gary Vaughan, Doug Lemmond & Terry Quesnel. *Wrangler:* John Scott. *Song:* Al Dubin & Joe Burke. *Title Design:* Phil Norman. *Opticals:* Westheimer Company. *Recording:* Goldwyn Sound Facility.

**CAST:** Charles Bronson (Albert Johnson), Lee Marvin (Sergeant Edgar Millen), Andrew Stevens (Officer Alvin Adams), Carl Weathers (Sundog/George Washington Lincoln Brown), Angie Dickinson (Vanessa McBride), Ed Lauter (Hazel Sutter), Scott Hylands (Hank Tucker), Henry Beckman (Bill Luce), William Sanderson (Ned Warren), Jon Cedar (Hawkins), James O'Connell (Hurley), Len Lesser (Lewis), Dick Davalos (Beeler), Maury Chaykin (Clarence), August Schellenberg (Deak de Clearque), Dennis Wallace, James McIntire, Rayford Barnes (Trappers), Maurice Kowalski (Charlie Rat), Sean McCann (News Reporter), Steve O.Z. Finkel (W.W. Douglass), Denis Lacroix (Jimmy Tom), Tantoo Martin (Indian Woman), Amy Marie George (Buffalo Woman).

Filmed on location in the Canadian Rockies and advertised under the title *Arctic Rampage*, *Death Hunt* was the first film from the combined production team of Albert S. Ruddy and Raymond Chow's Hong Kong–based Golden Harvest Group. With its production company headquartered in Banff, Alberta, Canada, the film used natural locales to tell its story, which was based on an actual manhunt in the Yukon Territory in 1931. That manhunt, which pitted Canadian Mounties and trappers against fugitive Albert Johnson, was the first time aircraft was used in a law enforcement trackdown. Noted pilot Vern Ohmert designed a replica of the craft the Mounties used in the manhunt, a Bristol open cockpit biplane from the World War I era. Actual dog sleds from the period were secured for the production which brought in 50 Siberian sled dogs from the Yukon for the chase sequences.

*Death Hunt* is the second telling of the famous Yukon manhunt as directors Tay Garnett and Ford Bebe told the story in *Mad Trapper of the Yukon* in 1972 starring Mike Mazurki in the title role. That film made a mint when it was four-walled in the U.S. in 1976 as *Challenge to Be Free*. This time out Charles Bronson essayed the role of the hunted trapper and like *Chato's Land* (1972) the part was far more physical than usual, with a minimum of dialogue. Still Bronson deftly portrayed the loner who, like Pardon Chato, knew how to use the terrain and live off the land as he avoided his pursuers. The actual character of Albert Johnson is open to speculation as little is really known about him. Some claim he was framed while others say he was a criminal. Both feature films, however, portray him as a decent man caught in a web of deceit and falsely accused of wrongdoing as any crimes he may have committed were in self defense.

In the Yukon Territory late in 1930, trapper Albert Johnson (Charles Bronson) comes upon a group of men watching a dog fight and when gambler Hazel (Ed Lauter) attempts to kill his white husky for losing, Johnson forcibly stops him and pays $200 for the injured animal. At the nearby Mountie outpost young recruit Alvin Adams (Andrew Stevens) arrives for duty, meeting the angry Hazel who takes him to Sergeant Edgar Millen (Lee Marvin), the drunken commander of the post. Hazel wants Johnson arrested for stealing his dog but Millen refuses the request, to the chagrin of the rookie. At the post Adams meets fellow officer, Sundog (Carl Weathers), a black American, who offers him his mistress, Buffalo Woman (Amy Marie George), who has taken a shine to the young man. Seeking revenge, Hazel and his cohorts surround Johnson's cabin and in a shootout one of them (Denis Lacroix) is killed as is the dog. At the post pretty widow Vanessa McBride (Angie Dickinson) arrives to claim the belongings of her late miner husband but she decides to stay with Millen. Hazel brings word that Johnson has killed one of his men so Millen, Sundog and Adams, along with Hazel and a group of trappers, go to Johnson's cabin. Millen, who respects Johnson and realizes he is being framed, tries to persuade him to come to town peacefully but one of the trappers starts shooting and in the fighting that ensues several of the trappers are killed. Old trapper Bill Luce (Henry Beckman) had previously warned Johnson that the Mounties and trappers were after him so Johnson was prepared for the attack. Millen then uses dynamite to blow up the fugitive's cabin but he escapes the explosion and kills more trappers before heading north into snow country. The Mounties and trappers pursue him using dog sleds and when the news media learns of the pursuit a bounty of $1,000 is placed on Johnson. Stopping for the night, Adams makes a comment about Hazel's name and the latter makes a pass at the young man who nearly beats him to death before being stopped by Millen and Sundog. With dozens of men on the trail of Johnson, the RCMP also sends cocky airplane pilot Hank Tucker (Scott Hylands) to run down the fugitive. Meanwhile Luce kills two of Hazel's friends for the gold in their teeth and then sets out to get the bounty on Johnson. As he nears the Alaska border Johnson, who has been running with the caribou to avoid Millen and his men, is spotted by Turner who tries to shoot him from the air. Instead he kills Sundog while Millen and Adams shoot at the plane, disabling the craft which crashes into a mountainside killing the pilot. Johnson stops Hazel by shooting him in the leg. Millen then orders the pursuers to halt as he and Adams go after Johnson, who has got the drop on Luce. Millen and Adams shoot Luce thinking it is Johnson and when they learn the truth they let the fugitive escape into Alaska, claiming they got their man.

*Death Hunt* not only provides a fine pictorial telling of the Albert Johnson legend but it is also populated with a number of interesting characters. While Charles Bronson dominates the feature as the taciturn Johnson, Lee Marvin has some amusing lines as the battle weary, heavy drinking Millen. In the scene just prior to Hazel's making a pass at Adams, Millen notes of the gambler, "Hazel's mother didn't know if he was a boy or a girl until he was fourteen. By that time he had turned mean and she didn't care." The trappers in the film exemplify the Yukon inhabitants of the period, men who know well the art of survival in the harsh land bordering the Arctic Circle.

Vincent Canby said in the *New York Times*, "Nothing in *Death Hunt* makes a great deal of sense, though the scenery is rugged and the snowscapes beautiful ... [it] has something of the manner of an old-time movie serial whose hero, at the end of each chapter, is put into an impossible corner from which, in the succeeding chapter, he escapes in a way that is never as clever as the circumstances demanded. Mr. Bronson and Mr. Marvin are such old hands at this sort of movie that each can create a character with ease, out of thin, cold air." Arthur Knight said in the *Hollywood Reporter* of Bronson and Marvin that "the presence of those two grizzled veterans effectively lifts it [the film] out of the category of just another chase movie" and Kevin Thomas in the *Los Angeles Times* noted "Marvin and Bronson are terrific." In *The Family Guide to Movies on Video* (1988), Henry Herx and Tony Zaza called it a "Routine outdoor melodrama ... with some strong language and violence."

Late in 1981 Charles Bronson was given The Golden Horse Award for being "The International Star of the Decade." The honor was presented at the Chiang Kai-shek Cultural Center in the Republic of China.

## *Death Wish* (Paramount, 1974) 93 minutes Color

*P:* Hal Landers, Bobby Roberts & Michael Winner. *EP:* Dino De Laurentiis. *D:* Michael Winner. *Sc:* Wendell Mayes, from the novel by Brian Garfield. *Ph:* Arthur J. Ornitz. *Ed:* Bernard Gribble. *Mus:* Herbie Hancock. *Prod Mgr:* Stanley Neufeld. *Prod Designer:* Robert Gundlach. *Asst Dir:* Charles Okun, Larry Albucher & Ralph Singleton. *Set Decorator:* George De Titta. *Dubbing Ed:* Alfred Cox & James Shields. *Casting Director:* Cis Corman. *Camera Operator:* Louis Barlia. *Recordist:* James Sabat. *Re-recordist:* Hugh Strain. *Wardrobe:* Joseph Dehn. *Director's Asst:* Steve Cory. *Makeup:* Philip Rhodes. *Costume Designer:* Joseph K. Aulisi. *Sc Supv:* Barbara Robinson. *Gaffer:* Willy Meyerhoff. *Property Master:* Conrad Brink. *Head Grip:* Charles Holb. *Scenic Artist:* Sante Fiore.

**CAST:** Charles Bronson (Paul Kersey), Vincent Gardenia (Inspector Frank Ochoa), Hope Lange (Joanna Kersey), William Redfield (Sam Kreutzer), Steven Keats (Jack Toby), Stuart Margolin (Aimes Jainchill), Stephen Elliott (Police Commissioner Dryer), Kathleen Tolan (Carol Toby), Jack Wallace (Hank), Fred Scollay (District Attorney), Chris Gampell (Ives), Robert Kya-Hill (Officer Joe Charles), Ed Grover (Lieutenant Briggs), Jeff [Goldblum] Goldberg (Tall Freak), Christopher Logan (Second Freak), Gregory Rozakis (Spraycan Freak), Floyd Levin (Desk Sergeant), Helen Martin (Alma Lee Brown), Hank Garrett (Andrew McCabe), Christopher Guest (Patrolman Jackson Reilly), Olympia Dukakis, Marsha Jean-Kurtz, Robert Dahdah.

To many, *Death Wish* was the peak of Charles Bronson's film career, as the role of sidewalk vigilante Paul Kersey is the one with whom he is most associated. In the film Bronson gives what is perhaps his greatest film performance, certainly one deserving an Academy Award; he was not even nominated. The feature takes Bronson's character from urban liberal pacifist to a modern day gunfighter ridding New York City of street scum. Throughout the film Bronson is both believable and personal. One great scene shows his reaction to learning of his wife's brutal murder. There is no dialogue, just a closeup of Bronson as the truth of the tragedy soaks in. Later when he sees punks breaking a car's windows he pulls down a blind as if to insulate himself from "the war zone" of his environment. After his first two retaliatory attacks Kersey is shown to be upset and shaky but as he continues to shoot creeps (always in self-defense) he becomes an assured gunman. Just before his final showdown, he tells his opponent "fill your hand"; when later told to leave town he asked "before sundown."

After an Hawaiian vacation, architect Paul Kersey (Charles Bronson) and his wife Joanna (Hope Lange) return to their New York City apartment. Later three freaks (Jeff [Goldblum] Goldberg, Christopher Logan, Gregory Rozakis) spot Joanna and her daughter Carol (Kathleen Tolan) in a supermarket and follow them back home. Breaking into the apartment, the men demand money and when they find little they sexually abuse Carol and beat Joanna to death. Kersey's son-in-law Jack Toby (Steven Keats) meets him at the hospital where Paul learns of his wife's murder. Following her funeral in Connecticut he goes to the police asking if they have any clues but is told there is little hope the murderers will be caught. As a result of the attack, Carol becomes nearly catatonic. To protect himself Kersey puts two rolls of quarters in a sock and when a mugger attacks him he beats the man in the face and the assailant runs away. The architect is then sent to Tucson, Arizona, to work with developer Aimes Jainchill (Stuart Margolin) on a proposed housing project which will conform to the land. While there Aimes teaches Paul to target shoot and when he returns to Gotham Paul opens a present Aimes has given him. It is a handgun. Jack tells Paul that Carol is not responding to treatment and that night Paul is attacked by a mugger and kills him. The shooting is investigated by Inspector Frank Ochoa (Vincent Gardenia). When Kersey comes across three men beating up another he kills the thugs with the beaten man refusing to identify him to Ochoa. By now Carol is in a sanitorium in New Hampshire as Ochoa tells his department the "vigilante" must be apprehended. After eating in a diner Kersey is followed by two men who try to rob him. He shoots them in a subway station but he is cut on the shoulder by a third mugger who escapes. By now people in New York consider the vigilante a hero and many are themselves fighting back when attacked. Ochoa and his department begin to close in on Kersey's neighborhood as the home of the vigilante with Paul as a suspect. Ochoa searches Paul's apartment and finds evidence of his being cut but later the district attorney (Fred Scollay), who admits muggings are down 50 percent thanks to the vigilante, tells Ochoa and Dryer (Stephen Elliott) not to apprehend the man. Ochoa agrees to try to scare off the vigilante and calls Kersey, warning him of police surveillance. Later Paul is pulled over by police and searched but that night he leaves his apartment building by the back way and goes to his office, where he has hidden his revolver. He shoots two thugs who attack him and is shot in the leg yet still pursues a third mugger before fainting. The police retrieve his gun and later in the hospital Ochoa tells Kersey to leave town. Paul relocates to Chicago and at the airport helps a young woman tormented by creeps.

*Death Wish* touched a nerve with the American public and became one of the most popular (it grossed nearly $9 million domestically) and controversial films of our time. This R-rated drama came at a time when America's morale was low. The Vietnam war had been lost, crime was rampant and the old mores of the past seemed to have fallen by the wayside. Suddenly Charles Bronson emerges on the scene as Paul Kersey, a Korean War conscientious objector, who evolves into a sidewalk vigilante after criminals defile his home and marriage. Audiences stood and cheered nationwide as Kersey turned on his tormenters—vicariously Americans were fighting back too and through *Death Wish* Charles Bronson went from international superstar to folk hero.

As expected from such a controversial film, *Death Wish* drew decided

Poster for *Death Wish* (Paramount, 1974).

mixed reviews although critics more than ever praised Charles Bronson for his performance. Rex Reed noted in the *New York Daily News*, "rarely have I found myself so caught between my own gut reactions and intellectual reservations. *Death Wish* is so cleverly constructed as entertainment that it bounces liberal challenges off its political back like a duck shaking raindrops.... People who are tired of being frightened, endangered and ripped-off daily in New York City are going to love Charles Bronson in *Death Wish* as much as I do." In a lengthy review in the *New York Times*, Vincent Canby had few kind words for the film or its star: "*Death Wish* is a movie produced by tourists ... For short-term fun it exploits very real fears and social problems and suggests simple-minded remedies by waving the American flag much in the fashion that former Vice President (Spiro) Agnew used to do." Regarding Bronson, Canby felt it was "a stroke of genius to cast Charles Bronson in the unlikely role of an upper middle-class New York liberal who sees the light. Almost any other actor I can think of would probably look very sheepish under the circumstances. Not Bronson, who seems no more capable of intellectual activity than a very old, tired circus bear. It's enough that he is able to walk around on his hind legs and occasionally shoot a gun." In another review, Judith Crist in *New York* magazine called the film "a first-rate suspenser set and filmed in New York City that provides, with bristling topicality, more empathy and Aristotelian purgation for the beleaguered city dweller than a monthful of Lone Rangers or a legion of Shanes in our innocent Western-oriented past.... What makes this fantasy work is the superb performance of Charles Bronson as the protagonist" *Variety* opined, "Poisonous incitement to do-it-yourself law enforcement is the vulgar exploitation hook on which *Death Wish* is awkwardly hung.... Bronson, who looks older than usual in keeping with his character of the father of an adult daughter, has here a role of greater depth than heretofore. To be sure, he mechanically guns down the heavies when the story gets rolling, but at least the script lets him manifest a third dimension." Ted Zehender wrote in *Films in Review*, "*Death Wish* is decked out in modern trappings and set down, cozily, in the Tombstone Gulches of NYC.... Dino De Laurentiis has given his fourth American-made film a handsome production. An eastern western? They said they could do it and they did." Regarding the star he wrote, "Bronson finds himself well cast: he's tough, cunning and menacing, in a way that owes no debt to [Gary] Cooper, [John] Wayne, or any other of his predecessors in the genre." Also associating *Death Wish* with Westerns, Lynn Minton noted in *Movie Guide for Puzzled Parents* (1984) that "the movie doesn't bother much to remind us of the drawbacks of frontier justice."

*Death Wish* marked Charles Bronson's third and final film commitment to Dino De Laurentiis, following *The Stone Killer* (1973) and *Valdez il Mezzosangue* (1973), since *The Valachi Papers* (1972) had been a one picture deal. De Laurentiis, along with Goffredo Lombardo's Titanus Pictures, announced at the time that Charles Bronson would play Hawkeye in a new version of *Last of the Mohicans* but the project never materialized. Bronson did reteam with De Laurentiis one last time in 1977 for *The White Buffalo.*

Ironically Charles Bronson and his agent Paul Kohner were at odds over whether or not Bronson should make *Death Wish.* Kohner apparently felt the film glorified vigilantism while Bronson thought it showed the futility of fighting outside the law. Fortunately Bronson relied on his own instincts and did the film with co-producer-director Michael Winner, their fourth teaming following *Chato's Land* (1972), *The Mechanic* (1972) and *The Stone Killer* (1973). While the last two films certainly were popular with United States audiences, *Death Wish* once and for all solidified Charles Bronson's immense popularity in his homeland. The film was also a blockbuster overseas where it sometimes played as *Vigilante in the Streets.* Bronson and Winner would reteam for two sequels, *Death Wish II* (1982) and *Death Wish 3* (1985) and Bronson would star as Paul Kersey in two more series outings, *Death Wish 4: The Crackdown* 1987) and *Death Wish V: The Face of Death* (1994). In many respects, the original *Death Wish* marks the apex of Charles Bronson's film career.

## *Death Wish II* (Filmways, 1982) 93 minutes Color

*P:* Menahem Golan & Yoram Globus. *EP:* Hal Landers & Bobby Roberts. *AP:* Christopher Pearce. *D:* Michael Winner. *Sc:* David Engelbach, from characters by Brian Garfield. *Ph:* Richard H. Kline & Tom Del Ruth. *Ed:* Arnold Crust & Julian Semilian. *Mus:* Jimmy Page. *Prod Designer:* William Hiney. *Sd Ed:* John Poyner, David Campling & Ron Davis. *Asst Dir:* Russell Vreeland & Roger Carlton. *Sp Eff:* Kenneth Pepiot. *Stunt Coordinators:* Ernie Orsatti & Chuck Couch. *Prod Mgr:* Tony Wade. *Casting:* Joe Scully & Beth Voiku. *Set Decorator:* Rich Gentz. *Sc Supv:* Aileen N. Nolman. *Prod Sd Mixer:* Tommy Overton. *Boom Man:* Dennis Jones. *Recorder:* Jim Thompson. *Mus Ed:* Robin Clarke. *Re-recordist:* Hugh Strain. *Camera Operator:* Tom Laughridge. *First Asst Cameramen:* Henry A. Lebo & Peter A. Santoro. *Second Asst Cameramen:* Kenneth Zunder & Robert A. Wise. *Property Master:* Kent H. Johnson. *Key Costumer:* Ron Archer. *Costumes:* Michelle Dittrick. *Makeup:* Philip Rhodes. *Hair Stylist:* Vivienne Walker. *Gaffer:* Danny Buck. *Key Grip:* Gene Kearney. *Transportation Captain:* Greg Van Dyke. *Transportation Coordinator:* Louis White. *Prod Accountant:* Marilyn Tasso. *Location Managers:* Jack English & Brad Aronson.

**CAST:** Charles Bronson (Paul Kersey), Jill Ireland (Geri Nichols), Vincent Gardenia (Inspector Frank Ochoa), J.D. Cannon (New York District Attorney), Anthony Franciosa (Los Angeles Police Commissioner), Ben Frank (Lieutenant Mankiewicz), Robin Sherwood (Carol Kersey), Silvana Gillardo (Rosaria), Robert F. Lyons (Fred McKenzie), Michael Prince (Elliott Cass), Drew Snyder (Hawkins), Paul Lambert (New York Police Commissioner), Thomas Duffy (Nirvana/Charles Wilson), Kevyn Major Howard (Stomper), Stuart K. Robinson (Jiver), Laurence Fishburne III

[Larry Fishburne] (Cutter), E. Lamont Johnson (Punkcut), Paul Comi (Senator McLean), Joseph Campanella (Judge), Hugh Warden (Minister), James Begg, Melody Santangello (Mugged Tourists), Robert Sniveley (Dr. Gofeld), Steffen Zaharias (Dr. Clark), Don Moss (Cabbi), Charles Cyphers (Kay), Peter Pan (Chinese Landlord), David Daniels (Lang), Don Dubbins (Mike), James Galante (Tim Shaw), Buck Young (Charles Pearce), Karsen Lee, Leslie Graves (Nirvana's Girls), Teresa Baxter, Cindy Daly (Nurses), Susannah Darrow (Nurse on Bus), Henry Capp, Joshua Gallegos (Policemen), Paul McCallum (Ambulance Man), Roberta Collins (Woman at Party), Diane Markoff (Prostitute), Cynthia Burr (New York District Attorney's Secretary), Michael Favon, Ezekiel Moss (Thugs), Ransom Walrod (Boat Captain), Gary Boyle, Ava Lazar (Soap Opera Actors), Fred Saxon (Newsman), Henny Youngman (Himself), Blair Farrington Group (Dance Group), Ginny Cooper, Lesa Weiss, Twyla Littleton, Diane Manzo (Diners).

*Death Wish II* marked Charles Bronson's return to the role of Paul Kersey from the controversial 1974 Paramount release *Death Wish*. This time the feature was produced by the Hollywood-based Cannon Group, for whom Bronson would make most of his 1980s features. The film marked the first of several teamings with producers Menahem Golan, chairman of Cannon, and Yoram Globus, while *Death Wish* producers Hal Landers and Bobby Roberts were the executive producers of this sequel. Michael Winner returned as the film's director with Cannon acquiring the rights to the Brian Garfield characters from producer Dino De Laurentiis and Paramount. Filmed mostly in Los Angeles on a $10 million budget, *Death Wish II* basically was a retelling of the first film's story set in a new locale. The original feature, however, did win some praise as did Bronson's performance in it but this time the liberal media had no kind words for the sequel, heavily lambasting it. As usual, the public paid no attention to the critics and *Death Wish II* was a major box office success when issued in the U.S. by Filmways. Overseas it was handled by Columbia–EMI–Warner and in West Germany the feature set a video cassette sales recording selling over 10,000 units in two months and making it produce over a half million dollars in royalties the first year of its video release.

Four years after being asked to leave New York City after killing nine muggers following the wanton murder of his wife and rape of his daughter, architect Paul Kersey (Charles Bronson) has begun a new life in Los Angeles. He is in love with beautiful radio news reporter Geri Nichols (Jill Ireland) and is happy that his once catatonic daughter Carol (Robin Sherwood) is beginning to show some improvement. When the three of them are at a street fair some thugs steal Kersey's wallet and go to his house where they rape his housekeeper Rosaria (Silvana Gillardo) and wait for his return. When he and Carol arrive, the thugs knock out Kersey, kill Rosaria when she tries to call for help and abduct Carol. They take her to an abandoned warehouse where they sexually abuse her and when the girl tries to escape she jumps

Poster for *Death Wish II* (Filmways, 1982).

through a window and is impaled on a fence. After Carol's funeral Kersey goes into the mountains for a rest but his anger builds and when he returns he refuses to help the police identify the killers. Instead he arms himself and begins hunting for the thugs. Seeing one of the men, Punkcut (E. Lamont Johnson), Kersey trails him and his friends to an abandoned Hollywood hotel where he kills the man. Coming upon a couple (James Begg, Melody Santangello) being attacked in a parking garage, Kersey comes to their defense, killing the muggers, two of whom had been part of the gang who broke into his home. Later the couple refuse to identify their rescuer to police Lieutenant Mankiewicz (Ben Frank). Realizing the city is dealing with a vigilante, the police commissioner (Anthony Franciosa) asks the aid of the New York City police since they dealt with a similar situation four years before. In Gotham, Inspector Frank Ochoa (Vincent Gardenia), who handled the original Kersey case there, is assigned to go to Los Angeles and stop Kersey's latest activities since they have pinpointed him as the vigilante. Hoping Geri can persuade her lover to give up street killing, Ochoa tells her of Kersey's past but later Paul denies this to Geri, saying Ochoa was mistaken. Meanwhile Ochoa tails Kersey who has spotted three of the original muggers and he follows them to a park area where they swap drugs for guns. When a sniper tries to kill Kersey, Ochoa opens fire and a shootout takes place with Ochoa being killed while Kersey shoots all the muggers but Nirvana (Thomas Duffy) who gets away. Later Nirvana is arrested and charged with Ochoa's murder. A lenient judge (Joseph Campanella) sends Nirvana to a mental hospital instead of ordering his execution. Through Geri, who he plans to marry, Kersey gets access to the hospital and in a brawl ends up killing Nirvana. Realizing Kersey really is the vigilante, Geri leaves him. Kersey is then left to continue hunting street scum.

In this outing the feeling is that a one-man force is superior to police dogged by court regulations in dealing with crime. The grey area that existed in the original *Death Wish*, where Kersey at first was shaken by his own violence, has disappeared and now the sidewalk vigilante does his thing with no remorse. Here Kersey has a chance to help the police catch the muggers who are responsible for the deaths of his housekeeper and daughter but he refuses to even look at mug books, knowing already he alone will exact the necessary revenge. In the scene where Inspector Ochoa is dying after a gun battle with the thugs, the lawman's last words encourage Kersey to finish his vendetta. The lethargy of the legal system with the coddling of criminals in deference to the protection of decent citizens has left Kersey a man of vengeance. He feels that if the system can let the scum of the earth destroy his home and murder his loved ones then he has the right to exact his revenge by taking the lives of those who commit such atrocities. Such is the theme of *Death Wish II* and while the critics were appalled the public loved it.

*Variety* called the film "ludicrous" saying "the more certain bet is that pic will enflame old passions with the cynicism of its manipulative and mocking plot." Sheila Benson wrote in the *Los Angeles Times* that "scene for scene, [it] seems even more objectionable than its predecessor. The brutality of the gang members is lingered upon, and the women victims are even more exploitatively revealed and photographed.... *Death Wish II* returns us to the level of cave men in a film lacking even the smallest humanity." In the *Los Angeles Herald Examiner* Peter Rainer wrote, "*Death Wish II* is, if that's possible, even more Neanderthal in its attitudes than *Death Wish*. That first film, which was one of Charles Bronson's biggest hits, exploited urban fears shamelessly; it strongly implied that the only effective way to combat crime was to take the law into your own hands. This new film does more than imply that message—it practically bleats it at you with a bullhorn."

As reported in the *Los Angeles Times*, Charles Bronson was paid $1.5 million for his work in *Death Wish II*. Three years later he and Michael Winner would team for the last time in another followup, *Death Wish 3*.

In 1982 Charles Bronson also lent his name to a national advertisement for the Motorcycle Industry Council in which he promoted the concept of responsible motorcycling.

## *Death Wish 3* (Cannon Group, 1985) 92 minutes Color

*P:* Menahem Golan, Yoram Globus & Michael Winner. *AP:* Michael Kagan. *D:* Michael Winner. *Sc:* Michael Edmonds, from characters created by Brian Garfield. *Ph:* John Stanier. *Ed:* Arnold Crust. *Mus:* Jimmy Page. *Prod Design:* Peter Mullins. *Stunt Coordinators:* Mark Doyle, Ernie Orsatti & Harry Madsen. *Stunts:* Gene Hartline, Alan Oliney, Rick Seaman, Jack Cooper, Paul Heaman, Jazzer Jeyes, Rocky Taylor, Tip Tipping, George Cooper, Thomas Delmar, Tracey Eddon, Elaine Ford, Michael Russo, Steve Whyment, Ray Ford, Terry Forrestal, Stuart St. Paul, Tim Condern & Lex Milloy. *Prod Supv:* Malcolm Christopher & Ron Purdie. *Second Unit Dir:* Ron Purdie. *Unit Prod Mgr:* George Manase. *Asst Dir:* Alan Hopkins & James Chory. *Casting:* Gery Walker & Michael Kara. *Asst Prod Mgr:* Michael Fadross. *Location Mgr:* Hugh O'Donnell. *Second Asst Dir:* Marcia Gay. *Prod Office Coordinator:* Jody Mulano. *Prod Asst:* Valerie Chamberlain. *Executive Ed:* Chris Barnes. *Sd Ed:* John Poynter, Brian Lintern, Tony Lenny, Mike Campbell, Nick Gaster & Stan Smith. *Mus Ed:* Alan Killick. *Camera Operators:* David Wynn-Jones, Dennis Kingston & Robert Wagner. *Camera Asst:* Alan Annand, Edward Pei, Zachary Winestine, Hamid Shams & Nigel Seal. *Sd Recordists:* Derek Ball & William Daly. *Boom Operators:* Ken Nightingall & Richard Murphy. *Re-recordist:* Hugh Strain. *Sc Supv:* Connie Willis, Eve Caberera & Susan Oldroyd. *AD:* David Mintz & James Taylor. *Set Decorators:* Robin Farnsane & Gretchen Rau. *Set Dresser:* Scott Rosenstock. *Construction Mgr:* Ron Coleman. *Construction Coordinator:* Michael Curry Sr. *Set Builder:* Michael Curry Jr. *Property Masters:* Ron C. Stone, John Chisholm & Ron Lofthouse. *Asst Property:* Karen Kater. *Costume Designer:* Peggy Farrell. *Wardrobe Supv:* Ron Beck. *Key Wardrobe:* Helen Butler. *Wardrobe Mistress:* Janet Tebrooke. *Asst Wardrobe:* Denise

Romano-Andres. *Makeup:* Richard Mills & Carla White. *Hairdressers:* Sue Love, Pattie Smith & Ron Abrams. *Sp Eff:* John Evans & Steven Krishoff. *Stills:* David Farrell & John Leakwood. *Prod Accountant:* Sue Wall. *Prod Auditor:* Heidi August. *Scenic Artist:* David Moon. *Executive Asst to Dir:* John Fraser. *Gaffers:* John Dimond & Sam Bender. *Best Boys:* Michael Woodland & Roberto Jiminez. *Key Grip:* Mitch Lillian. *Dolly Grips:* Alan Gates & Richard Kerekes. *Technical Advisor:* Wildey Moore. *Music Arranger & Conductor:* Mike Moran. *Recording Engineers:* Stuart Epps & Richard Dodd.

**CAST:** Charles Bronson (Paul Kersey), Deborah Raffin (Kathryn Davis), Ed Lauter (Inspector Richard S. Striker), Martin Balsam (Bennett Cross), Gavan O'Herlihy (Manny Fraker), Kirk Taylor (The Giggler), Joseph Gonzalez (Rodriguez), Alex Winter (Hermosa), Tony Spiridakis (Angel), Ricco Ross (The Cuban), Tony Britts (Tulio), David Crean (Hector), Nelson Fernandez (Chaco), Alan Cook, Bob Dysinger (Car Thieves), Topo Grajeda (Garcia), Barbie Wilde (Female Punk), Ron Hayes (Lieutenant), Jerry Phillips (Street Punk), Francis Drake (Charley), Leo Kharibian (Eli Kaprov), Hana Maria Pravda (Erica Kaprov), John Gabriel (Emil), Mildred Shay (Mrs. Emil), Kenny Marino (Used Car Seller), Birdie M. Hale (Mugging Victim), Marina Sirtis (Maria Rodriguez), Hayward Morse, Ronald Fernee (Interns), Sandy Grizzle (Rape Victim), Dinah May, Steffanie Pitt (Nurses), Billy J. Mitchell (Fraker's Lawyer), Lee Patterson (Television Newscaster), Olivia Ward (Protesting Woman), Manning Redwood (Lieutenant Sterns), Joe Cirillo, Ralph Monaco, William Roberts, Mac MacDonald, Sam Doublas, Sam Travis, Mark Stewart, Peter Banks, Nick D'Aviriro, Tom Hunsinger (Policemen).

*Death Wish 3* returned the character of Paul Kersey to New York City where he faced anarchy instigated by out-of-control street gangs and court handcuffed law enforcement. While the first two *Death Wish* movies were realistic in that the main character fought back against law breakers after losing his family to them, this outing was more urban fantasy than a factual exposé of street crime and gang warfare. Further blurring the area between fiction and reality the film's distributors rushed it into release in the fall of 1985 apparently to capitalize on Bernhard Goetz, dubbed the "Subway Vigilante" by the news media after he shot muggers in a Gotham subway. While *Death Wish 3* may have been the least realistic of the films in the series it certainly was one of the most action filled. Publicity claimed over 3,500 rounds of machine gun and small gun ammunition was used in the film and it took three stunt coordinators and some 20 stunt people to carry out the action sequences.

After a decade Paul Kersey (Charles Bronson) returns to New York City to visit an old friend, Charley (Francis Drake), who he finds dying in his apartment. The police arrive and arrest Kersey for the crime and take him to jail. There Inspector Striker (Ed Lauter) tells him he knows of his vigilante past and then throws him in the cooler where Kersey beats up one punk but attracts the hatred of gang leader Fraker (Gavan O'Herlihy). After attacking Kersey, Fraker is released but vows revenge. Striker meanwhile lets Kersey go telling him to rid the area of street scum. Kathryn Davis (Deborah Raffin) of the Public Defender's office wants Kersey to sue the city for false arrest but he refuses. Instead he goes to the Belmont apartment of his late friend and there meets local businessman Bennett Cross (Martin Balsam) who tells him street thugs have taken over the area and Fraker and his gang killed Charley. Kersey decides to stay and buys a car. When two punks try to rob the vehicle Kersey shoots them. Kathryn finds Kersey and invites him to dinner at her apartment and they begin a romance. Kersey helps the locals to rig booby-traps to keep the thugs out of their apartments but Fraker and his gang abduct and rape Maria (Marina Sirtis) who dies from their beating. When street punk The Giggler (Kirk Taylor) steals Kersey's camera he kills him and the neighbors witnessing the shooting applaud. Fraker tries and fails to kill Kersey but he does murder an old lady (Mildred Shay) and then trails Kersey to Kathryn's apartment. After making love, Kersey and Kathryn go out to dinner and when Paul stops to get his mail Fraker attacks Kathryn and puts her car in gear causing it to crash into another vehicle and explode. After Kathryn's death, Striker puts Kersey under protective custody as Fraker and his gang burn Bennett's store. The old man retaliates with a machine gun but it malfunctions and they throw him off a fire escape. Surviving, Bennett asks Kersey to wipe out the street gang. Kersey eludes the police and heads back to Belmont for a second machine gun stored in Bennett's apartment. By now Fraker has called in reinforcements as Kersey, aided by Rodriguez (Joseph Gonzalez), Maria's husband, opens fire on the thugs. As the hoodlums wreck the neighborhood citizens take up arms and join Kersey and Rodriguez in the fight. The police arrive to break up the riot and an all-out street war develops. Kersey goes back to his apartment for more ammunition and is followed by Fraker who is trailed by the wounded Striker. In the apartment Fraker tries to kill Kersey but is shot by Striker. Fraker, who wears a bullet-proof vest, is only stunned and again tries to kill Kersey but this time is blown through the wall by a missile launcher Kersey had stashed in the apartment. With Fraker's death the street war ceases and Striker permits Kersey to escape.

For action fans, *Death Wish 3* is a real crowd pleaser. Set in a slum neighborhood filled with street scum and embroiled in urban anarchy, the film moves at a fast clip and the violence is intense. Regarding the extermination of the punks, Kersey explains, "It's like killing roaches. You have to kill them all or what's the point?" The film is also laced with an endless array of weaponry, from regular handguns to machine guns, assault weapons and a missile launcher. There is little room for cerebral activity as the film is mainly based on the bad guys committing atrocities and Kersey getting revenge. A few scenes do stand out, including the one where the police harass an old couple by taking away their gun and threatening to put them in jail after they used the weapon to deter a house breaker. Another scene has Kersey telling Kathryn about the death of his wife and daughter and how, as a result, something changed inside him. A poignant scene has Kersey returning to the

**Charles Bronson and Joseph Gonzalez in *Death Wish 3* (Cannon Group, 1985).**

apartment of his murdered friend Charley and looking at the war medals and American flag hanging on the wall. When Striker tells Kersey to go out and kill street punks he announces he cannot because "I'm a cop," thus showing the impotence of law enforcement in dealing with street crime. Basically *Death Wish 3* is a war film transferred to the streets of Gotham, an action-filled tale of urban anarchy.

While the advertising for *Death Wish 3* read: "He's back in New York bringing justice to the streets," critics were not impressed. As before, the public bypassed the critics and the film was very successful; while issued in the U.S. in the fall of 1985 it did not see release abroad until early 1987. Walter Goodwin in the *New York Times* complained, "There is not a moment of credibility in the movie and the ending is sheer chaos, an anticlimactic at that. Mr. Winner runs out of imagination before Mr. Bronson runs out of ammunition. But that should not detract from its appeal. Along with the pleasure of seeing predators get their due, fans of the *Death Wish* series may also count on the usual vivid and noisy nature of their disposal and the imperturbability of the disposer. Even under stress, Mr. Bronson is as impassive as his Wideye." The Wideye was the assault weapon Kersey used in the film to wipe out half the muggers in Gotham—his weapon of choice as opposed to a regular handgun or bazooka. *Variety* noted, "*Death Wish 3* adds significantly to the body count scored to date in this street-rampant series. Thrills, however, are way down due to script's failure to build motivation for Paul Kersey's latest killing spree." In the *Chicago Sun-Times*, Roger Ebert opined, "One of the hypocrisies practiced by the *Death Wish* movies is that they ignore racial tension in big cities. In their horrible new world, all of the gangs are integrated, so that the movies can't be called racist. I guess it's supposed to be heartwarming to see whites, blacks and Latinos working side by side to rape, pillage and murder." Ebert felt the feature "marginally better" than its predecessor, "The action, direction and special effects are all better than the last time around." Patrick Goldstein in the *Los Angeles Times* wrote, "Although his film has a director, what it really needs is a munitions expert. Even the most minor car crashes are staged like the explosion of the Hindenburg." He called the film a "vile, cynical piece of junk." In the *San Gabriel (California) Valley Tribune Weekender*, Bill Hagen said "motivation even lags behind character development" in the film. He added, "This adventure could possibly find its way into a book the hero is coloring. In a book he's writing, never." Gannett News Service correspondent William Wolf noted, "There's no denying the film's crude, exploitative appeal; it's a tired retread of its two predecessors.... Bronson, continuing to play the role in his super-cool manner, gives his fans the catharsis of violence they pay to see. But the script by Michael Edmonds is scraping the barrel's bottom for plot and characterization." In the *Los Angeles Herald-Examiner*, David Chute wrote, "*Death Wish 3* marks a surreal new stage of escalation in the rhetoric of reactionary action films ... [it] is really a crude western with a safety pin in its nose.... Kersey has been transformed into a wandering black-clad stranger whose guns speak louder than he does." Tim Pulleine, in *The Film Yearbook 1987* (1988), said, "The situation is stylised in terms that deny any kind of realism, but the film is scripted with dark humor and realised with considerable gusto. Just because *Death Wish 3* is frankly unserious and sensationalist, it manages to sound a note of genuine provocation."

*Death Wish 3* was made on a $10 million budget, $1.5 million being Bronson's salary. It was mainly filmed in the Lambeth section of London, England, with two weeks location work in New York City. For one of the few times in his film career, Charles Bronson expressed displeasure with a feature. He told Marilyn Beck in the *Los Angeles Daily News* that the film was "too violent, needlessly violent." He also disapproved of director Michael Winner "shooting stuff with the extras—violence and blood and all that sort of thing—when I wasn't on the set. To me, it was awful and ridiculous."

*Death Wish 3* proved to be the final teaming of Charles Bronson and director Michael Winner although the star would headline two more features in the *Death Wish* series.

## *Death Wish 4: The Crackdown* (Cannon Group, 1987)

99 minutes Color

*P:* Pancho Kohner. *EP:* Menahem Golan & Yoram Globus. *D:* J. Lee Thompson. *Sc:* Gail Morgan Hickman. *Ph:* Gideon Porath. *Ed:* Peter Lee-Thompson. *Mus:* Paul McCallum, Valentine McCallum & John Bisharat. *AD:* Whitney Brooke-Wheeler. *Prod Executive:* Rony Yacov. *Prod Mgr:* John Zane. *Casting:* Peter Bullington & Robert MacDonald. *Asst Dir:* Robert J. Dougherty & Robert C. Ortwin Jr. *Prod Supv:* Marc S. Fisher. *Prod Coordinator:* Barbara A. Hall. *Sd Mixer:* Craig Fellburg. *Set Decorator:* Mark Andrew Haskins. *Costume Supv:* Michael Hoffman. *Sp Eff:* Michael Wood. *Asst Ed:* Mary E. Jochem & Christopher J. Notrathomas. *Mus Supv:* Paula Erickson. *Mus Coordinator:* Stephanie Lee. *Pyrotechnics Sp Eff Foreman:* Mike Edmondson. *Stunt Coordinator:* Ernie Orsatti. *Stunt Double:* J.P. Romano. *Stunts:* Brad Bovee, Bobby A. Burns, Richard E. Butler, Nick Ciarfello, Danny Costa, Yannick Derrien, Debbie Evans, Tom Harper, Lane Leavitt, Paul McCallum, Buck McDancer, Bobby McLaughlin, Noon Orsatti, Jimmy Ortega, Danny Perry, Diane Peterson, Carol Leslie Rees, Debbie Lynn Ross, Michael Tillman & Ted White. *Location Mgr:* Larry Pearson. *Prod Asst:* Patricia A. Payro. *Sc Supv:* Karin Cooper. *Prod Auditor:* Emily J. Rice. *Executive Trainee:* Tony Stafford. *Still Photographer:* Deanne Newcomb. *First Asst Cameraman:* Guy Skinner. *Second Asst Cameraman:* Nick Infield. *Asst Camera Trainee:* Bruce De Aragon. *Second Unit Ph:* Tom Neuwirth. *Additional Camera Operators:* Erik Bernstein & Sam Gart. *Additional First Asst Cameraman:* Richard Haas. *Additional Second Asst Camera:* Alicia Craft. *Boom Operator:* Cameron Hamza. *Cable Man:* Joe Rocheff. *Lead Man:* Scott J. Mullvaney. *Art Department Coordinator:* Mary E.A. Meyer. *On Set Dresser:* Scott W. Ambrose. *Set Dressers:* Phil Brandees & Jim Johnson. *Swing Gang:* Drew C. Williams & Dave Robinson. *Property Master:* Edwin Brewer. *Property Asst:* Mark X. Heiner & Daniel Isackson. *Costume Asst:* Hagit Jacqueline Farber. *Set Costumer:* Dallas Dornan. *Makeup & Protechnics:* Carla Fabrizi. *Makeup & Pyrotechnics Artists:* Lesa Nielsen. *Hair Stylist:* Annette Fabrizi. *Gaffer:* Paul F. Petzoldt. *Best Boy Electrician:* Larry Liddell. *Electricians:* Philip V. Trussell, John Vohlers & Anthony Caldwell. *Key Grip:* Robert J. Robin. *Best Boy Grip:* Christopher Hager. *Dolly Grip:* Michael Coo. *Grip:* Scott Lieu. *Equipment Technician:* John Overacker. *Extra Casting:* Dennis Hansen. *Office Prod Asst:* M. Ginanne Carpenter. *Prod Asst:* Gretchen Iversen, Joe Benn, John F. Karls & John Scott McCue. *Location Asst:* Kevin Platt. *Craft Service:* Robert Wishnefsky. *Stand-Ins:* John F. McCarthy & Sheila Gale. *Post Prod Supv:* Alan Jakowbuicz & Michael Alden. *Post Prod Coordinator:* Omneja "Nini" Mazen. *Apprentice Ed:* Joshua Alan Taft. *Supv Sd Ed:* Mike Le Maire. *Sd Ed:* Gary Sheffield. *Asst Sd Ed:* Steve Schwalbe. *ADR/Sd Mixer:* Tommy Goodwin. *Dialogue Ed:* Tony Polk. *Dialogue Asst:* Michael Hellwig. *Foley Ed:* Karola Storr. *Foley Asst:* Carolann Sanchez. *Rerecording:* Cannon Sound Studios. *Rerecording Mixers:* Frank Montano & Corey Bailey. *Mus Ed:* Elissa Assa. *Mus Mixer:* Peter T. Lewis. *Songs:* Michael Bishop. *Transportation Coordinators:* Jimmy Jones & John Renfro. *Transportation Captain:* Jeffrey S. Renfro. *Title Design:* Walter K. Baldwin & Kyle Seidenbaum. *Main & End Titles:* Main Street Imagery. *Negative Cutting:* Ron Vitello & Ann Marie Vitello. *Color Timer:* Angelo Russo. *Color:* TVC.

**CAST:** Charles Bronson (Paul Kersey), Kay Lenz (Karen Sheldon), John P. Ryan (Nathan White), Perry Lopez (Ed Zacharias), George Dickerson (Detective Reiner), Soon-Teck Oh (Sergeant Phil Nozaki), Dana Barron

(Erica Sheldon), Jesse Dabson (Randy Viscovich), Peter Sherayko (Nick Franco), James Purcell (Vince Montono), Michael Russo (Danny Moreno), Danny Trejo (Art Sanella), Daniel Sabia (Al Arroyo), Mike Moroff (Jack Romero), Dan Ferro (Tony Romero), Tom Everett (Max Green), David Fonteno (Frank Bauggs), Connie Hair (Angie), Mike Wise (Romero's Hood), Irwin Keyes (Joey, Bauggs' Chauffeur), Tim Russ (Jesse), Hector Mercado (JoJo Ross), Derek Rydall (Long Haired Teenager), Mark Pellegrino (Punk), Craig Curtis (White's Chauffeur), Margaret Howell (Rape Victim), Gary Rooney, J.P. Romano, Tony Borgia (Masked Men), Michelle Michaels (Marilyn, Kersey's Secretary), Charles Knox Robinson (Editor), Gerald Castillo (Lieutenant Higuera), Timothy Agee (Young Cop), Jason Scura (Cop), Linda Bukowski (Police Officer), David J. Partington (Morgue Attendant), Bruce Hansel (Dr. Rosenblatt), Michael MacDuff (Doctor), Sheila Gale, Joan Carangi, Noa Scott (Nurses), Gretchen Bryn (Intern), Gene Bori (Restaurant Owner), Robert Axelrod (Italian Restaurant Owner), Gene LaBell (Cannery Guard), Don Shapiro (Bus Boy), Mitch Pileggi (Cannery Lab Foreman), Alan Berger (Watchman), Dale Robinette (Fake Cop), Russell Solberg (Police Car Driver), Richard Nugent-Ahern (Real Nathan White), Terry Ward (White's Butler), Art Frankel (Pool Party Bartender), Roydon Clark (Cannery Workers), Elizabeth Scherrer, Debbie Solomon, Tyaes Connolly (Party Guests).

The successful teaming of Charles Bronson with director J. Lee Thompson and scripter Gail Morgan Hickman in Cannon Group's *Murphy's Law* (1986) resulted in their working together again in *Death Wish 4: The Crackdown*, a film which grossed $7 million domestically. Continuing in the vein of *Death Wish 3* (1985), the movie basically departed from the concept of the vigilante getting revenge on those who destroyed his family and again presented him as a universal avenger, this time out to destroy drug dealers. A slight return to the original theme was evidenced, however, in that Paul Kersey's new girlfriend's daughter dies from a cocaine overdose. The violence, as in the third entry, is in overdrive and the body count continues to mount as Kersey and an assault weapon destroy a drug processing plant along with taking out more than a score of drug dealers. While the plot was hardly realistic, it made for a strong, actionful film. Interestingly the movie opens with one of the most vivid scenes of the *Death Wish* series. A young woman is forced from her car by three masked thugs who prepare to rape her before they see Kersey. One of the thugs asks, "Who the fuck are you?" Kersey replies, "Death." Although it turned out to be one of Kersey's nightmares, it remains a powerful sequence.

Paul Kersey (Charles Bronson) has moved back to Los Angeles where he operates an architectural consulting firm. He also dates pretty reporter Karen Sheldon (Kay Lenz), a widow with a teenage daughter, Erica (Dana Barron). When Erica and her boyfriend Randy (Jesse Dabson) get drugs from pusher JoJo Ross (Hector Mercado) she dies of an overdose. Seeking revenge, Randy goes after JoJo but the latter knifes him. Kersey, who has followed

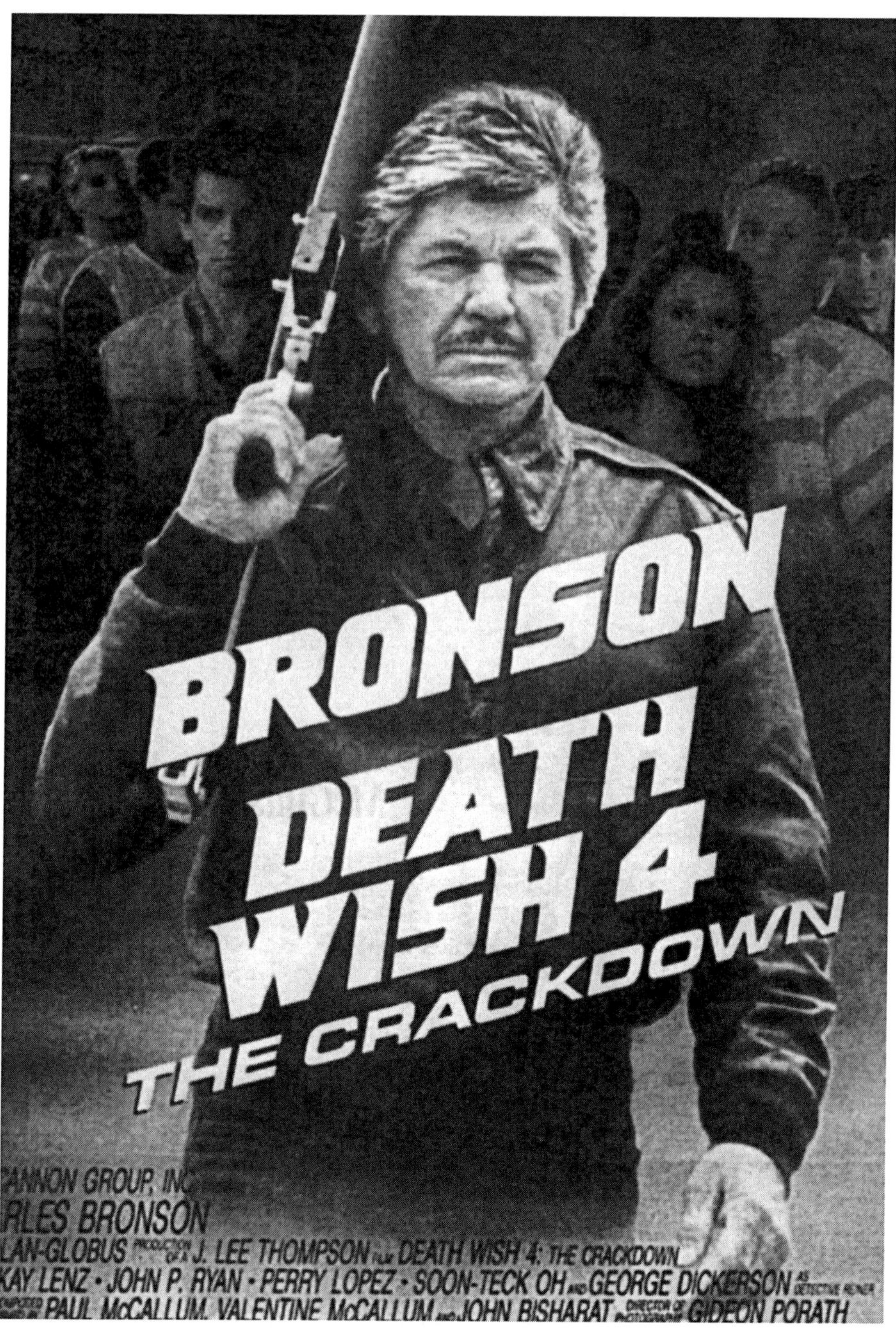


Poster for *Death Wish 4: The Crackdown* (Cannon Group, 1987).

Randy, kills the drug pusher. Kersey then gets a call and is asked to meet a mysterious man who turns out to be newspaper mogul Nathan White (John P. Ryan), who wants him to wipe out drug kingpins and rivals Ed Zacharias (Perry Lopez) and brothers Jack (Mike Moroff) and Tony Romero (Dan Ferro), because his daughter also died of an overdose. White offers Kersey money and weapons to do the job but he takes up the offer to get revenge for Erica's death. Meanwhile Zacharias thinks the Romanos are responsible for JoJo's death since JoJo was one of his pushers. Kersey infiltrates Zacharias' swank home as a caterer at his birthday party and there sees the Romano brothers, since the two rival groups have a truce. When he witnesses Zacharias kill corrupt partner Max Green (Tom Everett) Kersey is marked for murder but he escapes. Later he plants a bomb in an Italian restaurant, blowing up three of Zacharias' men and he also kills his right-hand man Frank Bauggs (David Fonteno) by throwing him off the balcony of his high rise apartment. Detective Reiner (George Dickerson) and his partner Sergeant Nozaki (Soon-Teck Oh) have been investigating the killings and Nozaki spots Kersey leaving the Bauggs murder scene. White tells Kersey that Zacharias uses a fish cannery in San Pedro as a front for his drug processing operations and Kersey infiltrates the plant and destroys it, making a getaway. Meanwhile, Nozaki, who is on the take from Zacharias tells his boss that Kersey is behind the killings but when he attempts to kill the architect it is he who gets shot. Zacharias asks the Romano brothers to meet him at an oil derrick near Los Angeles to talk over the situation and Kersey fires into the group precipitating a gang shootout. Only an injured Zacharias manages to survive and Kersey kills him after showing him Erica's picture. Reiner tells his superiors that Kersey is behind the killings, including Nozaki, but they tell him to stay away from the architect for fear he may sue the city. Meanwhile Kersey goes to meet White and is nearly killed when a car explodes. Going to White's house, he finds out the man who hired him was an imposter who wanted the war between the Romanos and Zacharias so he could take over the drug trade. Two fake cops (Dale Robinette, Russell Solberg) arrest Kersey but he realizes it is an abduction and causes them to wreck their car, killing the imposters. Returning home, Kersey is surprised by Reiner who plans to kill him but when the fake White calls and says he is holding Karen prisoner, Kersey knocks him out and sets out to rescue the woman. He finds her with "White" at a roller rink and a shootout ensues in which the gangster's men are all killed. Trying to escape, "White" kills Karen but is blown away by Kersey with a flame thrower. Reiner arrives and threatens to shoot Kersey but the architect walks away saying, "Do what you have to do."

"The new American way of life" is what a newspaper editor calls drug use in *Death Wish 4: The Crackdown*. A chilling scene has reporter Karen doing a story on teenage drug use and going to the morgue and seeing the corpses of four young people done in by drugs. "Anybody connected with drugs deserves to die," Paul Kersey says in the course of the movie and that appears to be the bottom line of its plot, a crusade against drugs and the drug trade. "This Time It's War" read the advertisements for the movie and Paul Kersey's war on dope proved popular with theatregoers, both here and abroad. An interesting sign of the times, however, found the film going directly to video for its release in Sweden.

As usual, Charles Bronson gives his solid and heroic performance as Paul Kersey in the feature and Kay Lenz is the attractive leading lady. Like all women who get too close to Kersey, however, she meets a bad end, being shot in the back by the fake mogul. Perry Lopez, who would next play Bronson's partner in *Kinjite: Forbidden Subjects* (1989), here is very good as the oily gangster Zacharias. The rest of the cast is quite good and one amusing scene has bitchy blonde Angie (Connie Hair) complaining about her black boyfriend, hitman Frank Bauggs (David Fonteno) as he makes her wait in his limousine while he gets opera tickets. "I wish he would drop dead" she tells the chauffeur just seconds before Kersey pushes Bauggs out of a high-rise balcony, thus landing on his own car.

Again the critics did not care for this latest *Death Wish* installment. Caryn James in the *New York Times* said it "is as efficient and predictable as Kersey himself, and inoffensive as long as you can root for a sociopathic hero." In the *Washington Post*, Richard Harrington complained, "This time around, there's barely any plot, just excuses for Bronson to blow people away.... Bronson, a chip off Old Mount Rushmore, sleepwalks through the film as though someone's dangling a paycheck just out of camera range. It's gotten to the point where the vigilante isn't really motivated anymore, he's just set off, like a bomb." *Variety* was more optimistic, "What raises *Death Wish 4* above the usual blowout is a semi-engaging script and sure pacing by veteran action director J. Lee Thompson." In the *Los Angeles Times*, Kevin Thomas wrote that the film was "an efficient, fast-moving, hard-action, good-looking comic-book fantasy.... By now Bronson's Paul Kersey is an architect in the same way that Clark Kent is a reporter. His vigilante has become as much an above-the-law mythological figure as Superman.... *Death Wish 4* may be preposterous, but on the level of technique it's a solid textbook example of crisp exploitation picture craftsmanship." Perhaps the *San Gabriel (California) Tribune* summed it up best: "For the Bernie Goetz in all of us."

An interesting footnote occurred early in 1988 when three independent Los Angeles television stations scheduled Charles Bronson movies against each other as part of the just-begun February ratings sweeps. The Bronson films not only blew away the competition but *Death Wish II* and *Death Wish 3* got the top ratings against other Bronson titles such as the original *Death Wish*, *The Stone Killer*, *Telefon* and *Mr. Majestyk*.

Following *Death Wish 4: The Crackdown*, the Cannon Group announced that Charles Bronson would star in a new screen version of *The Golem*, written by Michael Alan Canter and to be produced by Pancho Kohner. If the film had been made it would have been Charles Bronson's first horror film since *House of Wax* (1953).

## *Death Wish V: The Face of Death* (Trimark/21st Century, 1994) 95 minutes Color

*P:* Damian Lee. *EP:* Menahem Golan & Ami Artzi. *AP & Prod Mgr:* Helder Conclaves. *D-Sc:* Allan Goldstein. *St:* Michael Colleary & Allen Goldstein, from characters created by Brian Garfield. *Ph:* Curtis Petersen. *Ed:* Patrick Rand. *Mus:* Terry Plumeri. *Prod Design:* Csaba Andras Kertesz. *Costume Design:* Jay Du Boisson. *Prod Executive:* Yael Golan. *Asst Dir:* John Bradshaw, Marek Posival, Glenn MacIntosh & Andreas Schneider. *Sp Eff:* Ron Craig, Jeff Marsh, Peter Phillips & Stan Zuwala. *Stunt Coordinator:* J.P. Romano. *Stunts:* Marco Bianco, Shane Cardwell, Rick Forsaythe, Ted Hanlen, Jennifer Jarrett, Mike Jones, Mike Lee, Steve Lucescu, Patrick Mark, Dwayne McKean, Larry McLean, Christine McMahon, Susan Parker, Kenn Quinn, Buck Randall, Bryan Renfro & Helen Scott. *Doubles:* J.P. Romano, Shelley Cook, Randy Butcher, Watson Carlson, Eric Byrson, Jamie Jones & Alison Reid. *Casting:* Ann Tait & Kathy A. Smith. *Casting Associate:* Victoria Muspratt. *Extra Casting:* Dona Dupere. *First Asst Ed:* Mark Nedivi & Doug Caron. *Second Asst Ed:* Sean W. Menzies. *Financial Executive:* Daniel Boivin. *Mus Ed:* Richard C. Allen. *Transportation Coordinator:* Eric Beldowki. *Best Boy Grip:* Michael Bickel. *Construction Coordinator:* Lawrence Brandridge. *Sd Eff Designer:* Jimmy Busceme. *Dialog/ADR Ed:* Jeff Bushelman. *Foley Walker:* Patrick David Cabral. *Boom Operator:* Gavin Coford. *Best Boy Electric:* Yvon Comeau. *Steadicam Operator/Camera Operator:* Gilles Corbeil. *Key Set Decorator:* Jeff Cutler. *Color Timer:* Leslie D'Brass. *Sp Eff Makeup:* Francois Dagenais. "*B*" *Camera Focus Puller:* Richard Eagan. *Additional Sd Eff:* Lisle Engle. *Mus Supv:* Brian Gendece. *Sc Supv:* Barbara Gordon. *Sd Eff Designer/Supv Sd Ed:* Matt Green. *Second Asst Camera:* Lou Grezelier & Doug Nelson. *AD:* Ian Hall. *Key Grip:* Bill Heinz. *Set Nurse:* Lisa Greco. *Post Prod Supv:* Mark S. Hoerr. *ADR Mixer/Foley Mixer/Eff Mixer:* Steve Hollenbeck. *First Asst Camera:* Rick Kearney. *Unit Prod Manager:* Mike Kohne. *Boom Operator:* Geoffrey H. Layne. *Prod Coordinator:* Gaille Ledrew. *Choreographer:* Andrea Mann. *Still Photographer:* John Medland. *Supv Re-recording Mixer:* T.A. Moore Jr. *Focus Puller:* Durwin Partridge. *Property Master:* Kevin Pierson. *Orchestration:* Terry Plumeri. *Negative Cutter:* Catherine Rankin. *Gaffer:* Doug Reid. *Sd Recordist/Foley Walker:* Peter D. Saphier. *Key Makeup:* Cherre Van Dyk. *Key Hair Styles:* Leon Van Dyk. *Negative Cutter:* Erika Wolff.

**CAST:** Charles Bronson (Paul Kersey), Lesley-Anne Down (Olivia Regent), Michael Parks (Tommy O'Shea), Robert Joy (Freddie Fiskes), Chuck Shamata (Sal Pacconi), Kevin Lund (Chickie Pacconi), Saul Rubinek (District Attorney Brian Hoyle), Miguel Sandoval (Hector Vasquez), Kenneth Welsh (Lieutenant Mickey King), Lisa Inouye (Detective Janice Omori), Erica Lancaster (Chelsea Regent), Jefferson Maupin (Big Albert), Michael Dunston (Reg), Claire Rankin (Maxine), Sharolyn Sparrow (Dawn), Anna Starnino (Sister), Elena Kudaba (Housekeeper), Andrea Mann (Mrs. Hoyle), Scott Spidell

(Frankie), Tim MacMenamin (Mickey), Sandro Limotta (Angel), Alison Sealy-Smith (Doctor), Michelle Moffatt (TV Reporter), Allan Goldstein (Toy Store Clerk), Marcelle Meleca (Hoyle's Son), Tony Meyler (Agent), Dougie Richardson (Cab Driver), Tova Gallimore, Kimberley Cody, Mikki Greaves, Trish Olsthoorn, Jenni-Leigh Girard, Beverly Anderson, Lisa Heugham, Maxine Elaine, Kendal Hunder, Melissa Illes, Mara Matejic, Melissa Patile (Models).

After a lapse of seven years Charles Bronson returned to the role of Paul Kersey, the vigilante, for the fifth time in *Death Wish V: The Face of Death*. The locale is again New York City, the setting of the original *Death Wish* (1974) and *Death Wish 3* (1985), although the production was mostly filmed in Toronto, Canada. This outing gets back to the origins of the Kersey character—he is reluctant to take the law into his own hands until he is forced to do so by the murder of his fiancée and the inability of the police to bring in the culprit. "Sixteen years, it's a long time to be failing," Kersey tells a police lieutenant who has been after mob boss Tommy O'Shea (Michael Parks) for all those years without pinning anything on him. The movie is a well made, handsome production which is nicely paced and filled with interesting characterizations. The action does not really begin until near the end of the movie when Kersey takes his revenge on the mobsters. Here he is back to using a handgun and not the missile launchers or assault weapons of the two previous series outings. Overall, though, *Death Wish V: The Face of Death* is an entertaining thriller and a nice addition to the series. Ironically it has received poor writeups, especially in movie and video guides and TV magazines. It is as if the reviewers never watched the movie, they just judged it would be bad being the fifth entry in a series loved by the public but disdained by the critics.

Paul Kersey had returned to the New York City area under the guise of Professor Stewart, an instructor of architecture. He becomes engaged to beautiful fashion designer Olivia Regent (Lesley-Anne Down) whose business is being invaded by her mobster ex-husband Tommy O'Shea (Michael Parks) and his thugs, brothers Sal Pacconi (Chuck Shamata) and Chickie Pacconi (Kevin Lund). Kersey goes to his friend, District Attorney Brian Hoyle (Saul Rubinek), and tells him Olivia will testify as to O'Shea's illegal activities in the fashion industry. The night Kersey and Olivia become engaged, O'Shea hires transvestite Freddie Fiskes (Robert Joy) to scar Olivia's face by smashing it into a mirror. O'Shea and his thugs also torture Olivia's factory manager, Big Albert (Jefferson Maupin), and custodian Reg (Michael Dunston). Big Albert agrees to help police Lieutenant Mickey King (Kenneth Welsh) and his partner Janice Omori (Lisa Inouye) get the goods on O'Shea but the gangster finds out and has Freddie kill Big Albert and Janice, who gets in the way of his speeding car. While Olivia recuperates, Kersey takes her daughter Chelsea (Erica Lancaster) to his country home and realizing Hoyle's telephone is bugged, he tells the district attorney that Olivia will not testify against O'Shea. Later he goes to Hoyle's home and tells him Olivia will testify but Hoyle's assistant Hector Vasquez (Miguel Sandoval) is on the take from O'Shea and warns him. As a result the Pacconi brothers and Freddie invade Olivia's apartment and kill her but Kersey manages to escape. O'Shea then gets a custody order taking Chelsea from Kersey, who is knocked out by the thugs after hitting the mobster. Realizing the law can do nothing, Kersey sets out to kill off the gangsters, starting with Chickie, who he poisons. Vasquez tells O'Shea that Kersey is the vigilante of yore and that he killed Chickie. Next Kersey lures Freddie out of his security-laden house and kills him with a bomb hidden in a ball. Vasquez then tries to kill Kersey but instead gets shot. Kersey sends his body to O'Shea in a crate. Then he trails Sal who is picking up Chelsea to bring her to her father's office above the fashion design factory once owned by Olivia. The gangsters plan to trap Kersey but instead he kills two thugs (Scott Spidell, Tim MacMenamin) and ties up a third, Angel (Sandro Limotta). Sal accidentally shoots Angel and is killed by Kersey. As the police converge on the building, Kersey corners O'Shea but the latter gets a gun and injures Lieutenant King who arrives on the scene. Kersey overpowers O'Shea and throws him into a vat of boiling wax.

As *Variety* noted, Charles Bronson "still fit and fearsome at 72" dominates the action in *Death Wish V: The Face of Death*. Both in looks and movement he belies his age and proves he is still one of the movies' great action heroes. Unfortunately women who get too close to Paul Kersey do not fare well and Olivia Regent, nicely played by beautiful Lesley-Anne Down, is no exception. First she has her face scarred and then she is murdered. Michael Parks is one of the best villains of the series in his role as the quirky and thoroughly contemptible gangster. He is ably assisted by Chuck Shamata and Kevin Lund as the Pacconi brothers, Robert Joy as the dandruff-plagued Freddie Fiskes and Miguel Sandoval as the DA's corrupt assistant. Also nicely showcased are Saul Rubinek as the district attorney, Kenneth Welsh as the policeman and Erica Lancaster as Chelsea, the young girl who loves Kersey like a father and hates her real dad, gangster O'Shea.

Critics were mixed about the film. UPI correspondent Vernon Scott said it was "As good as, if not better than, the first [film]" and Satellite News Network's Bob Healy said it "Had more action than the first four put together. Bronson's still got the stuff of great action heroes." The majority of critics, however, as usual, disliked the movie. *Variety* opined, "Slackly paced and unexciting, *Death Wish V* comes off as a flat-footed, by-the-numbers programmer, that, judging from what's on screen, failed to spark much enthusiasm among the people who made it." Ed Leibowitz wrote in *LA Weekly* that it was "another cheap bastardization of his [Bronson] most famous role.... In *Death Wish V*, Bronson must still masquerade as the man of action, jumping off

Advertisement for *Death Wish V: The Face of Death* (Trimark/21st Century, 1994).

rooftops and dodging bullets and explosives. The only time he seems at ease is when he's allowed, however briefly, to play the old man." In the *Los Angeles Times*, Chris Willman called the film "cheap … a snoozer" but added "it is good to know, even in his early 70s [Bronson] can leap off tall buildings in a single bound and emerge unscathed." Matt Langdon in *LA Reader* said the feature was a "repulsive action drama" but added, "For someone who is older than Shelley Winters and way older than that whipper-snapper Wilford Brimley, Bronson is in remarkably good shape—a lot better shape than the film itself, which will please only his most devout fans."

Evidently *Death Wish V: The Face of Death* was intended for direct video release in the United States but instead it went to theatres first, grossing over $1.7 million, before video sales and cable television airplay.

## *De la Part des Copains (Cold Sweat)* (Films Corona/Conacico/Fair Film, 1971) 94 minutes Color

*P:* Robert Dorfmann. *EP:* Serge Lebeau. *AP:* Maurice Jacquin. *D:* Terence Young. *Sc:* Shimon Wincelberg, Albert Simonin, Jo Eisinger & Dorothea Bennett, from the novel *Ride the Nightmare* by Richard Matheson. *Ph:* Jean Rabier. *Ed:* Johnny Dwyre. *Mus:* Michel Magne. *AD:* Tony Roman. *Asst AD:* Eugene Roman. *Asst Dir:* Daniel Wronecki & Christian Raux. *Sd:* William R. Sivel. *Unit Mgr:* Clo D'Olban. *Makeup:* Marie Madeline Paris & Anatole Paris. *Hair Stylist:* Alain Scemama. *Set Decorator:* Fernand Bernardi. *Second Unit Camera:* Raymond Picon-Borel. *Camera Operator:* Alain Douarinou. *Continuity:* Jeanne Witta. *Administrators:* Stanko Grozdiano & Michele Girot. *Racing Stunts:* Remy Julienne & His Team.

**CAST:** Charles Bronson (Joe Martin/Joe Moran), Liv Ullmann (Fabienne Martin), James Mason (Captain Ross), Jill Ireland (Moira), Michel Constantin (Vermont), Jean Topart (Katanga), Yannick Delulle (Michelle), Luigi Pistilli (Fausto Gilarde); Natalie Varallo, Paul Boniface, Roger Maille, Remo Moscow, Dominique Crosland, Sabrina Suman.

Following making *Città Violenta* (1970) in Italy, Charles Bronson returned to France, this time to Nice where he starred in *De la Part des Copains*, originally known as *The Night Visitors*. He was paid $400,000 for this starring effort which teamed him with veteran British director Terence Young, best known for his James Bond features *Dr. No* (1962), *From Russia with Love* (1963) and *Thunderball* (1965). Jason Robards was originally set for the lead villain part which went to James Mason and the leading lady was Swedish actress Liv Ullmann who was mainly known at the time for her work in Ingmar Bergman features. The picture was shot at Port of Beaulieu Sur-Mer and at the La Victorine Studios. Remy Julienne, who had supervised the racing sequences in *Città Violenta*, here advised and executed three car chase sequences, the last of which lead to the climax of the feature.

Set in the south of France, the film tells of Joe Martin (Charles Bronson), an expatriate American who owns a boat which he uses both for tourism and fishing. He has a loving but edgy marriage to Fabienne (Liv Ullmann) who finds out about his past when Vermont (Michel Constantin) breaks into their home and tells Joe his past has caught up with him. Joe is forced to kill Vermont in a fight and he tells Fabienne that while spending time in a military prison for hitting a captain he became pals with black marketeer Captain Ross (James Mason) and agreed to become his driver when they escaped. During the break, however, one of the gang members, former Foreign Legionnaire Katanga (Jean Topart), killed a German policeman. Joe escaped with the car and the rest were caught and sent to prison. Now, seven years later, the gang is after Joe, whose real name is Joe Moran. Fabienne helps Joe dispose of Vermont's body but when they return home they find Ross, Katanga and Fausto Gilardi (Luigi Pistilli), another gang member, waiting for them. With Fabienne as a prisoner of the gang, Joe is forced to take Katanga on a rendezvous with a Turkish boat carrying heroin but Joe knocks him out and goes to the airport to meet Moira (Jill Ireland), Ross' hippie girlfriend, who is carrying the loot to pay for the drugs. Fausto is supposed to meet the girl but Joe waylays him and takes her to a remote shack, imprisoning her there. He then finds out that Fabienne and Ross have taken Michelle (Yannick Delulle) from camp and he returns home with a deal for Ross. For the safety of his wife and stepdaughter Michelle he will return Moira and take the gang to its rendezvous with the Turkish vessel. Ross agrees but at the shack he orders Katanga to shoot out the tires on the car Fabienne is driving. Joe attacks Katanga who fires wildly, killing Fausto and wounding Ross. Needing a doctor, Ross sends Joe with Moira to fetch one while he holds a gun on Katanga, who has tried to steal the money. Fabienne and Michelle try to aid Ross who is losing blood quickly. Joe and Moira get a doctor and speed back to the shack, trying to elude the police following them. At the cabin the dying Ross is overpowered by Katanga but Fabienne and Michelle escape and set a brush fire as a camouflage. Joe arrives on the scene and finds his wife and stepdaughter but Katanga gets the drop on them and orders Joe to take all of them aboard his boat in order to meet the Turkish ship. On board Katanga expresses a preference for 12-year-old Michelle as Joe uses a flare gun to set him on fire. Katanga falls overboard, along with the attaché case containing the money. Joe, Fabienne and Michelle return to a festive crowd celebrating Bastille Day.

Like *Città Violenta, De la Part des Copains* was very popular in Europe and elsewhere around the world. In Italy it was called *L'Uomo dalle Due Ombre*; it was a French-Italian co-production. To show the stature of his new-found stardom, Charles Bronson was billed on the screen in lettering larger than the rest of the cast and the plot found him in nearly every scene carrying off the action and emoting in equally good measures. Critics were upset to find

Advertisement for *Cold Sweat* (Emerson Film Enterprises, 1974), the U.S. release title of *De la Part des Copains* (Films Corona/Conacico/Fair Film, 1971).

**Charles Bronson and Liv Ullman in *Cold Sweat* (Emerson Film Enterprises, 1974).**

Bergman actress Liv Ullmann in the rather unglamorous role of Bronson's loyal wife while James Mason's American Southern accent was probably the most taxing part of the proceedings. Jean Topart was especially good as the sadistic degenerate Katanga while Michel Constantin, who had also appeared in *Città Violenta*, lent a fine cameo as the bumbling gang member sent to bring in Joe, only to end up at the foot of a deep ravine. While the finale was most suspenseful as to whether the dying Ross would stay alive long enough for Joe to return and save his family, one wonders why they simply just didn't tie up Katanga instead of having Ross hold a gun on him?

The feature did not see United States release until 1974 when it was released here by Emerson Film Enterprises as *Cold Sweat*. Ironically three days after having its first run in New York City it was shown on national television. The critics turned thumbs down on the film, the *Monthly Film Bulletin* called it "A flabbily effete thriller." It is really a rather picturesque and fairly entertaining outing which moves along quickly and provides all the elements of a Bronson production. Again Jill Ireland is in the cast, this time cast as a quirky hippie; she is not only very beautiful but is quite good in the part.

Despite Charles Bronson's popularity in his homeland in 1974, *Cold Sweat* got quick playoff. Today it is probably best known as a Bronson video perennial. The film is offered by several home video companies, often in tandem with other Bronson European features of the time, like his next feature *Quelqu'un Derriere la Porte* (1971).

## *Diplomatic Courier* (20th Century–Fox, 1952) 98 minutes B/W

*P:* Casey Robinson. *D:* Henry Hathaway. *Sc:* Casey Robinson & Liam O'Brien, from the novel *Sinister Errand* by Peter Cheyney. *Ph:* Lucien Ballard. *Ed:* James B. Clark. *Mus:* Sol Kaplan. *AD:* Lyle Wheeler & John De Cuir. *Sets:* Thomas Little & Stuart Reis. *Sp Eff:* Ray Kellogg. *Makeup:* Ben Nye. *Sd:* W.D. Flick & Roger Heman. *Mus D:* Lionel Newman. *Orchestrations:* Edward Powell. *Wardrobe D:* Charles Le Maire. *Costumes:* Elois Jenssen.

**CAST:** Tyrone Power (Mike Kells), Patricia Neal (Joan Ross), Stephen McNally (Colonel Cagle), Hildegarde Neff (Janine), Karl Malden (Ernie), James Millican (Sam Carew), Stefan Schnabel (Platov), Herbert Berghof (Arnov), Arthur Blake (Max Ralli), Helene Stanley (Stewardess), Michael Ansara (Ivan), Sig Arno (Chef de Train), Alfred Linder (Cherenko), Lee Marvin (Trieste Military Policeman), Tyler McVey (Watch Officer), Peter Coe (Zinski), Dabbs Greer (Intelligence Officer), Carleton Young (Brennan), Charles La Torre (French Ticket Officer), Tom Powers (Cherney), Monique Chantal (French Stewardess), Lumsden Hare (Jacks), Russ Conway (Bill), Charles Buchinski (Bronson, the Soviet Assassin), Mario Siletti (Man), Hugh Marlowe (Narrator).

High ranking State Department courier Mike Kells (Tyrone Power) is sent to Salzburg to obtain documents from the U.S. ambassador to Bucharest, Sam Carew (James Millican), which detail a planned Soviet invasion of Yugoslavia. At the appointed rendezvous at a train station, Mike finds Carew reluctant to talk and soon realizes he is being shadowed by two Soviet agents (Michael Ansara, Charles Buchinski) who later kill the ambassador. When Mike finds out the Russians did not get Carew's secret papers he is assigned by his boss, Colonel Cagle (Stephen McNally), to get in good with pretty Janine (Hildegarde Neff), a Soviet agent with whom Carew had worked. When slightly addled American tourist Joan Ross (Patricia Neal) becomes enamored with Mike he finds her romantic overtures getting in the way of his assignment. It is his relationship with the two women, however, which leads Mike to eventually bring the case to a satisfactory conclusion.

Made as the Cold War was getting hotter, *Diplomatic Courier* was a topical spy melodrama which benefitted from a good cast and a twist ending. For Charles Bronson it was another bit role, here as a Russian hitman who murders the ambassador played by James Millican. The same year the two would appear in an episode of TV's *Four Star Playhouse* called "The Witness." Ironically the character Charles Buchinski (as he was billed) played in the film was named Bronson; this being a full two years before the actor adopted Charles Bronson as his professional name.

Bosley Crowther in the *New York Times* claimed the film's deficiencies were with its writers who he said "haven't concocted a story that has clarity and suspense, and Mr. Hathaway hasn't been able to direct it so that it looks like anything on the screen." *Variety*, however, thought it "a top notch spy thriller" adding, "The cloak-and-dagger melodramatics spill out realistically and with suspense, slanting the film for good response." *Time* claimed "this particular diplomatic courier is traveling a well-worn movie-melodrama route, and that his diplomatic pouch contains nothing more momentous than a class-B screenplay." *Newsweek* felt the movie "spins the usual tangle of plot and counterplot of the spy melodrama and resolves it in the proper balance of action and suspense ... a satisfactory entertainment."

*Diplomatic Courier* reunited Charles Bronson with Henry Hathaway who had helmed his screen debut in *U.S.S. Teakettle* the year before. Despite the fact the film had many exotic European locales, it was shot entirely on the 20th Century–Fox soundstages. Some second-unit work with Tyrone Power done at the Trocadero night club was given a European look by the use of transparencies.

## *The Dirty Dozen* (Metro-Goldwyn-Mayer, 1967) 149 minutes Color

*P:* Kenneth Hyman. *AP:* Raymond Anzarut. *D:* Robert Aldrich. *Sc:* Nunnally Johnson & Lukas Heller, from the novel by E.M. Nathanson. *Ph:* Edward Scaife. *Ed:* Michael Luciano. *Mus:* Frank DeVol. *Songs:* Frank DeVol, Mack David & Sibylle Siegfried. *AD:* William Hutchinson. *Sd:* Franklin Milton & Claude Hitchcock. *Sd Ed:* John Poyner. *Sp Eff:* Cliff Richardson. *Asst Dir:* Bart Batt. *Makeup:* Ernest Gasser & Wally Schneiderman. *Main Title Design:* Walter Blake. *Prod Mgr:* Julian MacKintosh.

**CAST:** Lee Marvin (Major Reisman), Ernest Borgnine (General Worden), Charles Bronson (Joseph Wladislaw), Jim Brown (Robert Jefferson), John Cassavetes (Victor Franko), Richard Jaeckel (Sergeant Bowren), George Kennedy (Major Max Armbruster), Trini Lopez (Pedro Jiminez), Ralph Meeker (Captain Stuart Kinder), Robert Ryan (Colonel Everett Dasher Breed), Telly Savalas (Archer Maggott), Donald Sutherland (Vernon Pinkley), Clint Walker (Samson Posey), Robert Webber (General Denton), Tom Busby (Milo Vladek), Ben Carruthers (Glenn Gilpin), Stuart Cooper (Roscoe Lever), Robert Phillips (Corporal Morgan), Colin Maitland (Seth Sawyer), Al Mancini (Tassos Bravos), George Roubicek (Private Arthur James Gardner), Thick Wilson (General Worden's Aide), Dora Reisser (Blonde German Woman).

In order to prepare the Allied forces for the invasion of Normandy in 1944, military top brass in England led by General Worden (Ernest Borgnine) order renegade Major Reisman (Lee Marvin) to pick out and train a dozen soldier-criminals for a top secret mission—they are to be parachuted behind enemy lines to carry out sabotage by destroying specific targets, aimed at weakening the enemy before the invasion. At the military prison he chooses a motley crew, causing his top sergeant Bowren (Richard Jaeckel) to comment, "I think the first chance one of these mothers gets he'll shoot the major right in the head." Among those chosen are several convicted murderers due to be executed, including Joseph Wladislaw (Charles Bronson), religious fanatic Archer Maggott (Telly Savalas), hate-filled black Robert Jefferson (Jim Brown) and muscle bound Samson Posey (Clint Walker), who killed a man who was hassling him, with a punch that pushed his jawbone into his brain. Others chosen included Chicago gangster Victor Franko (John Cassavetes), convicted of a bank robbery after arriving in London, moronic Vernon Pinkley (Donald Sutherland) and Mexican Pedro Jiminez (Trini Lopez), who complains about not being allowed guitar strings in prison. Reisman warns all the men that if any of them fail all will be sent back to prison for the remainder of their sentences; if they survive their former ranks will be restored. Taken to a remote area the men construct their own barracks while undergoing tough training by Reisman and Bowren, who are also going on the mission. Working with the two men are Captain Kinder (Ralph Meeker), a psychiatrist, who thinks the group is a bunch of misfits and particularly warns Reisman to drop Maggott from the mission but the major refuses. Reisman's old enemy, Colonel Everett Dasher Breed (Robert Ryan), and his men invade the camp to find out what they are doing, and two of his men beat up Wladislaw. Reisman arrives and thwarts Breed's actions but ends up at a complaint board before General Worden and General Denton (Robert Webber). Both want to abort the mission but Reisman convinces them to give his men a chance at taking Breed's company in scheduled war games. Reisman and his "Dirty Dozen" (called so because they rebelled against shaving in cold water and were denied soap as a punishment) devise an intricate plan that not only causes them to win the war games but also results in making the arrogant Breed look like a fool since the group captures him in his own headquarters. With the mission on, the group parachutes into Normandy to a chateau where many top brass Nazis are having a conference and social holiday. Reisman and Wladislaw, who speaks some German, infiltrate the chateau posing as Nazi officers while the others surround the place. Just before the mission to kill as many German officers as possible begins Maggott murders a female guest (Dora Reisser), setting off the hostilities. The Nazi leaders and their women go to a basement bomb shelter where they are locked in by Reisman. As German troops open fire on the invaders, Reisman and his men drop scores of grenades down the air holes into the bomb shelter and then drench the area with gasoline. Jefferson, who was forced to shoot the crazed Maggott, is killed by a Nazi gunner before he can escape aboard a fortified jeep with Reisman, Bowren, Wladislaw, Posey and Sawyer (Colin Maitland).

Advertisement for *The Dirty Dozen* (Metro-Goldwyn-Mayer, 1967).

The survivors then plow through Nazi artillery and make it back to safety. In a military hospital, injured Reisman, Bowren and Wladislaw find themselves praised by generals Worden and Denton who want to see them back on the battlefield.

*The Dirty Dozen* was Charles Bronson's third all-male starring feature of the 1960s, preceded by *The Magnificent Seven* (1960) and *The Great Escape* (1963), and while those two were big moneymakers, *The Dirty Dozen* was the most successful with a domestic gross of over $20 million. The film also reunited Bronson with Ernest Borgnine and director Robert Aldrich from *Vera Cruz* (1957), while his career had several times crossed that of top billed Lee Marvin since their movie debuts in *U.S.S. Teakettle (You're in the Navy Now)* in 1951. Thanks to everyone being billed alphabetically following Lee Marvin, Bronson got third billing, right after Borgnine. The part of Joseph Wladislaw was also a good one and the actor does top notch work in the role with *Variety* referring to him as "a very capable actor." Wladislaw was a Polish-American sentenced to die by a military court for killing a fellow soldier who he tells Reisman was trying to desert during a fierce battle carrying away all the platoon's medical supplies. The major tells him his crime was not in shooting the deserter but in being seen doing the killing. Bronson also has the film's last and best line. After being praised by the two military brass for his heroism, he tells Reisman and Bowren, "Killin' generals could get to be a habit with me." Like *The Magnificent Seven* and *The Great Escape*, *The Dirty Dozen* solidified Charles Bronson's position as a top flight character star. Within three years he would be an international movie star and the next time he worked with Lee Marvin, in *Death Hunt* in 1981, it would be Bronson who got first billing.

*The Dirty Dozen* was shot on location at Hendon Aerodrome, 15 miles north of London; it was at this famed location that H.C. Baird made his first solo flight. Except for extras and eight actresses in bit parts as prostitutes, the only woman in the film was Bulgarian actress Dora Reisser who played the small part of the blonde German officer's girlfriend murdered by the demented Maggott. The film's only Academy Award went to sound editor John Poyner for his sound effects of explosives. On the minus side was Trini Lopez's brief vocalizing of the film's title song, the insipid "The Bramble Bush."

*Time* said the film "proves that Hollywood does best by World War II when it does it straight" and Arthur Knight noted in *Saturday Review*, "The realization that authority not only has its uses but, for some men, fulfills an aching need is a bitter pill that Aldrich coats with bountiful action, robust humor, and a uniformly superb cast." *Variety* thought it "an exciting Second World War pre–D-Day drama" while the *New York Times* complained, "A raw and preposterous glorification of a group of criminal soldiers who are trained to kill and who then go about this brutal business with hot, sadistic zeal is advanced in this astonishingly wanton and irresponsible war drama. Based on fact though it may be, it seems downright preposterous that a bunch of incorrigible felons, some of them psychopathic, would be committed by any American general to perform an exceedingly important raid that a regular commando group could do with equal efficiency." Just as critical was Gordon Drummond in *Films in Review*: "*The Dirty Dozen* is so full of socially deleterious propaganda that everyone connected with it should be ashamed." He added, "in the course of it the following occurs: the US command which authorizes the raid is made to seem as criminal, and as stupid, as the criminals; military discipline is mocked; black racism is condoned if not promoted; criminal and psychopathic forms of sadism are made to seem no different from those of war...." F. Maurice Speed in *Film Review 1968–1969* (1968) called it a "Good, well-handled war story...." In retrospect Danny Peary commented in *Guide for the Film Fanatic* (1986) it "was a box office smash despite the moviegoers' growing aversion to the genre in light of Vietnam. That's because it managed to stage exciting, brutal war sequences while simultaneously celebrating misfits, putting down authority figures and the military, and showing war to be a madman's game that can only be fought down and dirty." Peary also noted the film's similarity to the earlier *The Secret Invasion* (1964).

That Charles Bronson had become one of the screen's finest actors is evidenced by the fact that his performance in *The Dirty Dozen* excelled in a film populated by top notch emoting. In addition to Bronson, kudos go to Richard Jaeckel's tough top sergeant, John Cassavetes as the streetwise hoodlum, Ralph Meeker as the military psychiatrist, Robert Ryan as the calculating colonel, Donald Sutherland's moronic hick (he is particularly good in the scene in which he masquerades as an incognito general inspecting Breed's troops) and Robert Webber's brief scenes as a two-faced general.

Eighteen years after the theatrical release of *The Dirty Dozen*, Lee Marvin, Ernest Borgnine and Richard Jaeckel repeated their roles in the TV movie, *Dirty Dozen: The Next Mission* on NBC-TV. The plotline had them out to thwart an assassination plot against Adolf Hitler. Borgnine was back in *Dirty Dozen: The Deadly Mission* (NBC-TV, 1987) which also starred Telly Savalas from the original film, here cast as a major who leads his men in destroying poison gas. In 1988 two more "Dirty Dozen" TV sequels followed on NBC-TV—*The Dirty Dozen: The Fatal Mission* and *The Dirty Dozen: The Series, Danko's Dozen*. The first again co-starred Telly Savalas and Ernest Borgnine and added a female commando (Heather Thomas) in a plot involving the assassination of Nazis aboard the Orient Express; while the latter toplined Ben Murphy as a new leader, Danko, who heads a mission to blow up an enemy radar complex. It was the initial telefilm episode of the Fox network series *The Dirty Dozen: The Series* which was shown for four months in 1988.

Charles Bronson appeared with the rest of the film's cast and crew in the ten minute color theatrical short, *Operation Dirty Dozen* (1967). Produced by Professional Film Services, this promotional movie presented details on *The Dirty Dozen*'s location production in England. Bronson is shown briefly in a couple of scenes while the bulk of the footage is given to Lee Marvin as the film's star. Burt Sloane was the associate producer of this theatrical filler, with direction by Ronald Saland, photography by Ross Lowell and Al Mozell, script by Jay Anson and editing by Howard Kuperman.

## *Donato and Daughter (Dead to Rights)* (CBS-TV/ Multimedia, 1993) 95 minutes Color

*P:* Marian Brayton & Anne Carlucci. *EP:* Neil Russell & Brenda Miao. *D:* Rod Holcomb. *Sc:* Robert Roy Pool, from the novel by Jack Early. *Ph:* Thomas Del Ruth. *Ed:* Christopher Nelson. *Mus:* Sylvester Levay. *Prod Design:* Richard Sherman. *Costume Design:* Timothy D'Arcy. *Prod Sd Mixer:* Kim H. Ornitz. *Unit Prod Mgr:* Douglas S. Burdinski. *Casting:* Karen Hendel. *Set Decorator:* Michael Warga. *Property Master:* David Carpenter. *Sc Supv:* Karen Golden. *Asst Dir:* L. Dean Jones, Mark Glick & Ottie Brown. *Gaffer:* Danny Buck. *Makeup:* Marilyn Carbone & Ashley Scott. *Hair Stylist:* Charles Balsz. *Key Grip:* Lloyd Barcroft. *First Asst Camera:* Lex Rawlins. *Location Mgr:* Mark Cottrell. *Prod Coordinator:* Joan Cunningham. *Transportation Coordinator:* Fritz Braden. *Supv Sd Ed:* Peter Austin. *Post Prod Mixing & Sound Editing:* Todd A-O. *Titles & Opticals:* CFI.

**CAST:** Charles Bronson (Detective Sergeant Mike Donato), Dana Delany (Lieutenant Dena Donato), Xander Berkeley (Russ Loring), Jenette Goldstein (Detective Judy McCartney), Louis Giambalvo (Chief Hugh Halliday), Marc Alaimo (Detective Petsky), Tom Verica (Detective Keegan), Robert Gossett (Detective Bobbins), Bonnie Bartlett (Renata Donato), Michael Cavanaugh (Vinnie), Juliana McCarthy (Mrs. Loring); Richard Kuss, Kim Weeks, Charley Hayward, Patti Yasutake, Ian Patrick Williams, Sam Vincent, Sylvia Short, Malachi Pearson, Robin Cahall, Kathleen Coyen, David Gautreaux, Renee Golden, Gregory Itzin, Pine Jones, David McLain, Virginia Morris, Tony Pandolfo, Ronald Pitts, John Verea.

Charles Bronson returned to the police thriller format for his initial CBS-TV movie of the 1990s, *Donato and Daughter*. His previous telefeatures, *Raid on Entebbe* (1977), *Act of Vengeance* (1986) and *Yes Virginia, There Is a Santa Claus* (1991), had all cast him against type, but in *Donato and Daughter* he was doing the same kind of role he had been performing for the past two decades, the tough cop. This outing had the plot twist of having the Bronson character being the underling of his own daughter who outranks him on the force. Bronson and Emmy Award–winner Dana Delany handled the roles in good form although there is not much chemistry between them. This is mostly due to the fact that the character of the daughter is not particularly ingratiating. Allegedly the telefeature was the pilot for a proposed TV series that did not sell although it is hard to imagine that at this stage of his career Charles Bronson would want to be shackled with the rigors of doing a weekly series. As befitting a Charles Bronson vehicle, *Donato and Daughter* was the first TV movie of the 1993-94 season to carry a violence disclaimer. This was done to placate protests which had arisen in recent congressional hearings on small screen violence.

Two Catholic nuns are raped, murdered and mutilated in Los Angeles and Detective Sergeant Mike Donato (Charles Bronson) is on the scene of the first killing when his daughter, Lieutenant Dena Donato (Dana Delany) arrives, the two having been estranged since the death of her brother Tommy and Mike's demotion following the beating of a drug dealer. Upon the suggestion of police chief Hugh Halliday (Louis Giambalvo), Dena asks her father to join the task force looking into the murders, which they believe were committed by a serial killer. When a suspect tries to escape from his apartment building, Mike and Dena give chase but the man kills another officer, Detective Judy McCartney (Jenette Goldstein), Dena's best friend and Tommy's former girlfriend. A third nun is found murdered in Dena's neighborhood and an informant leads Mike to believe the killer had masqueraded as a nun. When the killer sends a severed finger to Dena's son Cal, the boy and Mike's wife (Bonnie Bartlett) are sent to stay with the boy's aunt. Disguised as a policeman, the madman kills another nun and leaves her body in an apartment elevator. Mike and Dena talk to the building's residents, including Kim Lyle and Russ Loring (Xander Berkeley), both of whom become suspects. Mike and Dena think Loring is the one they want and Mike heads to Arizona to the man's hometown. There the former local sheriff tells him that Loring's high school sweetheart mysteriously disappeared and the locals suspected Loring of killing her. He also talks to the man's mother (Julianna McCarthy) whose attitude further convinces him of Loring's guilt. Loring gets a restraining order stopping the police surveillance and Mike and Dena return home to find evidence the killer has been there. Mike tells Dena that Tommy, who had also been a cop, had overdosed on drugs and that he had beaten up Tommy's supplier. The two end their estrangement. Realizing the police are still after him, Loring returns to his apartment to destroy evidence only to learn his wife has found the police uniform. He tries to kill her as Dena arrives, attempting to stall him before the arrival of a search warrant. With Mike as backup, Dena goes into the apartment and talks to Loring, telling him the real killer has confessed. Loring makes a pass at Dena who finds bloodstains and calls for Mike. Loring takes Dena hostage and demands a helicopter in order to escape. Mike finds Mrs. Loring and calls for an ambulance and follows Loring and Dena to the apartment rooftop. Loring threatens to jump off the ledge, taking Dena with him, but when the helicopter arrives he becomes disoriented and Mike shoots and kills him. Dena is safe and reunited with her father.

Advertisement for *Donato and Daughter* (CBS-TV, 1993), released on video as *Dead to Rights* (Vidmark, 1995)

*Donato and Daughter* has much of the flavor of a Charles Bronson theatrical movie, which is to be expected since it was earmarked for theatres abroad following its U.S. TV debut on September 21, 1993. It was issued on video in the U.S. in 1995 as *Dead to Rights*. At the time of its telecast *Daily Variety* called it a "formulaic suspense thriller" adding, "Bronson may be a step slower, but his screen presence remains textured ... [he] delivers his customary spare and sinewy style, tailored for TV."

## *Drum Beat* (Warner Bros., 1954) 111 minutes Color

*P-D-Sc:* Delmer Daves. *EP:* Alan Ladd. *Ph:* J. Peverell Marley. *Ed:* Clarence Kolster. *Mus:* Victor Young. *AD:* Leo K. Kutter. *Sets:* William L. Kuehl. *Sp Eff:* H.F. Koenekamp. *Asst Dir:* William Kissel. *Tech Advisor:* Ben Corbett & George Ross.

**CAST:** Alan Ladd (Johnny MacKay), Audrey Dalton (Nancy Meek), Marisa Pavan (Toby), Robert Keith (Bill Satterwhite), Rodolfo Acosta (Scarface Charlie), Charles Bronson (Captain Jack), Warner Anderson (General Canby), Elisha Cook Jr. (Crackel), Anthony Caruso (Manok), Richard Gaines (Dr. Thomas), Edgar Stehli (Jesse Grant), Hayden Rorke (Ulysses S. Grant), Frank De Kova (Modoc Jim), Perry Lopez (Bogus Charlie), Willis Bouchey (General Gilliam), Peter Hansen (Lieutenant Goodsall), George Lewis (Captain Alonzo Clark), Isabel Jewell (Lily White), Frank Ferguson (Mr. Dyar), Peggy Converse (Mrs. Grant), Pat Lawless (O'Brien), Paul Wexler (William Brody), Richard Cutting (Colonel Meek), Strother Martin (Scotty), Rico Alaniz (Medicine Man), John Veitch (Young Soldier), George Ross, Victor Millan, Ken Smith (Sentries), Maurice Jara, Jonas Applegarth, Felix Noriego (Indians), James Griffith (Veteran), Frank Gerstle (Officer), Carol Nugent (Nellie Grant), Michael Daves (Young Man), Leonard Penn (Miller), Oliver Blake (Minister), Dan Borgaze, George Lloyd (Soldiers), Ron Hargrave (Singing Soldier).

*Drum Beat*, produced by star Alan Ladd's newly formed Jaguar Productions, was the first film in which Charles Bronson was billed under that name. Looking for a surname that was more common than Buchinsky, which he felt had limited the range of roles he received, the actor changed his last name to Bronson, after the street of the same name in Hollywood. Evidently the change brought him good luck as he drew considerable notice in *Drum Beat*, in which he played a Native American for the second time. The *Los Angeles Times* enthused, "Charles Bronson is only slightly less than sensational in the part. It is he who dominates the picture."

Like *Apache*, *Drum Beat* is based on historical fact and opens with President Ulysses S. Grant (Hayden Rorke) wanting to end the conflict between the U.S. Army and renegade Indians on the northern California-Oregon border. He sends for Johnny MacKay (Alan Ladd), a seasoned Indian fighter, and appoints him peace commissioner for the area. He wants Johnny to get the local Modoc Indians to sign a peace treaty without the use of armed

**Alan Ladd and Charles Bronson in *Drum Beat* (Warner Bros., 1954).**

force. Arriving in the area, Johnny finds out that many of the Modoc tribe want peace but that a band of rebels, led by Captain Jack (Charles Bronson), is the cause of the trouble. The murderous renegades kill soldiers and then proudly wear their uniforms as a badge of honor. The band make raids on the area and fight with soldiers at Fort Klamath before Johnny tracks Captain Jack and his men into the mountains. At the rebel camp Johnny challenges Captain Jack to combat and defeats him. As a result the insurrection is halted and Captain Jack is hung for his crimes, bringing peace to the area.

Filmed in Coconino National Forest in northern Arizona, *Drum Beat* is at its best in detailing the atmosphere of the old west, mainly due to producer-director-scripter Delmer Daves' love of the area, since he grew up in the West. Regarding the picture itself, the *New York Times* said, "It boils with commotion, with the fleeing Indians holing up atop towering mesa cliffs as the cavalry pursues them after a massacre. And the Arizona backgrounds come across ruggedly and vividly. But it's as standard and familiar as the day is long." In *The Western* (1983), Phil Hardy called it an "intriguing Indian Western" adding, "Daves' landscape photography is as majestic as ever." Also in retrospect Steven H. Scheuer wrote in *The Complete Guide to Videocassette Movies* (1987), "This is not a great Western but a surprisingly good one." It was Charles Bronson, and not star Alan Ladd or the film itself, which seemed to score best with the public. *Films and Filming* noted Ladd's "performance is dwarfed by that of Charles Bronson as Captain Jack..." while *Variety* said

Bronson portrayed the character "forcefully." The *Monthly Film Bulletin* felt "...only Charles Bronson as Captain Jack rises superior to the script." It should be noted that *Drum Beat* had two lovely female co-stars, Audrey Dalton for romantic interest and Marisa Pavan as one of the peaceful Modocs, but both were just window dressing in deference to action.

In his fine volume *The Films of Charles Bronson* (1980), Jerry Vermilye notes that Charles Bronson was ignored in the film's advertising campaign. He writes, "One imagines that perhaps executive producer Ladd did not fully appreciate Bronson's scene-stealing talents or the generous amount of close-ups allowed his thespian adversary by the movie's suitably impressed director, Delmer Daves."

While Charles Bronson made his name change in *Drum Beat* he would be billed as Charles Buchinsky one last time in *Vera Cruz*, which had been made earlier than the Alan Ladd feature but was released a month later, in December, 1954. *Drum Beat* is one of the most attractive of Bronson films having been lensed in CinemaScope and WarnerColor, thus enhancing the grandeur of its location scenery.

## *The Evil That Men Do* (Cannon Group, 1984)

90 minutes Color

*P:* Pancho Kohner. *EP:* Lance Hool. *AP:* Jill Ireland & David Pringle. *D:* J. Lee Thompson. *Sc:* John Crowther & David Lee Henry, from the novel by R. Lance Hill. *Ph:* Javier Ruvalcaba Cruz. *Ed:* Peter Lee-Thompson. *Mus:* Ken Thorne. *Executive in Charge of Prod:* Howard P. Alston. *Second Unit Dir/Stunt Coordinator:* Ernie Orsatti. *Prod Supv:* Marco Auerlio Ortiz. *U.S. Casting:* Hillary Holden. *Mexico Casting:* Claudia Baker. *Second Unit Prod Mgr:* Gordon A. Webb. *Asst Dir:* Gordon A. Webb & Terence B. Buchinsky. *Asst Dir—Mexico:* Jose Maria Ochoa & Javier Carreno. *Asst Prod Supv:* Anna Roth. *Prod Representative:* Robert Rose. *AD:* Enrique Estevez. *Wardrobe Designer:* Poppy Cannon. *Makeup:* Allan Marshall. *Second Unit Ph:* Daniel Lopez. *Camera Operator:* Manuel Gonzalez. *Camera Asst:* Javier Cruz Jr. *Steadicam Operator:* David Pringle. *Still Man:* Alfredo Rulvacara. *Sc Supv:* Jose Luis Ortega. *Sd Mixer:* Roberto Camacho. *Wardrobe Head:* Enedena Bernal. *Stuntman:* Ken Fritz. *Makeup Artist:* Esther Oropeza. *Hairdresser:* Esperanza Gomez. *Sp Eff:* Laurencio Cordero. *Gaffer:* Gabriel Castro. *Best Boy:* Garciano Perez. *Grip:* Adolpho Lara. *Property Master:* Antonio Mata. *Transportation Captain:* Salvatore Gutierrez. *Post Prod Supv:* James Potter. *Associate Ed:* Richard Marx. *Asst Ed:* Kimberley Bennett. *Apprentice Ed:* James Heller. *Mus Ed:* Steve Hope. *Sd Ed:* Michael Reborn, Richard Shorr, Joseph Holsen & John Post. *Re-recording Mixer:* Michael Winkler. *Prod Secretaries:* Abyzak Garcia & Sonia Troop. *Prod Estimator:* Lei Schmidt. *Second Unit Sc Supv:* Sara Tover. *Prod Asst:* Jason Bronson & Abelardo Delgadillo. *Unit Publicist:* Saul Cooper. *Titles/Opticals/Color:* CPI.

**CAST:** Charles Bronson (Holland), Theresa Saldana (Rhiana Hidalgo), Joseph Maher (Dr. Clement Molloch), Antoinette Bower (Claire Molloch),

Rene Enriquez (Max Ortiz), Jose Ferrer (Dr. Hector Lomelin), John Glover (Briggs), Raymond St. Jacques (Randolph Whitley), Joe Seneca (Santiago), Mischa Hausserman (Karl Hausmann), Jorge Luke (Cillero), Enrique Lucero (Colonel Victor Aristos), Constanza Hool (Isabel), Ernesto Gomez Cruz (Cafe Owner), Jorge Zepeda (Victim), Angelica Aragon (Maria), Alan Conrad (Fugitive), Rodrigo Pueblea (Farmer), Nicole Thomas (Sarah Hidalgo), Ania de Mblo (Dominique), Eduardo Lopez Rojas (Bartender), Carlos Romano (Cripple), Miguel Angel Fuentes (Latino), Richard Brodie (Driver Gunman), Angel Gutierrez (Gunman), Jorge Humberto Robles (Jorge), Fernando Saenz (Assael), Roger Cudney (Cannell).

*The Evil That Men Do* is one of the most violent of Charles Bronson's starring films and it is also one of the most visually attractive. Like *Caboblanco* (1980) it was filmed in Mexico and Javier Ruvalcaba Cruz' cinematography highlights that country's beauty. The film marked the first time that Jill Ireland worked on the production end of a Bronson film and he again teamed with producer Pancho Kohner and director J. Lee Thompson. As in *Città Violenta* (1970) and *The Mechanic* (1972), Bronson was cast as a hit man although this time he is a much more sympathetic character, one who loves the beauty of nature and who only returns to his old calling in order to eliminate a vicious sadist who uses horrible methods in his human rights violations. Outside of Academy Award-winner Jose Ferrer in a small role, Bronson is the only "name" in the cast and the film was just another example of how producers only needed Bronson to make a film and sell it to the public worldwide.

In South America journalist George Hidalgo (Jorge Zepeda) is tortured to death by Dr. Clement Molloch (Joseph Maher), who sells his services as a teacher of torture to Central and South American dictators who use his methods to keep rebels under control. Hidalgo had written an exposé on Molloch and the torture killing was the doctor's revenge. Dr. Hector Lomelin (Jose Ferrer) comes to the Cayman Islands to see retired hitman Holland (Charles Bronson) since both were friends of Hidalgo. He asks Holland to kill Molloch but he refuses even after watching tapes made of the madman's victims. In Guatemala City, where he is headquartered, Molloch is asked to leave by Colonel Victor Aristos (Enrique Lucero) because of increasing concern with his human rights violations. In Mexico City Holland tells Lomelin he has changed his mind and will kill Molloch and he takes Hidalgo's widow Rhiana (Theresa Saldana), and young daughter Sarah (Nicole Thomas) with him to Guatemala, masquerading as a tourist family. There they meet Max Ortiz (Rene Enriquez) who tells Holland of Molloch's habits and his associates, which includes his sister Claire (Antoinette Bower), right-hand man Randolph Whitley (Raymond St. Jacques) and cohorts Karl (Mischa Hausserman) and Cillero (Jorge Luke). Ortiz gets Holland weapons. At a low-life bar, Holland and Rhiana make the acquaintance of Randolph and offer to involve him in a sex party.

He goes back to their hotel with them and there Holland kills him. He later dumps the body in front of Molloch's compound. Although she is upset by the killing, Rhiana refuses to leave until Molloch is brought to justice. After Holland kills Karl, Molloch goes to corrupt U.S. representative Briggs (John Glover) and blames him and Aristos for the killing of his men. Briggs denies the charges as Holland kidnaps Claire and takes her to Ortiz for safekeeping. Ortiz and Sarah are captured by Molloch and the former is tortured by Molloch so he can find the whereabouts of his sister. Holland pretends he is blackmailing Molloch for Claire's return but soon realizes the doctor knows their whereabouts and the three head to the small village of Magdalena where Ortiz has another home. Along the way they engage in a shootout with Molloch's men, who Holland shoots, but Claire too is killed. Buying an old truck from a farmer, Holland and Rhiana head to the village but they are trailed by hired killer Cannell (Roger Cudney) and Briggs. In Magdalena Holland and Rhiana witness a funeral of men who were tortured to death by Molloch. They go to a nearby cafe and there Holland has a showdown with Cannell and Briggs, killing both men. He then telephones Molloch and tells him to meet

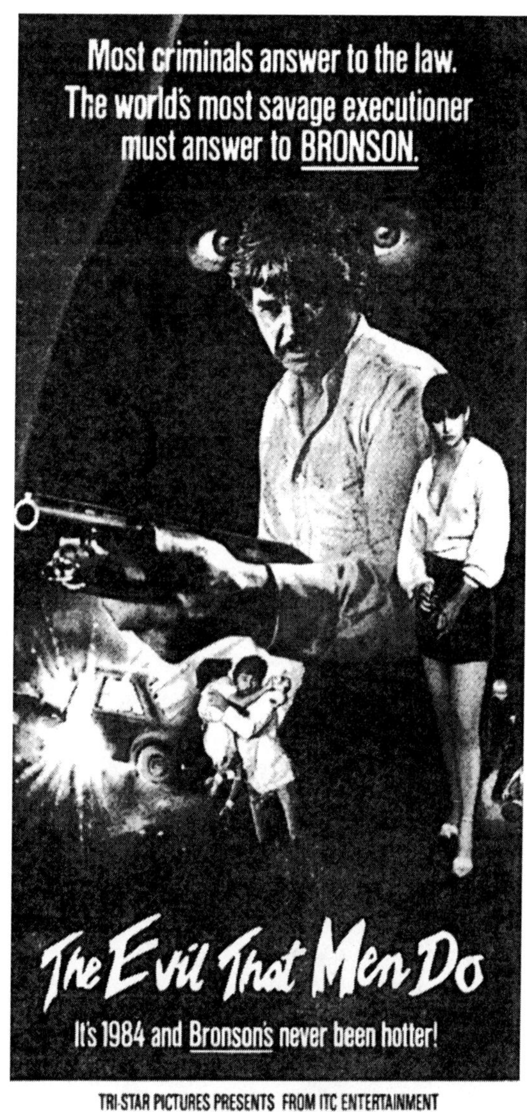


**Poster for *The Evil That Men Do* (Cannon Group, 1984).**

him at the abandoned opal mine outside of the village. Going there, Holland and Rhiana find the mine still being worked by dozens of men, most of whom have been disfigured by Molloch. The doctor arrives but has Sarah as his prisoner. Using a tape recorder to make Molloch think Claire is still alive, Holland manages to rescue Sarah as Molloch barricades himself in his limousine. Before Holland can kill him the workers converge on the car and beat Molloch to death. Holland, Rhiana and Sarah then return to Holland's home in the Cayman Islands.

Charles Bronson has a very action-packed role as hitman Holland in *The Evil That Men Do* and during the course of the feature he knocks off numerous Molloch allies. The film is particularly violent in that it not only depicts Molloch's torture devices (the opening scenes with Hidalgo being tortured to death with electrodes is particularly horrifying) but it also includes graphic shootings and even a cockfight. Holland is the hero out to kill the evil Molloch because "the doctor stands outside the law of civilized people" according to the professor character played by Jose Ferrer. When Rhiana wants to join Holland in getting revenge for her husband's death, Holland tells her, "Emotional vendettas are just another form of suicide." Joseph Maher played the torturer as an erudite monster, although he is more on the soft side rather than harsh as one would expect from such a character. Antoinette Bower is good as Molloch's cold-blooded lesbian sister. One amusing scene has Holland hiding under her bed while she has sex with a young girl. Raymond St. Jacques nicely handles the role of Molloch's henchman as does Enrique Lucero as the corrupt army colonel who protects the doctor. Roger Cudney projects menace in his brief role as a rival hitman while John Glover is the slimy American bureaucrat. J. Lee Thompson's direction keeps the plot moving along at a good clip—there are few lulls in *The Evil That Men Do*.

Janet Maslin noted in the *New York Times* that "There was plenty of audience participation" in the showing she caught at the National Theatre. A couple of scenes she noted included the one in the sleazy bar where a goon (Miguel Angel Fuentes) tries to molest Rhiana and Holland stops him by simultaneously choking him senseless with his foot and crushing his testicles. Another scene the audience enjoyed was when Holland killed Cannell by shooting him in the head and then announcing the other hitman was wearing a bulletproof vest. Ms. Maslin concluded her review with, "Mr. Bronson is stony as ever, and a little more nattily dressed." In *The Family Guide to Movies on Video* (1988) Henry Herx and Tony Zaza noted the "violent action vehicle is set against the background of an oppressive regime in Central America, but sidesteps any serious political commentary in favor of the usual excessively brutal melodrama." *LA Weekly*'s reviewer voted "to recommend the film, with heavy reservations, to anyone who believes they'll have a good time watching dozens of mugging actors being stabbed, shot and fiendishly tortured." *USA Today* noted, "Charles Bronson still has ice in his veins.... Mayhem in defense of liberty is no vice?" In the *Los Angeles Herald-Examiner*, Debba J. Kunk wrote that Bronson was "a man who wears his years gracefully" and that the film was "a slick enough vehicle for Bronson, if uninspired...." Jay Sharbutt in the *Los Angeles Times* noted the film contained 15 on-screen deaths in a script that "merely uses the headlines as an excuse to slay away for an hour and 37 minutes.... All of this is crisply directed by J. Lee Thompson. The film is workmanlike in its bloody way...." Owen Gleiberman wrote in *Video Times*, "Director J. Lee Thompson, a veteran of parish potboilers, supplies enough energy and heat to the scenario that builds to its climax as inexorably as a roller coaster careening around the curves. This comic-book vigilante picture has more anger, more live-wire chase scenes, and more blood-quickening thrills than Clint Eastwood's overrated *Tightrope*.... Say this for Bronson: After years of knocking off punks, the man still delivers." Michael J. Weldon in *The Psychotronic Film Guide* (1996) called the film "Bronson's most depraved."

## *Explosion!* (Warner Bros., 1957) 42 minutes B/W

*P:* Ellis St. Joseph. *EP:* William T. Orr. *D:* Don Weis. *Sc:* Jack Laird. *St:* Jack Laird & William T. Orr. *Ph:* Harold Stine. *Supv Ed:* James Moore. *Ed:* George Nicholson. *Mus:* David Buttolph. *AD:* Perry Ferguson. *Prod Mgr:* Oren W. Haglund. *Sd:* Eugene F. Westfall. *Set Decorator:* Bill Holland. *Makeup Supv:* Gordon Bau. *Asst Dir:* William Kissel.

**CAST:** Lyle Bettger (Harry Parker/William Bradley), Joy Page (Florence Parker), Charles Bronson (Brodsky/Johnson), Wilfred Knapp (Lieutenant Finch), James Garner (Burt Fowler), Terry Becker (Max), Roxanne Allen (Sadie Mayhew), Charles Maxwell (Sergeant Webster), Alan Reynolds (Morgan Hancock), Art Gilmore (TV Announcer).

Successful businessman Harry Parker (Lyle Bettger) was once a bookkeeper with the underworld. An organization gunman, Brodsky (Charles Bronson), and his partner Max (Terry Becker) trace him to a small Indiana town. Sent to silence Parker, the men plant a bomb in the wrong car and kill one of the man's employees. Realizing he will be next, Parker sells his business, puts his house up for sale and tells his wife Florence (Joy Page) to take their baby and go to her parents' home. Knowing the local police, lead by Lieutenant Finch (Wilfred Knapp), will also learn of his past, Parker plans to escape but Brodsky traps the man and his wife in their home, although the gunman is eventually outwitted by Parker.

Originally telecast March 27, 1956, on ABC-TV as a segment of *Warner Bros. Presents*, hosted by Gig Young, *Explosion!* was released theatrically in Great Britain the next year, making it Charles Bronson's first telefeature. The *Monthly Film Bulletin* noted, "Evidently intended for television, this short thriller manages to work up to a fairly exciting finish after a vague start. The only really worthwhile aspect of this poorly handled picture, however, is Charles Bronson's orthodox but effective study of the gunman." When it was first telecast on U.S. TV, *Variety* commented it was "not much" but added, "Charles Bronson is coldly convincing as the killer."

A particularly interesting plot twist had Bronson's gunman character Brodsky seduce a local clerk (Roxanne Allen) in order to find Parker's whereabouts so he could trap him.

## *The Family* see *Città Violenta*

## *A Family of Cops* (CBS-TV, 1995) 95 minutes Color

*P:* Peter Bray. *EP:* Douglas S. Cramer. *D:* Ted Kotcheff. *Sc-Executive Consultant:* Joel Blasberg. *Ph:* Francois Protat. *Ed:* Ron Wisman. *Mus:* Peter Manning Robinson. *Prod Design:* Trevor Williams. *Asst Dir:* Bruce Speyer. *Casting:* Margaret McSherry, Brad Warshaw & Clare Walker. *First Asst Camera:* Cam North. *Second Unit Camera Operator/Steadicam Operator:* Peter Rosenfeld. *Transportation Coordinator:* Bob Dennett. *Prod Executive:* Jean Desmoreaux. *Prod Mgr:* Noella Nesdoly. *Second Asst Dir:* Rocco Gismondi. *Prod Mgr:* Eleen Devine. *Asst Prod Mgr:* Card Urquhart. *Costume Design:* Vicki Graef. *Asst Costume Design:* Kei Yano. *Location Mgr:* Byron Martin. *Sc Supv:* Donna Gardon. *Camera Operator:* Andy Chumra. *Gaffer:* Billy Buttery. *Key Grip:* Richard Emerson. *Sd Recordist:* Daniel Latour. *Key Set Dresser:* Michael McShane. *Property Master:* Stephen Levitt. *Makeup Artist:* Maribeth Knezev. *Hair Stylist:* Lucy Orton. *Sp Eff:* Brock Jaliffe. *Stunt Coordinator:* Branko Racki. *Prod Coordinator:* Gaille Le Drew. *Prod Accountant:* Kelly Decooman. *Extra Casting:* Donna Dupere. *Unit Publicist:* Lisa Shamata. *Asst Ed:* Paul Whitehead. *Mus Supv:* Ron Proulx. *Re-recording Engineers:* Elius Caruso & Paul Williamson. *Sp Eff Design:* Brad Stephenson. *Dialogue/ADR Ed:* Jonas Kuhnemann. *Foley Artist:* Sol Eberman. *Post Prod Supv:* David Huband.

**CAST:** Charles Bronson (Detective Paul Fein), Daniel Baldwin (Ben Fein), Lesley-Anne Down (Anna Novacek), Angela Featherstone (Jackie Fein), Barbara Williams (Kate Fein), Sebastian Spence (Eddie Fein), Kate Trotter (Amy), Simon MacCorkindale (Adam Novacek), John Vernon (Frank Rampola), Blu Makuma (Philo), Cynthia Belliveau (Melanie Fein), Caroline Barclay (Laura Novacek), Robert Morelli (Lenny Glover), Real Andrews (Flo Burton), Robert Zeppieri (Tommy Rampola), Miguel Fernandes (Detective Lieutenant Swan), Stephen Russell (Horace Martin), Heather Gordon (Tali Fein), Ruby Smith-Merovitz (Maya Fein), Natascha La Force (Sarah Fein), Kim Weeks (Amy Myers), Richard Comar (Mr. Alexander), Claudette Mix (Marci Sullivan), Martha Christianson (Police Officer), John Freser (Judge), Sandi Ross (Judge Williams), Shannon Lawson (District Attorney), Harvey Atkin (Arum Weiss), Marvin Shapiro (Lawyer), Jilian Hart (Jailer), Gene Mack (McLemore), Judah Katz (Doctor), Christopher Tuah (Hezzie Ross), Robert King (Desk Sergeant), Jaque Halroyd (Kim), Sarahmaude Campbell (Cindy), Richard Fitzpatrick, Mark Wilson, Bill McDonald (Detectives), Lorne Campbell, Martin Doyle (Bar Patrons), Robnne Fanfair (Defendant), Noam Jenkins (Gym Attendant), Walter Alzar, David Bern, Phil No Nunes (Wise Guys).

Following *Donato and Daughter* (1993), Charles Bronson made a second CBS-TV movie, the family police drama *A Family of Cops*. Set in Milwaukee, Wisconsin, but filmed mostly in Canada, the telefeature was originally called *The Brewery*, which refers to the city's police headquarters. The movie centered around the Fein family's youngest daughter, misfit Jackie, being the chief suspect in the murder of a wealthy businessman. Charles Bronson, as Detective Paul Fein, a 37-year veteran of the police force, sets out to prove his daughter's innocence. The movie provides Bronson with a role which contains both physical action, such as his beating up two thugs in a bar, and tender scenes with his family. The telefilm proved to be a rating's success, one of the few such programs for CBS during the 1995-96 season, and spawned a sequel, *Breach of Faith: A Family of Cops II* (1997).

In Milwaukee, police Detective Paul Fein (Charles Bronson) arrests hoodlum Tommy Rampola (Robert Zeppieri), assisted by his policeman son Ben (Daniel Baldwin). Later Paul asks his oldest daughter, lawyer Kate Fein (Barbara Williams), to give him a birthday party but only with family members. He especially wants to see his youngest daughter Jackie (Angela Featherstone), who has become estranged from the family and is living in California. Both Kate and younger brother Eddie (Sebastian Spence), who is also a cop, ask Jackie to return home for the party and she finally agrees. Returning to Milwaukee, Jackie becomes involved with wealthy businessman Adam Novacek (Simon MacCorkindale) and spends the night with him after attending her dad's party. The next day she finds Adam murdered and calls Eddie who notifies his dad and brother. The two men arrive at Novacek's penthouse to find him dead and Jackie not knowing what happened. After talking with Novacek's pretty widow Anna (Lesley-Anne Down), Detective Fein goes to see gangster Frank Rampola (John Vernon), believing he set up Jackie because of his arrest of his son Tommy. Informant Lenny Glover (Robert Morelli) tells Inspector Fein that Mrs. Novacek hired hitman Horace Martin (Stephen Russell) to murder her husband and in a shootout Martin escapes but Ben is severely wounded. Jackie is charged with the Novacek killing and Lenny is found murdered. Mrs. Novacek is questioned in the murder of her husband but denies any knowledge of the crime. Jackie is released on bail and goes to see Ben, who is fighting for his life after two surgeries. On a tip, Detective Fein and other cops corner Martin but it turns out to be the wrong man. He then goes to see Novocek's first wife Laura (Caroline Barclay) who has been in a rest home for 20 years. The police believe she may have hired the assassin in order to get free of the rest home, since her bills there were paid by her ex-husband. She is brought in for questioning but proves to be innocent. Detective Fein locates Martin at his remote cabin and Eddie and his partner Philo (Blu Makuma), follow as backups. Paul kills Martin in a shootout but before dying the man says Mrs. Novacek hired him but he does not say which woman. In the cabin, Detective Fein locates the

Advertisement for *A Family of Cops* (CBS-TV, 1995).

evidence he needs and goes to Anna Novacek's mansion and accuses her of hiring Martin. He shows her Martin's bank statement which shows a $100,000 deposit from a charity she operates. Anna admits trying to frame Laura and then asks to change her clothes before going to jail. Fein agrees, not realizing she plans to shoot herself. Two months later the Fein family is reunited when Ben recovers and comes home from the hospital.

An actionful drama, *A Family of Cops* was rated PG-13 for violence and some sexuality when released on video by Vidmark. It also contained rougher language than usually heard on the small screen. Reviewing the telefilm, *TV Guide* said, "As the head of the family, Charles Bronson gives an understated (for him) performance ... the ends of the mystery are tied together a little too neatly."

## *Family of Cops III* (CBS-TV, 1999) 90 minutes Color

*P:* Nicholas J. Gray. *EP:* Douglas S. Cramer. *D:* Sheldon Larry. *Sc:* Noah Jubelirer. *Ph:* Bert Dunk. *Ed:* James Bredin. *Mus:* Fred Mollin. *Prod Design:* James McAteer. *Executive Consultant:* Joel Blasberg. *Executive in Charge of Production:* Eric Norlen. *Prod Mgr:* Michael Brownstone. *AD:* Ken Watkins. *Sc Supv:* Anna Rane. *Asst Dir:* Elizabeth Scherberger & Alison Jones. *Location Mgr:* Erik T. Snyder. *Asst AD:* Mark Duffield. *Stunt Coordinator:* Matt Bierman. *Stunts:* Roy T. Anderson, Matt Bierman, Leigh Brinkman, Eric Bryson, Randy Butcher, Tommy Chang, Maxine Dumont, Bobby Hannah, Danny Lima, Steve Lucescu, Carson Manning, Loren Peterson, Robert Racki, Morris Santia, John Stoneham Sr., Anton Tyuhody, Rod Wilson & Ron Van Hart. *Toronto Casting:* Gail Carr & Claire Hewitt. *Casting Executive:* John Buchan. *Art Department Coordinator:* Sharon Kohne. *Construction Mgr:* Frans Van Gerwen. *Head Carpenter:* Allan Crawly. *Set Decorator:* Brendan Smith. *Leadman:* Arlindo Vicente. *Set Dressers:* Ken Sinclair, Matthew Badger & Jesse O'Connor. *Property Master:* Gary Honcharuk. *Weapons:* John Berger. *Costume Designer:* Resa McConaghy. *Asst Costume Designer:* Gersha Phillips. *Set Supv:* Erika Larner-Corbet. *Asst Set Supv:* Carole Griffin. *Costumer:* Barbara Somerville. *Hair Stylist:* Moira Verwijk. *Makeup Artist:* Marysue Heron. *Camera Operator:* Michael Soos. *Asst Camera Operator:* Brian White. *Focus Puller:* Kevin Dutchak. *Sound Mixer:* Brian Avery. *Boom Operator:* Gavin Coford. *Gaffer:* Ira Cohen. *Best Boy Electric:* Antony Ellis. *Electrics:* Paul Michel & Ron Hodgson. *Key Grip:* Cynthia Barlow. *Best Boy Grip:* Christian Drennan. *Dolly Grip:* Michael John. *Grips:* Nick Swyntlich & Chris Wilson. *Special ETX Coordinator:* Brock Joliffe. *Extra Casting:* Rita Bertucci. *Still Photographer:* Ben Mark Holtzberg. *Post Prod Supv:* Connie McKinnon. *First Asst Ed:* Valerie Weiss. *Colorist:* Deborah Holland. *On-Line Ed:* Bernie Clayton. *Sd Eff Ed:* Dan Sexton. *Dialogue ADR Ed:* Jonas Kuhnemann. *Foley Artist:* Paul Edwards. *Re-recording Mixers:* Mike Baskerville & Jamie Sulek.

**CAST:** Charles Bronson (Inspector Paul Fein), Joe Penny (Detective Ben Fein), Sebastian Spence (Eddie Fein),

Barbara Williams (Kate Fein), Kim Weeks (Amy Myers), Nicole De Boer (Jackie Fein), Torry Higginson (Caroline Chandler), Sean McCann (Jim Grewkowski), Sabrina Grdevich (Fran Mullins), Jan Filips (William Warden), Cynthia Belliveau (Melanie Fein), Chris Leavins (Coello), Diego Chambers (Gasparra), Art Hindle (Mayor Edwards), Greg Spottiswood (Evan Chandler), Jesse Collins (Deputy Mayor Albright), Jonathan Potts (Sam), Phillip Javarett (Millihen), Dian A'Quila (Orientation Cop), Pat Moffatt (Rose), Doug Lennox (Lungren), Kyrin Hall (Vondra), Conrad Bergschneider (Police Captain), Clive Cholerton (Phillip), Laura Catalano (Woman in Bar), Philip Akin (Desk Sergeant), Louis del Grande (Sean the Bartender), Mark Humphrey (Matthew), Andrew Tarbet (Policeman at Paul's), Steve Mousseau (Detective Dillon).

Filmed in Toronto, Canada, in the fall of 1997, *Family of Cops III* marked Charles Bronson's third appearance in the role of Inspector Paul Fein, the patriarch of a family of law enforcers. Repeating their roles were Joe Penny, Barbara Williams and Sebastian Spence as Fein's grownup children, Kim Weeks as his girlfriend, and Cynthia Belliveau as his daughter-in-law. The telefilm was not telecast by CBS-TV until January 12, 1999, although it had been issued months earlier overseas, including Australia and Germany. In the latter country, *Videotip: Das Home Entertainment Magazin* (August 8, 1998) noted "classic crime film action is mixed with family items ... spectacular action."

Preceded by *A Family of Cops* (1995) and *Breach of Faith: A Family of Cops II* (1997), this outing had Milwaukee police Inspector Paul Fein (Charles Bronson) and his son, Detective Ben Fein (Joe Penny), investigating the murders of a rich man and his wife, the bodies having been discovered by their daughter Caroline Chandler (Torry Higginson). When her stepbrother Evan Chandler (Greg Spottiswood) tries to run away he becomes a suspect but he has an alibi and is represented by his family's attorney, William Warden (Jan Filips). Fein's youngest son Eddie (Sebastian Spence), a uniformed cop, loses his nerve during a drug bust and almost costs his partner (Clive Cholerton) his life. Meanwhile the police chief (Sean McCann) plans to retire and the mayor (Art Hindle) offers the post to Inspector Fein, who accepts. Ben learns that his father ordered an investigation of the dead man's bank stopped two years before. Paul then asks the police chief why he ordered him to close the case and finds out the chief was involved in a money laundering operation run by Ernesto Gasparra (Diego Chambers). Inspector Fein approaches Gasparra about being cut in on the payoffs, but someone tries to kill him and does fatally wound the police chief. Both Inspector Fein and Ben are taken off the Chandler case but continue to seek out the truth and Ben and his attorney sister Kate (Barbara Williams), who is pregnant, find out the brains behind the money laundering operation is Vincent Coello (Chris Leavins), the operator of a swank Milwaukee cigar club frequented by the city's top politicians, including the mayor. After an attempt is made on Caroline's life she accuses Coello of killing her parents. She tells Inspector Fein that her half-brother Evan, who has been mysteriously murdered, let Coello use the family bank to carry out his illegal operations and that the mayor is also involved. Inspector Fein confronts the mayor about the allegations and later he and his girlfriend, Detective Amy Myers (Kim Weeks), who is Ben's partner, go to Coello's club. Eddie and Caroline become lovers, since it was Eddie who saved her life when she was attacked, but friction develops when she admits she had once been Coello's girlfriend. With the aid of information obtained from a TV reporter (Sabrina Grdevich), the Fein's lead a police raid on Coello's cigar club, confiscate contraband and bring in the mayor, Coello and Gasparra, all of whom are represented by attorney Warden. It is then Inspector Fein reveals the motive for the murders and unmasks the killer, who tries unsuccessfully to escape from the law, meeting death in a fiery car crash.

*Family of Cops III* was a taut thriller which housed an intricate plot that balanced itself well between the subplots of solving three murders, political and police corruption, drug money laundering and graft, and Inspector Fein's grappling with the trials in the lives of his children, including Eddie's wanting to leave the police force and Kate's pregnancy by a man (Mark Humphrey) she no longer loves. The mystery aspects of the storyline are especially well handled, with a plethora of red herrings nicely masking the identity of the killer until the finale. The film's biggest weakness was a lack of sustained action, something usually associated with a Charles Bronson movie.

Now in his mid–70s but playing a character a dozen years younger, Charles Bronson dominates the proceedings although actionwise he participates only in a couple of brief shootouts. *Daily Variety* reported, "He's very much the old-timer now. He's got a gut. His cheeks are puffy. But make no mistake, Charles Bronson is still Charles Bronson. That squinty-eyed glint that leaves strong men quaking is still there...." The reviewer found the film to be "moderately compelling."

Just prior to the U.S. telecast of *Family of Cops III*, Charles Bronson and Kim Weeks were married on December 28, 1998.

## *4 for Texas* (Warner Bros., 1963) 124 minutes Color

*P-D:* Robert Aldrich. *EP:* Howard W. Koch. *AP:* Walter Blake. *Sc:* Teddi Sherman & Robert Aldrich. *Ph:* Ernest Laszlo. *Second Unit Ph:* Carl Guthrie, Joseph Biroc & Burnett Guffey. *Ed:* Michael Luciano. *AD:* William Glasgow. *Sets:* Raphael Bretton. *Mus:* Nelson Riddle *Orchestrations:* Gil Grau. *Second Unit Dir:* Oscar Rudolph. *Asst Dir:* Tom Connors & Dave Salven. *Sd:* Jack Solomon. *Stunt Supv:* John Indrisano. *Costumes:* Norma Koch. *Makeup:* Robert Schiffer. *Prod Supv:* Jack E. Berne.

**CAST:** Frank Sinatra (Zack Thomas),

Dean Martin (Joe Jarrett), Anita Ekberg (Elya Carlson), Ursula Andress (Maxine "Max" Richter), Charles Bronson (Matson), Victor Buono (Harvey Burden), Edric Connor (Prince George), Nick Dennis (Angel), Mike Mazurki (Chad), Richard Jaeckel (Mancini), Wesley Addy (Mr. Trowbridge), Marjorie Bennett (Miss Ermaline), Jack Elam (Dobie), Fritz Feld (Fritz), Percy Helton (Ansel), Jonathan Hole (Renee), Jack Lambert (Monk), Paul Langston (Mr. Beauregard), Ellen Corby, Jesslyn Fax (Widows), Allison Ames (Elya's Maid), Juanita Moore (Burden's Maid), The Three Stooges [Moe Howard, Larry Fine, Joe Da Rita] (Delivery Men), Arthur Godfrey (Guest), Teddy Buckner & His All Stars (Band), Grady Sutton (Messenger), Bob Steele (Gang Member), Virginia Christine (Woman).

Following the success of *What Ever Happened to Baby Jane?* (1962), producer-director Robert Aldrich again teamed with Warner Bros. to make this glossy, but basically empty, comedy-drama western which contained a few chuckles and a bit of well-staged action, but overall was an overlong and lifeless effort. The film did provide Charles Bronson with co-star billing under the film's title, after the quartet of stars (Frank Sinatra, Dean Martin, Anita Ekberg, Ursula Andress) who were billed above the title. He also received billing before Victor Buono, who had a larger role in the proceedings. Bronson, however, was quite good as cold-blooded killer Matson and he played the part straight in deference to the tongue-in-cheek attitude of the rest of the film's major players. He was particularly good in the scene where he shoots cohort Jack Elam for "just wonderin'" why he had failed to capture the stagecoach in the film's opening sequence. Another fine scene had him bullying boss Victor Buono just as the latter was about to enjoy a huge meal. Bronson's death scene at the finale is somewhat stark, compared to the lighthearted antics in the rest of the feature, with him being shot between the eyes by Frank Sinatra and falling back into a gambling boat's paddle wheel and pulled underwater.

Plotwise *4 for Texas* opens with Matson (Charles Bronson) and his gang failing to rob a stagecoach and to kill Zack Thomas (Frank Sinatra), the corrupt lawman in Galveston, whose boss, banker Harvey Burden (Victor Buono) wants him dead. Also on the stage is vagabond lawyer Joe Jarrett (Dean Martin) who ends up taking Zack's $100,000 when the stagecoach is wrecked following the thwarted robbery attempt. Jarrett uses part of the money to pay off the debt of a school owned by his mentor Miss Ermaline (Marjorie Bennett) and then heads to Galveston where he deposits the rest of the cash in Burden's bank. Zack decides to get the money back by having his girlfriend Elya (Anita Ekberg) romance Joe but when Matson, who hates Zack, gets the drop on him it is Joe who shoots the badman who swears revenge on Zack as he is thrown out of town. Meanwhile Joe decides to invest in a gambling boat proposition offered to him by sexy widow Max (Ursula Andress) and he also finds out that a boat which Zack had insured was sabotaged for its insurance money. When the gambling ship opens for business Zack and his men try to take over while Burden has double-crossed Zack by hiring Matson, and his men to blow up the vessel. Zack and Joe decide to fight to the finish, winner take all, as Burden signals Matson to carry out his plan. During the fight Matson cannot resist a chance to shoot Zack but instead wings Joe and is killed by Zack. With his plan thwarted, Burden is taken into custody by the U.S. marshal and Zack and Joe marry their girlfriends.

The most enjoyable part of the film is the bevy of character players who make appearances, with Victor Buono especially good as the crooked banker, and Mike Mazurki equally so as Sinatra's dense right-hand man. An especially hilarious scene has The Three Stooges attempting to deliver a nude painting of Ursula Andress but being stymied not only by their own incompetence but also by two angry widows (Ellen Corby, Jesslyn Fax) who claim the picture is obscene. Outside of its cast and good production values, *4 for Texas* has little to offer. The *New York Times* commented, "This hand-me-down Christmas Tree magnanimously offers Frank Sinatra and Dean Martin in a wisecracking, double-cross marathon, gaudily colored and clothed in an 1870 Galveston setting and almost clothed by Anita Ekberg and Ursula Andress, who conduct a chest contest throughout the lumpy course of this flapdoodle." Phil Hardy in *The Western* (1983) called it a "disaster" adding the film "suffers from Aldrich's recurrent tendency to exaggerate in the name of satire when precision is required." In his biography of Dean Martin, *Dino* (1992), Nick Tosches referred to the film as "a half-witted Western comedy." *Variety* noted, "A Western too preoccupied with sex and romance to enthrall sagebrush-happy moppets and too unwilling to take itself seriously to sustain the attention of an adult." The same reviewer did single out Victor Buono and Charles Bronson who "make an impression" but felt "the editing tends to add to the confusion."

Charles Bronson and director Robert Aldrich would team once more, albeit more successfully, four years later in *The Dirty Dozen*, having already worked together on television and the feature *Vera Cruz* (1954).

Worth noting is that when *4 for Texas* went into production it was claimed that Bette Davis, who had been Oscar-nominated for her work in Aldrich's *What Ever Happened to Baby Jane?* the year before, would make a guest appearance in the film. She does not—perhaps she read the script.

## *From Noon Till Three* (United Artists, 1976) 99 minutes Color

*P:* M.J. Frankovich & William Self. *D-Sc:* Frank D. Gilroy, from his novel. *Ph:* Lucien Ballard. *Ed:* Maury Winetrobe. *Mus:* Elmer Bernstein. *Song:* Elmer Bernstein, Marilyn & Alan Bergman. *Prod Design:* Robert Clatworthy. *Asst AD:* Dick Lawrence. *Sets:* George R. Nelson. *Sp Eff:* Augie Lohman. *Asst Dir:* Russell Saunders & Mike Kusley. *Costume Designer:* Mos

Mabry. *Set Designers:* Lester Gobruegge & Harry Kemm.

**CAST:** Charles Bronson (Graham Dorsey), Jill Ireland (Amanda Starbuck), Douglas V. Fowley (Buck Bowers), Stan Haze (Ape), Damon Douglas (Young Man), Hector Morales (Mexican), Bert Williams (Sheriff), William Lanteau (Rev. Cabot), Betty Cole (Edna), Davis Roberts (Sam), Don "Red" Barry (Red Roxy), Fred Franklyn (Postmaster Hall), Sonny Jones (Dr. Finger), Hoke Howell (Deke), Howard Brunner (Mr. Foster), Larry French (Mr. Taylor), Michael Le Clair (Cody Taylor), Anne Ramsey (Large Woman), Elmer Bernstein, Alan Bergman (Songwriters).

*From Noon Till Three* is a paradox in Charles Bronson's career. For once the critics liked his performance and many thought the film both amusing and entertaining. On the other hand, the public, especially in the United States, was lukewarm to the production and it proved to be Bronson's least popular film to date. Some critics blamed director-scripter Frank D. Gilroy, Pulitzer Prize–winner for his play *The Subject Was Roses*, for the film's troubles. In retrospect, a stronger director more attuned to the Western would probably have helped. Overall, though, the film is a fragile serio-comedy and all concerned probably did the best possible, resulting in an amusing, but minor, effort. For the Bronson's the film must have held special pleasure. Both got good reviews and in terms of their working as co-stars, *From Noon Till Three* shows them both to good advantage. Their love for each other is especially evident in the scenes where romance blossoms between the two lead characters.

The Buck Bowers gang, made up of Buck (Douglas V. Fowley), Graham Dorsey (Charles Bronson), Ape (Stan Haze), a young man (Damon Douglas) and a Mexican (Hector Morales), arrive in what appears to be a deserted town and easily rob the bank. As they ride out they are ambushed and all are killed except Dorsey who suddenly awakens from his nightmare. The next day they ride to rob a bank but Dorsey's horse breaks its leg and has to be shot. They stop at the luxurious home of widow Amanda Starbuck (Jill Ireland) with Dorsey remaining behind while the others ride off to town. Dorsey, who has lied about the widow not having a horse because he did not want to participate in the robbery, is attracted to Amanda and her beautiful home. Feigning impotence, Dorsey seduces the widow who suddenly blooms into a passionate woman. They have an idyllic three-hour love affair until a neighbor boy (Michael Le Clair) brings news that the holdup was thwarted, the Mexican killed and the other three gang members are to be hung. Amanda convinces the reluctant Dorsey to try and save his cohorts but instead he waylays Dr. Finger (Sonny Jones) and changes clothes with him. A posse kills Finger thinking it is Dorsey and when the widow learns her lover has been killed she proudly confesses her love affair to the town. A writer (Howard Brunner) turns the story into a worldwide best-selling novel while Dorsey gets a year in jail because of the dental fakery of Finger, who he closely

Charles Bronson in *From Noon Till Three* (United Artists, 1976).

resembles. Getting out of prison and wearing a fake beard, Dorsey goes to Amanda's home with a tour and there confronts her with the news he is really alive. At first Amanda does not believe him but finally convinced she commits suicide rather than taint the legend of their love. Becoming a drifter, Dorsey is unable to convince anyone of his true identity, even outlaw cohorts like Red Roxy (Don "Red" Barry). Finally he suffers a complete breakdown and is sent to a mental hospital where the inmates accept him as the true Graham Dorsey.

Particularly good are the love scenes between Charles Bronson and Jill Ireland in *From Noon Till Three* and a later sequence when Graham Dorsey debunks the image of the outlaw life in the old West, telling Amanda the Buck Bowers gang was a third rate one and that being an outlaw was a miserable way to exist. Many felt the main thrust of the feature was to taint the aura of the West, to tell the truth about its hard ways, but the romance angle so overshadowed this premise it got lost in the shuffle of low key comedy and passion. Certainly Charles Bronson and Jill Ireland do all they can to sustain the momentum of the feature and they succeed more often than not. Bronson proves himself quite at home with the character of Dorsey, basically a charlatan who finds love and riches and does not want to part with them. Instead he becomes famous and in the end loses his identity. Jill Ireland, usually not a favorite with critics, here shines as the lonely widow who becomes radiantly beautiful and alive during three hours of passionate love. Composers Elmer Bernstein and Alan Bergman (who appear as song pluggers in the film), along with Marilyn Bergman, wrote the title theme, "Hello and Goodbye," which Jill Ireland sang quite effectively over the end credits. She also recorded the song for United Artists Records and it was issued on a 45 rpm single, number 853.

*The Miami Herald* said "much of the problem in this frolicsome western is attributable to director-screenwriter Frank D. Gilroy's script ... Mrs. Bronson conveys the right edge of inviting gullibility throughout; her hubby constantly strives to be James Coburn–cocky, something even Coburn would have a difficult time doing with this material." *Variety* thought it "an offbeat and amiable, if uneven and structurally awkward, western comedy ... [a] good-looking production." Steve Swires in *Films in Review* said the feature "has been completely sabotaged by the heavyhandedness of writer-director Frank D. Gilroy." He said the feature "has the flat, monotonous look of a made-for-T.V.-movie." He also criticized the leads, "Since becoming a star, Bronson has lost the lean and hungry vitality which provided his earlier supporting performances with their distinctive dynamism, and while Ireland looks stunning, she speaks her lines as if reciting them from a blackboard. Consequently, what should have been a potent star chemistry becomes a romance between two zombies." Henry Herx and Tony Zaza wrote in *The Family Guide to Movies on Video* (1988), "The cast's wooden performance, the script's utter

Poster for *From Noon Till Three* (United Artists, 1976).

banalities and Frank Gilroy's inept direction obscure the theme of mistaken identities and half-truths becoming the basis for a legend." *The Independent Film Journal* opined, "When all is said and done, *From Noon Till Three* amounts to little more than a personal showcase for Mr. and Mrs. Bronson, one that probably proved far more enjoyable and worthwhile for them to make than it will for audiences to sit through." Vincent Canby in the *New York Times* felt the film "is an ebulliently cheerful satire of contemporary myth-making and celebrity, cast as a fable of the Old West." He also noted that Charles Bronson "is funny without ever lunging at a laugh...." In *The Western* (1983), Phil Hardy wrote, "Despite its intriguing and novel idea, this is neither successful as a comic Western nor as a Bronson vehicle ... Sadly neither Gilroy's direction nor his cast do justice to his literate and, at times, very funny script."

As time passes and *From Noon Till Three* is seen by new generations of viewers via television and video, perhaps Los Angeles' *Galaxy Cable TV* best summed it up by saying, "This overlooked gem deserves far greater attention than it has received to date."

## *Gang War* (20th Century–Fox, 1958) 75 minutes B/W

*P:* Harold E. Knox. *D:* Gene Fowler Jr. *Sc:* Louis Vittes, from the novel *The Hoods Take Over* by Ovid Demaris. *Ph:* John M. Nickolaus Jr. *Ed:* Frank Baldridge. *Mus:* Paul Dunlap. *AD:* John Mansbridge. *Set Decorators:* Walter M. Scott & Bertram Granger. *Asst Dir:* Frank Parmenter. *Sd:* Engene Irvine. *Sc Supv:* Mary Gibson. *Mus Ed:* George Brand. *Props:* Fred Simpson. *Wardrobe:* James Taylor. *Makeup:* Jack Orbinger. *Hair Styles:* Ann Kirk. *Transportation:* Joe Padovich.

**CAST:** Charles Bronson (Alan Avery), Kent Taylor (Bryce Barker), Jennifer Holden (Marie), John Doucette (Maxie Matthews), Gloria Henry (Edie Avery), Gloria Grey (Marsha Brown), Barney Phillips (Sam Johnson), Ralph Manza (Axe Duncan), George Eldredge (Sergeant Ernie Tucker), Billy Snyder (Mr. Tomkins), Jack Reynolds (Joe Reno), Dan Simmons (Bob Cross), Larry Gelbmann (Little Abner), Jack Littlefield (Johnny), Ed Wright (Henchman), Shirle Haven (Nicki), Arthur D. Gilmore (Captain Finch), Don Giovanni (Mike Scippio), Jack Finch (Police Sergeant), Stephen Masino (Hoodlum), Stacey Marshall (Millie), Lynn Guild (Diane Barker), Lenny Geer (Slick Connors), Helen Jay (Street Girl), Marion Sherman (Agnes), Whit Bissell (Mark).

*Gang War* is a very important motion picture for Charles Bronson in that it is the first time he received star billing on the big screen. After seven years of supporting roles, the actor finally obtained a starring part and he made the most of it in this taut, well-made "B" melodrama which some see as a precursor to his most popular U.S. feature, *Death Wish* (1974). In both films he portrays a basically decent man who is drawn into retaliation for the murder of loved ones by the scum of society. While his vigilante in the *Death Wish*

**Lobby card for *Gang War* (20th Century–Fox, 1958).**

movies actually takes the law into his own hands, in *Gang War* his Alan Avery is always on the verge of doing so but is more often restrained by the law itself than his own aversion to vigilante activity. In watching *Gang War* one can see the beginnings of the ultimate Bronson screen image, that of the strong, basically good man who can become violent and even homicidal when pushed too far.

Los Angeles high school teacher Alan Avery (Charles Bronson) witnesses a gangland killing in a Hollywood parking lot and is reluctant to get involved in the prosecution of the case. Finally he identifies the murderers and agrees to testify against them in court. Gangster Maxie Matthews (John Doucette) tells his lawyer Bryce Barker (Kent Taylor) to buy off Avery and for further insurance he also sends his bodyguard Little Abner (Larry Gelbmann) to persuade Avery's pregnant wife Edie (Gloria Henry) to have her husband keep silent. The thug gets too violent, however, and Edie dies from a beating. Consumed with revenge, Alan stalks Matthews, intending to kill him but is thwarted by police Sergeant Tucker (George Eldredge). Meanwhile Barker reluctantly gets the gangland killers set free on the false alibi of one of Matthews' hoodlums. Not realizing the syndicate is unhappy with all the adverse publicity Matthews has engendered and that they plan to get him out of the way, the gang overlord hires two out-of-town hit men to kill Avery. When he learns of this, Barker leaves Matthews' employ and he too is ordered killed by the gangster. When Avery narrowly escapes being shot by the killers he decides to retaliate and he goes to see Barker who he finds dying after being shot by the hit men. Barker gives Avery his gun and the latter goes to Matthews' house, intent on killing him. Meanwhile Matthews' wife Marie (Jennifer Holden) has threatened to leave him and in a rage he strangles her. When Avery gets to Matthews' home he finds the gang leader is stark raving mad and instead of shooting him, he leaves the crazed hoodlum to the law.

Typically Charles Bronson received good reviews for his portrayal of the schoolteacher turned avenger. "Charles Bronson, in underplaying his role of the teacher, keeps a sympathetic interest centered on himself," wrote *Variety* which also said the film itself "holds up as a bang-bang opus with more than enough excitement for a second feature life." The *Monthly Film Bulletin* felt the lead role was "well acted by Charles Bronson." *Harrison's Reports* said "the story is interesting and it has been produced well.... Everyone in the cast does fine work, thanks to the expert direction."

*Gang War* was made by Regal Films for release through 20th Century–Fox and it was the first of two "B" features in which Charles Bronson was to star. *Gang War* was issued theatrically April, 1958, and two months later came the second feature, *Showdown at Boot Hill*, which reteamed him with producer Harold E. Knox, director Gene Fowler Jr., writer Louis Vittes and cinematographer John M. Nickolaus Jr.

It is interesting to note that *Gang War*'s credits carried the statement that Charles Bronson was formerly known as Charles Buchinsky, although he had not used that billing for four years!

## *The Great Escape* (United Artists, 1963) 168 minutes Color

*P-D:* John Sturges. *Sc:* James Clavell & W.R. Burnett, from the book by Paul Brickhill. *Ph:* Daniel L. Fapp. *Ed:* Ferris Webster. *Mus:* Elmer Bernstein. *AD:* Fernando Carrere. *Sd:* Harold Lewis. *Sp Eff:* Paul Pollard. *Asst Dir:* Jack Reddish. *Makeup:* Emile Lavigne. *Wardrobe:* Bert Henrikson. *Technical Advisor:* C. Wallace Floody. *Prod Asst:* Robert E. Relyea.

**CAST:** Steve McQueen (Hilts–Cooler King), James Garner (Hendley–The Scrounger), Richard Attenborough (Roger Bartlett–Mr. Big X), James Donald (Senior Officer Ramsey), Charles Bronson (Danny Velinski), Donald Pleasence (Blythe–The Forger), James Coburn (Sedgwick–The Manufacturer), David McCallum (Ashley Pitt), Gordon Jackson (MacDonald), John Leyton (Willie), Angus Lennis (Ives–The Mole), Nigel Stock (Cavendish), Jud Taylor (Goff), William Russell (Sorren), Robert Desmond (Griffith–The Taylor), Tom Adams (Nimmo), Lawrence Montaigne (Haynes), Hannes Messemer (Von Luger), Robert Graf (Werner), Harry Riebauer

(Strachwitz), Hans Reiser (Kuhn), Robert Freytag (Posen), Heinz Weiss (Kramer), Til Kiew (Frick), Ulrich Beiger (Preissen), George Mikell (Dietrich), Karl Otto Alberty (Steinbach).

A written on-screen prologue explains *The Great Escape* is based on a real story but the characters are composites and the plot time compressed. At 168 minutes, the film is leisurely paced with a detailed accounting of the intricate plans made and carried out by Allied soldiers in trying to escape from a maximum security Nazi prison camp. Aided by Elmer Bernstein's rousing score, a set of very interesting characters and an intriguing plot, the movie moves fairly quickly but the overall script cannot bear close scrutiny. In particular it is hard to understand how the Germans subjected such well-known escape artists to so little supervision while in the compound. Even more surprising is the fact that the character played by Richard Attenborough, a known leader of Allied escape attempts, was given free rein to plan still more escapes instead of being placed in solitary confinement. Of course if either of these obvious actions had been taken there would have been no plotline to carry out this "simply great escapism" (*Time*).

Set at the German maximum security prison camp Stalag Luft Nord in 1942, *The Great Escape* tells the story of a diverse group of Allied prisoners who plan to constantly harass the enemy by escaping 200 to 300 men at a time via three tunnels dug under the prison walls into a nearby forest. While British Senior Officer Ramsey (James Donald) is the nominal chief of the Allied prisoners, the brains behind the scheme is Squadron Leader Robert Bartlett (Richard Attenborough), known as "Big X." Among the leading participants in the master plan, each with a specific task, are Hendley (James Garner), who scrounges whatever is needed; Danny Velinski (Charles Bronson), who supervises the digging of the tunnels despite being claustrophobic; Blythe (Donald Pleasence), a forger who is going blind; Sedgwick (James Coburn), who can manufacture items like a breathing apparatus used while the men dig; and Griffith (Robert Desmond), a tailor who supplies the uniforms the men will need for camouflage once they escape into the German countryside. Operating apart from the group are American flier Hilts (Steve McQueen) and his buddy from Scotland, Ives (Angus Lennis), known as "The Mole," who are caught making endless attempts to escape and spend most of their time in solitary confinement. After months of preparation and digging one of the tunnels is nearly complete but while the prisoners are celebrating the Fourth of July with homemade brew concocted by Sedgwick a Nazi soldier (Robert Graf) accidently discovers the tunnel. The disappointment causes Ives to have a mental breakdown and he is shot to death trying to climb the barbed wire fence surrounding the camp. As a result Hilts joins the conspirators and escapes, then lets himself get caught, returning with valuable information needed for the final tunneling out of the compound.

When the tunnel is completed it is discovered it is 20 feet short of the forest but many of the men manage to escape before the caper is uncovered. The Nazis begin immediately to hunt down the escapees with Hilts leading them on a merry motorcycle chase before being apprehended, while Bartlett and his associate MacDonald (Gordon Jackson) are found as they try to board a bus. Ashley Pitt (David McCallum), another British escapee, gives up his life in order to try and save Bartlett. Hendley and the now-blind Blythe procure a Nazi plane but it crashes and Blythe is killed by the Nazis. Sedgwick manages to make it to France where he is aided by the underground and is smuggled into Spain. Velinski and his pal Willie (John Leyton) steal a boat and eventually board an Allied ship. Nearly all of the others, however, are captured and as punishment the Nazis kill 50 of the escapees. When Hilts and Hendley arrive back at the prison camp they are greeted as heroes while the commandant (Hannes Messemer) is replaced for his failure to prevent the escape. With Hilts back in solitary the plans for a new escape begin.

Working for the third time with director John Sturges, *The Great Escape*, filmed on location in Munich, West Germany, gave Charles Bronson another fine screen role and he made the most of it. Although fifth billed he gave a standout performance and his work is one of the best remembered performances in this star-studded vehicle. Very effectively using a Polish accent, Bronson played "The Tunnel King," Danny Velinski, a flier who had escaped to England in order to continue the fight against the Nazis. Early in the film he unsuccessfully masquerades as a Russian prisoner in order to get out of the camp but then joins the escape plot by starting his seventeenth tunnel. After a time his fear of enclosed places gets the best of him and he nearly backs out of the escape attempt once the tunnel is completed, but he is urged on by his friend Willie (John Leyton) and the two are among the few who actually elude the Nazis. An especially well done sequence is Bronson's reaction to being caught in the escape tunnel during an air raid. When the film was premiered in the United States Bronson's billing was listed as third on all advertising material, thus proving his box office appeal. The movie became one of the year's most successful, grossing $5.52 million domestically.

In the *New York Herald-Tribune*, Judith Crist called *The Great Escape*, "A first-rate adventure film, fascinating in its plot, stirring in its climax, and excellent in performance." *Variety* said director John Sturges "has fashioned a motion picture that entertains, captivates, thrills and stirs" while the *New York Times* opined "the picture churns ahead vividly, as directed by John Sturges, with mounting tension. Energetically, at least, it is performed to the hilt." In *Film Review 1964–1965* (1964), F. Maurice Speed wrote, "Meticulous, detailed, intermittently thrilling and amusing but very long...." Tony Thomas said in *The Great Adventure Films* (1976), "*The Great Escape* is one of those films which prove that style is something more important than subject matter.... It makes no bones about war being hell but it also presents war as man's greatest crack at adventuring. And with the highest of stakes—life and death, victory or defeat, submission or surmount." James Robert Parish noted in *The Great Combat Pictures* (1990) "the film has a carefully crafted blend of tension, actions, stunts, and comedy relief with the focus swinging back and forth among its diverse cast of characters. And in the typical tradition of the early 1960s, it is oversized in star names, running length, widescreen, and a big story."

Not only was *The Great Escape* a big box office success in the United States, but it was also the fourth biggest-grossing film in Great Britain in 1963. The film not only reteamed Charles Bronson with director John Sturges from *The Magnificent Seven*, but also with Steve McQueen who also appeared in the 1960 western. Bronson and John Sturges would reteam for a final time in *Valdez il Mezzosangue* in 1973.

Some sources mistakenly claim *The Great Escape* is a remake of the 1958 British Lion release *Danger Within* (called *Breakout*, also the name of Charles Bronson's 1975 feature) which also starred Richard Attenborough. That production, however, was based on a novel by Michael Gilbert and dealt with attempted Allied escapes from a military prison camp in Northern Italy in 1943.

A sequel to *The Great Escape* appeared a quarter of a century after the original with *The Great Escape II: The Untold Story* (NBC-TV, 1988). It starred Christopher Reeve (who would appear with Charles Bronson in *The Sea Wolf* in 1993) who leads the post-war survivors on a quest for their former Nazi captors. In the cast from the 1963 feature was Donald Pleasence but this time he was cast as a German SS officer. Initially telecast in two parts, it has a total running time of 200 minutes, and retold much of the initial film's story.

## *Guns for San Sebastian* (Metro-Goldwyn-Mayer, 1968)

111 minutes Color

*P:* Jacques Bar. *AP:* Ernesto Enriquez. *D:* Henri Verneuil. *Sc:* James R. Webb, from the novel *A Wall for San Sebastian* by William Barby Faherty. *Ph:* Armand Thirard. *Ed:* Francoise Bonnot. *Mus:* Ennio Morricone. *AD:* Robert Clavel & Roberto Silva. *Sp Eff:* Lee Zavitz. *Sp Visual Eff:* J. McMillan Johnson. *Asst Dir:* Claude Pinoteau & Juan Luis Bunuel. *Prod Mgr:* Paul Joly. *Makeup:* Monique Archamabault & Alex Archamabault. *Sd:* William Monique.

**CAST:** Anthony Quinn (Leon Alastray), Anjanette Comer (Kinita), Charles Bronson (Teclo), Sam Jaffe (Father Joseph), Silvia Pinal (Felicia), Jorge Martinez de Hoyos (Cayetano), Jaime Fernandez (Golden Lance), Rosa Furman (Agueda), Jorge Russek (Pedro), Leon Askin (Vicar General), Jose Chavez (Antonito), Ivan Desny (Captain Calleja), Fernand Gravey (Governor), Pedro Armendariz Jr. (Father Lucas), Aurora Clavel (Magdalena), Julio Aldama (Diego), Ferrusquilla (Luis), Pancho Cordova (Kino), Enrique Lucero (Renaldo), Chano Urueta (Miguel), Noe Murayama (Captain Lopez), Guillermo

Hernandez (Timoteo), Francisco Reiguera (Bishop), Carlos Berriochoa (Pablo), Armando Acosta (Pascual), Guy Fox, Rico Lopez (Villagers).

In 1746 rebel leader Leon Alastray (Anthony Quinn) is being chased by Spanish soldiers in Mexico. Elderly Franciscan priest Father Joseph (Sam Jaffe) gives him sanctuary after finding Alastray wounded in his remote church. When he refuses to give the wanted man up to authorities, church officials send Father Joseph to the far-off village of San Sebastian, which is being raided by Yaqui Indians. Disguised as a monk, Alastray accompanies Father Joseph and once they arrive at the village after a difficult desert trek, they find the place is uninhabited due to a raid. Only Kinita (Anjanette Comer), a pretty young girl, remains. When a sniper kills Father Joseph, Alastray is mistaken for a priest by half-breed Teclo (Charles Bronson), who has been trying to get the villagers to abandon Christianity in order to avoid the Yaqui raids. He wants to hang Alastray but the girl saves him and when the people return they accept the rebel-bandit as their new priest. In order to aid the villagers, Alastray shows them how to build a dam to irrigate their crops and then travels to the capitol where he gets his former mistress (Silvia Pinal), now the wife of the area governor (Fernand Gravey), to persuade her husband to give him weapons for the village's defense. The villagers then repel the attacking Yaquis and Alastray blows up the dam, killing most of the raiders. He then fights Teclo in hand-to-hand combat and kills the half-breed. As a result troops arrive to help celebrate a victory mass and when one of the soldiers recognizes Alastray he manages to escape, taking Kinita with him.

Filmed in Mexico at San Miguel Allende and Durango, this French (CIPRA Films)–Mexican (Pelliculas Enresto Enriquez)–Italian (Filmes Cinematografica) co-production was lensed in 1967 in Franscope and Eastman Color. While veteran western scripter James R. Webb is credited with the screenplay in the English language release, the French, Italian and Spanish language versions were written by Serge Ganze, Ennio De Concini and Miguel Morayta. In production the film was called *Wall for San Sebastian* (the name of the novel on which it was based) and *Miracle for San Sebastian*. In Italy it was called *I Cannoni di San Sebastian* and when released in Paris in 1969 (one year after its U.S. and British debuts) it was dubbed *La Bataille de San Sebastian* with a running time of 120 minutes, nine minutes longer than its English-language counterpart.

For Charles Bronson, *Guns for San Sebastian* was familiar ground with its plot reminiscent of *The Magnificent Seven* (1960) and his part close to that of Captain Jack in *Drum Beat* (1954). As *This Property Is Condemned* (1966) was a vehicle for Natalie Wood, so this feature highlighted Anthony Quinn as historical Mexican rebel leader Leon Alastray. As usual, Bronson managed to attain some good reviews in a film criticized for its dubbing techniques. Don

Gordon in the *Hollywood (California) Citizen-News* said the actor was "excellent ... wallowing in a pagan existence" while John Mahoney noted in *The Hollywood Reporter*, "Bronson's delivery is reminiscent of Jackie Mason, though he scores in the demands of physical action that would bring a flush of pride to Sergio Leone." The latter is prophetic since Bronson would score an international success the next year in Leone's *C'Era una Volta il West (Once Upon a Time in the West)*.

**Poster for *Guns for San Sebastian* (Metro-Goldwyn-Mayer, 1968)**

Critical reaction to *Guns for San Sebastian* was mixed. Kevin Thomas in the *Los Angeles Times* said the film "was pretty much doomed from the start" and he felt star Anthony Quinn and "Armand Thirard's color photography of the rugged settings are the picture's only strong points." *The Hollywood (California) Citizen-News* reviewer, Don Gordon, said "James Webb's treatment emerges as a taut, masterful screenplay lifting what might have become an ordinary Western into compelling drama of the frontier period." In *The Films of Anthony Quinn* (1975), Alvin H. Marrill called the feature an "apocryphal tale" which was "lengthy, sporadically exciting." *Time* opined "it is not very much."

*Guns for San Sebastian* was the only western of popular French director Henri Verneuil, a native of Turkey whose real name was Achod Malakian. He is probably best known for his Jean Gabin–starrers, *Any Number Can Play* (1963) and *The Sicilian Clan* (1969).

While the film was released in the United States in 1968, it was shown in the United Kingdom, West Germany, Sweden and Denmark the same year, but as noted earlier it was not debuted in France until 1969, no doubt to coincide with Charles Bronson's newfound popularity in *Adieu l'Ami*.

## *Guns of Diablo* (Metro-Goldwyn-Mayer, 1964) 76 minutes Color

*P:* Boris Ingster. *D:* Boris Sagal. *Sc:* Berne Giler, from the novel *The Travels of Jamie McPheeters* by Robert Lewis Taylor. *Ph:* John Nickolaus Jr. *Ed:* Harry Coswick. *Mus:* Walter Scharf, Harry Sukman & Leigh Harline. *AD:* George W. Davis & Addison Hehr. *Sets:* Harry Grace & Jack Miller. *Recording Supv:* Franklin Milton. *Asst Dir:* Eddie Saeta. *Prod Asst:* Norman Siegel & Ariel Wray.

CAST: Charles Bronson (Linc Murdock), Susan Oliver (Maria Gerard Macklin), Kurt Russell (Jaimie McPheeters), Jan Merlin (Rance Macklin), John Fiedler (Ives), Douglas Fowley (Knudson), Rayford Barnes (Dan Macklin), Robert Carricart (Mendez), Ron Hagerthy (Carey Macklin), Russ Conway (Dr. McPheeters), Morris Ankrum (Mr. Macklin), Maurice Wells (Girard), Mike De Anda (Blacksmith), Susan Flannery (Molly), Byron Foulger (Hickey), Marguerita Cordova (Florrie).

Charles Bronson joined the cast of the ABC-TV series *The Travels of Jaimie McPheeters* after it went into production, appearing in a dozen of the 26 one-hour episodes. His character of Linc Murdock was the wagon master leading settlers to California in 1849 with Bronson being added to the cast in order to boost ratings, as was done earlier in *Empire* on NBC-TV. The series' final episode, "The Day of Reckoning," telecast March 15, 1964, was filmed in an alternate version and released in Great Britain that year as a feature film entitled *Guns of Diablo*. In January 1965, it was shown in West Germany as *Und Knallten ihn Nieder* and by the end of the decade it was playing on U.S. television. Following Charles Bronson's rise to international stardom in the late 1960s and early 1970s, European distributors began using some of his television films for theatrical consumption. *Guns of Diablo* was given new life, showing up in 1971 as *El Californien (The Californian)* in France, *Il Californiano (The Californian)* in Italy, *Diablo—Laglos Stad* in Sweden and *Den Enarmede Haevner* in Denmark.

During the fording of a river by the wagon train he is leading, wagon master Linc Murdock (Charles Bronson) saves the life of a man whose condition causes the train to stop for a few days. Taking advantage of the situation Linc and Jaimie McPheeters (Kurt Russell), the young son of Dr. McPheeters (Russ Conway), the leader of the settlers, ride into the nearby town of Devil's Gap to leave mail and pick up supplies. There Linc finds Maria (Susan Oliver), the girl he once loved and who he thought was dead.

She is cold to him and he finds out she is married to Rance Macklin (Jan Merlin) who with his brothers Carey (Ron Hagerthy) and Dan (Rayford Barnes) run the hotel/saloon along with cohort Ives (John Fiedler). From the locals he also learns the Macklins run roughshod over the area. Jaimie meanwhile befriends Knudson (Douglas Fowley), an old man who claims to be a millionaire, but is stranded in the town due to a bad heart. Linc remembers he met Maria five years before when he drifted into the Macklin ranch and was forced to beat up Rance in a fight. The ranch owner, Mr. Macklin (Morris Ankrum), liked Linc and hired him but after he and Maria, whose father also works for Macklin, fall in love, the three brothers ambush him and leave him for dead. Maria nurses Linc back to health and the two make love and agree to run away together. That night Rance and his brothers get the drop on Linc but in a shootout Maria is shot and Linc escapes thinking he has killed her. Now, in the night Linc goes to Maria's room and she tells him she waited for him but when he did not return she married Rance, who lost his right arm in the shootout. Wanting to avoid trouble for Maria, Linc decides to leave town the next day but Carey and Dan arrive and take him prisoner. That night Maria gives Linc a gun but Carey catches them together just as Rance returns. He shoots Linc in the wrist and then forces a showdown in front of the saloon. From an upstairs window, Jaimie and Knudson warn Linc of an ambush and Knudson kills Dan before being shot by Rance. Linc kills Carey and in a final showdown mortally wounds Rance. The dying Knudson then gives Jaimie his gold mine claim and Linc, Maria and Jaimie rejoin the wagon train on its journey to California.

A well-made and fairly exciting western, *Guns of Diablo* adapted fairly well to the big screen with its added footage mostly being a lengthy flashback sequence. One scene had Linc and Maria in a postcoital embrace with only a tree branch hiding the girls' naked body. Such a sequence was hardly intended for 1964 primetime television audiences. Charles Bronson brought strength and compassion to his low-key playing of Linc Murdock while Susan Oliver, here a brunette, is very sexy as the love-starved Maria. The supporting cast too is quite good, especially Kurt Russell as Jaimie, Jan Merlin, Ron Hagerthy and Rayford Barnes as the Macklin brothers, Morris Ankrum as their father, and Douglas Fowley as the old man too sick to fight the town bullies. Although originally made-for-TV, *Guns of Diablo* holds its own as a feature film.

Running times vary for the feature. When issued in England in 1964 it timed in at 56 minutes but by the time it was being shown in Europe in the early 1970s the running time had been beefed up to 81 minutes. The MNTEX Entertainment video version runs 76 minutes, although the video box lists a 91 minute running time and an R-rating.

Because of its origins, *Guns of Diablo* has garnered few reviews. When issued in England in 1964 the *Monthly Film Bulletin* called it "a completely routine, small-scale horse opera" and added, "A great waste of Charles Bronson, as carved and weather-beaten a face as ever graced a totem pole." *Elliott's Guide to Films on Video* (1993) said it was a "routine oater ... Interestingly, Bronson gives a better performance in this one than in just about any of his later films." The French publication *La Saison Cinématographique 1971* said the film "does not offer interest."

## *Hard Times* (Columbia, 1975) 97 minutes Color

*P:* Lawrence Gordon. *EP:* Paul Maslansky. *AP:* Fred Lemoine. *D:* Walter Hill. *SC:* Walter Hill, Bryan Gindroff & Bruce Henstell. *St:* Bryan Gindroff & Bruce Henstall. *Ph:* Philip Lathrop. *Ed:* Roger Spottiswoode. *AD:* Trevor Williams. *Mus:* Barry DeVorzon. *Orchestrations:* Al Sendry. *Sets:* Dennis Peeples. *Asst Dir:* Michael Daves & Nathan Haggard. *Stunt Coordinator:* Max Kleven. *Harmonica Solos:* Eddy Lawrence Manson. *Sc Supv:* Bonnie Prendergast. *Prod Asst:* Karen Rasch. *Costume Designer:* Jack Bear. *Camera Operator:* William Johnson. *First Asst Cameraman:* Garrett Graham. *Sd Mixer:* Donald Johnson. *Boom Man:* Jules Strasser III. *Gaffer:* Wilbur Kinnett. *Best Boy:* Carl Manoogian. *Generator Operator:* Robert Teasley. *Transportation Captain:* J.W. Coffman. *Still Photographer:* Jim Coe. *Unit Publicist:* Ernie Anderson. *Property Master:* Allan Gordon. *Asst Property Master:* David Coleman. *Sp Eff:* Jerry Endler. *Location Mgr:* Tony Plakiotis. *Makeup:* Philip Rhodes & Joe DiBella. *Hairdresser:* Vivienne Walker. *Asst Ed:* Dennis Dolan. *Sketch Artist:* Alex Tavoularis. *Cameramen:* Vincent Saizis, Louis Noto & Salavatore Camacho. *Second Grips:* Ford Clark & Robert Applewhite. *Dolly Grip:* Lee Krosskove. *Electricians:* Richard Kinnett, William A. Bosio, Ellis William Harwell, Stephen Herbert, Wayne A. Hill & Robert Paul Sperier. *Lead Man:* Gary Antista. *Swing Men:* Joseph Meyer & Henry C. Keith III. *Casting:* Michael Fenton & Jane Feinberg. *Location Auditor:* Norman Webster. *Construction Coordinator:* Lee Levy. *Carpenters:* Walter Weysham Jr., L.J. Arthur, John Calacas, Robert Levy, Lucien Mistrot Jr., Joseph Riggio Jr., Jimmy Victor Salva, Pascal Warner & Myron M. Waysham. *Set Painter:* James Woods. *Executive Secretaries:* Elaine Gyorke, Lynda Gordon, Sandy Siegel, Marcia Fenker Curtis, Judy Patricia Miller & Shirley Harrison. *Wardrobe Asst:* Daniel Chichester, Edna Taylor & Katherine Tilley. *Drivers:* Tom Yardley, David Jernigan, Merril Townsend, Joseph Jones, Charles Kirsch, Roger Leoncavallo, Hal Grist, John Webb, Jack Daniels, Paul English, Leroy Chaplin, Melvin Theriot, A.J. Marquez, Bertand White & Joseph Gugliuzza.

CAST: Charles Bronson (Chaney), James Coburn (Spencer "Speed" Weed), Jill Ireland (Lucy Simpson), Strother Martin (Poe), Maggie Blye (Gayleen Schoonover), Michael McGuire (Chick Gandil), Robert Tessier (Jim Henry), Nick Dimitri (Street), Felice Orlandi (Le Beau), Bruce Glover (Doty), Edward Walsh (Pettibon), Chrys Forbes (Chrystal), Maurice Kowalewski (Caesare), Don Hood (Pickpocket), Sid Arroyo (Pigeon), Pamela Verges (Decoy), Al Scott (Blindestiff), Lyla Hay Owen (Diner Waitress), John Creamer (Apartment Manager), Fred Lerner, Chuck Hicks (Fighters), Frank McRae (Hammerman), Naomi Stevens (Madam), Robert Castleberry (Counterman), Becky Allen (Poe's Date), Joan Kleven (Carol), Anne Welsch (Secretary), Jim Nickerson (Barge Fighter), Walter Scott, Max Kleven (Pool Players), Valerian Smith (Handler), Bob Minor (Zack), Larry

Martindale (Driver), Charles W. Schaeffer Jr., LeslieBonano (Card Players), Ronnie Philips (Cajun Fighter); Greater Liberty Baptist Church Choir & Congregation.

The year 1975 proved to be a very good one at the box office for Charles Bronson's movies. The combination of *Breakout* and *Hard Times*, both Columbia releases, brought in receipts in excess of $50 million worldwide. Bronson was paid one million dollars for each feature and his popularity proved his salary was a wise investment for both movies' producers. In addition *Hard Times* also gave the star some of the best notices of his career. Many reviewers were enthusiastic about Bronson's performance in the feature and lauded his acting ability, something his fans had been doing for some two decades. The movie also was the directorial debut of Walter Hill, who collaborated on the script, and its feel for the Depression-era in which it is set is very authentic.

Filmed on location in New Orleans, *Hard Times* used the sites of the city to good advantage. Among them were the Chalmette Railroad Yards, Magazine Street, the French Quarter, the Cornstalk Hotel (used as the residence of James Coburn's character), the Irish Channel, St. Vincent de Paul Cemetery on Desire Street, Chartres Street in the Ninth Ward, Jackson Street and the Algiers Ferry. One sequence was filmed in Cajun country near Lafitte, Louisiana, and featured the steamboat *Mark Twain*.

In the early 1930s hobo Chaney (Charles Bronson) jumps off a freight and in a small town encounters a street fight match. Later he offers his services as a fighter to promoter-hustler Speed Weed (James Coburn) who thinks Chaney is too long in the tooth to be a fighter. Since his man was beaten, Speed takes the chance and Chaney knocks out his first opponent with one punch. The two travel to New Orleans, where Speed is headquartered with his girlfriend Gayleen (Maggie Blye). Chaney gets an apartment and meets lonely Lucy Simpson (Jill Ireland), a pretty young woman with a husband in jail and no prospects. Chaney and Speed become partners and they take on Speed's pal Poe (Strother Martin), a medical student turned opium addict, as their cut man. Speed borrows money from loan shark Le Beau (Felice Orlandi) and uses it to promote a match for Chaney in the bayou country. Chaney easily defeats promoter Pettibon's (Edward Walsh) fighter (Ronnie Philips) but Pettibon refuses to pay off. That night Chaney breaks into Pettibon's roadhouse and takes the money as well as shooting up the place. Back in New Orleans Chaney begins to see Lucy regularly while Speed sets up a fight for him with the champion city street brawler Jim Henry (Robert Tessier), who is managed by Chick Gandil (Michael McGuire), a fish merchant. Chaney batters Henry into submission and he and Speed make $5,000 each from the fight. Speed immediately loses his take in a dice game and is upset when Chaney refuses Gandil's offer to buy one-half of his contract since

**Charles Bronson and Jill Ireland in *Hard Times* (Columbia, 1975).**

Speed needs the money to pay off Le Beau whose man Doty (Bruce Glover) has been strong-arming him. Chaney and Speed break up their partnership over the offer but Gandil pays off Speed's loan to Le Beau in order to force Chaney into fighting tough import Street (Nick Dimitri). When Poe tells Chaney that Speed will be killed if Chaney refuses to fight Street, Chaney goes ahead with the match. He is also unhappy over the breakup of his relationship with Lucy, who has found a more steady man. Chaney and Street square off in a warehouse with Chaney betting his own $5,000 that he will win. After a gruelling altercation Chaney beats Street senseless and he and Speed collect their winnings. Before leaving New Orleans, heading north, Chaney gives money to both Poe and Speed.

Charles Bronson's character of Chaney is a man of few words. He tells girlfriend Lucy that street fighting is "better than workin' at the gas station changin' tires for two bucks a day" and it has "no reason about it—just money." When she asks him what it feels like to knock an opponent down he laconically replies, "It makes me feel a hell of a lot better than him." Although well into his early fifties, Charles Bronson is more than physically fit for the part of the street fighter, a character who is silent without being morose. Chaney also has an affinity for animals—he cares for a cat in his slum apartment and at the Bayou fight scene he is appalled to find a bear kept in a cage. Certainly

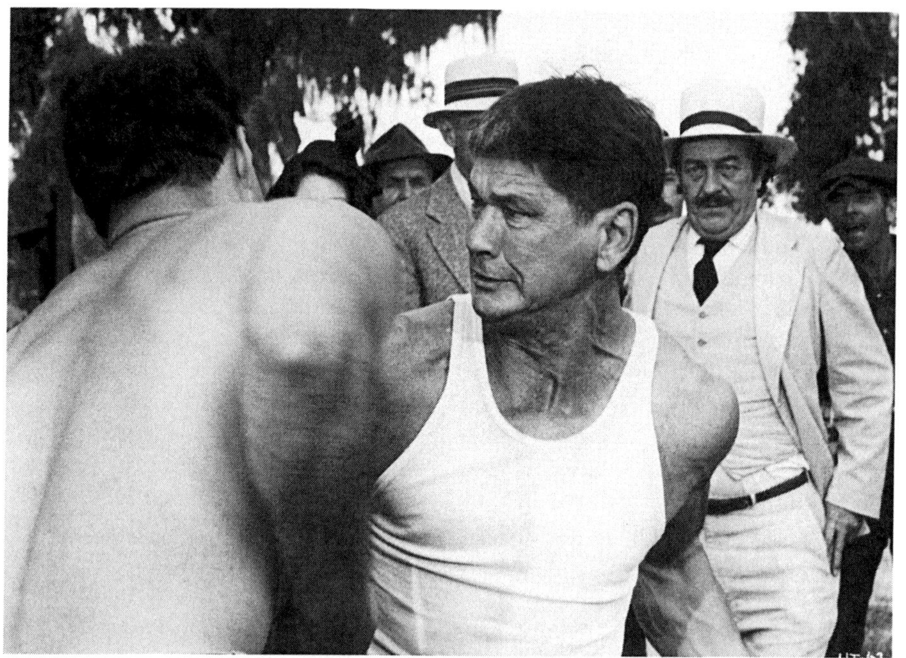

**Ronnie Philips, Charles Bronson and Strother Martin in *Hard Times* (Columbia, 1975).**

Chaney is one of Charles Bronson's most appealing film roles and one that earned much praise. James Coburn, with whom Bronson has worked in *The Magnificent Seven* (1960) and *The Great Escape* (1963), nicely counterbalances Bronson's quiet character with a larger-than-life portrayal of the slick Speed. Jill Ireland has a few good scenes as the rather dour girl Chaney is attracted to while Maggie Blye is fine as Coburn's fun-loving but level-headed fiancée. Strother Martin underplays the part of the drug-addicted cornerman while Felice Orlandi and Michael McGuire excel as slimy crooks. Robert Tessier and Nick Dimitri are especially good as the cruel street fighters Chaney must oppose.

Although *Hard Times* got some of the best reviews given a Charles Bronson starrer, they were still mixed. *Variety* complimented the producers for "a sincere attempt to broaden Charles Bronson's role spectrum" saying the film "has a very handsome mid–Thirties New Orleans period flavor, but there is a fatal lack of 'center' in the story...." The same reviewer thought Jill Ireland "is excellent in a touching performance." Richard Eder in the *New York Times* said the film "is a stylish, sharp, ingratiating movie" and in a later review for the same newspaper Vincent Canby said it "is a terrific directorial debut for Walter Hill. The movie recalls classic Westerns about godlike heroes who come out of nowhere, set things straight and then move on, as well as more mundane movies of the thirties about men working at their jobs." He said Bronson "is to acting what a monolith is to sculpture." Candice Russell in *The Miami Herald* called *Hard Times* "Passable entertainment because it's several cuts above what we've come to expect from the world's highest-paid actor.... Bronson never seems to be performing because he's the same unflappable fellow each time out." Alan Jenkins in the *Palm Beach Post* felt it was a "sorry excuse for a movie" while the *Hollywood Reporter* said the film had "some strong pluses and some curious minuses." That reviewer, Arthur Knight, said of the star, "Bronson is—Bronson, cold, hard, implacable, keeping his emotions to himself." Lewis Weinberg in the *UCLA Daily Bruin* wrote, "*Hard Times* is a film whose characters work their way into your heart by working their fists into each other's faces. If there is any sentiment in the film, it is the love for contusions and multiple fractures." In the *Toronto (Ontario) Star*, Clyde Gilmour called the film "a taut, richly atmospheric story about the Great Depression of the early '30s, when men would do almost anything for the price of a meal." Jay Cocks in *Time* opined, "Surprise: a good Charles Bronson movie. *Hard Times* is unassuming, tough and spare, a tidy little parable about strength and honor." He also said it contained "Charles Bronson's best performance to date" noting the film is "evidence that there may be larger ones on the way." Charles Champlin in the *Los Angeles Times* said the film "is what you could call a perfect example of the escapist movie. But it is also perfect proof of what a bore total escapism can be." Regarding the star, he wrote, "Bronson is a better actor (by far) than most of his roles ask him to be. He is a strong personality but he is not a granite statue, and one of these days he will get paid a lot for letting more of himself out."

In the British publication *Films & Filming*, Eric Braun wrote of *The Streetfighter* (the title given the film in Great Britain so as not to confuse it with the Charles Dickens novel) that it "can be safely recommended to anyone who enjoys watching grown men beating hell out of one another, which means it should please a pretty large public."

It should be noted that *Hard Times*' locale of New Orleans was also the backdrop of an earlier Charles Bronson–Jill Ireland feature, *Città Violenta* (1970). During the filming of *Hard Times* Charles Bronson was offered the lead role by Tennessee Williams in the latter's new play, "The Red Devil Battery Sign." Bronson, however, had to decline due to upcoming movie commitments.

## *House of Wax* (Warner Bros., 1953) 89 minutes Color.

*P:* Bryan Foy. *D:* Andre De Toth. *Sc:* Crane Wilbur. *St:* Charles Belden. *Ph:* Bert Glennon & Peverall Marley. *Ed:* Rudi Fehr. *Mus:* David Buttolph. *AD:* Stanley Fleischer. *Natural Vision Supv:* M.L. Gunsburg. *Makeup:* Gordon Bau & (uncredited) George Bau. *Sets:* Lyle B. Reifsnider. *Orchestrations:* Maurice de Packh. *Wardrobe:* Howard Shoup. *Visual Consultant:* Julian Gunzburg,

M.D. *Natural Vision Consultant:* Lothrop Worth.

**CAST:** Vincent Price (Professor Henry Jarrod), Frank Lovejoy (Lieutenant Tom Brennan), Phyllis Kirk (Sue Allen), Carolyn Jones (Cathy Gray), Paul Picerni (Scott Andrews), Roy Roberts (Matthew Burke), Angela Clarke (Mrs. Andrews), Paul Cavanaugh (Sidney Wallace), Charles Buchinsky (Igor), Ned Young (Leon Averill), Dabbs Greer (Sergeant Jim Shane), Reggie Rymal (Barker), Philip Tonge (Bruce Allison), Lyle Latell (Waiter), Frank Ferguson (Coroner), Terry Mitchell, Ruth Whitney, Trude Wyler (Women at Opening), Merry Townsend (Ticket Taker), Jack Kenney, Darwin Greenfield (Boarders), Riza Royce (Ma Flanagan), Ruth Warren (Cleaning Woman), Richard Benjamin, Jack Mower (Detectives), Eddie Parks, Jack Woody (Morgue Attendants), Oliver Blake (Pompous Man), Leo Curley (Heavy Set Man), Mary Lou Holloway (Millie), Joanne Brown, Shirley Whitney (Girlfriends).

On a rainy night New York City art critic Sidney Wallace (Paul Cavanaugh) comes to see the work of Professor Henry Jarrod (Vincent Price), a master sculptor in wax who runs a historical museum exhibiting his superb wax figures. Wallace is so impressed he considers becoming Jarrod's partner and buying out the sculptor's present partner Matthew Burke (Roy Roberts). Saying he will be away for six months Wallace departs and Jarrod tells Burke the good news but the latter does not want to wait and instead decides to collect the insurance on the exhibition by setting it on fire. Jarrod tries to stop him but is knocked out in the scuffle. Burke carries out his scheme and sets the fire which destroys the place and badly burns Jarrod. Months later Burke collects the $25,000 insurance money but is soon killed by a phantom-like figure with a badly scarred face. Also killed by the phantom is Cathy Gray, (Carolyn Jones) the girlfriend of Burke, and the murder is witnessed by her friend Sue Allen (Phyllis Kirk) who is chased through the deserted streets by the phantom but finds refuge in the home of her boyfriend Scott Andrews (Paul Picerni), also a sculptor, and his mother (Angela Clarke). Sue tells her story to police Lieutenant Brennan (Frank Lovejoy) and his partner (Dabbs Greer) while the phantom steals Cathy's body from the morgue. Wallace returns to New York and is summoned to the workshop of Jarrod, who he thought had been killed in the fire. Instead he finds Jarrod a cripple who now directs the work of his assistants, mute Igor (Charles Buchinsky) and alcoholic Leon Averill (Ned Young). Jarrod tells him of his plans to open a chamber of horrors and asks Wallace's financial aid. The latter agrees. Through Wallace, Jarrod meets Scott and he hires him to work for him while he wants Sue to pose as his model of Marie Antoinette. At the opening Sue notices the strong resemblance of the waxworks of Joan of Arc to Cathy, and Jarrod tells her he used Cathy's newspaper photo as a model. When the phantom comes to her room at night Sue thinks it was a dream but she still feels there is something mysterious about the Joan of Arc statue. Again talking to Brennan, the policeman decides to investigate Jarrod and while Wallace vouches for him he and his partner bring in Averill who eventually breaks down and

**Vincent Price, Charles (Bronson) Buchinsky and Paul Cavanaugh in *House of Wax* (Warner Bros., 1953).**

says it was Jarrod who murdered Burke and Cathy. Meanwhile Sue is to meet Scott at the closed museum that night and Jarrod sends Scott on an errand as Sue is stalked in the locked waxworks by Igor. Scott returns and fights with Igor and is knocked out while Jarrod plans to cover Sue's body with wax and turn her into Marie Antoinette. Brennan and his men arrive and subdue Igor, and in trying to stop Jarrod, the latter falls into the boiling vat of wax.

Filmed in 3-D with WarnerPhonic Sound (actually RCA Stereophonic sound), *House of Wax* was a major box office success grossing $4.65 million in its initial release. Its success was mainly due to its 3-D gimmick (who can forget barker Reggie Hymal and his ping-pong paddles?) rather than its horror elements which were pale compared to the film on which it was based, Warner Bros.' *Mystery of the Wax Museum* (1932) starring Lionel Atwill, Fay Wray, Glenda Farrell and Frank McHugh and filmed in two-color Technicolor. That film kept the sculptor's horribly scarred face a secret until the finale while *House of Wax* ruined the shock effect by exposing Vincent Price in the monster makeup throughout the feature. *House of Wax* does contain a

Reissue poster for *House of Wax* (Warner Bros., 1953).

few good shock effects, such as Price pretending to be a corpse in the morgue before stealing a girl's body and Charles Bronson's Igor as he stalks Sue Allen in the spooky wax museum. In one memorable scene Bronson pretends to be one of several wax heads as he watches Sue's movements.

Despite being a mute, the part of Igor brought Charles Bronson one of his best-remembered early film roles. His Igor is not only menacing and strong but is played with an undercurrent of evil detachment. At the finale it is a bust of Bronson which Frank Lovejoy shoves into theatre patrons' faces as he announces the character has been sent to Sing Sing.

In 1971 *House of Wax* was reissued by Sherpix in StereoVision 3D and by this time Charles Bronson was billed under his own name and moved up the cast list to second billing, just behind star Vincent Price. Warner Bros. re-released the film again in 1982 and it has had several revivals since then.

While *Mystery of the Wax Museum* was in a modern setting, *House of Wax* was set in turn-of-the century New York City.

Charles Bronson would co-star with Vincent Price in *Master of the World* in 1961.

## *The Indian Runner* (Metro-Goldwyn-Mayer/United Artists, 1991) 126 minutes Color

*P:* Don Phillips & Patricia Morrison. *EP:* Stephen K. Bannon, Thom Mount & Mark Bisgeier. *D-Sc:* Sean Penn. *Ph:* Anthony B. Richmond. *Ed:* Jay Cassidy. *Mus:* Jack Nitzsche. *Mus Supv:* Danny Bramson. *AD:* Bill Groom. *Prod Design:* Michael Haller. *Costume Design:* Jill Ohanneson. *Asst Dir:* Artist W. Robinson, Eric Haller & John Wildermuth. *Location Mgr:* Lawrence Banks. *Sc Supv:* Carol De Pasquale. *Sp Eff:* Gary Elmendorf. *Set Decorator:* Derek R. Hill. *Supv Sd Ed:* James J. Klinger. *Asst AD:* Sarah Knowles. *Camera Operator:* Buzz Feitschans. *Second Unit Camera Operator:* Andy Anderson. *Title Design:* David L. Aaron. *Sd Mixer:* Gary Alper. *Casting:* Dee Dee Wehle. *Local & Extra Casting:* Jackie Beavers. *Transportation Coordinator:* Jon Bergholz. *Makeup Supv:* Hallie D'Amore. *Special Makeup:* Jo-Anne Smith-Ojeil. *Additional Makeup:* Nancy Glissman. *Hair Styles:* Frank Bianco. *Foley Walker:* Robert Friedman. *Dolby Consultant:* Douglas Greenfield. *Prod Mgr:* David Shamroy Hamburger. *Stunt Coordinator:* Jeff Jensen. *Helicopter Pilot:* Gress Horne. *Best Boy Grip:* Jeffrey Johnson. *Key Grip:* Lloyd Moriarty. *Foley Walker:* Keith Olsen. *Re-recording Mixer:* Michael Minkler. *Mus Coordinator:* Leslie Morris. *Prod Coordinator:* Maureen Osborne-Beal. *Negative Cutter:* Brian Ralph. *Boom Operator:* Andrew Schmetterling. *Property Master:* Tom Shaw Jr. *Rigging Gaffer:* Tommy Ray Sullivan. *Still Photographer:* Michael Tighe. *Best Boy Electric:* James Tomaro. *Mus Ed:* Richard Whitfield. *Construction Coordinator:* Hank Wynands. *Construction Foreman:* Mike Wynands. *Drivers:* Kip Parker, Ray Holmes, Marvin Runge, Arthur Campbell, Steve Miller & James Maddox.

**CAST:** David Morse (Joe Roberts), Viggo Mortensen (Frank Roberts), Valeria Golino (Maria Roberts), Patricia Arquette (Dorothy), Charles Bronson (Mr. Roberts), Sandy Dennis (Mrs. Roberts), Dennis Hopper (Caesar), Jordan

Rhodes (Deputy Randall), Enzo Rossi (Raffael Roberts), Harry Crews (Mr. Baker), Eileen Ryan (Mrs. Baker), Trevor Endicott (Joe Roberts, Age 12), Brandon Fleck (Frank Roberts, Age 7), Kathy Jensen (Woman at Carwash), Jim Devney (Deputy), Dr. Leland J. Olson (Doctor), Annie Pearson (Hotel Manager), Thomas Blair Levin (Clyde), V. Stacy Klein (Lucy), Benicio Del Torro (Miguel), James J. Luxa (Randall's Partner), Adam Nelson, Eddie Katz (Cellmates), Kenny Stabler (Indian Runner), Don Shanks (Young Indian Runner), Neal Star (Midget), Elaine Schoonover (Bearded Lady), Larry Hoefling (Larry), Phil Gould (Man at Del Mar), Chuck Ulmer (Frank's Boss), Joe Martin, Helen Halmes (Dorothy's Parents), Jimmy Intveld (Kid on Highway), John Blyth Barrymore, Allison Caine (Voices).

Charles Bronson returned to the screen in 1991 in a cameo appearance in *The Indian Runner*, a film which marked the screenwriting and directing debut of actor Sean Penn. The film was dedicated to the memories of Hal Ashby, Frank Bianco and John Cassavetes. After a two year big screen absence, Bronson evidently took the role to ease himself back into movie work. He appears in about a half-dozen scenes although he thoroughly dominates them. It is interesting that critics fell all over themselves praising Bronson's work in the movie. While his performance is a telling one, it is little different from what he had been doing for the past 40 years. The same critics who usually turned up their noses at Bronson's movies now lauded him. The reason for this is that he was appearing in a film which appealed to critics instead of the action thrillers which won him worldwide fame.

*The Indian Runner* is basically a boring, unpleasant study of two alienated brothers who do not know how to communicate. One has become a lawman after failing as a farmer while the other is a Vietnam War veteran, a tattooed rebel who his sibling calls "the angriest man I know." All of this is set against the backdrop of a small midwestern town and the legend of the Indian Runner, who runs so fast he becomes his own message. Writer-director Sean Penn throws everything into the feature except the kitchen sink, including a graphic birth sequence. Mostly, though, the main characters sit and stare off into space and contemplate and speak in short, clipped sentences. Nearly everyone (except Bronson and Sandy Dennis) smoke, either cigarettes or dope. Only Charles Bronson gives solid characterization and his scenes are too brief to bring much life to the proceedings. He is especially good in the scene where he tells his oldest son Joe that he was wrong when he objected to his marrying a Mexican girl. Later he tells Joe, "The same thieves who took your farm and now you work for them."

Taking place in a small midwest town in the late 1960s, the film begins with local sheriff Joe Roberts (David Morse) being forced to shoot a local man in self-defense and being accused of murder by the dead man's parents (Harry Crews, Eileen Ryan). Joe's younger brother Frank (Viggo Mortensen) returns from service in Vietnam and the two siblings realize they are strangers. Frank, who was a hellraiser before joining the army, leaves town without seeing his parents and six months later his mother (Sandy Dennis) dies. Frank cannot attend the funeral because he is in jail on an assault charge. After his release, Joe finds Frank and tells him their mother has died and that he wants them to be close again. Frank steals a car and robs a service station and then runs off with his girlfriend Dorothy (Patricia Arquette). In the meantime Joe and Frank's father (Charles Bronson) commits suicide. Frank and Dorothy arrive in town and live in Joe and Frank's parents' home and Frank gets a job on a bridge construction crew. When Dorothy finds out she is pregnant the two get married. Later Frank and Dorothy quarrel and Frank beats up a man in a bar. Frank feels remorse and tells Joe he is sorry about the past. Just as Dorothy is about to give birth, Frank ducks out to a bar. Joe follows him and tries to get him to come home but fails. Frank goes berserk in the bar and kills the bartender (Dennis Hopper). Joe is forced to pursue Frank just as the baby is born. Both Joe and Frank stop on a highway, but when Frank leaves, Joe knows he will never again see his brother.

The critics waxed enthusiastic over *The Indian Runner* although the public stayed away in droves. The film's domestic gross was less than $200,000. The film was based on the Bruce Springsteen song "Highway Patrolman" and its soundtrack included music by Janis Joplin and Bob Dylan. Janet Maslin in the *New York Times* said that writer-director Sean Penn "has reached for a ragged emotional reality that recalls the films of John Cassavetes ... and he has framed even his film's most unruly episodes with unexpected delicacy. Loose, rambling and sometimes rudderless as it is, *The Indian Runner* has a fundamental honesty that gives it real substance." She added, "Mr. Bronson and Ms. Dennis are unlikely but strangely effective as the dazed, determinedly polite parents who have lost their moorings." *Variety* reported, "Rambling, indulgent and joltingly raw at times, Sean Penn's first outing as a director takes a fair amount of patience to get through but has an integrity that intermittently serves it well." In *Roger Ebert's Video Companion 1995 Edition* (1994), critic Ebert said, "It's impressive, how thoughtfully Penn handles this material. The good brother isn't a straight arrow, and the bad brother isn't romanticized as a rebel without a cause, and there are no easy solutions or neat little happy endings for this story." In regards to Charles Bronson's work in the film, Ebert wrote, "It is a performance of quiet, sure power. After his recent string of brainless revenge thrillers, I wondered if Bronson had sort of given up on acting and was just going through the motions. Here he is so good it is impossible to think of another actor one would have preferred in his place." In *Film Review 1993* (1992), James Cameron-Wilson felt the movie was "a surprisingly mature, well-crafted melodrama that serves both the actor and cinematographer particularly well."

It has been noted that although Sean Penn expanded on Bruce Springsteen's song for his script, it is also reflective of some of his own experiences, including sibling rivalry, incarceration and childbirth. Penn cast his mother, actress Eileen Ryan, as the vindictive mother of the man shot in the film's first sequence.

Also in 1991 NBC-TV telecast *Reason for Living: The Jill Ireland Story* on May 20. The film recounted Jill Ireland's battle with cancer and her struggle to save her adopted son, a heroin addict. Jill Clayburgh portrayed Jill Ireland, Lance Henriksen played Charles Bronson and Neill Barry portrayed the young man. *TV Guide* noted, "The movie wisely downplays the Hollywood and soap-opera elements and concentrates instead on the kind of illness-caused tensions (her fight against breast cancer) and drug-related pain (her adopted son's addiction) that can hobble any family, whether yours or Charles Bronson's."

## *Jubal* (Columbia, 1956) 101 minutes Color

*P:* William Fadiman. *D:* Delmer Daves. *Sc:* Russell S. Hughes & Delmer Daves, from the book *Jubal Troop* by Paul I. Wellman. *Ph:* Charles Lawton Jr. *Ed:* Al Clark. *Mus:* David Raksin. *Mus Conductor:* Morris Stoloff. *AD:* Carl Anderson. *Sd:* Harry Smith. *Recording Supv:* John Livadary. *Gowns:* Jean Louis. *Asst Dir:* Eddie Saeta. *Color Consultant:* Henri Jaffa. *Second Unit Ph:* Ray Cory. *Set Decorator:* Louis Diage. *Makeup:* Clay Campbell. *Hair Stylist:* Helen Hunt. *Orchestrations:* Arthur Morton.

**CAST:** Glenn Ford (Jubal Troop), Ernest Borgnine (Shep Horgan), Rod Steiger (Pinky Pinkham), Valerie French (Mae Horgan), Felicia Farr (Naomi Hoktor), Basil Ruysdael (Shem Hoktor), Noah Beery Jr. (Sam), Charles Bronson (Reb Haislipp), John Dierkes (Carson), Jack Elam (McCoy), Robert Burton (Dr. Grant), Robert Knapp (Jake Slavin), Juney Ellis (Charity Hoktor), Don C. Harvey (Jim Tolliver), Guy Wilkerson (Cookie), Larry Hudson (Bayne), Mike Lawrence, Robert "Buzz" Henry (Tolliver Boys), William Rhinehart (Matt), John Cason (Cowboy), Ann Kunde (Girl).

Rejected by his mother after the death of his father, Jubal Troop (Glenn Ford) becomes a saddle tramp. Lost in a blizzard and having lost his horse, he is found half-frozen by Shep Horgan (Ernest Borgnine) who takes him to his ranch. Immediately ranch hand Pinky (Rod Steiger) takes a dislike to Jubal although he is befriended by the other cowboys, Sam (Noah Beery Jr.) and Carson (John Dierkes) as well as the ranch cook (Guy Wilkerson). After breaking a tough horse, Jubal is asked to stay on by Shep and he agrees but Shep's unhappy wife Mae (Valerie French) makes a pass at him. Mae has had an affair with Pinky but rejects him in favor of Jubal who does not want her. Shep asks Jubal to be his foreman which makes Pinky jealous. The latter tries to run off a group of religious travelers who have stopped on the Horgan ranch after Jubal tells them they can stay and rest. There he meets their leader, Shem Hoktor (Basil Ruysdael), and his pretty daughter Naomi (Felicia Farr) as well as cowboy Reb Haislipp (Charles Bronson), who he hires to work on the ranch. Again rejecting Mae's advances and telling Shep to be kinder to his wife, Jubal becomes attached to Naomi and tells her about his past. The girl's intended, Jake Slavin (Robert Knapp), becomes jealous and tells Jubal that Shem has promised him his daughter. As the travelers plan to leave Naomi goes to Jubal and says goodbye and tells him she does not care for Jake. That night Mae rides out to camp with a letter for Shep who asks Jubal to escort her home. Back at the ranch Jubal again rejects Mae but Pinky tells Horgan the two are having an affair. Shep returns to the ranch to hear his wife call out Jubal's name in her sleep and he accuses her of infidelity. She lies and says she and Jubal are lovers. Reb rides into town to warn Jubal about Horgan but the latter arrives in the saloon and tries to shoot Jubal. Reb gives his unarmed friend a gun and Jubal is forced to shoot Horgan in self-defense. When Pinky is told of the shooting he rouses the other cowboys into forming a posse to find Jubal who was injured in the shooting and has been taken to the traveler's camp by Reb. There he is tended by Naomi but the jealous Jake rides to the posse and tells them where to find Jubal. Meanwhile Pinky has tried to force his attentions on Mae and when she refuses he beats her badly, believing he has killed her. Against Naomi's objections, Jubal rides back to the ranch where he finds Mae. The posse locates the Hoktor wagon but when they do not find Jubal they head to the ranch. The dying Mae tells Dr. Grant (Robert Burton) that it was Pinky who beat her and the posse turns on him. Jubal is reunited with Naomi and he and the girl and Reb ride away from the Horgan ranch.

As *Apache* (1954) had been based on a Paul I. Wellman work, so was *Jubal*. This adult psychological western had been kicking around Columbia Pictures since 1942 and had at one time been intended as a vehicle for Gary Cooper. It gave Charles Bronson a solid, sympathetic character role as the tough cowpoke who proves to be a true friend to the hero. A highlight of the picture had pals Jubal and Reb exchange their handguns by tossing them in the air and then firing at the moment each caught the other's gun. Glenn Ford and Charles Bronson did the difficult trick without the aid of doubles. Regarding Bronson's performance in the film, the *Hollywood Reporter* captured the essence of a Bronson portrayal calling it "outstanding without overemphasis."

Set in the beautiful locales of Wyoming's Teton Mountains, *Jubal* was filmed in CinemaScope and Technicolor. The film reunited Charles Bronson with director Delmer Daves (they made *Drum Beat* in 1954) and *Variety* wrote of the movie, "Oddly enough, much of the footage is free of actual physical violence, but the nerves are stretched so taut that it's almost a relief when it does come." In *The Western* (1983), Phil Hardy called *Jubal* "gripping" and added, "Daves presents the characters forcefully, his swooping camera creating a sense of boxed-in tensions and sense of depth unusual in a Western." *Photoplay*, at the time of the film's release, noted it "is not at all the conventional Western" as "Bunkhouse scenes with Noah Beery Jr., Charles Bronson and John Dierkes suggest the Old West of fact and not fiction...."

In keeping with the vagaries of Hollywood, *Jubal* was the second screen pairing of Charles Bronson and Ernest Borgnine within a period of little more than one year. They had been together in *Vera Cruz*, released late in 1954, and *Jubal* was issued in the spring of 1956. In *Vera Cruz* they had nearly equal roles as gang members but by the time *Jubal* was released Ernest Borgnine had won an Academy Award for *Marty* (1955) and had been elevated to stardom.

## *Kid Galahad* (United Artists, 1962) 95 minutes Color

*P:* David Weisbart. *D:* Phil Karlson. *Sc:* William Fay, from the novel by Francis Wallace. *Ph:* Burnett Guffey. *Ed:* Stuart Gilmore. *Mus:* Jeff Alexander. *AD:* Cary Odel. *Sets:* Edward G. Boyle. *Sp Eff:* Milt Rice. *Sd:* Lambert Day. *Wardrobe:* Bert Hendrikson & Irene Caine. *Makeup:* Lynn Reynolds. *Hair Styles:* Alice Monte. *Prod Supv:* Allen K. Wood. *Prod Mgr:* Robert E. Relyea. *Asst Dir:* Jerome M. Siegel. *Songs:* Ruth Batchelor, Bob Roberts, Fred Wise, Ben Wiseman, Dee [Dolores] Fuller, Sharon Gilbert, Sherman Edwards & Hal David. *Technical Advisor:* Mushy Callahan.

**CAST:** Elvis Presley (Walter Gulick), Gig Young (Willy Grogan), Lola Albright (Dolly Fletcher), Joan Blackman (Rose Grogan), Charles Bronson (Lew Nyack), Ned Glass (Lieberman), Robert Emhardt (Maynard), David Lewis (Otto Danzig), Michael Dante (Joie Shakes), Judson Pratt (Zimmerman), George Mitchell (Sperling), Richard Devon (Martin), Jeffrey Morris (Ralphie), Liam Redmond (Father Higgins).

Upon his release from the army, Walter Gulick (Elvis Presley) gets a job working as a sparring partner at a training camp in the Catskill Mountains run by sleazy Willy Grogan (Gig Young) and his lady friend, Dolly Fletcher (Lola Albright). Walter proves to be such a good boxer that Willy decides to make him a professional although Dolly opposes the idea. When hoodlums try to collect debts owed to them by Willy, the thugs try to hurt Dolly who is saved by Walter, who is then dubbed "Kid Galahad." Aided by his handler, trusty former boxer Lew Nyack (Charles Bronson), and falling in love with Willy's pretty sister Rose (Joan Blackman), Walter carries off a series of victories in the ring, becoming a sensation. When Rose agrees to marry him, however, Walter decides to give up boxing after one more bout. The gangsters bet against him and warn Willy that Walter must not win the fight. When she finds out about the fight, Dolly leaves Willy, and Lew has his fingers broken because he refuses the gangsters' offer of $500 for not working in Walter's corner. Walter finds out what happened to Lew and beats up the hoodlums and then goes on with the fight. After a grueling encounter in the ring, he is the victor. Finding out the truth, Dolly reconciles with Willy and Walter retires from the ring to wed Rose and start his own garage to repair automobiles.

**Poster for *Kid Galahad* (United Artists, 1962).**

At first glance his fifth-billed appearance in *Kid Galahad* might appear to be a downward step cinematically for Charles Bronson. It must be remembered, however, that at the time the *Motion Picture Herald* named Elvis Presley the fifth most popular film star at the box office and thus his appearance in a Presley feature offered the actor exposure to a large audience. His role of trainer Lew Nyack was also a sympathetic one and it garnered him some good reviews while the film itself proved to be a potent box office success, both at home and in England.

A loose remake of the 1937 Warner Bros. film of the same title, *Kid Galahad* became a semi-musical populated by seven songs which failed to chart for the film's singing star. Wayne Morris made his screen debut in the title role of the 1937 feature, with Edward G. Robinson and Bette Davis in the roles refashioned for Gig Young and Lola Albright. The first version was filmed as *Battling Bellhop*, the title it reverted to when sold to TV in the early 1960s, so as not to conflict with the Presley vehicle.

Publicity for *Kid Galahad* noted that Elvis Presley was trained in the boxing sequences by Mushy Callahan, the former junior welterweight boxing champion of the world. Callahan had also trained such cinema greats as Errol Flynn, John Garfield, Burt Lancaster and Kirk Douglas for boxing roles, but according to Callahan, Presley was "my best pupil. He has a natural rhythm. He would have made a great boxer." In training for the film, Presley allegedly worked out on light and heavy bags, spent many hours boxing with Callahan and other fighters and lost 12 pounds before the film went into production.

*Variety* reported, "The story may be old, the direction not especially perceptive, the performances, in several cases pretty poor, but United Artists' *Kid Galahad* is apt to be a moneymaker in spite of all this." Bosley Crowther wrote in the *New York Times* that the film "makes a moderately genial entertainment. It's not explosive, but it has the cheerful top of a lightly romantic contrivance that ranges between comedy and spoof."

## *Kinjite: Forbidden Subjects* (Cannon Group, 1989) 97 minutes Color

*P:* Pancho Kohner. *Ed:* Menahem Golan & Yoram Globus. *AP:* Patricia G. Payro. *D:* J. Lee Thompson. *Sc:* Harold Nebenzal. *Ph:* Gideon Porath. *Ed:* Peter Lee-Thompson & Mary E. Jochem. *Mus:* Gregg De Belles. *AD:* W. Brooke Wheeler. *Prod Mgr:* Sheridan "Dar" Reid. *Asst Dir:* Robert C. Ortwin Jr. & George Van Noy. *Executive in Charge of Prod:* Marc S. Fisher. *Casting:* Nancy Lara & Perry Bullington. *Second Unit Coordinator:* Ernie Orsatti. *Stuntmen:* Kenny Endoso, Brian Snader, Alan Oliney, Frank Orsatti, Buck McDancer, Dan Bradley, Carl Ciarfello, Jon Epstein, Glory Foramontoni, Mickey Gilbert, Jeff Imada, James Lew, Noon Orsatti, Burford McClerkins, Dennis Madalone, Stuart Quin, Bill Ryusaki & Rick Wagner. *Prod Coordinator:* M. Ginanne Carpenter. *Asst Prod Coordinator:* John Siavano. *Locations Mgr:* John Pearson & Gary Kessel. *Sd Supv:* Karin Cooper. *Prod Auditor:* Emily J. Rice. *Asst Prod Auditor:* Nicola Lubitsch. *First Camera Asst:* Guy L. Skinner. *Second Camera Asst:* John Karis. *Additional Ph:* Roland Vidor. *Additional Ph Operators:* D.R. Boyd, Sean McClinn & Vladimir Tukan. *Additional Camera Asst:* Mark Ludwig, Alicia Craft, Peter Norkus, Scott E. Steele, Dennis S. Hall, Lance Fisher, Michael Riba, F. Mako Korwai & W.L. Peterson. *Additional Second Camera Asst:* Edward L. Rich, Bruce De Aragon & Pierre Chenally. *Prod Sd:* Skyland Sound, Inc. *Sd Mixer:* Carl Felburg. *Boom Operator:* Cameron Hamza. *Set Decorator:* Margaret C. Fisher. *Asst AD:* Robert Miasto. *Art Department Coordinator:* Marjorie J. Costner. *Asst Set Decorator:* Masako Mazuda. *Lead Man:* Drew C. Williams. *On Set Dresser:* Donnie Merrell. *Set Dressers:* Lance Clarke, Craig Gadsby & Neil B. Wolfson. *Property Master:* Edwin M. Brewer. *Property Asst:* Mark Heiner. *Costume Designer:* Michael Hoffman. *Costume Supv:* Agnes J. Lyon. *Costumer:* Tony Velasco. *Key Makeup & Hair:* Carla Fabrizzi. *Asst Makeup:* Linda A. Vallejo. *Hair Stylist:* Annette Fabrizzi. *Gaffer:* Paul F. Petzoldt. *Best Boy Electrician:* Tony N. Marshall. *Electricians:* Larry Liddell, William

James Gray & Robert A. Petzoldt III. *Asst Gaffer:* Danny "G" Graff. *Additional Best Boy Electrician:* Vance Trussell. *Equipment Technician:* Danny Azzolt. *Key Grip:* Robert J. Rabin. *Best Boy Grip:* Scott Lieu. *Additional Best Boy Grips:* Christian Silver. *Dolly Grip:* Michael Coo. *Grips:* Todd Griffith & Mark E. Kline. *Additional Key Grip:* Cobie Fair. *Still Photographers:* Garry Farr & Said Adzani. *Asst Auditor:* Marilyn Febus. *Extra Casting:* Dennis Hansen. *Extra Wrangler:* Don L. Morton. *Key Prod Asst:* Joe Benn. *Prod Asst:* Amy Perlmutter, Natalie Sara Rooney, Andrew Singer & James F. Reid. *Catering:* The Arrangement. *Craft Services:* Robert Wishnefsky. *Stand-Ins:* Sheila Gale Kandlebinder & John F. MacCarthy. *Sp Eff:* Bruce C. Dalton. *Sp Eff Asst:* Frank L. Pope. *Post Prod Supv:* Alan Jakubowicz & Michael Alden. *Post Prod Coordinator:* Omneya "Nini" Mazen. *First Asst Ed:* Doron Regev. *Second Asst Ed:* Jason Taft & Laura Lee Bong. *Apprentice Ed:* Anthony Bronson. *Supv Sd Ed:* Tony Garber. *Sd Ed:* Birl Van Daalen, Jeffrey L. Sadler, Richard Burton, Albert Gasser, Thierry Courtorier & Tara Lynn Howell. *Foley Ed:* Kurt N. Forshanger. *Asst Sd Ed:* Mark F. Cafolla & Susanne Spain. *Apprentice Sd Ed:* Peter Elliott. *Foley Artists:* Robert Friedman & Theresa Algarin. *Ade/Foley Mixer:* Tommy Goodwin. *Ade/Foley Recordist:* Dean St. John. *Voice Casting:* Burton Sharp. *Re-recording:* Cannon Sound Studio. *Re-recording Mixers:* Patrick Cyccone Jr., Frank A. Montero Jr. & David Cunningham. *Songs:* Craig De Belles, Lisa Raggio, Robert J. Walsh & Shosuke Ichikawa. *Recordists:* Tony Pascuzzo & Tina Canny. *Mus Ed:* Virginia S. Ellsworth & John S. Salandra. *Music Producer & Recorder:* Guy Townley. *Mus Supv:* Joachim C. Hansch. *Mus Coordinator:* Lisa Drew. *Construction Coordinator:* Alan MacRae. *Carpenters:* Greg Rachall, John Reynolds & Theo Van Den Heuuel. *Scenic Painters:* Richard Huston & Donna Slager. *Transportation Coordinators:* Jimmy Jones & Joel Renfro. *Transportation Captain:* Joel Renfro. *Transportation Secretary:* Kat Werner. *Title Design:* Weldon K. Baldwin & Kyle Seidenbaum. *Negative Cutting:* Ronald Vitello & Ann-Marie Vitello. *Main Title & Opticals:* Pacific Titles, *Color Timer:* Angelo Russo. *Color:* TVC.

**CAST:** Charles Bronson (Lieutenant Crowe), Perry Lopez (Eddie Rios), Juan Fernandez (Duke), James Pax (Hiroshi Hada), Peggy Lipton (Kathleen "Cathy" Crowe), Sy Richardson (Lavonne), Marion Kodama Yue (Mr. Karuko Hada), Bill McKinney (Father Burke), Gerald Castillo (Captain Tovar), Nicole Eggert (DeeDee), Amy Hathaway (Rita Crowe), Kumiko Hayakawa (Fumiko Hada), Michelle Wong (Setsuko Hada), Sam Chew Jr. (McLane), Sumant (Pakistani Hotel Clerk), Alex Hyde-White (English Instructor), Jim Ishida (Nakata), Jill Ito (Tokyo Hostess), Leila Lee Olsen (Nobu-Chan), Richard Egan Jr. (Vinnie), Deonca Brown (Louise), Sheila Gale Kandlbinder (Swimming Coach), Chris Bennett (School Photographer), George Van Noy (Swimming Meet Starter), Helen Lin (Tokyo Subway Girl), Richard E. Butler (Deli Owner Joey), James Ogawa (Kokudan Representative), Bill Cho Lee (Ota), Cynthia Crow (Los Angeles Hostess), Veronica Carothers (Blonde Hostess), Alonzo Brown Jr. (Mugger), Michael Chong (Lieutenant Lim), Yung Sun (Gray-Haired Japanese), Shaun Shimoda (Japanese Calligraphy Teacher), Mindy Simon (School Girl), Samuel E. Woods (Vendor), Rob Narita (Japanese School Principal), Yuri Ogawa (Mrs. Ota), Shelli Rae, Jessica Younger (Duke's Girls), William Brochtup (Hairdresser), Laura Crosson (Officer Petrini), Tom Morgan (Krieger), Kim Lee (Porno Actress), Marilyn Frank (Lesbian Pedophile), John F. McCarthy (Porno Theatre Manager), Jerome Thor (Rich Client), Erez Yoaz (Rosario), Robert Axelrod (Security Guard), Elisabeth Chavez (Maria Rios), Simon Maldonaldo (Eddie Rios Jr.), Don Morton

(Turnkey), Jay S. York (Cellmate), Lance Lane, Gary Mitrea, Danny Trejo (Prisoners), Lane Leavitt (Crane Operator), Jophery C. Brown, Clifford Strong (Duke's Thugs).

*Kinjite: Forbidden Subjects* (pronounced Kin-ja-ta) closes a chapter in Charles Bronson's film career. Not only was it his final film of the 1980s but it was also the last one he made before the death of his wife Jill Ireland in 1990. It was also his last feature with producers Menahem Golan and Yoram Globus (he would work with Golan again on *Death Wish V: The Face of Death* in 1994) and their Cannon Group and also the last of his nine films with director J. Lee Thompson. It is also one of his most violent thrillers, a film which features heavy doses of nudity, brutality and profanity. It also had an underlying racial prejudice judging from the fact it featured Japanese, blacks and Hispanics in less than heroic roles. At one point in the film Bronson's character complains about the Japanese taking over the country and, letting off steam, he harasses a group of Japanese people at an ethnic event. On the other hand, *Kinjite* is a harrowing look at the underbelly of child pornography and takes aim at the slime who put little girls on the street as hookers. Solidifying the whole affair is the film's presentation of the clash of Eastern and Western cultures in the confines of crime-ridden Los Angeles. At 68 Charles Bronson proved he was still more than a viable action hero, engaging in several fights and other athletic encounters with the bad guys, when not blowing them away or dropping them off a balcony as he did with one pimp who would not give the whereabouts of his boss. Certainly *Kinjite* contained enough action to satisfy Bronson followers.

In Los Angeles vice squad police Lieutenant Crowe (Charles Bronson) and his partner Eddie Rios (Perry Lopez) bust a man planning to sexually torture a young girl supplied to him by pimp Duke (Juan Fernandez). At the same time in Tokyo businessman Hiroshi Hada (James Pax) is having trouble with his wife (Marion Kodama Yue) but finds out he is being transferred to Los Angeles for three years. Hada and his family, which includes daughters Fumiko (Kumiko Hayakawa) and Setsuko (Michelle Wong), get settled as Crowe corners Duke and makes him eat his $25,000 watch before setting fire to his Cadillac and promising to put him out of business. Later Duke attempts to kill Crowe in a diner but only succeeds in shooting up the place and murdering the owner (Richard E. Butler). After a business dinner, Hada takes the bus home after having too much to drink and he gropes Rita (Amy Hathaway), the 15-year-old daughter of the policeman. Feeling rage at what happened to his daughter, Crowe goes to his priest (Bill McKinney) for help as Duke and cohort Lavonne (Sy Richardson) abduct Fumiko at her school. Duke takes the little girl to his apartment where he initiates her into sex and drugs, grooming her to be one of his prostitutes. Crowe and Rios are assigned to find Fumiko as Duke peddles her to a rich pervert (Jerome Thor) and a

**Advertisement for *Kinjite: Forbidden Subjects* (Cannon Group, 1989).**

lesbian (Marilyn Frank). Getting word that Fumiko has been seen at a downtown hotel, Crowe and Rios raid a room where they find a porno operation making a movie but they do not find the missing child. Crowe asks DeeDee (Nicole Eggert), one of Duke's ex-hookers, for help but she warns the pimp as Crowe tails him to his apartment. Duke and the girls get away but Lavonne ends up being dropped from the balcony by Crowe and Rios when he will not reveal Duke's whereabouts but they do find Fumiko and return her home. In thanks for saving their daughter Hada and his wife bring Rita a present and she recognizes Hada as the man who tried to molest her but says nothing. That day Fumiko commits suicide. Crowe and Rios trace Duke to a boat but before they can catch him their car is deliberately crushed by a crane, killing Rios. Crowe manages to get out of the car unharmed and Duke tries to run him down with his car but it goes out of control and lands in the water. Duke cannot swim and begs Crowe to save him. Later Crowe is with

Duke as he begins his prison term and the policeman makes sure his cellmate is a brutal homosexual. Crowe leaves Duke to his cellmate, what he refers to as poetic justice.

As expected most critics did not care for *Kinjite*, which grossed $3.5 million domestically. *Variety* reported, "Pic unravels at tortuously slow pace, with poor dialog and several howler scenes that ultimately turn it into low camp." *People Weekly* reported, "Bronson seems carved out of wood.... Bronson has let too many formula action flicks drain the life out of him. His acting style is now limited to two expressions: combative and comatose." Janet Maslin said in the *New York Times* that *Kinjite* "is one of Mr. Bronson's better-made if more rabidly xenophobic efforts ... Mr. Bronson seems to require a little more editing help to get through the action sequences than he has before. But in fight scenes he can still manage quite a nice high kick." Richard Harrington complained in the *Washington Post* that the film "could be the worst Charles Bronson film ever, and that's saying something. If it were any slower, it would be running backward.... Bronson seldom acts these days; he simply endures, sleeptalking through his lines." In the *Chicago Sun-Times*, Roger Ebert reported, "Charles Bronson has played so many avenging fathers in so many different movies in the past 15 years that he seems almost to have settled into the role, as William Boyd eventually became Hopalong Cassidy." Ebert called the film "an odd, well-made and thoroughly unpleasant thriller ... Bronson's most polished movie in a long time; it's slimy, but slick." Noting the movie was one of several Bronson had done with director J. Lee Thompson and producer Pancho Kohner, he concluded by saying, "It's ironic that their best-made film is also their most distasteful." *LA Weekly* noted "gritty L.A. locales aren't enough to rescue J. Lee Thompson's film from backsliding into feel-good mayhem and wedding-cake symmetry, into a world of wide-eyed innocents vs. the kind of human pus who gave up just saying no a long time ago." In the *Los Angeles Herald-Examiner*, Andy Klein wrote, "Consider this for a moment: Charles Bronson is 68 years old. That's right: older than Peter Ustinov, older than Wilford Brimley, older than most of the Golden Girls. But here he is, in *Kinjite (Forbidden Subjects)*, yet one more action thriller, ready to kick ... well, you know what he's ready to kick. If you're only as old as you feel, Bronson is feeling young. And mean." He added, "As an action film, *Kinjite* is competently made...." Michael Wilmington in the *Los Angeles Times* called *Kinjite* "just another Charles Bronson thriller—a bit sleazier and more repellent than most—in which Bronson is put through his patented paces and car chases by director J. Lee Thompson, a brazen old pro who apparently doesn't care any more who he offends." Noting that Bronson and Thompson had made nine films together since *St. Ives* (1976), he said this one was "the strangest, most intense of the lot." He also called it "a pretty odd, murky stew. If you think you might be offended by it, don't go. You will be." In the same newspaper, Charles Champlin said *Kinjite* "is a fairly standard mix of heavy action and sleazy villains, but it does have quieter, subtler moments when the culture shock is seen from both sides of the gulf and some violence, at least, is forestalled."

*Kinjite: Forbidden Subjects'* title refers to subjects (such as sex, child molesting, prostitution) which are forbidden topics in Japanese culture.

Following the release of *Kinjite* early in 1989, Charles Bronson ended his association with Cannon Group. Although he still had two movies to do for the company he voluntarily remained off screen for over two years while his wife Jill Ireland fought a valiant, but losing, battle with cancer. She died in 1990 and the next year NBC-TV telecast the movie *Reason to Live: The Jill Ireland Story* starring Jill Clayburgh as Jill Ireland and Lance Henriksen as Charles Bronson. He returned to the screen that year in *The Indian Runner.*

***Lola*** see *Twinky*

## *Love and Bullets* (Associated Film Distribution Corporation, 1979) 103 minutes Color

*P:* Pancho Kohner. *EP:* Sir Lew Grade. *D:* Stuart Rosenberg. *Sc:* Wendell Mayes & John Melson. *Ph:* Fred Koenekamp & Anthony Richmond. *Ed:* Michael Anderson. *Mus:* Lalo Schifrin. *Asst Dir:* Jack Aldworth. *Prod Design:* John De Cuir. *Prod Mgr:* Hal Klein. *Prod Supv:* George Van Noy. *Dialogue Coach:* Robert Easton. *AD:* Colin Grimes. *Wardrobe:* Ron Beck. *Women's Costumer:* Yvonne Kubis. *Men's Costumer:* Ed Wyrigear. *Asst AD:* George Richardson. *Casting:* Hilary Holden. *Wardrobe Mistress:* Janet Tebrooke. *Hairdresser:* Vivienne Walker. *Sp Eff:* Richard Parker & Gene Gregg. *Re-recording Mixer:* Tex Rudoloff. *Still Photographers:* Paul Ronald & Kenny Bell. *Sd Eff:* Jack Cheap, Paul Hochman & Dan Walden. *Prod Accountants:* Ruth West & John Beharrell. *Electrical Supv:* Martin Evans. *Prod Coordinators:* Virginia Cook, Iris Rose & Dominique Lefevre. *Prod Secretary:* Terri Farnsworth. *Gaffer:* Gene Stout. *Key Gaffers:* John Murray & John West Sr. *Set Decorators:* Richard Goddard & Joe Chevalier. *Second Asst Dir:* Benjamin Rosenberg & Robert T. Ortwin. *Asst Ed:* John W. Carr, Chuck Ellison & William Zaballa. *Costumes:* Dorothy Jeakins. *Camera Operators:* Gordon Hayden, Colin Corby, Mike Benson & Steve Yaconelli. *Property Masters:* John Chisholm & Earl Huntoon. *Prod Asst:* Terry Buchinsky. *Prod Mgr:* George Casati & Basil Rayburn. *Associated Ed:* Stanford C. Allen. *Publicist:* Earl Anderson. *Asst Publicist:* Anthony Huston. *Mus Ed:* Ken Hall. *Sd Prod:* John Bramwell & Gene Garvin. *Transportation Coordinator:* Frank Ballou, *Makeup:* Philip Rhodes & Joe Di Bella. *Stunt Coordinator:* Bennie Dobbins. *Sc Supv:* Hope Williams. *Set Design:* Russ Menzer.

**CAST:** Charles Bronson (Lieutenant Charlie Congers), Jill Ireland (Jackie Pruit), Rod Steiger (Joe Bomposa), Henry Silva (Vittorio Farroni), Bradford Dillman (FBI Agent Brickman), Strother Martin (Louis Monk), Michael V. Gazzo (Lobo), Paul Koslo (Huntz), Sam Chew (Cook), Val Avery (Caruso), William [Billy] Gray (Patrolman Mike Durant), Andy Romano (FBI Agent Marty), Robin Clarke (FBI Agent George), Albert Salmi (FBI Chief), Cliff Fellows (Police Captain), Lorraine Chase (Farroni's Girlfriend), Joe Roman (Carpenter), Alan

Brye (Freddo), Rik Colletti (Carlo), Jerome Thor (Senator), Richard Gideon (Council), Ramon Chavez (Mexican Policeman), Joe Bellucci (Albain), Karen Wyeth (Stewardess), James Keane (Director), John Hallan (Council), Sidney Keene (Manchoni), Remy Julienne (Stunt Driver), Ray Le Fre, Richard Brose, Lon Carli (Gangsters).

*Love and Bullets* was Charles Bronson's first feature film in over a year since *Telefon* had been released late in 1977. This new feature premiered in London in March 1979 some 15 months later. Oddly enough, *Love and Bullets* (filmed as *Love and Bullets, Charlie*) was completed early in 1978 but kept on the shelf while new projects for the star could be developed. The film was supposed to be the first of four Bronson was to do for producer Sir Lew Grade and it was announced he would appear with Sophia Loren in *Firepower* (1979) for director Michael Winner, but the male lead was played by James Coburn. When *Love and Bullets* was finally released it drew a critical lambasting while drawing no more than average attention from U.S. moviegoers, although, as expected, it did well overseas. While more than a competently made production the film simply did not jell. Its main drawbacks were co-stars Jill Ireland and Rod Steiger. Here Mrs. Bronson was cast as a hillbilly girl who is the mistress of a big time mobster. Jill Ireland was simply out of her element although she probably did as well with the part as anyone could have, the role would even have flattened Garbo. Rod Steiger, as the stuttering Mafioso who likes Jeanette MacDonald and Nelson Eddy movies, has to be Bronson's quirkiest co-star since Anthony Perkins in *Quelqu'un Derrière la Porte* (1971). Still *Love and Bullets* is moderately entertaining and unlike some movies it gets better with each viewing.

When the pretty fiancée of a policeman (William Gray) is given a drug overdose by gangsters, the lawman is comforted by his superior, Lieutenant Charlie Congers (Charles Bronson). Local gangster Joe Bomposa (Rod Steiger) is behind all the illegal activities in Phoenix and the young cop vows to kill him. Charlie warns him to forget the idea but the young man returns to his car only to be mortally wounded in an explosion. Charlie is then asked by the FBI to go to Switzerland and smuggle out Bomposa's mistress, Jackie Pruit (Jill Ireland), who other mobsters want out of the way because they are afraid she will testify about the rackets. She is guarded by two of Bomposa's hoods, Lobo (Michael V. Gazzo) and Huntz (Paul Koslo), in a chateau. Charlie arrives in Switzerland to get the girl while Huntz finds out Lobo has turned FBI informant and kills him. Thinking Charlie is a confederate of Bomposa, Jackie leaves with him while back in the States the gangster's lawyer Monk (Strother Martin) tells him he has no choice but to have the girl killed. A contract is put out on her with hit man Vittorio Farroni (Henry Silva), who also hires Huntz. As they flee, Jackie realizes Charlie is a cop and he tells her that Bomposa wants her killed. Farroni and Huntz get on their trail but Charlie kills two of their confederates. After they take sanctuary in a deserted farmhouse, Charlie is forced to kill Farroni's henchman and they flee across country finally boarding

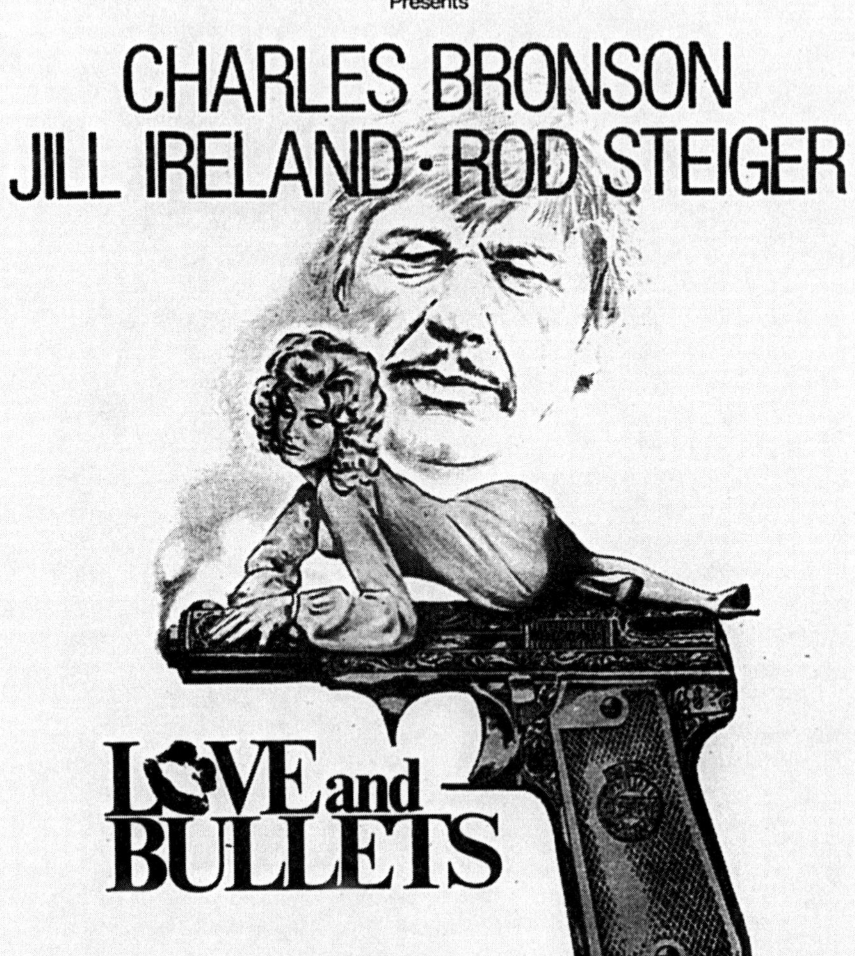


Poster for *Love and Bullets* (Associated Film Distribution Corporation, 1979).

a train. Stopping at a hotel, Charlie rigs up a blow gun device which he uses to kill three more of his followers as he and Jackie escape by boat to Geneva. There they are met by FBI Agent Brickman (Bradford Dillman) but Farroni and Huntz are also there and Huntz kills Jackie before being gunned down by lawmen. Back in the U.S. Charlie is chewed out by the FBI chief (Albert Salmi) for leaving a trail of corpses all over Switzerland and he is also told to stay away from Bomposa. Meanwhile the gangster chief has put out a contract on Farroni as Charlie forces Monk to reveal who paid for Jackie's killing. Charlie and Jackie had been lovers on the boat where he learned she was innocent of mob activities. Pretending to be a mortuary worker, Charlie brings a coffin to Bomposa's mansion saying it contains Jackie's body and it was sent by Farroni. As Bomposa reads the card on the coffin which says, "Love and Bullets, Charlie," he opens the lid and an explosion blows up his home.

To show Jill Ireland's character is Southern she affects an Arkansas accent and wears a beehive wig. She also listens to Tammy Wynette sing "Stand By Your Man." To show Bomposa's cultural bent he is seen watching Jeanette MacDonald and Nelson Eddy in *New Moon* (1940) as they sing "Wanting You."

*The Hollywood Press* called *Love and Bullets* "one of those star-stuffed travelogues" but thought it "does afford Rod Steiger with the best part he's had since his Oscar-winning turn in *In the Heat of the Night*." *Variety* noted, "Refreshing to report, this essentially family thriller refrains from gratuitous sadism and nudity.... At worst, *Love and Bullets* is bland and fails to thrill. But it's never offensive." The *Los Angeles Times* said the movie "is an instance of familiar made diverting through some decent writing, taut direction and solid principal performances by Charles Bronson, Jill Ireland and Rod Steiger.... Indeed, this modest venture is one of the best of the Bronson–Ireland efforts." Peter Rainer wrote in the *Los Angeles Herald-Examiner*, "The one virtue of *Love and Bullets* is that, despite soupy direction, listless plotting, overscaled acting and blotchy cinematography, Bronson doesn't go soft on us." The *New York News* said, "Improbable is the key word for this one ... Bronson has killed on screen with far more purpose than in this one." Richard Freedman in the *Newark (New Jersey) Star-Ledger* noted, "For all its silliness, *Love and Bullets* has several virtues" and he said Bronson "can get more mileage out of not showing any facial expression than any other actor around, with the possible exception of Clint Eastwood." *Entertainment Today* opined of the film's star, "This tough-guy-with-a-soft-center personality Bronson radiates on-screen is an important key to his phenomenal success. He is one of the top-grossing actors of all time."

British prints of *Love and Bullets* were a few minutes shy of footage which the censor removed. It showed Charles Bronson putting together a blowgun using such items as part of a lamp, nail and paper. Also of note is that actor Michael V. Gazzo, who played the crusty-voiced informant Lobo, was the author of the noted play, *A Hatful of Rain*.

## *Machine Gun Kelly* (American International Pictures, 1958)

84 minutes B/W

*P-D:* Roger Corman. *EP:* James H. Nicholson & Samuel Z. Arkoff. *Sc:* R. Wright Campbell. *Ph:* Floyd Crosby. *Ed:* Ronald Sinclair. *Mus:* Gerald Fried. *AD:* Dan [Daniel] Haller. *Sets:* Harry Reif. *Prod Mgr:* Maurice Vaccarino. *Asst Dir:* Jack Bohrer. *Sd:* Philip Mitchell. *Makeup:* Dave Newell. *Wardrobe:* Marge Corso. *Property Master:* Karl Brainard. *Title Design:* Bill Martin.

**CAST:** Charles Bronson (George "Machine Gun" Kelly), Susan Cabot (Flo), Morey Amsterdam (Fandango), Jack Lambert (Howard), Wally Campo (Maize), Barboura Morris (Lynn Grayson), Richard Devon (Apple), Frank De Kova (Harry), Connie Gilchrist (Ma), Dawn Menzer (Cheryl Vito), George Archambeault (Frank), Bob Griffin (Andrew Vito), Larry Thor (Drummond), Ted Thorp (Teddy), Shirley Falls (Martha), Mike Fox (Clinton), Jay Sayer (Philip Ashton), Mitzi McCall (Harriet).

*Machine Gun Kelly* was made at a time when screen biographies about real life gangsters were very popular. The vogue had started in the mid–1950s with the release to theatres of films like *Gangbusters* (1955) and *Guns Don't Argue* (1957), made up to footage from television programs, and it hit its stride with the popular TV series *The Untouchables* (ABC-TV, 1959–1963). Among the era's big screen gangster biopics were *Baby Face Nelson* (1957), *The Rise and Fall of Legs Diamond* (1959), *Al Capone* (1959), *Mad Dog Coll* (1959), *Ma Barker's Killer Brood* (1960) and *Pretty Boy Floyd* (1960). *Machine Gun Kelly* was double-billed with *The Bonnie Parker Story* starring Dorothy Provine and both films got a boost by having their stars headlining television series; Charles Bronson in *Man with a Camera* (ABC-TV, 1958–1960) and Dorothy Provine's *The Roaring Twenties* (ABC-TV, 1960–1962). Still the double bill mainly played drive-ins and small theatres and it was not until *Machine Gun Kelly* was released in France in 1963 that critics really began to notice not only the film but also its star. The first momentum that would lead to international stardom for Charles Bronson began with his portrayal of George "Machine Gun" Kelly.

The film carries a statement saying the title character is based on a real person while everyone else in the film is fictional. Actually *Machine Gun Kelly* is a thinly veiled account of hoodlum George R. Kelly who was a small time bootlegger until he married Kathryn Coleman Thorne in 1927. After that she publicized him as a major bank robber proficient with a machine gun, thus his nickname. In 1933 they kidnapped an Oklahoma businessman and demanded a $200,000 ransom. Two months later they were captured in Memphis, Tennessee, and George spent the rest of his life in prison, dying in Alcatraz in 1954 at the age of 57. Kathryn was released from prison in 1958, the year *Machine Gun Kelly* was issued, thus the need for the film's opening disclaimer.

The movie opens with Machine Gun Kelly (Charles Bronson) and

**Poster for *Machine Gun Kelly* (American International Pictures, 1958).**

cohorts Howard (Jack Lambert) and Maize (Wally Campo) successfully pulling off a bank heist with Fandango (Morey Amsterdam) as the bag man. The gang splits up for their escape with Kelly going with girlfriend Flo (Susan Cabot) to a service station operated by Harry (Frank De Kova), a drunk who was once a big game hunter. When Harry tries to get money from Kelly by scaring him with a mountain lion he has captured, Kelly beats him badly. Later at a meeting to split the stolen loot, Kelly finds out Fandango has tried to hold out on some of the loot. Kelly meets Fandango by the cat's cage and pushes him into it, causing Fandango to lose his left arm. The next robbery the gang plans is muffed when Kelly becomes scared after two men carry a coffin across his path. Howard is forced to shoot a teller and in the getaway Maize is killed by the police, but Howard escapes. Kelly and Flo hide out at a brothel run by her mother Ma (Connie Gilchrist) and father Frank (George Archambeault) where Flo learns from Philip Ashton (Jay Sayer), a friend of Fandango's, that Howard has joined a new gang and plans to kill Kelly. As a result, Kelly surprises the gang as they are playing cards and guns them down with his machine gun, killing them all, including Howard. Next Kelly plans a kidnapping caper and he and Flo abduct little Cheryl Vito (Dawn Menzer) and her nurse Lynn Grayson (Barboura Morris) and demand a $100,000 ransom from the girl's steel magnate father (Bob Griffin). Joining in the kidnapping is hoodlum Apple (Richard Devon) who tries to molest Lynn as they hide out at a remote cabin. Kelly stops Apple but the gang has to flee when a local cop spots New York license plates on Flo's car. They take refuge at Harry's place and there Flo makes up to Apple and turns on Kelly, calling him a coward. Apple beats up Kelly but the latter kills him and then calls Fandango to make the ransom money pickup. Kelly plans to take half the ransom money and kill the child and her nurse so that he and Flo can leave the country. Fandango is picked up for questioning by federal agents but gives them the slip and then gets the ransom money. Harry, however, trails him and forces Fandango to drive to his place where Kelly is waiting for the money. When the feds surround the place, Harry shoots Fandango who admitted leading them there, but is killed by a lawman's bullet. Kelly turns yellow and wants to give up but Flo starts shooting and Kelly knocks her out. The feds break into the house and rescue Cheryl and Lynn, taking Kelly and Flo into custody.

At 84 minutes, *Machine Gun Kelly* is a compact and thoroughly entertaining gangster yarn enhanced by a fine cast and an actionful script. Especially effective are Floyd Crosby's fluid photography and Gerald Fried's bouncy music score. The highlight of the movie, though, is its performances, topped by Charles Bronson's work as Machine Gun Kelly. He presents the gangster as a cold-blooded conniver who alternates between cowardice and sympathy. He is shown bullying the cripple Harry and the effeminate Fandango, squirming under the thumb of the ambitious Flo, being the victim of his own superstitions, and as a coward. Yet he shows Kelly as an intelligent planner who seems to have a soft spot for the child he kidnaps, even though he plans to kill her. A memorable scene has Kelly afraid of the captured mountain cat when he thinks it can get out of its cage but when he finds it cannot he spits soda pop in its face and later torments the caged animal by throwing rocks at it. At the finale when they are surrounded by the law, Kelly tells Flo, "Why die for nothing." When captured, the federal agents ask Kelly why he did not fight and he replies, "Because I knew you'd kill me." As he is being led away one of the agents called him "pop gun Kelly."

Susan Cabot gives one of her best screen performances as the manipulative and seductive Flo and Morey Amsterdam is very good as the double-crossing Fandango, who Kelly derisively calls "Fanny." Frank De Kova is quite good as the alcoholic henchman, as is Connie Gilchrist as Flo's smart-mouthed mother, who runs a brothel but shows sympathy to the kidnapped little girl. Jack Lambert and Richard Devon are good as cold-blooded cohorts of Kelly who end up being killed by their boss and Barboura Morris nicely underplays the role of the child's nanny.

A minor mistake can be spotted in *Machine Gun Kelly*. Although the feature takes place in the 1930s, a scene in a federal agent's office has a picture of J. Edgar Hoover on the wall, although the photograph is obviously a recent one, taken a quarter of a century after the events portrayed in the film took place.

Produced in eight days on a budget of less than $200,000, *Machine Gun Kelly* garnered only slight critical attention when it was released. *Variety* thought it "a first-rate little picture" adding, "Bronson gives a brooding, taut performance that somehow takes the curse off the character without lessening the horror of the casual slayings." In retrospect producer-director Roger Corman said in *The Movie World of Roger Corman* by Philip di Franco (1979) that Bronson "was excellent. It is a further testimony to his gifts as an actor when you remember that there was almost no rehearsal time, and we very seldom went beyond a second or third take—this had to be the rule on those limited shooting schedules."

Corman made the film because American International bosses James H. Nicholson and Samuel Z. Arkoff wanted a gangster film and George Kelly was chosen because he had been the FBI's Most Wanted Man after the 1933 kidnapping of wealthy oilman Charles F. Urschel. Scripter R. Wright Campbell fashioned his screenplay to star his brother William Campbell. Although Dick Miller had been the initial choice for the title role, the part finally went to Charles Bronson. It is claimed that Alain Delon screened *Machine Gun Kelly* when he was looking for a co-star for the film *Adieu l'Ami* (1968) and chose Charles Bronson, who he knew slightly due to their mutual interest in art, because of his performance as Machine Gun Kelly.

## *The Magnificent Seven* (United Artists, 1960) 129 minutes Color

*P-D:* John Sturges. *EP:* Walter Mirisch. *AP:* Lou Morheim. *Sc:* William Roberts. *Ph:* Charles Lang Jr. *Ed:* Ferris Webster. *Mus:* Elmer Bernstein. *AD:* Edward Fitzgerald. *Sets:* Rafael Suarez. *Prod Mgr:* Chico Day. *Asst Dir:* Robert Relyea & Jaime Contreras. *Sd:* Jack Lawrence & Rafael Esparza. *Makeup:* Emile La Vigne & Daniel Striepke. *Sp Eff:* Milt Rice. *Prod Supv:* Allen K. Wood. *Property:* Sam Gordon. *Sp Eff Ed:* Del Harris. *Dialogue Dir:* Thom Conroy. *Script Continuity:* John Franco.

CAST: Yul Brynner (Chris), Eli Wallach (Calvera), Steve McQueen (Vin), Charles Bronson (Bernardo O'Reilly), Robert Vaughn (Lee), Horst Buchholz (Chico), Brad Dexter (Harry Luck), James Coburn (Britt), Vladimir Sokoloff (Old Man), Rosenda Monteros (Petra), Jorge Martinez de Hoyos (Hilario), Whit Bissell (Undertaker Charmlee), Val Avery (Henry), Bing Russell (Robert), Rico Alaniz (Sotero), Robert Wilke (Wallace), Alex Montoya (Cowboy), Natividad Vacio, Pepe Hern, Mario Navarro, Danny Bravo, John Alonso, Enrique Nicerno (Villagers).

Charles Bronson kicked off the 1960s theatrically with a blockbuster, *The Magnificent Seven*. Not only was the film a big box office success but it also gave the actor a memorable role, one that eventually paved his way to stardom. Again he worked with director John Sturges with whom he had just done *Never So Few* (1959). Unlike that film, however, the actor had a part with which the audience could identify, that of an Irish-Mexican mercenary with a soft spot for children. Shown to be a powerful, intelligent man, his Bernardo O'Reilly is given good advantage throughout the feature and Bronson is particularly effective in the scenes where he gives a little girl a whistle he has just whittled and when he tells three boys their fathers are not cowards. He explains to the youngsters that he is really much more of a coward than their fathers because they accept the responsibility for their families while he has never had the courage to do more than fight for a living. Regarding the film's fine cast, *Variety* noted, "Bronson fashions the most sympathetic character of the group."

A gang of bandits led by Calvera (Eli Wallach) make their annual raid on the Orozco peasants in the Mexican province of Cuernavaca. The villagers decide the next time they will fight and three of them head to a border town where they see gunman Chris (Yul Brynner) team with drifter Vin (Steve McQueen) in taking the body of an Indian to boot hill for burial while standing up to townsmen who oppose this action. The three farmers ask Chris to aid them against the bandits and he finally agrees and enlists the aid of Vin, old pal Harry Luck (Brad Dexter), mercenary Bernardo O'Reilly (Charles Bronson), knife expert Britt (James Coburn) and bounty hunter Lee (Robert Vaughn). On the way to the village they are joined by another young man, Chico (Horst Buchholz). On arrival they kill three bandit spies and then begin teaching the villagers how to defend themselves. When Chico captures pretty Petra (Rosenda Monteros) Chris realizes the villagers have hidden their women from them and orders them to be returned to the village. When the bandits arrive they are met with force from the mercenaries and the villagers, suffering heavy losses, although Calvera escapes into the hills. Chico infiltrates the gang and finds they are starving and planning another attack to get food. Hoping to weaken them further Chris and his men head to the bandits' camp in order to scare off their horses. Upon arrival they do not find the gang and return to the village only to be surrounded by Calvera and his men. Saying he does not want trouble from the United States, Calvera offers to let the seven go without their weapons, which he will later return to them, and they accept. The seven men ride away from the village but after Calvera's man returns their guns they decide to go back to the village for a final showdown, although Harry rides off by himself. The remaining six men attack the village and shoot it out with the gang. When Chris is about to be shot, Harry returns to save him but is himself mortally wounded. Also killed are Lee, Britt and O'Reilly. Chris kills Calvera as the villagers rise up to defend their village and the gang is defeated. Chris and Vin ride away while Chico stays with Petra.

Advertisement for *The Magnificent Seven* (United Artists, 1960).

An adaptation of the classic 1954 Japanese film *The Seven Samurai*, directed by Akira Kurosawa, *The Magnificent Seven* was filmed in Panavision and DeLuxe Color. With its strong cast, beautiful panoramas and Elmer Bernstein's memorable music score (which sadly was later used on television to advertise a tobacco product), the film, despite its careful pacing and two hours plus running time, was highly entertaining and quite exciting. Its success kept Charles Bronson in the $50,000 per picture salary range and enabled him to sign with the powerful MCA agency for exclusive representation.

Despite audience popularity, the film itself met with mixed critical reaction. The *New York Times* called it "A loud, pretentious and overlong Western-style shoot-'em-up.... There's an endless, dawdling prologue and William Roberts' scenario increasingly blunts the action with philosophical talk and some easy cliches." *Time* magazine said, "*Seven* is not a great picture—not nearly as good as the Japanese *Magnificent Seven*.... Nevertheless, it is the best western released so far in 1960, a skillful, exciting, and occasionally profound contemplation of the life of violence." *Newsweek* asserted, "The result is a hard-pounding adventure movie full of exciting characters and topped off with a message that goes down as easily as nutmeg in an eggnog.... The acting is strong and individual, and Elmer Bernstein has provided a sturdy score, while Sturges' direction sets some nice, small touches against his nice, big Mexican background." Tony Thomas wrote in *The Great Adventure Films* (1976), "*The Magnificent Seven* should not be made the subject of academic discussion. It's an adventure yarn with some fine action sequences, good color photography by Charles Lang Jr. of rugged Mexican settings and most conspicuously a music score by Elmer Bernstein that is not so much background as up-front."

Charles Bronson would again work with director John Sturges in *The Great Escape* (1963) and *Valdez il Mezzosangue (Chino)* (1973).

*The Magnificent Seven* would have three follow-up theatrical features: Yul Brynner in *Return of the Seven* (1966), George Kennedy headlining *Guns of the Magnificent Seven* (1969) and Lee Van Cleef in *The Magnificent Seven Ride!* in 1972.

## *The Marrying Kind* (Columbia, 1952) 92 minutes B/W

*P:* Bert Granet. *D:* George Cukor. *Sc:* Ruth Gordon & Garson Kanin. *Ph:* Joseph Walker. *Ed:* Charles Nelson. *Mus:* Hugo Friedhofer. *AD:* John Meehan. *Sets:* William Kiernan. *Sd:* Jay Goodrich. *Makeup:* Clay Campbell. *Asst Dir:* Earl Bellamy. *Mus Dir:* Morris Stoloff. *Gowns:* Jean Louis. *Hair Styles:* Helen Hunt. *Second Unit Dir:* Harry Howe & Larry Buchanan.

**CAST:** Judy Holliday (Florence Keefer), Aldo Ray (Chet Keefer), Madge Kennedy (Judge Carroll), Sheila Bond (Joan Shipley), John Alexander (Howard Shipley), Rex Williams (George Bastian), Phyllis Povah (Mrs.

Derringer), Peggy Cass (Emily Bundy), Mickey Shaughnessy (Pat Bundy), Griff Barnett (Charlie), Susan Halloran (Ellen), Wallace Acton (Newhouse), Elsie Holmes (Marian), Joan Shawlee (Dancer), Barry Curtis (Younger Joey), Christie Olsen (Older Joey), Thomas Browne Henry (Mr. Jenner), Frank Ferguson (Mr. Quinn), Don Mahin (Roy), Larry Blake (Benny), Tom Farrell (Cliff), Gordon Jones (Steve), John Elliott (Minister), Joe McGuinn (Bus Driver), Richard Gordon (Lawyer), Patrick Butler (Child), Malna Mills (Charlotte), Charles Buchinski (Eddie), Nancy Kulp (Edie), Robert Hartley, Charles Brewer, Johnnie Kiado (Musicians), Mary Chamberlain (Leona), Jean Wardley (Peggy), James MacColl (Subway Man), George Auld (Spec), Raymond Largay (Postmaster General), Frank Krigg (Hank), Ethan Laidlaw, Robert Evans, Guy Teague, Allen Pinson, Alexis Davinoff, Jeffrey Sayre, John Sheffield, Margaret Roberts, Tommy Kingston, Ethel Sway, Kathleen Field, Shirlee Allard, Vera Burnett, Terry Kingston, Clint Dorrington, William O'Brien, Alan Marston, Carl Laviness.

Judy Holliday's follow-up to her Academy Award–winning performance in *Born Yesterday* (1950) was this comedy-drama which launched the 40 year starring career of Aldo Ray, who had previously done bits billed under his own name, Aldo Da Rae, and as John Harrison. Held over from *Born Yesterday*, which Ms. Holliday first popularized on Broadway, were director George Cukor, co-scripter Garson Kanin and cinematographer Joseph Walker. *The Marrying Kind* was a major success for Columbia Pictures, although it garnered mixed notices. For Charles Bronson it provided only a brief bit as Eddie, a post office co-worker of Aldo Ray's character Chet Keefer.

*The Marrying Kind* opens at a divorce court hearing presided over by Judge Carroll (Madge Kennedy) who listens to the stories of an estranged couple, Florence (Judy Holliday) and Chet Keefer (Aldo Ray). They each relate their side of the drama beginning with their meeting in a park, quick courtship and marriage, and their married life, including the death of a son in an accident, and the events which led to the breakup of their marriage. Told in flashbacks with dream sequences, the movie alternated between high comedy and tragedy but managed to retain a proper balance needed for good entertainment value, thanks in part to the two stars and a fine supporting cast.

Bosley Crowther in the *New York Times* felt the film "will undoubtedly stand up as one of the happiest entertainments of the year." *Variety* said the movie owed much of its success to the teaming of Judy Holliday and Aldo Ray: "The pairing is a good one in meeting requirements of plot characters, and the team does excellently in carrying out story and directorial aims." *Time* said it "is the kind of picture that is best described as average" while Manny Farber wrote in *The Nation*, "(George) Cukor is a fine technician who has lately been imagining himself as an American Rossellini.... The actors make Anna Magnani seem soft-spoken and even tempered." *Newsweek* noted "the film's chief claim to verisimilitude stems from the flashes of perceptive writing by the Kanins and from the performances of the two principal players."

# *Master of the World* (American International Pictures, 1961)

104 minutes Color

*P:* James H. Nicholson. *EP:* Samuel Z. Arkoff. *D:* William Witney. *SC:* Richard Matheson, from the novels *Master of the World* and *Robur the Conqueror* by Jules Verne. *Ph:* Gil Warrenton. *Ed:* Anthony Carras. *Mus:* Les Baxter. *AD:* Daniel Haller. *Sets:* Harry Reif. *Makeup:* Fred Philips. *Sd:* Karl Zint, Bill Warmarth, Vinnie Vernon & Jerry Alexander. *Song:* Les Baxter & Lenny Adelson. *Orchestration:* Albert Harris. *Special Props & Eff:* Pat Dinga. *Wardrobe:* Marjorie Corso. *Asst Dir:* Robert Agnew. *Sp Eff:* Tim Barr, Wah Chang & Gene Warren. *Photographic Eff:* Ray Mercer. *Aerial Photography:* Kay Norton.

**CAST:** Vincent Price (Robur), Charles Bronson (John Strock), Henry Hull (Mr. Prudent), Mary Webster (Dorothy Prudent), David Frankham (Philip Evans), Richard Harrison (Alistair), Vito Scotti (Topage), Wally Campo (Mr. Turner), Steve Masino (Weaver), Ken [Kenneth] Terrell (Shanks), Peter Besbas (Wilson), Gordon Jones (Townsman).

American International Pictures, for whom Charles Bronson had starred in *Machine Gun Kelly* in 1958, produced this medium budget science-fiction feature in one of its initial attempts to break away from "B" features. Thanks to Daniel Haller's superb art direction and Gil Warrenton's lensing in Magna-Color, *Master of the World*, based on two Jules Verne novels, is a pleasant feature to watch. Its plot, however, is somewhat convoluted and at past 100 minutes in running time, the feature has trouble retaining viewer interest. Fortunately the five lead players do well by their roles, compensating for the overall emptiness of the proceedings.

Filmed at Republic Studios with process shots done over the High Sierras, *Master of the World* benefits from the handsome looking airship, the *Albatross*, but is hurt by poor special effects, especially when the vessel is shown flying over various locales or against mountain backdrops. Publicity for the film claimed that part of the shooting was done on a small stage where the temperature hit 120 degrees until wind machines blowing over ice were utilized to drop the temperature eight degrees!

Some sources have indicated that Charles Bronson was not happy being cast in *Master of the World* but, if so, this certainly does not show in his performance. *Film Daily* said he was "excellent … imbuing his role with quiet charm…." The *New York Times* said, "The hero, quietly played by Charles Bronson, is a likeable type, homely, modest, and altogether noble." Bill Warren wrote in *Keep Watching the Skies!, Volume II* (1986), "Bronson is, in fact, excellent as the atypical hero. The part was written as a standard apparent-coward-but-true-hero, often seen in war films, prison pictures, and the like, but Bronson plays Strock in a manner effectively at odds with (Richard) Matheson's rather shallow characterization. Bronson is relaxed, controlled and confident at all times; despite his homeliness, it's easy to understand why the heroine is so swiftly attracted to him."

*Master of the World* starts with a black and white comedy prologue about early flying contraptions and then begins its story in 1868 in Morgantown, Pennsylvania, where the citizens are frightened by what they believe is the voice of God and jolts from a nearby mountain crater. In Philadelphia government agent John Strock (Charles Bronson) goes to the Welden Balloon Society and asks the aid of Mr. Prudent (Henry Hull), a wealthy munitions manufacturer, in the use of his balloon in observing the crater from the air. Going along on the flight are Prudent's pretty daughter Dorothy (Mary Webster) and her fiancé Philip Evans (David Frankham), the balloon's co-builder. Upon reaching the site a rocket from the crater shoots down the balloon which crashes. When the quartet awakens they find they are on a flying ship, the *Albatross*, piloted by Robur (Vincent Price). When Robur attacks an American vessel and destroys it with bombs he declares he is using his ship to rid the world of warfare. When the ship hovers over Ireland to take on water, Prudent, Dorothy and Philip plan to escape but Strock, knowing they will fail, tells Robur who punishes Philip by forcing him to hang from the balloon by a rope. When Prudent is given the same punishment, Strock takes his place and he saves Philip's life when the latter's rope breaks. Prudent offers Robur ten million dollars and amnesty to turn his ship over to the United States. Robur refuses as does Strock when the former asks him to join his cause. Robur then destroys naval fleets in several world capitals while the four captives agree to sabotage the airship. While trying to stop a war in Egypt, Robur is injured when a bomb explodes too close to the craft. The vessel is damaged but manages to stay aloft. When the ship anchors at an island for repairs, the captives make their move and Strock sets off a fuse linked to gun powder. Prudent and his daughter make their escape by sliding down the anchor coil but Evans, who is jealous of Strock, stays behind and knocks him out before escaping. When he comes to, Strock also slides down the coil but is wounded by one of the crewmen. Making it to land he is aided by Evans as they cut the coil rope and the ship rises just as the explosion takes place. The captives are safe on land and Robur gives orders to abandon ship but his loyal crew refuses and joins him in the *Albatross*' last moments.

Vincent Price and Charles Bronson shared top star billing in *Master of the World* and just as Bronson's hero was no stereotype, neither was Price's Robur. While not totally sane, the character was far from a villainous madman who used his futuristic ship and its armaments in an effort to bring about world peace by forcefully ending global conflicts. Like Bronson, Vincent Price did a fine job with a multi-layered characterization. Henry Hull played the role of the munitions manufacturer in a zestful manner while comely Mary Webster was fine as the young woman who finds herself falling in love with Bronson's character, Strock. David Frankham nicely handles the role of the jealous fiancé while some comedy relief is provided by Vito Scotti as the harried ship's cook. Wally Campo is also good as Robur's loyal assistant, Mr. Turner.

Critical reaction to *Master of the World* was decidedly mixed. *Film Daily* called it "an opulent mixture of spectacle and fantasy that results in an entertainment delight for the entire family" while *Variety* terms it a "Fairly lavish production based on the Jules Verne fantasy, but sluggishly paced and loosely written." The *New York Herald-Tribune* felt the film was "well below the level of interest adult moviegoers would expect" while the *Monthly Film Bulletin* thought it "watered down Jules Verne." In *Science Fiction* (1984), Phil Hardy wrote, "Script and direction are both surprisingly lightweight, perhaps because the problem of unifying the mood of the two novels was so great. The first (published in 1886) sees Robur as a visionary and idealist, the second (published in 1904) marks Verne's growing disenchantment and conceives of its hero as a clumsy, power-hungry megalomaniac. These tensions are repressed in the film in favor of an atmosphere in which adventure dominates." Donald C. Willis in *Horror and Science Fiction Films: A Checklist* (1972) thought it "Fairly enjoyable."

While most countries saw release of *Master of the World* during the 1961-62 film season, it was not shown in France until 1972, no doubt then due to Charles Bronson's international popularity.

## *The Meanest Men in the West* (Universal, 1976) 92 minutes Color

*P:* Charles Marquis Warren & Joel Rogosin. *AP:* David Levinson. *D:* Samuel Fuller & Charles S. Dubin. *Sc:* Ed Waters & Samuel Fuller. *Ph:* Lionel Lindon, Enzo A. Martinelli & Alric Eden. *Ed:* Gene Palmer & Jean-Jacques Bertholet. *Mus:* Hal Mooney. *AD:* George Patrick. *Sets:* John McCarthy, Glen L. Daniels & James M. Walters Jr. *Asst Dir:* George Risk & Lou Watt. *Makeup:* Bud Westmore & Leo Lotito. *Hair Stylists:* Larry Germain & Florence Bush. *Unit Prod Mgr:* Abby Singer & Frank Arrigo. *Color Consultant:* Robert Brower. *Color Coordinator:* Alex Quiroga. *Sd:* Frank W. Wilkinson & William A. Russell.

**CAST:** Lee J. Cobb (Judge Henry Garth), Charles Bronson (Harge Talbot), Lee Marvin (Kaligh), Miriam Colon (Eva Talbot), James Drury (The Range Boss), Albert Salmi (Quinn), Don Mitchell (Preble), Sara Lane (Liz Garth), Brad Weston (Keeler), Charles Grodin (Arnie Dodd), Ross Hagen (Bassett), Gary Clarke (Shorty), Michael Conrad (Harge Talbot Sr.), Warren Kemmerling (Sharkey), Michael Mikler (Cord), Jan Stine (Eddie), Lance Kerwin (Young Kaligh), Betty Baird (Sarah Ann Talbot), Regis Cordic (Doctor), Bonnie Bartlett (Aunt Myrtle), Ron Soble (Mungo), Doug McClure (Trampas).

In 1864 young Kaligh (Lance Kerwin) loses his mother in childbirth and winds up hating his new little brother Harge and his stepfather, Harge Sr. (Michael Conrad), who he kills when the man threatens to beat him for trying to steal money. Growing up, Kaligh (Lee Marvin) nurtures a festering hate for his younger brother Harge (Charles Bronson), as both become gang leaders. During a bank robbery, Harge and his men are ambushed by the law and Harge and four others escape. Seven years later Kaligh convinces Harge that the local Range Boss (James Drury) from the Garth Ranch is the one who turned him over to the law. Kaligh plans to use Harge to get rid of the Range Boss so he can steal cattle belonging to Judge Garth (Lee J. Cobb), the man who sentenced him to prison. Harge's men kidnap Liz Garth (Sara Lane), the judge's daughter, and plan to use her as bait to capture her sweetheart, the Range Boss. The plan works but Liz helps Harge's wife Eva (Miriam Colon) deliver their new son and afterward she is able to help the Range Boss escape. Back at the Shiloh Ranch, the Range Boss finds a note from Judge Garth, who has been captured by Kaligh and his gang, demanding a $100,000 ransom. As the Range Boss is taking the money to the rendezvous point he is ambushed by Harge and his men. The Range Boss, however, is able to prove that he did not turn in Harge and the culprit turns out to be gang member Bassett (Ross Hagen), who is shot by Harge. The Range Boss is then free to deliver the ransom money but he finds out Kaligh will not set the Judge free. Before dying, Bassett tells another gang member, Preble (Don Mitchell), that he took the money from Kaligh to double cross Harge. Preble tells Harge the truth as the Range Boss teams with Trampas (Doug McClure) and Shorty (Gary Clarke), two Shiloh cowboys, in pursuing Kaligh and his gang. They are joined by Harge. Near a river the quartet corner the outlaws and in a shootout the Judge is set free while Harge kills Kaligh.

Like the earlier *Bull of the West* (1970), *The Meanest Men in the West* is made up of two episodes of *The Virginian* (NBC-TV, 1962–1971) television series. In this case, "It Tolls for Thee," telecast November 21, 1962, guest starring Lee Marvin; and "The Reckoning," telecast September 13, 1967, toplining Charles Bronson. The two previously unrelated segments are combined in a strained fashion, making for a fairly lackluster feature film. As usual, Charles Bronson provides the lion's share of entertainment as the basically good outlaw who is unknowingly betrayed by his half-brother. Overall, though, the telefeature tends to drag with even a slight color contrast in the editing together of the two disparate episodes. The film also has some billing problems. James Drury is never called The Virginian (he is the Range Boss), Doug McClure as Trampas is unbilled and Gary Clarke, who played Steve in the series, here is dubbed Shorty. Sara Lane plays Judge Garth's daughter but at the time she was featured in the TV series the Garth character had been replaced by a rancher played by Charles Bickford and she played his niece!

Although it carries a 1976 copyright date, *The Meanest Men in the West* was not shown theatrically until 1978 when it was released in Sweden and Denmark. The next year it was issued to theatres in England and France, in the latter country by Group 3 Distribution as *Il Etait une Fois Deux Salopards*.

## *The Mechanic* (United Artists, 1972) 100 minutes Color

*P:* Robert Chartoff & Irwin Winkler. *EP:* Lewis John Carlino. *AP:* Henry Gellis. *D:* Michael Winner. *Sc:* Lewis John Carlino. *Ph:* Richard Kline. *Ed:* Freddie Wilson. *Mus:* Jerry Fielding. *AD:* Roger E. Maus. *Asst Dir:* Jerome M. Siegel. *Prod Supv:* Hal Polaire. *Sp Eff:* Richard F. Albain. *Sd:* Burdick S. Trask. *Prod Asst:* Jeff Benjamin. *NYC Grip:* Clyde W. Hart. *Dialogue Dir:* Russ Hill. *Gaffer:* Colin J. Campbell. *Stunt Coordinator:* Alan R. Gibbs. *Transportation:* Alfred F. Schultz. *Camera Operator:* Al Bettcher. *Property Master:* Eugene T. Booth. *Sc Supv:* Betty Cosby. *Prod Secretary:* Janet Crosby. *Costumes:* Lambert Marks. *Casting:* Lynn Stalmaster. *Makeup:* Philip Rhodes. *European Sequences: Ph:* Robert Paynter. *AD:* Herbert Westbrook. *Second Unit Dir:* Antonio Tarruella. *Asst Dir:* Peter Price & Francesco Cinieri. *Property Master:* Ray Traynor. *Camera Operator:* Norman Jones. *Continuity:* Pamela Carlton. *Prod Mgr:* Clifton Brandon & Mario Mariani. *Re-recordist:* Brian Paxton. *Dir Asst:* Steven Cory. *Sd:* Terence Rawlings.

**CAST:** Charles Bronson (Arthur Bishop), Jan-Michael Vincent (Steve McKenna), Keenan Wynn (Harry McKenna), Jill Ireland (Call Girl), Linda Ridgeway (Louise), Frank De Kova (Mafia Don), Lindsay H. Crosby (Policeman), Takayuki Kubota (Karate Master), Martin Gordon (American Tourist), James Davidson (Intern), Steve Cory (Messenger), Patrick O'Moore (Old Man), Celeste Yarnell (The Mark's Girl), Athena Lorde (Old Woman), Howard Morton (Car Polish Man), Gerald Peters (Butler), Alison Rose (Young Girl), Enzio Fiermonte (The Mark), Stephen Vinovich, Ken Wolger, Trina Mitchum (Hippies), Father Amando De Vincenzo (Priest), Kevin O'Neal (Cam), Linda Grant (Girl in Tub), Louise Fitch (Librarian), Hank Hamilton (Kori), Kiroysu Fujishima (Aikido Master), Michael Hinn (Rifle Range Attendant), Christine Forbes (Waitress in Bikini), Ernie Orsatti (Fast Food Truck Driver), J.N. Roberts (Gang Leader), John Barclay (Garden Party Host), Sara Taft (Woman at Garden Party), Alan Gibbs (Guard).

Filmed in Hollywood and Italy on an eight week schedule, *The Mechanic*, Charles Bronson's second feature with director Michael Winner, again proved to be an international sensation but this time its United Artists release in the United States resulted in a success in the star's homeland. For stateside viewers, most of whom had not seen Charles Bronson on screen since the mid–1960s, the star was a revelation. Now sporting his pencil-thin mustache and modest haircut, Bronson cut such a handsome figure that he now assumed matinee idol status, a far cry from the days when some critics called him pug-ugly. At the age of 50 Bronson was now a star in his homeland, attracting a new generation of moviegoers and becoming the romantic ideal of young women half his age. From this time onward Charles Bronson would never again want for audience recognition in the United States for his popularity at home would be as great as abroad.

*The Mechanic* cast Charles Bronson in a part similar to the one he played in *Città Violenta* (1970), that of a hit man who stood apart from organized crime, one who was his own man. Jan-Michael Vincent co-starred as his protégé and Jill Ireland had a brief role as a high-class hooker who sees to the mechanic's (underworld parlay for a hired killer) erotic needs. Keenan Wynn has a cameo as Vincent's father, an underworld figure who becomes a victim of his organization. Interestingly, Bronson's character is independently wealthy, who works not for money but to be "standing outside of it all, on your own." In one sequence, when Bronson and Vincent are touring a wax museum he tells the young man, "People who stand outside the law often end up as heroes." As in *Città Violenta*, the mechanic's independence is not popular with his bosses and the Mafia don (Frank De Kova) tells the hit man, "What you and I want is unimportant, only the rules." In addition to attractive location shooting in California and Italy, the film contains exciting motorcycle and car chase sequences. Also of interest is the film's recording of the mechanic's methodical work habits and his multilayered personality—he lives in a mansion, appreciates good wine, art, music, food and women, he is a judo expert and a pilot. He also takes pills and at one point blacks out while visiting an aquarium.

Plotwise *The Mechanic* is not involved but its characters and action keep it moving at a good clip. The film opens with hit man Arthur Bishop (Charles Bronson) promising to intercede with the mob for the life of old-time racketeer Harry McKenna (Keenan Wynn), a friend of his late father's, one of the organization's founders. At MacKenna's home he meets the man's son Steve (Jan-Michael Vincent) who has no respect for his father's activities. In reality Bishop has been assigned to kill the elder McKenna. He carries it out and then goes to see his steady girlfriend, a high-priced call girl (Jill Ireland). At McKenna's funeral Arthur again sees Steve and goes with the young man when the latter's girlfriend Louise (Linda Ridgeway) tries to commit suicide due to Steve's indifference. The two men become friends and when Steve learns of Bishop's occupation he wants to join him and the hit man decides to train him as an associate. After teaching him the tricks of the trade, Bishop takes Steve along on the rubbing out of a trio of drug dealers but they almost muff the hit and as a result Bishop is called to the mansion of a Mafia don (Frank De Kova) and warned to do a better job. He is told to go to Naples and kill a suspected informant (Enzio Fiermonte). Going to Steve's house to tell him of the job, Bishop accidentally finds his own dossier and realizes he has been marked for assassination. Taking Steve with him to Italy the two successfully blow up their mark with his yacht but they are chased by the law and barely escape. Back at their hotel and just before leaving the two share a drink, with Bishop realizing his wine has been poisoned. Steve tells his dying mentor his weakness was that he could not work alone and that he, Steve, would operate independently. Returning to California, Steve goes to Bishop's house to retrieve his car only to find he too has made a fatal error.

Audiences liked *The Mechanic*, both for Charles Bronson's slick hit man and also for its surprise twist ending. Even some critics were beginning to like Bronson's films, like Sherman Morley in *Films and Filming* who called it "one of the best thrillers of the year." David Castell in *Films Illustrated* said it was, "A neat, crisp piece of mayhem, done with a dash." *Variety* tended to approve, "Possibilities of limning such a character (the mechanic) are realistically pointed up in this action-drenched gangster yarn burdened with an overly-contrived plot development." Steven H. Scheuer in *The Complete Guide to Videocassette Movies* (1987) opined, "This is a slickly made B action melodrama that contains a few tense moments and Bronson's usual low-key performance, but is basically formula fare." Roy Hemmings wrote in *Video Review's Movies on Video* (1983) that director Michael Winner "creates an unusually sharp and interesting character study of Bronson's hitman ... the twist ending is the best part." "Director Michael Winner has turned out a slick, suspenseful and not very pleasant crime movie," wrote Henry Herx and Tony Zaza in *The Family Guide to Movies on Video* (1988). *Gossip* (February, 1973) wrote, "*The Mechanic* is so full of tricks that it must have been made from discarded clips from old *Mission Impossible* episodes." The writer added, however, of Charles Bronson, "His marvelous face reveals parts of his character that a script could never touch."

While *The Mechanic* dealt with a hit man working for the underworld, Bronson's next starrer, *The Valachi Papers* (1972), was about the heart and soul of organized crime.

## *Messenger of Death* (Cannon Group, 1988) 91 minutes Color

*P:* Pancho Kohner. *EP:* Menahem Golan & Yoram Globus. *AP:* Patricia G. Payro. *D:* J. Lee Thompson. *Sc:* Paul Jarrico, from the novel *The Avenging Angel* by Rex Burns. *Ph:* Gideon Porath. *Ed:* Peter Lee-Thompson. *Mus:* Robert O. Ragland *AD:* W. Brooke Wheeler. *Costume Design:* Shelley Komarov. *Asst Dir:* Robert C. Ortwin Jr. & George Van Noy. *Prod Mgr:* Sheridan (Dar) Reid. *Executive in Charge of Prod:* Marc C. Fisher. *Casting:* Peter Bullington. *Additional Ph:* Tom Neuwirth. *Stunt Coordinator:* Ernie Orsatti. *Stunts:* Bob Bickel, Bob Brown, Justin de Rosa, Debbie Evans, Al Jones, Bob Herron, Whitey Hughes, Jane Leavitt, Buck McDancer, Burt Marshall, Noon Orsatti, Jean-Pierre Romano, George E. Sack Jr., Rich Seaman, Brian Smrz & Jim Wilkey. *Prod Coordinator:* Gretchen Iverson. *Asst Prod Coordinator:* M. Ginanne Carpenter. *Location Mgr:* Larry Pearson. *Sc Supv:* Karin Cooper. *Prod Auditors:* Emily J. Rice & George Sweney. *First Asst Ph:* Guy Ladd Skinner. *Second Asst Ph:* Richard Haas & John F. Karls. *Additional Camera Operator:* Sean McLin. *Additional Camera Asst:* Victor De Palma. *Sd Mixer:* Craig Felburg. *Boom Operator:* Cameron Hamza. *Cable Man:* Christopher Taylor. *Set Decorator:* Shawn Castello-Smith. *Asst AD:* Phil Brandees. *Construction Coordinator:* Robert Maisto. *Lead Men:* Tim Keegan & Michael Allowitz. *On Set Decorator:* Grant Witt. *Set Dressers:* Craig Gadsby, Kevin Long & Loy Hopkins. *Property Master:* John Kaye. *Asst Property/Weapons Technician:* Gerry Wade. *Wardrobe Supv:* Sherry Reavis Wade. *On Set Costumer:* Tony Velasco. *Wardrobe Asst:* Scilla Sandiuzzi. *Key Makeup & Hair:* Carla Fabrizi. *Asst Makeup:* Linda A. Vallejo. *Hair Stylist:*

Manny Benmoshe. *Best Boy Electrician:* Van Phillips. *Electricians:* Lon Thompson, Lloyd M. Moriarty & David Wood. *Equipment Technician:* David K. Goodwin. *Key Grip:* Robert J. Rabin. *Best Boy Grip:* Scott Lieu. *Dolly Grips:* Christopher Hager & Frank Ellison. *Grips:* Richard Crompton & Brian Devin. *Still Photographer:* Brian McLaughlin. *Extra Casting:* David Hansen. *Asst Auditor:* Kelly A. Snyder. *Prod Asst:* Joe Benn, Robert Wishnefsky, Virala Kardash, Fabricio De Santo & Tommy Bartee. *Extra Wrangler:* Don L. Morton. *Catering:* The Arrangement. *Sp Eff:* Pioneer FX. *Post Prod Supv:* Alan Jakubowicz & Michael Alden. *Post Prod Coordinator:* Omneya "Nini" Mazen. *First Asst Ed:* Mary E. Johem. *Second Asst Ed:* Rolf Johnson. *Apprentice Ed:* Laura Lee Bong & Lucy Hoffert Rose. *Supv Sd Ed:* Tony Garber. *Sd Ed:* Birl Van Daalen, Christine Dalenski, Godfrey Marks, Richard Burton, Jeff Burman & Thomas Giles Burke. *Foley Ed:* Cathy Siegel. *First Asst Sd Ed:* Kurt N. Forshanger. *Second Asst Sd Ed:* Mark S. Cafolla, Susanne Spain, John Varoday & Laura Lee Bong. *Apprentice Sd Ed:* Thomas P. Crocker. *ADR/ Foley Mixer:* Tommy Goodwin. *Voice Casting:* Burton Sharp. *Re-recording:* Cannon Sound Studio. *Re-recording Mixers:* Robert Cyconne Jr., Frank A. Montano Jr. & David Cunningham. *Sd Recordists:* T-Bone Pascuzzo & Tina Canny. *Mus Supv:* Joachim H. Hansch. *Mus Ed:* Elisha Assa. *Mus Coordinator:* Lisa Hulac. *Transportation Coordinators:* Jimmy Jones & Joel Renfro. *Transportation Captain:* Edward Flotard. *Transportation Secretary:* Kay Werner. *Title Design:* Weldon K. Baldwin & Kyle Seidenbaum. *Main Titles & Opticals:* Pacific Titles. *Negative Cutting:* Ronald Vitello & Ann-Marie Vitello. *Color Timer:* Angelo Russo. *Color:* TVC.

**CAST:** Charles Bronson (Garrett Smith), Trish Van Devere (Jastra Watson), Laurence Luckinbill (Homer Foxx), Daniel Benzali (Chief Barney Doyle), Marilyn Hassett (Josephine Fabrizio), John Ireland (Zenas Beecham), Charles Dierkop (Orville Beecham), Jeff Corey (Willis Beecham), Penny Peyser (Trudy Pike), Gene Davis (Junior Assassin), John Solari (Senior Assassin), Jon Cedar (Saul), Tom Everett (Wiley), Duncan Gamble (Lieutenant Scully), Bert Williams (Sheriff Yates), Jerome Thor (Jimmy), Sydna Scott (Sarah Beecham), Cheryl Waters (Magda Beecham), Patricia Allison (Florinda Beecham), Maria Mayenzet (Esther Beecham), Sheila Gale Kandlbinder (Ursula Beecham), Margaret Howell (Naomi Beecham), Warner Loughlin (Ruth Beecham), Kimberly Beck (Piety Beecham), Beverly Thompson (Mrs. Lucy Bigelow), Don Kennedy (Cyrus Pike), Susan Bjurman (Mrs. Doyle), John P. McCarthy (Sergeant Purdue), Phil Zuckerman (Caleb Beecham), David Cooper (Willis' Follower), Jeffrey Conklin (Priest Joshua), William Edward Phipps (Doc Turner), Jim Bullock (Neighbor), Saladin James (Maitre d'), Enrica Gaspari (Willis' Daughter), Joseph Darrell (Contributor), Eric Fry (Timothy Beecham).

Charles Bronson continued his association with Cannon Group producers Menahem Golan and Yoram Globus and director J. Lee Thompson with *Messenger of Death*, a taut thriller dealing with an alleged death feud between two Mormon siblings. Filmed on location at Colorado National Monument, the film is picturesque as well as being an entertaining mystery. Here Bronson portrays a newspaperman who stumbles onto a story which shakes the political foundations of the area. For action fans there was the usual bloodletting, car chases and fist fights, all part of the

**Jeff Corey (left) and Charles Bronson (center) in *Messenger of Death* (Cannon Group, 1988).**

formula expected by the star's fans. In the U.S. the movie grossed $3.1 million.

When the wives and children of Mormon Orville Beecham (Charles Dierkop) are massacred in a remote Colorado town, Denver newspaper ace Garrett Smith (Charles Bronson) is assigned to the story at the behest of police chief Barney Doyle (Daniel Benzali), who is planning to run for mayor with the support of wealthy businessman Homer Foxx (Laurence Luckinbill). Orville is held in protective custody for a time and from him Smith learns that his father, Willis Beecham (Jeff Corey), preaches in a remote Mormon community. Going there the newsman is not welcomed by Willis who informs him the murders were ordered by his brother, Zenas Beecham (John Ireland). With the aid of his girlfriend and co-worker Josephine Fabrizio (Marilyn Hassett), Smith finds Zenas on the Colorado tax rolls and goes to the small town near where he has his farm. There he meets Jastra Watson (Trish Van Devere), a young widow who runs the local weekly. Since she is Zenas' cousin she takes Smith to the remote farm where he confronts Zenas who denies killing his nephew's family. Returning to town Smith and Jastra are bothered by the driver of a Colorado Water Company truck. Back in Denver Doyle opens his campaign for mayor with Smith learning Homer has won the chief the support of rich Cyrus Pike (Don Kennedy) and his young

Advertisement for *Messenger of Death* (Cannon Group, 1988).

beautiful wife Trudy (Penny Peyser), who is the owner of the Colorado Water Company. Smith again confronts Willis, who has been reunited with his son Orville, but the old man dies of heart failure. Attending the funeral the next day, the newsman realizes it was all a ploy to keep him in town while Willis, Orville and their cohorts go to kill Zenas and his family in a blood feud revenge action. Smith flies to the town near Zenas' home and he and Jastra go to the farm to warn him but it is too late as Willis and his men attack. Smith is able to initiate a truce but a sniper shoots Zenas and one of Zenas' sons kills Willis as a bloodbath between the family members ensues. Realizing that a professional killer was the sniper, Smith and Jastra head back to town but are nearly killed when three trucks from the Colorado Water Company run them off the road. Escaping unharmed the reporter goes back to Denver where an informant (Gene Davis) who worked with the hit man (John Solari) arranges a meeting but he is murdered before he can talk. The hit man also tries to kill Smith but is overpowered by the reporter, although he manages to escape. At the campaign kickoff party for Doyle at the home of Homer Foxx, the hit man again tries to kill Smith but is badly beaten by the reporter who forces him to reveal the person who hired him to instigate the blood feud since that individual wanted to buy Zenas' farm, which was located over an artesian lake.

Charles Bronson is in good form as the investigative reporter and he is capably supported by a fine cast including John Ireland and Jeff Corey as the feuding brothers, Marilyn Hassett as his attractive lady friend, Trish Van Devere as the rural newspaper editor and Laurence Luckinbill as the somewhat seedy millionaire. John Solari is especially menacing as the hitman and his cohort is played by Gene Davis, who co-starred as the psychotic killer in Bronson's *10 to Midnight* (1983). Gideon Porath's on-location photography in Colorado is a highlight of the feature, one of Bronson's most visually appealing. For the most part the plot is tightly fitted and moves at a believable pace. Keeping the red herrings to a quartet to be revealed at the finale is also an asset.

*The Film Yearbook 1990* (1989) called *Messenger of Death* "an above-average mystery" adding Bronson turns in "one of his better recent performances." *Variety* wrote, "In the old days this would have been regarded as a routine programmer, but in these days of mindless mayhem and random plotting, Paul Jarrico's script at least offers some substance." The reviewer added, "It takes the sleuthing Bronson a reasonably engaging 90 minutes to put all the pieces together, and he manages to do so without shooting anybody, even though the baddies try to get him out of the way any number of times." *LA Weekly* said of *Messenger of Death*, "A very odd Charles Bronson movie, one seemingly calculated to disappoint fans and detractors alike. True believers are sure to be frustrated by the fact that Bronson not only doesn't kill anybody, but he doesn't even get into a fistfight until the last 15 minutes."

The latter review is interesting in that it criticizes a Bronson film for not being more violent, when critics in the past have complained about the amount of violence in the star's vehicles. Charles Bronson told *Los Angeles Times* writer Charles Champlin in 1986, "Every script that comes my way is violent. I don't know what to do, except go for the ones that have something to say...."

## *Miss Sadie Thompson* (Columbia, 1953) 90 minutes Color

*P:* Jerry Wald. *D:* Curtis Bernhardt. *Sc:* Harry Kleiner, from the story "Rain" by W. Somerset Maugham and the play by John Colton and Clemence Randolph. *Ph:* Charles Lawton Jr. *Ed:* Viola Lawrence. *AD:* Carl Anderson. *Mus:* George Duning. *Mus Dir:* Morris Stoloff. *Songs:* Lester Lee, Ned Washington & Allan Roberts. *Technicolor Consultant:* Francis Cugat. *Sets:* Louis Daige. *Choreography:* Lee Scott. *Gowns:* Jean Louis. *Makeup:* Clay Campbell. *Hair Styles:* Helen Hunt. *Sd:* George Cooper. *Prod Asst:* Lewis J. Rachmil. *Asst Dir:* Sam Nelson.

**CAST:** Rita Hayworth (Sadie Thompson), Jose Ferrer (Alfred Davidson), Aldo Ray (Sergeant Phil O'Hara), Russell Collins (Dr. Robert MacPhail), Diosa Costello (Ameena Horn), Harry Bellaver (Joe Horn), Wilton Graff (Governor), Peggy Converse (Margaret Davidson), Henry Slate (Griggs), Rudy Bond (Hodges), Charles Buchinsky (Edwards), Frances Morris (Mrs. MacPhail), Peter Chong (Chung), John Grossett (Minister), Billy Varga, Teddy Pavelec, Frank Stanlow, Harold T. Hart, Ben Harris, Ted Jordan, Eduardo Cansino Jr., John Duncan (Marines), Clifford Botelho, Erlynn Botelho, Elizabeth Bartilet, Dennis Medieros (Children), Robert G. Anderson (Dispatcher), Joe McCabe (Native), Al Kikume (Secretary), Fred Letuli (Messenger).

First staged by Sam H. Harris on Broadway in 1922, W. Somerset Maugham's story "Rain," as adapted for the stage by John Colton and Clemence Randolph, had made a star of Jeanne Eagles and had provided screen roles for Gloria Swanson in *Sadie Thompson* (1928) and Joan Crawford in *Rain* (1932). This updated version of the old chestnut was filmed in Hawaii and modernized with Rita Hayworth giving a superb performance in the title role. She was ably assisted by Jose Ferrer as the pious missionary with a yen for Sadie and Aldo Ray as the young Marine enamored by the gilded lily. For Charles Bronson the film gave him a role which brought quite a bit of screen time since he often shared scenes with Rita Hayworth and Aldo Ray. As one of the many Marines taken with Sadie's charms, Bronson was seen to good advantage in the role of one of Aldo Ray's three buddies (Henry Slate and Rudy Bond played the other two) and received some critical attention for his work as the earthy and fun-loving Edwards. When the feature was revived theatrically in Los Angeles in 1977 Charles Champlin wrote in the *Los Angeles Times*, "...Charles Buchinsky, instantly recognizable as the present Charles Bronson and even then, in a very minor supporting role, suggesting the suppressed power that would eventually earn him stardom." The film's plot updated the story to the World War II–era. The dull lives of marines stationed on a remote Pacific isle are suddenly enlivened by the arrival of night club singer Sadie Thompson (Rita Hayworth), who arrives on the same freighter as Alfred Davidson (Jose Ferrer) and his wife Margaret (Peggy Converse). Davidson is the chairman of a mission's board who has come to the island to inspect a hospital run by a missionary (John Grossett). It is Sadie, however, who excites Davidson but she is quickly attracted to Sergeant Phil O'Hara (Aldo Ray), and his buddies Griggs (Henry Slate), Hodges (Rudy Bond) and Edwards (Charles Buchinsky). Becoming the main attraction at the local bar and hotel, Sadie spends nights entertaining the men with song and dance much to the chagrin of the religious Davidson and his cold wife. Davidson objects to Sadie's activities and tries to reform her but is ignored by the woman and her lover O'Hara. When Davidson learns that Sadie is wanted by the San Francisco police in connection with the killing of a gambler, she pleads with him not to turn her over to the island's governor (Wilton Graff) who will have her deported back to the United States. Overcome with lust, Davidson attacks Sadie and she unsuccessfully tries to fend him off before he rapes her. Sadie then denounces Davidson who kills himself in shame over what he has done. Sadie then takes the next freighter to New Guinea for her next engagement.

*Miss Sadie Thompson*, originally conceived as a musical to star Jane Russell, was filmed in 3-D with a new four-way camera process. After its initial release, the movie, however, got mass release in a flat 2-D version which ran one minute more than its 3-D counterpart. By the time the film hit theatres the 3-D craze was dying and Columbia felt that the film could stand on its own without the additional 3-D hype. While the musical aspects were downplayed, the movie did contain a quartet of songs, "The Heat Is On," "Hear No Evil, See No Evil" and "Blue Pacific Blues," all sung by Rita Hayworth but dubbed by Jo Ann Greer, and "A Marine, A Marine, A Marine."

*Daily Variety* stated, "The dramatic pacing of Curtis Bernhardt's direction achieves a frenzied jazzlike tempo, quite in keeping with the modernization...." while Bosley Crowther in the *New York Times* felt the film "is a thoroughly and oddly shampooed version of the old John Colton sex drama...." In his 1977 review of the 3-D revival, Charles Champlin, in the *Los Angeles Times*, said, "In its naivete and restraint and simplicity of character *Miss Sadie Thompson* is very much a period piece, its figures surprisingly shallow even for 1954 and despite the process."

## *Mr. Majestyk* (United Artists, 1974) 103 minutes Color

*P:* Walter Mirisch. *D:* Richard Fleischer. *Sc:* Elmore Leonard. *Ph:* Richard H. Kline. *Ed:* Ralph E. Winters. *Mus:* Charles Bernstein. *AD:* Cary Odell. *Sp Eff:* Richard N. Dawson. *Sd:* Harold M. Etherington. *Sd Ed:* Frank Warner. *Sd Rerecording:* Richard Portman. *Prod Mgr:* Jim Henderling. *Asst Dir:* Buck Hall. *Titles:* Pacific Title/Steven H. Smith. *Stunt Arranger:* Paul Baxley.

**CAST:** Charles Bronson (Vince Majestyk), Al Lettieri (Frank Renda), Linda Cristal (Nancy Chavez), Lee Purcell (Wiley), Paul Koslo (Bobby Copas), Taylor Lacher (Gene Lundy), Frank Maxwell (Detective Lieutenant McAllen), Alejandro Rey (Larry Mendoza), Richard Erdman (Renda's Lawyer), Jordan Rhodes (Deputy Sheriff Harold Ritchie), Bert Santos (Julio Tamaz), Vern Porter (Gas Station Attendant), Allen Pinson, Robert Templeton (Kopas' Henchmen), Bill Morris (Police Officer), Jim Reynolds (Black Prisoner), Eddy Reyes, Larry Cortinez (Chicano Prisoners), Howard Beasley (Ron Malone), Bus Gindhart, Tom Hickman (TV Camera Crew), Kenny Bell, Max Reed (Photographers), Luis Ramirez (Labor Contractor), Alma Lawrentz (Mrs. Mendoza).

Lensed in La Junta and Rocky Ford, Colorado, *Mr. Majestyk* was another international box office success for Charles Bronson with its theme of a loner taking on criminals predating only a few months his most memorable feature, *Death Wish* (1974). Here he plays a former war hero who served a brief prison term on trumped up charges, now trying to go straight as a melon farmer but first battling labor problems, and then organized crime. The part was tailor-made for Bronson and one in which he excelled: that of the basic loner who uses both brain and brawn to combat evil adversaries. As in *Death Wish* law enforcement is seen as more of a hindrance than a help. With lots of action, well-delineated characters and even a lengthy vehicle chase sequence, the film hit the spot as far as Bronson fans were concerned. Archer Winston correctly reported in the *New York Post*, "Hard-face Bronson has done it again for his immense worldwide following."

Melon farmer Vince Majestyk (Charles Bronson) befriends migrant worker Nancy Chavez (Linda Cristal) and her co-workers, hiring them to pick the ripe melons on his 160-acre farm. Labor contractor Bobby Kopas (Paul Koslo) wants him to hire his men but Majestyk refuses and in a fight he beats up Kopas. The latter files assault charges and Majestyk is taken to jail where in the lockup he meets Frank Renda (Al Lettieri), a hit man being held on a murder charge. During a bus ride to court, Renda's gang tries to free him but in a bloody shootout it is Majestyk who abducts the criminal. While Renda offers Majestyk $25,000 for his freedom, the farmer makes a deal with Detective Lieutenant McAllen (Frank Maxwell) to turn over Renda in return for dropping the assault charge. When Wiley (Lee Purcell), Renda's mistress, shows up, the trio head to the police but Wiley slips Renda a gun and Majestyk barely escapes. Vince goes to Allen and turns himself in while Renda's lawyer (Richard Erdman) gets him released on bond and urges him to lay low, but Renda vows to kill Majestyk. Back at his ranch and still lacking a crew, Majestyk, along with Nancy and her friends, manage to harvest many of the melons. That night while Vince and Nancy are at a nearby bar, Renda and his men show up and harass the migrant workers and tell them to leave, before shooting up Vince's harvest. Renda then comes to the bar and threatens Vince who knocks him down. Finding out what Renda has done to his crop, Majestyk salvages what he can and sends his friend and foreman, Larry Mendoza (Alejandro Rey), to sell the melons. Renda's men, however, drive a car into Mendoza, crushing his legs. After visiting Larry in the hospital, Vince returns home to find Nancy there and the place surrounded by Renda's thugs. Deciding to turn the situation around, he and Nancy lead the men away from the ranch and during a long chase disable two cars carrying Renda's men. Realizing he is now the hunted, Renda returns to his lodge hideout with right hand man Lundy (Taylor Lacher) and Copas. Since Majestyk has them cornered, Renda sends Wiley to talk to him but the girl deserts her lover and Vince sends her into town with Nancy. Renda uses Lundy as a decoy and Vince kills him and he tries to do the same with Copas who turns on him, leaving Majestyk and Renda to a final showdown.

As usual, the critics were not positive about *Mr. Majestyk.* Tim Allen in *The Village Voice* called it "a quiescent action movie untouched by aspiration or, in other words, a B movie without a soul" while the *Palm Beach Post* reviewer Jerry Renninger complained, "Structurally the film is overly distended, with odd scenes dragging on the ground from start to finish. Tighter editing and direction might have trimmed off enough of the excess to make the whole thing smoother." He added, "The PG rating on *Mr. Majestyk* is totally out of line with its content of brutality...." Judith Crist wrote in *New York*, "It is all mindless violence, with a score of men being slaughtered and a dozen automobiles crashing and exploding to incinerate the occupants." Lynn Minton noted in *Movie Guide for Puzzled Parents* (1984) the "one scene in which the villains try to destroy the hero's hopes by shooting up his watermelons is more effective and integral to the plot than the sadist's entire repertoire of brutishness."

On the plus side was the on-location Colorado landscapes and the film's early look at the plight of migrant workers. The script had hero Majestyk paying workers $1.40 per hour, far above the cut rate offered by seedy Bobby Copas and his cohorts. Critics, however, complained about the film's turn when Majestyk takes on the mob but, of course, this is just what Bronson's legion of fans wanted to see happen. What few critics ever realized is Charles Bronson's fans did not pay to see social issues. Instead they wanted to see their hero in action and *Mr. Majestyk* more than filled that requirement.

Co-star Al Lettieri was enjoying a screen vogue at the time he made *Mr. Majestyk* thanks to his gangster roles in *The Godfather* (1972) and *The Don Is Dead* (1973). His career, however, was cut short by his death at age 47 in 1975.

## *The Mob* (Columbia, 1951) 87 minutes B/W

*P:* Jerry Bresler. *D:* Robert Parrish. *Sc:* William Bowers, from the story "Waterfront" by Ferguson Findley. *Ph:* Joseph Walker. *Ed:* Charles Nelson. *Mus:* George Duning. *AD:* Cary Odell. *Sd:* Lodge Cunningham. *Sets:* Frank Tuttle. *Asst Dir:* James Nicholson. *Makeup:* Clay Campbell. *Mus Dir:* Morris Stoloff. *Hair Styles:* Helen Hunt.

**CAST:** Broderick Crawford (Johnny Damico), Betty Buehler (Mary Kiernan), Richard Kiley (Thomas Clancy), Otto Hulett (Lieutenant Banks), Matt Crowley (Smoothie), Neville Brand (Gunner), Ernest Borgnine (Joe Castro), Walter Klavun (Sergeant Bennion), Lynne Baggett (Peggy), Jean Alexander (Doris), Ralph Dumke (Police Commissioner), John Marley (Tony), Frank De Kova (Culio), Jay Adler (Russell), Duke Watson (Radford), Emile Meyer (Gas Station Attendant), Carleton Young (District Attorney), Fred Coby (Plainclothes Cop), Ric Roman (Policeman), Michael McHale (Talbert), Kenneth Harvey (Paul), Don Megowan (Bruiser), Robert Foulk (Gunman), Al Mellon (Joe), Joe De Leo (Cigar Store Owner), Ernie Venneri (Crew Member), Robert Anderson (Mate), Art Millan (Officer), Richard Irving (Driver), Peter Prouse (Fred), Sidney Mason, David McMahon (Cops), Jess Kirkpatrick (Mason), Charles Buchinski (Jack), Harry Lauter (Daniels), Mary Alan Hokanson, Virginia Chapman (Nurses), Charles Marsh (Waiter), William Pullen (Plotter), Peter Virgo (Bakery Truck Driver), Paul Bryar (Officer), Lawrence Dobkin (Doctor), Paul Dubov (Johnson), Tom Greenway, Dick Pinner, Jack Finley (Men).

When a fellow policeman is murdered by mobsters, cop Johnny Damico (Broderick Crawford) is assigned to the case, forcing him to postpone his upcoming nuptials to fiancée Mary Kiernan (Betty Buehler). The case takes him from California to New Orleans where he uncovers a connection with racketeers shaking down dock workers. Along the way the hoodlums try to sidetrack him with two party girls (Lynne Baggett, Jean Alexander) as he works undercover on the case. Finally the trail takes him back to the West Coast and to his own department where he nabs the brains behind the gangland operations.

Broderick Crawford was a box office name when *The Mob* was released theatrically, having won an Academy Award the previous year for *All the King's Men*. The film proved to be a good follow-up to this triumph and it was popular with audiences. "A bold melodrama, it makes no attempt to be pretty, and its violence is as exciting and as fast-paced as you could ask for.... What it offers, precisely, is an hour and a half of physical mayhem, served up hot with pistols and blackjacks," Oscar Godbout reported in the *New York Times*. *Variety* noted, "Fist fights, gunfire and some salty dialog and sexy interludes involving Crawford and Lynne Baggett enliven the proceedings considerably.... Scripter William Bowers has studded the Ferguson Findley original with some logically developed clues designed to throw the customers off the track. It's definitely a surprise when the true culprit is exposed." *Newsweek* wrote the film "is a regulation cops-and-robbers thriller that deserves extra points for generating a little more action and suspense than might have been expected under the deceptively familiar circumstances." *Time* said the movie "rates a B-plus for its efforts with a B-picture plot.... Director Robert Parrish serves this rehash expertly, pointing up the tart flavor and inventive trimmings of William Bowers' script."

In *The Mob* Charles Bronson gained more cinematic experience but the movie only provided him with a brief bit as a dock worker. Still the feature introduced him to the violence genre and much of its action takes place in New Orleans, the setting of his later starrer *Città Violenta* (1970). When issued in Great Britain in 1953 *The Mob* was called *Remember That Face*, its intended U.S. title. Bronson would again work with Broderick Crawford in the violent prison feature *Big House, U.S.A.* in 1955.

## *Murphy's Law* (Cannon Group, 1986) 101 minutes Color

*P:* Pancho Kohner & Jill Ireland. *EP:* Menahem Golan & Yoram Globus. *AP-Sc:* Gail Morgan Hickman. *D:* J. Lee Thompson. *Ph:* Alex Phillips Jr. *Ed:* Peter Lee-Thompson & Charles Simmons. *Mus:* Marc Donahue & Valentine McCallum. *Prod Design:* William Cruse. *Prod Executive:* Jeffrey Silver. *Unit Prod Mgr:* George Van Noy. *Asst Dir:* Steve Lazarus & Robert C. Ortwin Jr. *Casting:* Peter McDonald & Peter Bullington. *Extra Casting:* Dennis Hansen. *Stunt Coordinator:* Ernie Orsatti. *Asst Stunt Coordinator:* Beau Van Der Ecker. *Stunt Players:* David Bilson, George Novak, May Boss, Alan Oliney, Hal Burton, Karen Price, Carrie Cullen, Carol Rees, Christopher Doyle, Debbie Lynn Ross, Tom Elliott, John Sherrod, Eurlyne Epper, Bob Norm Stephens, Jeannie Epper, Joe Stone, Debbie Evans, Harry Wowchuk, Buck McDancer & David Ziletti. *First Asst Cameraman:* Ed Giovanni. *Second Asst Cameraman:* Kevin

Kuh, Pat Swovelin & Josh Bleibtreu. *Asst Costume Designers:* Heidi Freundich Giller & Beverly Brown. *Makeup & Hair Supv:* Lily Benyair. *Makeup:* Dee Mansao. *Asst Hairdresser:* Melanie Nadine Clerice. *Property Master:* Edwin Brewer. *Asst Property Master:* Mark Heiner. *Asst AD:* Joseph S. Culp. *Set Decorator:* W. Brooke Wheeler. *Set Dressers:* Rodger M. Pitts, Jane Elyea & James Shipley. *Art Department Coordinators:* Catherine Schlessinger & Lynn Risdom. *Costumes:* Shelley Kamarov. *Sd:* Craig Felburg. *Sp Eff:* Pioneer FX. *Best Boy Electrician:* Newton Termeer. *Electricians:* Hugh McCallum, Dino Parks, John M. Maniger, Eric A. Ward & Charles W. Smith. *Asst Prod Executive:* Caroline Baron. *Sc Supv:* Karin Cooper. *Prod Coordinator:* Alan Gershenfeld. *Prod Asst:* Patricia A. Payro. *Prod Asst:* Erez Yoaz, Gretchen Iversen, Shelly Mills & Amy Grandrath. *Still Photographer:* Andrew Cooper. *Sp Eff Men:* Michael A. Clifford & John Hixon. *Post Prod Supv:* Michael R. Sloan. *Scenic Artist:* Aimee D. Orkin. *Boom Operators:* Darwin Jay Lollar & Mike Clark. *Cable Man:* Dennis Fuller. *Key Grip:* John Morgan. *Best Boy Grips:* Caleb Edwards & Anthony Caldwell. *Grips:* Anthony D. Manzucci, Jamie Young, Joan Geduld & Jess Tango Jr. *Gaffer:* John P. English. *Additional Editing:* Daniel J. Guthrie & Michael Lowenthall. *Asst Ed:* Mary E. Jackson, Joanne L. Bennett, Karen Joseph, Craig Weintraub, Scott Stephenson & Anne Couk. *Supv Sp Eff Ed:* Sandy Gendler. *Sd Eff Ed:* Elliott Peech, Richard King & Julie Ball. *Asst Sd Ed:* Lowell Gibbons, Christine Daleinsho & Ralph Stewart. *Supv Dialogue Ed:* George Berndt. *Dialogue Ed:* James A. Bogardt, Victor Grodecki & Ruth Shell. *Mus Ed:* Barbara Pokras. *Asst Mus Ed:* Bill Black. *Policy Ed:* John Duval, David Le Brun & Barry Rubinow. *Asst Dialogue Ed:* Jessica Gallavan. *Re-recording:* Lion's Gate Studios. *Re-recording Mixers:* Dick Portman & Ron Glass. *Location Mgr:* Larry Pearson. *Prod Accountant:* Jonathan D. Wolf. *Asst Prod Accountant:* Leslie Linville. *Aerial Coordinator:* Mischa Haussermann. *Construction Coordinators:* John Karras & Rene Veluzat. *In-House Transportation:* Jimmy Jones. *Transportation Coordinator:* Joel A. Renfro. *Transportation Captain:* Edward Flotard. *Drivers:* John A. Burnette, John Conte, Ross Ellis, Allen Henderson, Joseph Killian, Tim McHenry, George Meteks, Jim Rogers, Charles Rothstein, Daniel Rothstein, Danny Swanson, Chip H. Wilson & John David Yarbrough. *First Aid Craft Services:* Kevin B. Platt. *Catering:* Starwagon Catering. *Chef/Driver:* George Panevics. *Cook's Helper:* Robert Shaurman. *Security:* Michael Madl. *Signage:* Nacola Design. *Titles:* Pacific Title. *Songs:* Paul McCallum, Kathleen Wilhoite, John Bisharat, Jim Cushinberry & Val McCallum. *Music Supv:* Paula Erickson. *Title Design:* Weldon K. Baldwin & Kyle Seiderenbaum. *Color Timer:* Angelo Russo. *Negative Cutting:* Ron Vitello & Ann-Marie Vitello. *Color:* TVC.

**CAST:** Charles Bronson (Jack Murphy), Kathleen Wilhoite (Arabella McGee), Carrie Snodgrass (Joan Freeman), Robert F. Lyons (Art Penney), Richard Romanus (Frank Vincenzo), Angel Tompkins (Jan Murphy), Bill Henderson (Ben Wilcove), James Luisi (Ed Reineke), Clifford A. Pellow (Lieutenant Nachman), Janet MacLachman (Dr. Lovell), Lawrence Tierney (Cameron), Jerome Thor (Judge Kellerman), Mischa Haussermann (Dave Manzarek), Cal Haynes (Rees), Hans Howes (Santana), Joseph Spallina Roman (Carl), Chris De Rose (Tony Vincenzo), Frank Annese (Kelly), Paul McCallum (Hog), Dennis Hayden (Sonny), Tony Montero (Max), David Hayman (Jack), Lisa Vice (Blonde), Janet Rotblatt (Mrs. Vincenzo), Greg Finley (Booking Sergeant), Jerry Lazarus (Lawyer), Robert Axelrod (Hotel Clerk), John Hawker (Hotel Guest), Bert Williams (Police Captain), Daniel Halleck (Lead Cop), Randall Carver (Mechanic), Gerald Berns

(Young Cop), Don L. Brodie (Old Man), Graham Timbes (Detective), David K. Johnson (Guard #1), Paul McCauley (Bailiff), Brooks Wachtel (Maitre d'), Richard Hochberg (Man withGlasses), John F. McCarthy (PatrolCop), Leigh Lombardi (Stewardess), Charlie Brewer (Security Guard), Charles A. Nero (Liquor Clerk), Wheeler Henderson (Woman in Bathroom), Frank Bove (Guard #2), Chris Stanley (Ambulance Assistant), Linda Harwood (Waitress), Nancie Clark (Restaurant Patron).

Coming out of a supermarket, police detective Jack Murphy (Charles Bronson) sees his car being stolen by teenager Arabella McGee (Kathleen Wilhoite). He gives chase but she gets away. The next day the heavy drinking Murphy is assigned to the murder of a young hooker and he finds evidence implicating hoodlum Tony Vincenzo (Chris De Rose), the brother of dope pusher Frank Vincenzo (Richard Romanus). Meanwhile Joan Freeman (Carrie Snodgrass), who spent ten years in a mental institution for killing her boyfriend, murders a private detective (Lawrence Tierney) who she hired to get the addresses of the men who put her behind bars. These include Murphy and his former partner, now crippled Ben Wilcove (Bill Henderson). Murphy gets a tip that Tony is trying to leave town and at the airport the gangster opens fire and kills a young woman before being blown away by Murphy. As a result his brother Frank vows to have Murphy killed. Meanwhile Murphy spots Arabella at a market and captures her and takes her to jail to be booked. Murphy, who has been drinking heavily because his wife Jan (Angel Tompkins) has left him for another man and is working as a stripper, is knocked out by Joan who uses his gun to kill Jan and her boyfriend. Murphy is blamed for the crime and is arrested by his arch-enemy Ed Reineke (James Luisi) who promises to send him to prison. Murphy is handcuffed to Arabella at the lockup but he knocks out a guard, takes a gun and the two escape by a police helicopter. He lands the craft on an old barn which turns out to be a drug hideout and they are attacked by three thugs but Murphy shoots their way out and they get away in a truck. They drive to Wilcove's remote cabin where Murphy is treated by his ex-partner for a concussion. The next day Murphy and Arabella return to Los Angeles while Joan murders Wilcove. That night they learn that Murphy has been accused of killing Wilcove and that Arabella helped him. Believing Frank Vincenzo is behind framing him, Murphy breaks into the hoodlum's penthouse suite and tries to make him confess, only to realize the cowardly gangster had nothing to do with the killings. Murphy then asks for help from former co-worker Art Penney (Robert F. Lyons) who gets him the names of three recently released murderers who Murphy and Wilcove put behind bars. Only Joan Freeman matches the modus operandi for the recent killings and he and Arabella go to her apartment and find the body of her psychiatrist (Janet MacLachman), recently strangled by Joan. The duo then head to Malibu to see the prosecutor

Poster for *Murphy's Law* (Cannon Group, 1986).

who sent Joan to jail, since the judge (Jerome Thor) in the case has already been murdered by the crazed woman. There Joan abducts Arabella leaving a message for Murphy that they will be at the Bradley Building in Los Angeles, the place where Joan murdered her boyfriend a decade before. Murphy calls headquarters and talks to Reineke, telling him to send a squad to the Bradley Building as he is going there to save Arabella. Arriving at the deserted building, Murphy finds himself stalked not only by Joan but also by Vincenzo and his goons, who have been tipped off by the corrupt Reineke. The latter is killed by Joan while Murphy disposes of Vincenzo and his hit men. He also saves Arabella from being crushed by an elevator only to have Joan shoot the girl with an arrow. She attacks Murphy with an axe, cutting his midsection but he manages to knock her over the side of the elevator shaft. Joan begs for help but Murphy lets her drop to her death. Later he and Arabella are taken via ambulance to the hospital.

*Murphy's Law* was one of Charles Bronson's most popular 1980s features, with a domestic gross of $10 million. Again he teamed with executive producers Menahem Golan and Yoram Globus and their Cannon Group, along with director J. Lee Thompson, with Jill Ireland as co-producer. Especially enjoyable was the repartee between tough cop Bronson and foul-mouthed teenager Wilhoite. The latter tells the policeman she would rather steal cars than be a whore. Several subplots (the homicidal woman after Murphy, the policeman's estranged wife turned stripper, crooked co-workers) abound in the film which moves at a fast clip. Like most Bronson-Thompson films of the 1980s, it was loaded with action, sex and violence. It also was very entertaining with Bronson being nicely supported by Kathleen Wilhoite as the sailor-sounding teenager, Carrie Snodgrass as the deranged killer, James Luisi as the crooked cop, Angel Tompkins as the ex-wife and Lawrence Tierney as the ill-fated private eye.

For the record, the movie's title refers not to the old axiom that anything that can possibly go wrong will. Instead in the movie Charles Bronson's character says "Murphy's Law" is "Don't [expletive deleted] with Jack Murphy." For the TV ads for this R-rated feature, it was cleaned up as "Don't mess with Jack Murphy."

As usual, most critics were not impressed. The *New York Times* called it "sleazy" while *People Magazine* said, "The pace lags periodically, but true-blue Bronson buffs will get their money's worth." *Variety* called the film "a very violent urban crime meller ... tiresome but too filled with extreme incidents to be tiring." In the *Los Angeles Herald-Examiner*, David Chute noted "Charles Bronson doesn't really make movies anymore, he allows other people to make movies around him. *Murphy's Law* is the snappiest recent Bronson picture by a wide margin, but it still isn't much.... If you like your burgers rare with ketchup, you could do a lot worse." Kirk Honeycutt, film critic for the *Los Angeles Daily News* said, "*Murphy's Law* is one of those overwhelmingly silly films that is constantly though unintentionally funny. It's every Charles Bronson movie rolled into one, with the moves and attitudes ritualized into a cartoon."

## *My Six Convicts* (Columbia, 1952) 104 minutes B/W

*P:* Stanley Kramer. *AP:* Edna Anhalt & Edward Anhalt. *D:* Hugo Fregonese. *Sc:* Michael Blankfort, from the book by Donald Powell Wilson. *Ph:* Guy Roe. *Ed:* Gene Havlick. *Mus:* Dimitri Tiomkin. *AD:* Edward Ilou. *Prod Design:* Rudolph Sternard. *Sd:* Lambert Day. *Asst Dir:* James Casey.

**CAST:** Millard Mitchell (James Connie), Gilbert Roland (Punch Pinero), John Beal (Doc), Marshall Thompson (Blivens Scott), Alf Kjellin [Christopher Kent] (Clem Randall), Henry [Harry] Morgan (Dawson), Jay Adler (Steve Kopac), Regis Toomey (Dr. Gordon), Fay Roope (Warden Potter), Russ Conway (Dr. Hughes), John Marley (Knotty Johnson), Byron Foulger (Doc Brint), Charles Buchinsky (Jocko), Jack Carr (Higgins), Carol Savage (Mrs. Randall), Joe McTurk (Big Benny), Henry Stanton (Banker), Fred Kelsey (Store Detective), Edwin Parker (Dump Truck Guard), Joe Palma (Convict Driver), Barney Phillips (Foreman), Dick Curtis (Guard), John Monaghan (Test Guard), George Eldredge, Frank Mitchell, Peter Virgo, Joe Haworth, Paul Hoffman, Dick Cogan, Allen Mathews, H. George Stern, Danny Jackson, Chester Jones, Vincent Renno (Convicts), Billy Nelson (Himself), Charles Sullivan (Driscoll), Charles Perry (Man), Shirley C. Mills (Blonde Tilly), Grace Lenard (Waitress).

After a series of bit roles following his noticeable screen debut in *U.S.S. Teakettle (You're in the Navy Now)* in 1951, Charles Bronson (billed as Charles Buchinsky) got a fairly good role as the hardened thug Jocko in this off-beat prison melodrama which contains a good deal of humor. While Jocko is not one of the title characters, the role enabled Bronson to give a deft interpretation of the mean, wisecracking convict who takes part in a prison break. Although several more bits would follow, *My Six Convicts* helped solidify Charles Bronson as a recognizable Hollywood character actor.

Psychiatrist Doc (John Beal) arrives at Harbor State Prison to begin a program of psychological testing in order to rehabilitate inmates. The warden (Fay Roope) has misgivings as do most of the staff and Doc finds his program is not popular with the inmates. He selects six prisoners: safe cracker James Connie (Millard Mitchell), gangster Punch Pinero (Gilbert Roland), drunken Blivens Scott (Marshall Thompson), who is doing time for a crime committed by his girlfriend, holdup man Clem Randall (Alf Kjellin), crazed killer Dawson (Henry Morgan) and embezzler Steve Kopac (Jay Adler). Doc rejects many other inmates, including the sarcastic thug Jocko (Charles Buchinsky). Doc makes a breakthrough when James Connie agrees to go along with his plans and is further aided by hit man Punch Pinero, who turns out to have well-above-average intelligence. As a result Connie is paroled for one day to legally open a safe but when Blivens gets drunk and destroys months of paperwork, the program gets a temporary setback. Dawson stages a breakout with the aid of Jocko and Knotty Johnson (John Marley), using Doc as a shield. By now the psychiatrist is so popular with the inmates that hated dentist Doc Brint (Byron Foulger) is substituted. Once the breakout is thwarted and the culprits punished, Doc's program is proved to be a success.

While a bit overlong at 104 minutes, *My Six Convicts* does not lag in interest or entertainment value. Filmed at San Quentin and retaining dour prison atmosphere, the movie has many light moments and among the cast Gilbert Roland shines as the mobster with a high I.Q. In the *New York Times*, A.H. Weiler called the film "a compassionate, thoughtful, incisive and above all, genuinely humorous account of life behind prison walls." *Newsweek* reported, "The film establishes a suffocating sense of the forced enclosure within walls, and of the iron world of their own into which the inmates have withdrawn.... About many of the prison proceedings there is a wry, acid humor ... the figures are believable and moving, both as convicts and men." *Time* accused the movie, based on Donald Powell Wilson's 1951 best-seller, of "accenting the corn instead of the criminology" adding, "The picture is a fairly lively but less legitimate account of these not-so-legitimate characters."

## *Never So Few* (Metro-Goldwyn-Mayer, 1959) 126 minutes Color

*P:* Edmund Grainger. *D:* John Sturges. *Sc:* Millard Kaufman, from the novel by Tom T. Chamales. *Ph:* William H. Daniels. *Ed:* Ferris Webster. *Mus:* Hugo Friedhofer. *AD:* Hans Peters & Addison Hehr. *Sets:* Henry Grace & Richard Pefferle. *Sp Eff:* Robert R. Hoag & Lee LeBlanc. *Asst Dir:* Robert E. Relyea. *Gowns:* Helen Rose. *Makeup:* William Tuttle. *Color Consultant:* Charles K. Hagedon. *Sd:* Franklin Milton. *Hair Styles:* Sydney Guilaroff. *Mus Cond:* Charles Wolcott.

**CAST:** Frank Sinatra (Captain Tom C. Reynolds), Gina Lollobrigida (Carla Vesari), Peter Lawford (Captain Grey Travis), Steve McQueen (Bill Ringa), Richard Johnson (Captain Danny de Mortimer), Paul Henreid (Nikko Regas), Brian Donlevy (General Sloane), Dean Jones (Sergeant Jim Norby), Charles Bronson (Sergeant John Danforth), Philip Ahn (Nautaung), Robert Bray (Colonel Fred Parkson), Kipp Hamilton (Margaret Fitch), John Hoyt (Colonel Reed), Whit Bissell (Captain Alofson), Richard Lupino (Mike Island), Aki Aleong (Billingsly), Maggie Pierce (Nurse).

Based on an actual World War II incident, *Never So Few* (filmed as *Sacred and Profane*) brought Charles Bronson back to big budget films but in a supporting role and one of his least memorable of the 1950s. Although he was good as Native American soldier Sergeant John Danforth, his ninth billing was hardly fitting the star buildup he had received in his four previous features (*Gang War, Showdown at Boot Hill, Machine Gun Kelly, When Hell Broke Loose*) and his stardom on TV in "Man with a Camera." Further the feature, although a box office success, was a violent affair which seemed to condone massacre and excessive violence. Director John Sturges, however, specifically chose Charles Bronson for the film having previously worked with him in *The People Against O'Hara* (1951) and, more importantly, his work here led Sturges to request him for his next big screen assignment, *The Magnificent Seven* (1960), one of the high water marks of Charles Bronson's film career.

Set in Burma during World War II, *Never So Few* told the story of Captain Tom C. Reynolds (Frank Sinatra) who is the leader of Allied troops, the bulk of which are some 600 Kachin soldiers. They are assigned to stop some 40,000 Japanese troops, in the northern part of that country, who are hurting the Allied offensive in completing the Burma Road. When Reynolds is forced to kill a dying servant because of the lack of medical facilities, he flies to Calcutta seeking help and there falls in love with exotic Carla Vesari (Gina Lollobrigida) the mistress of wealthy businessman Nikko Regas (Paul Henreid). Returning to the jungles with his British ally Captain Denny de Mortimer (Richard Johnson) and a physician, Captain Grey Travis (Peter Lawford), the troops, which include Americans Bill Ringa (Steve McQueen), Jim Norby (Dean Jones) and John Danforth (Charles Bronson), find that an Allied convoy has been massacred on the China-Burma border by Chinese warlords with official permission from the Chinese government. Seeking revenge, Reynolds leads his men into China where they kill those responsible for the duplicity. Later Reynolds is court-martialed but is found innocent. Carla, who with Regas was an Allied spy, agrees to return to the United States with Tom.

*Variety* wrote, "*Never So Few* is one of those films in which individual scenes and sequences play with verve and excitement. It is only when the relation of the scenes is evaluated, and their cumulative effect considered, that the threads begin to unravel like an old, worn sack." The *Chicago Daily News* said the film "is a better love story than a war drama, but honest as either" while the *Fort Lauderdale (Florida) News* called it "an above par action and drama war story" adding, "The battle and action scenes are exciting and well-filmed. There are some excellent panoramas of the Burmese countryside." *The Sign Magazine* called the feature "a high-powered drama of explosive action.... It has suspense, excellent photography, and provocative portrayals to recommend it but bogs down on a moral issue and makes serious accusations against the Nationalist Government of Chiang Kai-shek.... Its major errors rule out recommendation." The *New York Times* opined, "Put this down as a romantic fabrication by which intelligence is simply repelled."

While the bulk of *Never So Few* was shot at MGM, it did interpolate some well-done on-location Far East photography.

## *Once Upon a Time in the West* see *C'Era una Volta il West*

## *La Passager de la Pluie (Rider on the Rain)* (Greenwich Film Productions/Medusa Distribuzione, 1970) 119 minutes Color

*P:* Serge Silberman. *D:* Rene Clement. *Sc:* Sebastien Jasprisot & Lorenzo Ventavoli. *Ph:* Andreas Winding. *Ed:* Francoise Javet. *Mus:* Francis Lai. *Sd:* Jacques Gallios. *AD:* Pierre Guffroy. *Asst Dir:* Georges Grodzenczyk & Jacques Bourdon. *Prod Mgr:* Ulrich Pickardt. *Asst AD:* Albert Rajain. *Asst Cameraman:* Jean Harnois. *Sd Engineer:* Noelle Balenci. *Makeup:* Jacqueline Lipard. *Wardrobe:* Rosine Delamare. *Unit Manager:* Jean Lara.

CAST: Charles Bronson (Colonel Harry Dobbs), Marlene Jobert (Melancholie "Mellie" Mau), Gabriele Tinti (Tony Mau), Jill Ireland (Nicole), Jean Gaven (Inspector Toussaint), Annie Cordy (Juliette), Corinne Marchand (Tania), Marc Mazza (Max Duffin/Bruno Caccai), Marika Green (Tania's Hostess), Jean Piat (M. Armand), Ellen Bahl (Madeleine Legauff), Marcel Peres (Station Manager); Steve Eckhardt, Jean-Daniel Ehrman, Yves Massart.

*Rider on the Rain* was such a success that it solidified Charles Bronson's rise to international stardom. The film was even successful in the United States, where it often played in art theatres. For once critics realized what audiences had known for years, Charles Bronson was a very fine actor capable of being a very commanding screen presence. The film broke all attendance records in France, giving him three spectacular successes in a row with *Adieu l'Ami* and *Once Upon a Time in the West* preceding it. The success of the film elsewhere brought the realization that Charles Bronson was now a star and the image he projected in the film, that of the strong, low-key hero capable of both compassion and sudden violence would remain with him for the rest of his career. He sported the thin mustache which seemed to enhance that image and in only a very few subsequent movies has he been without it.

Serge Silberman, who had produced *Adieu l'Ami*, wanted Bronson for the male lead in *Rider on the Rain*, which was shot in both French and English language versions, and recommended him to director Rene Clement, who had worked in films since 1931 and was noted as one of France's best helmsmen for features like *Gervaise* (1955), *Plein Soleil (Purple Noon)* (1959) and *Is Paris Burning?* (1966). The biggest part in the film went to Marlene Jobert but after the movie's completion it was evident that Charles Bronson so dominated the proceedings that he was given top billing and heavy press coverage. Bronson and Jobert worked well together, as evidenced by what appears on the screen, but an attempt to reteam them was not successful. Jill Ireland also has a supporting role in the film and for the first time she and her husband shared a scene together on screen, albeit a brief one in which her character walks in on Bronson and Jobert with the latter wanting Ireland's character to think they are lovers.

**Charles Bronson and Marlene Jobert in *Le Passager de la Pluie (Rider on the Rain)* (Greenwich Film Productions/Medusa Distribuzione, 1970).**

While working with her mother (Annie Cordy) at the latter's bowling alley, Mellie (Marlene Jobert) sees a stranger (Max Duffin) get off a bus. Later while trying on a dress at the shop of her friend Nicole (Jill Ireland) she again sees the man peering at her through a window. That night he breaks into her home and rapes Mellie. When she finds him hiding in her basement she kills him with a shotgun and then takes his body to the nearby ocean and disposes of it. Her flight engineer husband Tony (Gabriele Tinti) returns home and they go to a wedding where he meets Harry Dobbs (Charles Bronson) who tells them he is there "hunting." When her husband goes on another flight Dobbs confronts Mellie saying he wants the TWA bag the stranger was carrying when she saw him get off the bus. She locates the bag at the local bus station and Dobbs takes it away from her. In it he finds a picture of Tony, implicating him in some kind of an illegal deal with the stranger who Dobbs accuses her of murdering. Calling Mellie "Love, Love" he gets her drunk but she will not confess to the killing. She threatens to go to the police and Harry takes her there. Instead she confronts Nicole who admits having an affair with Tony. Back at her house Dobbs gives Mellie more liquor and tells her the stranger was carrying $60,000 in the TWA bag, money stolen from the mental hospital from which he had escaped because he was a vicious sex maniac. Nicole arrives and Mellie lets her think she and Harry are lovers but after she leaves Mellie falls asleep. The next day her mother finds the stranger's real TWA bag in the back of her car and Mellie realizes the other bag and the picture had been a hoax by Dobbs to make her talk. She goes to his hotel and finding him gone goes through his belongings and finds out he is with the U.S. military. When he returns Dobbs admits Tony had no connection with the missing stranger but that the missing man's mistress has been charged with his murder. Seeing the woman at the beach, Mellie then eludes Harry and flies to Paris where she sees the woman's sister (Corinne Marchand), a madam whose cohorts then try to force Mellie to reveal where she hid the money found in the bag. They do not know she has mailed it back to herself. Harry follows Mellie to Paris where he finds her in the brothel and beats up her tormenters. He then takes her to a hotel to rest and then returns her to her home. Back home with Tony, Mellie gets the money in the mail and hides it again. Meanwhile the stranger's body has washed ashore and Dobbs finds a button from Mellie's dress clenched in his hand. Although he now has the proof to send her to jail, Harry closes the case and leaves Mellie to fly with Tony to London.

An exceedingly well-acted, directed and paced thriller, *Rider on the Rain* is top notch entertainment. Charles Bronson and Marlene Jobert excel in their parts and their scenes are highly entertaining. Several underlying themes are handled, including Mellie's being haunted by her mother's infidelity, the desertion by her father and her husband's affair with her best friend. Mellie always wears white, the color scheme in contrast to the dark thoughts which haunt the young woman, especially after she is brutally raped and then kills her attacker. The cat-and-mouse scenes in which Bronson tries to pry the truth out of Mellie are most entertaining as is the realization that an attraction has developed between the two adversaries. Running throughout the plot is the trick Dobbs uses of cracking nuts by throwing them against a window pane—if the glass breaks then the thrower is in love. This theme is used to wrap up the feature following its many taut dramatic sequences. Like with many thrillers, the threads of the plot take a long time to come together, especially the realization that Dobbs is a military man after an escaped prisoner who has stolen a great deal of money.

Although the cast is very good and the production a top notch one, its success belongs to Charles Bronson. The *Los Angeles Times* said, "It is Bronson's most memorable role." *Films and Filming* said he played the part "in perfect balance between menace and charm" and Wanda Hale in the *New York Daily News* thought he was "marvelous." Perhaps *New York Times* reviewer Vincent Canby hit the right chord when he wrote, "It is one of the ironies of national taste that the very qualities that the French pretend to find so abhorrent in American foreign policy becomes so beloved in an American savior figure," referring to Bronson's character. Henry Herx and Tony Zaza in *The Family Guide to Movies on Video* (1988) called the film "an intriguing French thriller.... Director Rene Clement has hit the mark with this suspenseful melodrama, with plenty of moody atmosphere and engaging characters." *Video Review's Movies on Video* (1983), edited by Roy Hemming, noted "an offbeat atmosphere and the kind of serious approach that adds depth to a would-be run-of-the-mill adventure."

## *Pat and Mike* (Metro-Goldwyn-Mayer, 1952) 95 minutes B/W

*P:* Lawrence Weingarten. *D:* George Cukor. *Sc-St:* Ruth Gordon & Garson Kanin. *Ph:* William Daniels. *Ed:* George Boemler. *Mus:* David Raksin. *AD:* Cedric Gibbons & Urie McCleary. *Sets:* Edwin B. Willits & Hugh Hunt. *Sd:* Douglas Shearer. *Makeup:* William Tuttle. *Sp Eff:* Warren Newcombe. *Montage:* Peter Ballbusch. *Wardrobe:* Orry-Kelly. *Asst Dir:* Jack Greenwood.

**CAST:** Spencer Tracy (Mike Conovan), Katharine Hepburn (Pat Pemberton), Aldo Ray (Davie Hucko), William Ching (Collier Weld), Sammy White (Barney Grau), George Mathews (Spec Cauley), Loring Smith (Mr. Beminger), Phyllis Povah (Mrs. Beminger), Charles Buchinski (Hank Tasling), Frank Richards (Sam Garsell), Jim Backus (Charles Barry), Chuck Connors (Police Chief), Joseph E. Bernard (Gibby), Owen McGiveney (Harry MacWade), Lou Lubin (Lindy's Waiter), Carl "Alfalfa" Switzer (Bus Boy), William Self (Pat's Caddy), Jeanne Wardley (Secretary), Lois Messler (Assistant Coach), Frankie Darro, Paul Brinegar, Billy McLean, "Tiny" Jimmie Kelly, Gil Patric, Arnold Hedberg, Joseph Bretherton, Spec O'Donnell (Caddies), Mae Clarke, Helen Eby-Rock, Elizabeth Holmes (Golfers), Crauford Kent (Tennis Umpire), Hank Weaver (Commentator), Tony Hughes (Press Official), Kay English, Jerry Schumacher, Sam Pierce, Bill Lewin, A. Cameron Grant (Reporters), Tom Harmon (Sportscaster), Roger Moore, Larry Harmon, Tom Quinn, John McKee, Gene Coogan, Frank Sully, Robert Nelson, J. Lewis Smith, Donald Kerr, John Raven, Jack Rogers, Ross Carmichael, Harry Cody, Jack Bonigul, Margaret Hedin, Paul Raymond, Michael Dugan, Lucy Largay (Photographers), Babe Didrikson Zaharias, Gussie Moran, Don Budge, Alice Marble, Frank Parker, Beverly Hanson, Betty Hicks, Helen Dettweiler (Themselves), John Sheehan (Starter), John Fell (Gallery Voice), Pat Flaherty (Man with Walkie Talkie), Wilson Wood, Doug Carter, Frank Pershing, Pinkie Woods (Spectators), Bobby Walberg (Boy), Stanley Briggs (Tennis Instructor), Sam Hearn (Lawyer), Russ Clark, John Close, Fred Coby (Troopers), Frank Sucack (Chairman), Tom Gibson, Kay Deslys (Shooting Gallery Owners), Kathleen O'Malley, Virginia Lindblad, Maxine Doviat, Tanya Somova (Golf Contestants), Forbes Murray, Steve Mitchell (Golf Officials), John Bishop, Peter Adams, Estelle Etterre, Jo Anne Aehle, Shirley Kimbell (Collier's Tennis Guests), Barbara Kimbrell, Elinor Cushingham, Jane Stanton (Tennis Players), King Mojave (Linesman), Val Ray (Tennis Umpire), Louis Mason (Railroad Conductor).

Young widow Pat Pemberton (Katharine Hepburn) is a physical education coach at Pacific Technical College and she is being romanced by administrative assistant Collier Weld (William Ching) who she plans to marry. When Collier is present, however, he jinxes her abilities at sports and he causes her to foul up a golf match with a prospective big donor (Loring Smith) and his talkative wife (Phyllis Povah). Pro golfer Charles Barry (Jim Backus) sees potential in Pat and enters her in a golf tournament. There she meets promoter Mike Conovan (Spencer Tracy) and his partner Barney Grau (Sammy White) who offer her big money to throw the match. Pat refuses but loses anyway when Collier shows up and jinxes her again. Upset, Pat runs out on plans to wed Collier and goes to New York City, signing with Mike who becomes her manager. He also manages a heavyweight boxer, Davie Hucko (Aldo Ray), and a race horse, Little Nelle. Under Mike's management Pat becomes a top pro golfer and tennis player and when mobsters (George Mathews, Charles Buchinski) move in on Mike she physically manhandles them. At a big tennis match with Gussie Moran (herself) Collier appears and again causes Pat to lose. That night Pat realizes she loves Mike and when Collier finds them together he walks out on her for good. With Collier gone Pat has lost her jinx and she and Mike continue their association, both professionally and romantically.

*Pat and Mike* marked Charles Bronson's second film with director George Cukor who had been impressed with his work in *The Marrying Kind*, released in April 1952, followed by *Pat and Mike* that June. This time Bronson (billed as Charles Buchinski) did not share scenes with featured star Aldo Ray (who is very good as the thick-headed heavyweight boxer) but it was his second outing with Spencer Tracy, with whom he had worked the year before in *The People Against O'Hara*. Unlike that film and *The Marrying Kind*, Charles was seen in more than a bit role. This time he had a well-scripted role as gangster Hank Tasling with Bosley Crowther in the *New York Times* saying he and George Mathews "are also fun" as the two would-be thugs. Bronson, in fact, is downright funny in his three scenes and he appears to be right at home acting alongside Spencer Tracy and Katharine Hepburn and scene-stealer George Mathews. His first scene has Bronson, Mathews and Frank Richards, as another "investor" who the two soon buy out, being forced to drink milk as they negotiate with Tracy and Hepburn about the latter's throwing sporting events. Unsuccessful at their attempt, the gangsters leave with Bronson asking a pardon for not finishing his milk because it "gives me the gas." The next scene has the two thugs interrupting Tracy and Hepburn's dinner in a restaurant and taking Tracy into the parking lot where Hepburn dispatched Bronson with his own weapon as well as breaking Mathews' glasses and dropping him with a judo chop. Bronson really shines in his third scene at the police station where he and Mathews try to explain what happened to the police chief, played by Chuck Connors, then the Los Angeles Angels' first baseman. Charles is particularly funny in explaining his aliases to Connors and demanding justice for the manhandling he received from Hepburn. The scene's finale has the two crooks being held by the law for not obeying a court order denying them the right to take part in business deals in the state.

Overall *Pat and Mike* is a pleasing light comedy with an appealing cast but overcrowded with sports sequences which tend to slow up the plot. The film's script was nominated for an Academy Award. The film was Katharine Hepburn's final one under her MGM contract. *Time* magazine called it "One of the season's gayest comedies...."

## *The People Against O'Hara* (Metro-Goldwyn-Mayer, 1951) 102 minutes B/W

*P:* William H. Wright. *D:* John Sturges. *Sc:* John Monks Jr., from the novel by Eleazar Lipsky. *Ph:* John Alton. *Ed:* Gene Ruggiero. *Mus:* Carmen Dragon. *AD:* Cedric Gibbons and James Basevi. *Sets:* Edwin B. Willits & Jacques Mapes. *Sp Eff:* A. Arnold Gillespie & Warren Newscombe. *Asst Dir:* Herbert Glazer.

**CAST:** Spencer Tracy (James P. Curtayne), Diana Lynn (Virginia Curtayne), Pat O'Brien (Vince Ricks), John Hodiak (Louis Barra), Eduardo Ciannelli (Knuckles Lanzetta), James Arness (John O'Hara), William Campbell (Frankie Korvac), Jay C. Flippen (Sven Norson), Yvette Duguay (Carmelita Lanzetta), Richard Anderson (Jeff Chapman), Henry O'Neill (Judge Keating), Arthur Shields (Mr. O'Hara), Louise Lorimer (Mrs. O'Hara), Ann Doran (Betty Clark), Emile Meyer (Captain Tom Mulvaney), Regis Toomey (Fred Colton), Katherine Warren (Mrs. Sheffield), Paul Bryar (Howie Pendleton), Peter Makamos (James Korvac), Perdita Chandler (Gloria Adler), Frank Ferguson (Al), Don Dillaway (Monty), C. Anthony Hughes (George), Lee Phelps (Emmett Kimbaugh), Lawrence Tolan (Vince Korvac), Jack Lee (Court Clerk), Tony Barr (Little Wolfie), Ned Glass (Judge), Charles Buchinski (Angelo Korvac), Celia Lovsky (Mrs. Korvac), Mae Clarke (Receptionist), Jack Kruschen (Detective), Richard Landry (Sailor), Jan Kayne, Virginia Hewitt (Young Women), Bill Fletcher (Pete Korvac), Richard Bartlett (Tony Korvac), Lou Lubin (Eddie), William Schallert (Intern), Frank Sully, Ernesto Morelli (Fishmongers), Jeff Richards (Ambulance Driver), George Magrill (Court Attendant), Sailor Billy Vincent (William Sheffield), Michael Dugan (Charlie), Jim Toney (Officer Abrams), Benny Burt (Sammy), Paul McGuire (Stenographer), Julius Tannen (Toby Baum), Michael Mark (Workman), Fred Essler (Augie), John Sheehan (Postal Clerk), William Self (Technician), Bud Wolfe (Fingerprint Man), Frankie Hyers (Bartender), Lennie Bremen (Harry), John Maxwell (Thayer Connolly), Kay Scott (Secretary), Angi O. Poulis (Watchman), Dan Foster (Assistant District Attorney), Harry Cody (Photographer), John Butler (Clerk), Phyllis Graffeo (Mary), Maurice Samuels (Papa Lanzetta), Joyce Otis (Thelma), Tiny Jimmie Kelly (Leigh Keighly), John Albright (Waiter), Jonathan Cott (Policeman), Sammy Finn, Brooks Benedict (Gamblers).

Age and alcohol have dulled the skills of one-time criminal attorney James P. Curtayne (Spencer Tracy) who takes on the defense of John O'Hara (James Arness), a young man accused of murdering an old family friend. District Attorney Louis Barra (John Hodiak) is convinced O'Hara is guilty of the crime. His thorough prosecution outweighs Curtayne's defense and the defendant is convicted of the crime. Believing his client has been framed, Curtayne, supported by his daughter Virginia (Diana Lynn) and homicide detective Vince Ricks (Pat O'Brien), delves deeper into the case and unravels the events behind the framing of his client. Setting a trap to catch the killer, Curtayne meets his death as a result but not before getting the evidence the police and the district attorney need to exonerate O'Hara.

Charles Bronson (billed as Charles Buchinski) has a brief bit as Angelo Korvac, one of the sons of a middle-class working family interviewed at their mealtime by Curtayne as he looks into the O'Hara murder case. For Bronson the film's chief assets were working with Spencer Tracy and a seasoned supporting cast, further learning the ropes of filmmaking and having his initial job with director John Sturges who would later help direct Bronson's career toward stardom with *Never So Few* (1959), *The Magnificent Seven* (1960) and *The Great Escape* (1963).

Critics took little notice of Charles Bronson's brief bit in *The People Against O'Hara* and the film itself got mixed reviews and lukewarm audience reaction, despite being a fairly stout mixture of courtroom drama and whodunit detection. Howard Thompson in the *New York Times* thought it "old-fashioned" while *Variety* noted, "A basically good idea for a film melodrama is cluttered up with too many unnecessary side twists and turns, and the presentation is uncomfortably overlong." Manny Farber in *The Nation* reviewed, "An adroit scholarly example of sound storytelling ... also highly enjoyable for its concerns about a 'static' subject—the legal profession." *Newsweek* said it "is a crime melodrama with so many plot strands that even Spencer Tracy has trouble weaving his way through them ... director John Sturges manages to work up suspense when the screenwriters give him the time." *Time* noted "the film is played as though everyone concerned enjoyed making it. Director John Sturges draws a distinctive gallery of urban characters...."

Issued stateside in 1951, the film was shown the next year in Sweden and Denmark and in France in 1953.

## *Quelqu'un Derrière la Porte (Someone Behind the Door)*

(Lira Film/Medusa, 1971) 97 minutes Color

*P:* Raymond Danon. *AP:* Maurice Jacquin. *D:* Nicolas Gessner. *Sc:* Jacques Robert, Marc Behm, Lorenzo Ventavoli & Nicolas Gessner, from the novel by Jacques Robert. *Ph:* Pierre Lhomme. *Ed:* Victoria Mercanton. *AD:* Marc Frederix. *Mus:* A. Dvorak. *Mus Arrangers:* George Garvarentz & M.J. Helison. *Sd:* Jacques Lebreton. *Makeup:* Anatole Paris & Francois Leclerc. *Prod Mgr:* Ludmila Goulian & Ralph Baum. *Asst Dir:* Michel Lang, Guy Sauteret & Jean-Marie Duran. *Hairstyles:* Alain Scemana. *Unit Mgr:* Suzanne Weisenfeld. *Set Design:* Louis Seuret. *Wardrobe:* Claudia Teray & Raymond Ventura. *Continuity:*

Alice Zeller. *Camera Operator:* Gilbert Duhalde. *Asst Camera Operators:* Guy Testa Rosa & Jacques Renard. *Asst Ed:* Carole Thiller. *Furs:* Chombert. *Boom-man:* Gaston Demade. *Property Masters:* Robert Giron & Louis Testard. *Sd Ed:* Renee Dechamps. *Medical Consultant:* Dr. P. Pertuiset. *Accountant:* Pauline Montel. *Secretaries:* Odette Darrigol & Blanche Weisenfeld. *Stills:* Raymond Voinquel.

**CAST:** Charles Bronson (The Man), Anthony Perkins (Dr. Laurence Jeffries), Jill Ireland (Frances Jeffries), Henri Garcin (Paul Damian), Adriano Magestretti (Andrew), Agathe Natanson (Lucy), Andre Penvern (Intern), Vivian Everly (Girl on Beach), Carl J. Studer (Fisherman), Denise Peronne, Isabelle Del Rio (Nurses), Silvana Blasi (Mrs. Evans), Colin Mann (Sergeant Gordon), Yves Elliot (Man).

Charles Bronson was reportedly paid over $500,000 to star in *Quelqu'un Derrière la Porte (Someone Behind the Door)* for producer Raymond Danon. This, and perhaps because Jill Ireland co-starred, might be the reason the actor appeared in a mostly dismal affair, which fortunately did nothing to dampen his international popularity. Three writers, including director Nicolas Gessner, helped Jacques Robert adapt his novel (which was published by Hachette in France) to the screen but nothing could help this sad brew of cat-and-mouse psychological melodrama and darkly photographed, pseudo-film noir. Bronson was not only stuck playing a brutish character more suited for Lon Chaney Jr. in his prime, but he also had to contend with the oddball characterization of Anthony Perkins in the second lead. Slow moving and talky, the film's story of personality transfer was punctuated by a twisting plot, culminating in a long, brutal rape-murder flashback sequence. The production was shot at Paris Studios Cinema and did get release in the U.S. by GSF Films as *Someone Behind the Door.* In Italy it was called *Qualcuno Distro la Porta.* Miracle Films released the feature in England in 1973.

Opening with gory scenes of brain surgery, the feature relates the story of Dr. Laurence Jeffries (Anthony Perkins), who practices in the small English seaport town of Bowston. A stranger (Charles Bronson), found wandering on the East Cliff beach and suffering memory loss, is brought to the clinic where Jeffries practices by a fisherman (Carl J. Studer). The man says he was lost and Jeffries takes an interest in him because his specialty is memory failure. The doctor takes the man to his home for observation, telling him he lives alone. There they realize the stranger is married because he wears a wedding ring. Also, the doctor finds a gun in his overcoat. After the stranger goes to sleep from a sedative the doctor gave him, Jeffries goes to his bedroom and talks with his just-waking wife Frances (Jill Ireland), who is planning to go to London to visit her brother Andrew (Adriano Magestretti). Jeffries, realizes, however, she is actually going to Paris to meet her lover, Paul Damian (Henri Garcin). After refusing her husband's advances, Frances leaves on her rendezvous and the doctor drives their maid Lucy (Agathe Natanson) to the station for a four day holiday with her sailor lover, so he can be alone to carry

**Anthony Perkins and Charles Bronson in *Quelqu'un Derrière la Porte (Someone Behind the Door)* (Lira Film, 1971).**

out a scheme of revenge against Frances and Paul. Returning with a suitcase he claims to be the stranger's, he shows the man a picture of a naked girl (actually Frances) and convinces him it is his wife. He then makes the man believe that Paul has killed Frances causing the unbalanced stranger to become angry and want to go to Paris and kill Paul. Andrew arrives and Jeffries asks him to have Paul come to the house as he secretly plans to have the stranger murder his wife's lover upon his arrival. A policeman (Colin Mann) tells the doctor a man has escaped from a local mental institution and is suspected of raping and murdering a young woman (Vivian Everly) on the beach. Since the stranger had told the doctor he had tried to help an injured woman on the beach, he realizes the stranger is the killer. As they wait for Paul, the stranger begins to unravel but when Paul arrives the two have a showdown over Frances. When the stranger, who now thinks Frances is his wife, accuses Paul of murdering her, the man produces the confused woman. As Paul is about to leave the angry stranger kills him and then tries to rape Frances, recalling a similar scene on the dunes with the young woman. He tries to strangle Frances but Jeffries intervenes and tells the stranger the woman is not his wife and to go back to the beach to find his real spouse. The confused stranger wanders away from the Jeffries home and the doctor tells his wife the truth about his scheme. She tells him it was all unnecessary and that he is a fool.

The ambiguous ending of the feature did nothing to sort out an already confusing plot premise. Charles Bronson handled the role of the stranger (billed as The Man in the end credits) as best he could but he obviously received very little aid from either the director or the script. That he made the character as convincing as he did shows the depth of his acting talent; in lesser hands the stranger and the film would have become a farce. Little help also came from Anthony Perkins who seemed to be in his own world as the doctor; he hardly exuded the qualities of a jealous husband. In fact his character seems misogynistic. In an early scene an attractive nurse shows interest in him and he turns away. About the only sign of interest the doctor shows in his wife is a tepid attempt at seduction which she easily repulses. Only Jill Ireland has any kind of a defined role—that of the two-timing wife—but her screen time is limited, although she makes the most of her scenes.

Although *Someone Behind the Door* did get U.S. playdates at the time of its release (unlike *Città Violenta* and *De la Part des Copains*, both of whom had to wait until the mid–1970s for stateside showings) it did only tepid business. Most critics found it boring, *Variety* calling it "a surface affair." In *The Family Guide to Movies on Video* (1988), Henry Herex and Tony Zaza opined it was a "Plodding murder melodrama ... the dull and static movie contains a rape scene that is ludicrous despite its ferocity." Despite the brutal rape and a nude picture of Jill Ireland, the feature was given a PG rating.

Sadly *Someone Behind the Door*, like *Cold Sweat*, is one of the most widely available of Bronson features on video. Fortunately his run of mediocre scripts came to a halt with this outing, for his next feature was the highly regarded and very popular *Soleil Rouge (Red Sun)*, issued the same year.

Despite being a bad film, *Quelqu'un Derrière la Porte* proved popular internationally and the actor's next work was a commercial made for Japanese television. Receiving $100,000 for four day's work (two on location in Monument Valley) he advertised a men's cologne produced by Mandom. When the commercial aired in Japan (with Bronson dubbed) it became a sensation and the product became a best-seller.

## *Raid on Entebbe* (NBC-TV/20th Century–Fox, 1977) 152 minutes Color

*P:* Edgar J. Scherick & Daniel H. Blatt. *AP-Prod Mgr:* Robin S. Clark. *D:* Irvin Kershner. *Sc:* Barry Beckerman. *Ph:* Bill Butler. *Ed:* Bud S. Isaacs, Nick Archer & Art Seid. *AD:* Kirk Axtel. *Mus:* David Shire. *Set Decorator:* Fred Price. *Asst Dir:* Mack Harding & Max Kleven. *Prod Mgr:* W. Stewart Campbell. *Sp Eff:* Terry Frazee. *Second Unit Ph:* Terry Meade. *Post Prod Supv:* Cleve Landsburg. *Sd Ed:* Bernard F. Pincus. *Mus Ed:* Ken Johnson. *Second Unit Prod Mgr:* R.J.

Louis. *Camera Operator:* Jim Connell. *Hairstylist:* Jan Van Ucheen. *Mus Supv:* Dan Perry. *Mixer:* Glenn Anderson. *Boom Man:* Tom Cunlee. *Makeup:* Jack Petty. *Property Masters:* Bill Hudson & Matt Springman. *Asst Ed:* Janice Hampton. *Sc Supv:* Jeanette Lewis Hoyle. *Prod Coordinator:* Barbara Allyne Bennett. *Key Grip:* George Hill. *Wardrobe:* Fran Tauss & Dorothy Barkley. *Featured Women's Wardrobe:* Patty Woodward. *Men's Wardrobe:* Botany 500. *Location Auditors:* Lloyd Leidman & Associates. *Sd Eff Services:* Echo Films. *Gaffer:* Colin Campbell. *Director'sAsst:* Pennfield Jensen. *Castings:* Melnick/Holstra. *Special Optical Eff:* Howard A. Anderson Co. *Technical Advisors:* Shmuel Erde & Ahron Ipale. *Stunt Coordinator:* Rock Walker.

**CAST:** Charles Bronson (General Dan Shomron), Peter Finch (Yitzhak Rabin), Yaphet Kotto (Idi Amin Dada), Jack Warden (General Mordecai Cur), Horst Bucholz (Wilfred Boese), Eddie Constantine (Michel Bacos), Martin Balsam (Daniel Cooper), John Saxon (General Benny Peled), Sylvia Sidney (Dora Bloch), Tige Andrews (Simon Peres), Allan Arbus (Pasco Cohen), Robert Loggia (Yigal Allon), David Opatoshu (Menachem Begin), Mariclare Costello (Gabriele Krieger), Stephen Macht (Colonel Yonatan "Yonni" Netanyahu) Warren Kemmerling (Yaakobi), James Woods (Sammy Berg), Lou Gilbert (Bar Lev), Alex Colon (Fifteenth Terrorist), Robin Gammell (Mr. Sager), Ahron Ipale (Lieutenant Crut), Harvey Lembeck (Mr. Harvey), Billy Sands (Goldbaum), Pearl Shear (Mrs. Loeb), Millie Slaven (Mrs. Sager), Rene Assa (Thirty-Eighth Terrorist), Allyne Bennett (First Relative), Anna Berger (Mrs. Berg), Stanley Brock (Gallili), Peter Brocco (Scharf), Fred Cardoza (Uri Rosen), Lauren Frost (Julie Darin), Larry Gelman (Mr. Berg), Bill Gerber (Nathan Darin), Dov Gottesfeld (Meteorologist), Hanna Hertelendy (Mrs. Gordon), Dinah Manoff (Rachel Sager), Caryn Matchinga (Mrs. Bennett), Harlee McBride (Air France Stewardess), George Petrie (Zadok), Louis Quinn (Delegation Member), Kim Richards (Alice), Tom Rosqui (Amos Eran), Steve Shaw (Jonathan Sager), Martin Speer (Second Delegation Member), John Chancellor, Steve Delaney (TV Newsmen).

Charles Bronson returned to network television for the first time in a decade in the role of General Dan Shomron, the Israeli military man who planned and led the daring rescue of some 100 hostages at the Uganda airport at Entebbe on July 4, 1976. The event so captured the public's fancy that a number of theatrical projects were quickly announced, including Universal's *Rescue at Entebbe*, Paramount's *90 Minutes at Entebbe, The Odyssey of Flight 139* from Merv Griffin Productions and a $20 million epic from Warner Bros. to star Steve McQueen as Shomron. None of these projects developed although Menahem Golan (who would co-produce most of Charles Bronson's films in the 1980s) directed *Operation Thunderbolt* (1977) with Klaus Kinski and Sybil Danning, in Israel. In the United States ABC-TV and NBC-TV produced all-star versions of the event with the intent of showing them on television and then releasing them abroad theatrically. ABC's version, *Victory at Entebbe*, made it to TV first but it is generally considered inferior to NBC's *Raid on Entebbe.* The latter was telecast January 9, 1977, but was shown in Danish theatres the previous month. It was filmed in a three week period in August–September, 1976, at a budget of $2.5 million. It was shown

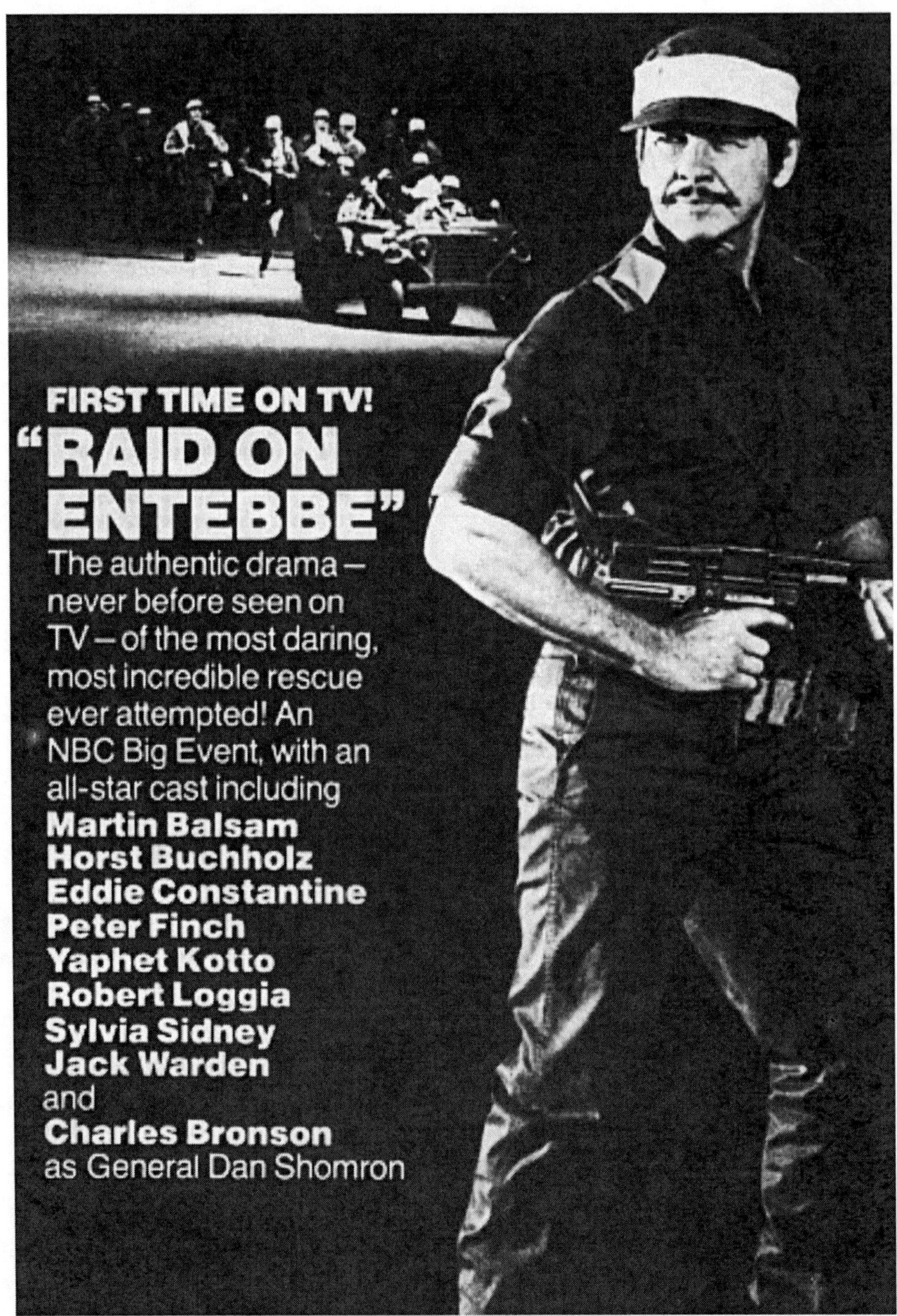


Advertisement for *Raid on Entebbe* (NBC-TV/20th Century–Fox, 1977).

theatrically in England, France, West Germany and Sweden early in 1977. In Sweden it was released January 5, 1977, by Europa Film and had an attendance of slightly over 89,000 compared to *Breakheart Pass* which had an attendance in that country of over 120,000.

The factual production begins June 26, 1976, with Air France flight 139 from Athens to Paris being hijacked by four terrorists, Germans Wilfred Boese (Horst Bucholz) and Gabriele Krieger (Mariclare Costello) and numbers 15 (Alex Colon) and 38 (Rene Assa). They announce to the passengers that they represent the Popular Front for the Liberation of Palestine and that they will blow up the plane unless their orders are followed. The flight first sets down in Libya but the pilot (Eddie Constantine) is forced to fly to Uganda, landing at Entebbe. The captors want the release of 53 prisoner comrades. Israeli Prime Minister Yitzhak Rabin (Peter Finch) wants to develop a military plan while also negotiating. Israeli General Dan Shomron (Charles Bronson) proposed Operation Thunderbolt, in which the military makes a swift invasion of Entebbe and rescues the hostages. Meanwhile at the airport Ugandan President Idi Amin Dada (Yaphet Kotto) tells the 240 plane passengers that he is their host and hopes to resolve the problems as soon as possible. The terrorists say that if the 53 prisoners are not released they will destroy the plane and kill the passengers. Those with Israeli passports are separated from the rest of the passengers as Amin announces the release of 47 women and children. He also gets the terrorists to extend their deadline three days until July 4 and then announces the release of all non–Israeli passengers, although the pilot and crew refuse to leave until all are freed. The terrorists now demand five million dollars for the plane and the release of more prisoners. Shomron meanwhile formulates Operation Thunderbolt as the captured passengers write a letter asking that the terrorists' demands be met. Rabin and opposition leader Menachem Begin (David Opatoshu) agree to Thunderbolt as Shomron and his men hone the operation. When word comes from Kenya that the Israeli planes can refuel there, Rabin gives the go-ahead to start the mission which is approved by the Israeli cabinet while the military is airborne. At touchdown in Entebbe, the United States, France and Great Britain are informed of Operation Thunderbolt as Shomron leads the invasion. Seven terrorists are killed, including Boese and Gabriele. Ugandan planes are destroyed on the ground and local reinforcements are repulsed although a sniper kills one of the raid leaders, Yonni (Stephen Macht). The hostages make it to the rescue plane safely and are returned home.

When first shown on network television, *Raid on Entebbe* ran 152 minutes but it was cut to 113 minutes for theatrical and later TV showings. It proved to be a well-made and nicely paced film highlighted by a series of fine performances, including Bronson as Shomron, Peter Finch (in his final performance) as Rabin, Martin Balsam as the spokesman for the hostages, Jack

Warden as Army General Mordecai Cur and Eddie Constantine as the French pilot. Yaphet Kotto contributed a very engaging performance as Ugandan President Idi Amin Dada as did Sylvia Sidney as Dora Bloch, the grandmother who defied Amin and disappeared from a Ugandan hospital (she had been taken there due to a choking spell) following the raid. Even small roles were nicely crafted, such as George Petrie as Israeli cabinet member Zadok, Kim Richards as a young hostage from California and David Opatoshu as Menachem Begin. Perhaps the real surprise was Charles Bronson's "with" billing beneath the film's title. It is difficult to explain why the world's most popular movie star would accept feature billing in a medium-budget TV feature. Interestingly when the film was released abroad his billing was still after the title but in large letters with his character name given, thus special billing.

Critics generally liked *Raid on Entebbe.* Judith Crist in *TV Guide* said, "This carefully made film opts for authenticity, rather than theatricality" and she thought Bronson was "outstanding." Alvin H. Marill in *Films in Review* (March 1977) noted the film was "Superior in most respects" to its rival *Victory at Entebbe* and it "focused not only on the raid itself but on the debate with Rabin's cabinet and the intensive commando training for the operation." Regarding Bronson he said "he combined equal doses of easy leadership and soft-spoken Bronson-style heroics at the head of his commandos." *Variety* reported, "Whatever the truth of the affair, the *Raid* version had the virtue of methodically building its narrative by logical steps that projected believability...." The same reviewer also wrote that the part of Shomron was "uniquely suited to Charles Bronson." In *The Complete Guide to Videocassette Movies* (1987), Steven H. Scheuer stated, "This by-the-book unfolding of the Israelis' rescue of the planeload of hostages held at Uganda's Entebbe Airport is politically correct—Israelis/good, terrorists/bad, Idi Amin/real bad—and crisply executed." *Leonard Maltin's 1998 Movie & Video Guide* thought it an "Intelligent drama."

An interesting aspect of the telefeature is the way it treated the terrorists. Instead of crazy-minded, blood thirsty thugs, the movie presented the leader, played by Horst Bucholz (who worked with Bronson in *The Magnificent Seven* in 1960), as a man who is politically motivated but not a murderous savage. During the shootout the character has the choice of blowing up the hostages with a hand grenade or shooting it out with the commandos. He chooses the latter and is killed. Also good is Mariclare Costello as the other terrorist leader who plays the part in a methodical, cold-blooded, but again politically motivated, manner.

Bill Butler won an Emmy Award for his camera work on *Raid on Entebbe* and Emmy nominations went to Peter Finch, Martin Balsam and Yaphet Kotto for acting, director Irvin Kershner, Barry Beckerman for his script, David Shire for his music score and the editing of Bud S. Isaacs, Nick Archer and Art Seid.

Dick Maurice in the *Glendale (California) News-Press* said that in a recent popularity poll taken in 60 countries, Charles Bronson was voted the most popular film star. He also noted Bronson "was recently paid the highest salary ever given an actor for 10 days' television work" on *Raid on Entebbe*.

## *Real Heroes* (United Way of America, 1981) 10 minutes Color

*P-D-Sc:* Mario Pellegrini

**CAST:** Charles Bronson, Jill Ireland, Orson Welles (Themselves).

For many years the United Way of America produced annual short films to promote its organization and to aid it in obtaining monetary donations. Often these films featured a well-known personality as a spokesperson. In 1981 Charles Bronson and Jill Ireland starred in *Real Heroes* in which they discussed the United Way and its budget allocations. They also talked with United Way recipients, like a blind Boy Scout and a middle-age couple helped by the organization. In the film's introduction Orson Welles described Charles Bronson's movie image.

In advertising *Real Heroes* in its 1981 Communications Catalog, the United Way said, "Charles Bronson is the most widely known and liked spokesman United Way has ever had. His face and no-nonsense image insure immediate identification and credibility in audiences everywhere. In more than 60 [sic] motion pictures, Mr. Bronson has become a hero to millions. He has a unique quality with which people identify. It's that deep sense of honesty that grows from a first hand knowledge of the hard side of life." In conclusion, the advertising stated: "Discover the unprecedented popular appeal of Charles Bronson and see his straightforward delivery that makes giving and commitment to the United Way the bottom line."

While seen by many people at their work sites and through United Way promotions, this film is no longer available for viewing. According to United Way archivist Ann Chenoweth the music rights to *Real Heroes* expired and for copyright reasons the film cannot be shown, not even to the United Way's own local agencies.

Charles Bronson and Jill Ireland were named the United Way of America's 1981 international ambassadors.

## *Red Skies of Montana* (20th Century–Fox, 1952) 98 minutes Color

*P:* Samuel G. Engel. *D:* Joseph M. Newman. *Sc:* Harry Kleiner. *St:* Art Cohn. *Ph:* Charles G. Clarke. *Ed:* William Reynolds. *Mus:* Sol Kaplan. *AD:* Lyle Wheeler & Chester Gore. *Sets:* Thomas Little & Bruce MacDonald. *Mus Dir:* Lionel Newman. *Orchestrations:* Edward Powell. *Makeup:* Ben Nye. *Sd:* William H. Leverett & Roger Heman. *Wardrobe Dir:* Charles Le Maire. *Costume*

*Designer:* Edward Stevenson. *Special Photograph Eff:* Fred Sersen.

**CAST:** Richard Widmark (Cliff Mason), Constance Smith (Peg Mason), Jeffrey Hunter (Ed Miller), Richard Boone (Dryer), Warren Stevens (Steve), James Griffith (Boise), Joe [Joseph] Sawyer (Pop Miller), Gregory Walcott (Randy), Richard Crenna (Noxon), Bob Nichols (Felton), Ralph Reed (Piney), William Murphy (Winkler), Charles Buchinsky (Neff), Lawrence Dobkin (Spotter), Robert Adler (McMullen), Mike Mahoney (Kenner), John Close (Lewisohn), Grady Calloway (Sabinson), Henry Kulky (Dawson), Harry Carter (Phillipe), Charles Tannen (Pilot), Ron Hargrave (Grayson), Robert Osterloh (Dispatcher), Ted Ryan (Foreman), Johnny Kennedy (Telegraph Operator), Parley Baer (Doctor), Barbara Woodell (Nurse), Ray Hyke, Wilson Wood (Inspectors), Ann Morrison (Mrs. Miller), Dr. S.M. Morrison (Second Doctor), Steve Henault (Loadmaster).

Another small part for Charles Bronson came in *Red Skies of Montana* (also called *Smoke Jumpers*) as Neff, a recruit in the U.S. Forestry Service firefighting division, commonly known as Smoke Jumpers. The movie was Bronson's first Technicolor release and it moved him back to the 20th Century–Fox lot where he debuted a year earlier in *U.S.S. Teakettle (You're in the Navy Now)*. Again he got more learning experience than screen time or audience or critical notice.

The plot had Richard Widmark topcast as Cliff Mason, the chief of a division of Smoke Jumpers who parachute into a forest fire only to have all his men trapped and killed with Cliff the only survivor. Not remembering just what happened he does not know if he is a coward or not, although he finds support from his loyal wife Peg (Constance Smith). Cliff is hated, however, by Ed Miller (Jeffrey Hunter) who accuses him of cowardice in the fire which took the life of his father (Joe Sawyer). Cliff is given the job of training raw recruits and then is assigned to battle a blaze ignited by summer heat in Montana's timber country. Among his recruits is Ed Miller who realizes Cliff's innocence when the latter saves his life while fighting the fire the paratroops eventually bring under control.

Highlighted by Charles G. Clarke's superb color photography, *Red Skies of Montana* was a moderately entertaining male dominated feature. *Variety* stated, "the dramatics are contrived and rather ordinary, but the setting and the way (Joseph M.) Newman's direction keeps the film and the excitement moving insure high interest for the action fan."

Three years after is release, the movie was remade for TV by 20th Century–Fox as *Smoke Jumpers*. Telecast on CBS-TV on November 14, 1956, as a segment of *The Twentieth Century–Fox Hour*, it starred Dan Duryea, Joan Leslie, Dean Jagger, Richard Jaeckel and series host John Conte.

## *Red Sun* see *Soleil Rouge*

## *Rider on the Rain* see *La Passager de la Pluie*

## *Riding Shotgun* (Warner Bros., 1954) 75 minutes Color

*P:* Ted Sherdeman. *D:* Andre De Toth. *Sc:* Tom Blackburn. *St:* Kenneth Perkins. *Ph:* Bert Glennon. *Ed:* Rudi Fehr. *AD:* Edward Carrere. *Sets:* Benjamin S. Bone. *Mus:* David Buttolph. *Orchestrations:* Maurice De Packh. *Asst Dir:* James McMahon. *Makeup:* Gordon Bau.

**CAST:** Randolph Scott (Larry DeLong), Wayne Morris (Deputy Tub Murphy), Joan Weldon (Orissa Flynn), Joe Sawyer (Tom Biggert), James Millican (Dan Maraday), Charles Buchinsky (Pinto), James Bell (Dock Winkler), Fritz Feld (Fritz), Richard Garrick (Walters), Victor Perrin (Mar–M Rider), John Baer (Hughes), William Johnstone (Colonel Flynn), Kim Dibbs (Ben), Alvin Freeman (Johnny), Ned Young (Manning), Paul Picerni (Bob Purdee), Jack Lawrence (Lewellyn), Jack Woody (Hardpan), Richard Benjamin (Blackie), Boyd "Red" Morgan (Red), Mary Lou Holloway (Cynthia Biggert), Lonnie Pierce (Ellie), Evan Lowe, Holly Brooke (Saloon Girls), Allegra Varron (Fritz' Wife), Edward Coch Jr. (Pablo), Frosty Royce (Outlaw), Jimmy Mobley (Petey), Ruth Whitney (Petey's Mother), George Ross (Lam), Jack Kenney (Sam), Maura Murphy (Mrs. Purdee), Phil Chambers (Abel), Harry Hines (Cooky), Carol Henry, Bud Osborne, Frank Ferguson, Ray Bennett, Clem Fuller, Joe Brockman, Opan Evard, George Selk, Dick Dickinson (Townsmen), Merry Townsend (Young Woman), Buddy Roosevelt (Rifleman), Mira McKinney (Lady), Dub Taylor (Eddie), Morgan Brown, Bob Stephenson (Players).

In the three years since Dan Marady (James Millican) and his gang caused the deaths of his sister and her son, Larry DeLong (Randolph Scott) has ridden shotgun on stagecoaches throughout the West as he trails the gang. Knowing Larry is after him, Marady sets a trap for him and DeLong is captured by the gang. Despite orders to shoot him, gang member Pinto (Charles Buchinsky) leaves Larry hogtied to die in the sun as the gang attacks the stage Larry was to ride. This ploy is designed to lead the law away from the nearby town of Deep Water so the gang can raid the local gambling palace. The stage is attacked and the substitute guard (Paul Picerni) is killed. Meanwhile Larry escapes and rides into town where he is met with hostility by everyone except the local doctor (James Bell), and Orissa Flynn (Joan Weldon), the girl he loves and the daughter of the gambling house owner (William Johnstone). The head of the stage line (Joe Sawyer) accuses Larry of complicity in the holdup and the townspeople will not let him ride for the sheriff, who is out investigating the stage incident. Larry is pinned down in Fritz' (Fritz Feld) seedy saloon while Deputy Tub Murphy (Wayne Morris) is reluctant to arrest him due to lack of evidence. The townspeople try to flush Larry out of the cantina but he escapes through the roof just as Marady and Pinto arrive in town to case the gambling house. Recognizing Pinto, Larry makes it to the gambling house as the gang arrives and a shootout takes place in which Larry kills Marady and later Pinto. Finally the townspeople realize Larry was telling them the truth.

A thoughtful, slow-paced western with some scenic appeal, *Riding*

*Shotgun* is an interesting Randolph Scott vehicle about a just man who gets into trouble due to circumstantial evidence going against him. Scott, an old hand at such fare, was both rugged and vulnerable as the hero with lesser roles being handled nicely, especially Wayne Morris as the over-eating but intelligent deputy, and Joan Weldon as the girl who has faith in her man's innocence. The *New York Times* did not like the feature: "This tired, boney little horse opera starring Randolph Scott, photographed in rather faded-looking color, remains as ordinary as they come." More on the mark was Phil Hardy in *The Western* (1983) who called it "A lively budget film … Both (Tom) Blackburn's script and (Andre) De Toth's forceful and imaginative direction bring an extra lease of life to the cliched story."

*Riding Shotgun* was Charles Bronson's first western and his second feature with director Andre DeToth, following *Crime Wave* the same year. Bronson's character of outlaw Pinto is highlighted at the start and finish of the feature. At the beginning he is the vengeful Marady cohort who disobeys orders and leaves Larry DeLong to die in the sun in revenge for a similar death DeLong had caused his pal by chasing them through Utah salt flats. Pinto returns at the finale as the gang pulls off the robbery and he mingles with the townspeople, urging them to kill DeLong who he thinks is cornered in the cantina. Pinto's final effort to kill the hero is thwarted by a young boy with a sling shot who causes Pinto to miss Larry and then be killed by him. *Riding Shotgun* proved Charles Bronson and the western movie were quite compatible.

## *Run of the Arrow* (RKO Radio/Universal-International, 1957) 86 minutes Color

*P-D-Sc:* Samuel Fuller. *Ph:* Joseph Biroc. *Ed:* Gene Fowler Jr. *AD:* Jack Okey & Albert D'Agostino. *Sets:* Bert Grainger. *Mus:* Victor Young. *Makeup:* Harry Maret Jr. *Hair Styles:* Larry Germain. *Asst Dir:* Ben Chapman.

CAST: Rod Steiger (O'Meara), Sarita Montiel (Yellow Moccasin), Brian Keith (Captain Clark), Ralph Meeker (Lieutenant Driscoll), Jay C. Flippen (Walking Coyote), Charles Bronson (Blue Buffalo), Olive Carey (O'Meara's Mother), H.M. Wynant (Crazy Wolf), Neyle Morrow (Lieutenant Stockwell), Frank De Kova (Red Cloud), Colonel Tim McCoy (General Allen), Stuart Randall (Colonel Taylor), Frank Warner (Singer), Billy Miller (Silent Tongue), Chuck Hayward (Corporal), Chuck Roberson (Sergeant), Don Orlando (Private Vinci), Carleton Young (Doctor), George Ross (Archer), Bill White Jr. (Sergeant Moore), Tex Holden (Peg Leg), Frank Baker (General Robert E. Lee), Emile Avery (General Ulysses S. Grant), Roscoe Ates, Frank O'Connor, Ray Stevens (Men Near Pier), Angie Dickinson (Voice of Yellow Moccasin).

On the last day of the Civil War, Irish Confederate O'Meara (Rod Steiger) shoots Union soldier Driscoll (Ralph Meeker) and then takes him back to camp where a doctor (Carleton Young) saves his life just as General Lee (Frank Baker) surrenders to General Grant (Emile Avery). Hating the Union and turning his back on his mother (Olive Carey) and homeland, O'Meara heads West where he teams with aging scout Walking Coyote (Jay C. Flippen) who has a bad heart and is going back to his Sioux tribe to die. They are captured by renegade Crazy Wolf (H.M. Wynant) and his drunken braves and made to endure the run of the arrow. Walking Coyote dies of a heart attack as a result but O'Meara is found by pretty Yellow Moccasin (Sarita Montiel) who takes him back to her village. There he asks the chief, Blue Buffalo (Charles Bronson), for permission to join the tribe and it is granted. After surviving a terrible fever, O'Meara joins the tribe, marries Yellow Moccasin and adopts her charge, mute boy Silent Tongue (Billy Miller). General Allen (Tim McCoy) and Red Cloud (Frank De Kova) agree on a site for the building of Fort Lincoln and the Indian chief insists that O'Meara be the party's lead scout. Driscoll joins the party as an escort and in command is Captain Clark (Brian Keith) who is killed by renegades led by Crazy Wolf. The latter is captured by O'Meara and made to partake in the run of the arrow but Driscoll shoots and wounds the brave, who is returned to Blue Buffalo by O'Meara. Driscoll disobeys orders and leads the caravan to another spot where the building of the fort is begun. O'Meara warns him the Sioux will attack but he knocks out O'Meara and the Indians destroy the fort, killing most of the soldiers. Crazy Wolf lets Driscoll survive in order to torture him but O'Meara kills the soldier to put him out of his misery. With Yellow Moccasin and Silent Tongue he then leads the survivors back to Fort Laramie.

Filmed on location near St. George, Utah, *Run of the Arrow* (the title refers to a Sioux endurance test) was co-produced by RKO Radio with producer-director-writer Samuel Fuller's Globe Enterprises. RKO, however, ceased distribution before the film's release and it was picked up for domestic issuance by Universal-International. Highlighted by Joseph Biroc's gorgeous Technicolor photography, the film was an adult western which dealt with hatred and yet avoided being preachy. A particularly good supporting cast added zest to the proceedings with Rod Steiger handling the title assignment in fine form. Co-star Sarita Montiel was dubbed by Angie Dickinson. Charles Bronson made the most of his scenes as intelligent Indian chief Blue Buffalo, his third big screen portrayal of a Native American, following *Apache* and *Drum Beat*, both 1954 releases. Also noteworthy were Jay C. Flippen as the Indian Scout, Olive Carey as Steiger's mother and cowboy star Colonel Tim McCoy as General Allen.

*Variety* said, "Production is strong on visual values to bolster Samuel Fuller's sometimes meandering screenplay," while the *New York Times* opined, "This is just an ordinary cavalry–Indian movie, conspicuous for a lot of raw blood-letting...." Richard B. Jewell and Vernon Harbin wrote in *The RKO Story* (1982), "A crazy, mixed-up western that had nothing to do with cowboys, rustlers, sheriffs or schoolmarms, *Run of the Arrow* was worth seeing for its unbridled audacity." The *Monthly Film Bulletin* took note, "The climactic scene of torture, with the cavalry officer being cut to pieces by vengeful Indians, remains a disturbing experience."

*Run of the Arrow* did only tepid business in the United States but it was popular in Europe, particularly in France where it was issued in 1959. It did not see release in Denmark until 1961.

The editor of *Run of the Arrow* was Gene Fowler Jr. who would direct Charles Bronson in his next two feature films, *Gang War* and *Showdown at Boot Hill*, both 1958 releases which would mark the first time the actor would receive star billing theatrically.

## *St. Ives* (Warner Bros., 1976) 94 minutes Color

*P:* Pancho Kohner & Stanley Canter. *D:* J. Lee Thompson. *Sc:* Barry Beckerman, from the novel *The Procane Chronicle* by Oliver Bleeck. *Ph:* Lucien Ballard. *Ed:* Michael F. Anderson. *Mus:* Lalo Schifrin. *Unit Prod Mgr:* Hal Klein. *Sd:* Harlan Briggs & Arthur Plantadosi. *Prod Design:* Philip M. Jeffries. *Sets:* Robert De Vestel. *Casting:* Jack Baur. *Asst Dir:* Ronald L. Schwary & Ed Ledding. *Stunt Coordinator:* Max Kleven. *Stunts:* Dar Robinson. *Sp Eff:* Gene Grigg. *Makeup:* Philip Rhodes. *Hairdresser:* Shirley Padgett. *Mus Ed:* Eugene Marin. *Re-recording Mixer:* Michael Minkler.

CAST: Charles Bronson (Raymond St. Ives), Jacqueline Bisset (Janet Whistler), John Houseman (Abner Procane), Maximilian Schell (Dr. John Constable), Harry Guardino (Detective Deal), Harris Yulin (Detective Oller), Dana Elcar (Detective Charlie Bount), Michael Lerner (Myron Green), Dick O'Neill (Hesh the Counterman), Elisha Cook (Eddie the Desk Clerk), Val Bisoglio (Finley Cummings), Burr De Benning (Officer Frann), Michael J. Travanti (Johnny Parisi), Olan Soule (Man at Union Station), Robert [Bob] Terhune (Mike Kluszewski), Jerome Thor (Chasman), Benjie Bancroft (Patrolman), Lynn Borden (Party Girl), Ben Young (Detective), George Sawaya (Arab Bagman), Joe Roman (Seymour), Walter Brooke (Mickey), Robert Englund, Jeff Goldblum, Mark Thomas (Thugs), Tom Pedi (Fat Angie Polaterra), Dan Robinson (Jimmy Peskoe), Jerry Brutsche (Jack Boykins), John Steadman (Willie), Morris Buchanan (Police Sergeant), Don Hanmer (Punch), Rosalyn Marshall (Girl at Table), Joseph De Nicola (No Nose), Glenn Robards (Procane's Butler), Stanley Brock (Night Clerk), Larry Martindale (Station Man), Louis H. Kelly (Croupier), Owen Hith Pace (Slim), Gayla Gallaway, Jill Stone (Nurses), Edward Cross (Orderly), George Memmoli (Shippo), Norman Palmer (McDuff).

*St. Ives* not only had Charles Bronson on a modern murder case for the first time since *The Stone Killer* (1973) but it also marked the first of his lengthy associations with director J. Lee Thompson and producer Pancho Kohner, the son of his agent, Paul Kohner. Bronson and Thompson would make nine films together in the next baker's dozen years. Britisher Thompson had been directing since 1950 and his credits included *The Good*

*Companions* (1957), *Tiger Bay* (1959), *The Guns of Navarone* (1961), *Cape Fear* and *Taras Bulba* (1962), *MacKenna's Gold* (1968) and *The Reincarnation of Peter Proud* (1974). Bronson and Thompson worked well together; Bronson once commented he liked working with Thompson because the latter only required two setups for each shot, while other directors wanted three or more. Certainly *St. Ives* was a fine launching of their cinematic collaborations as it was a good old-fashioned film noir melodrama, which if done in the 1940s would probably have starred Humphrey Bogart, Lauren Bacall and Sydney Greenstreet. Its fine use of seedy Los Angeles locales and lots of night shooting, give it the feel of a Raymond Chandler–era yarn.

Raymond St. Ives (Charles Bronson), a one-time ace crime reporter and now a struggling novelist, gets a job through his lawyer, Myron Green (Michael Lerner). He is to act as a go-between for wealthy Abner Procane (John Houseman) and blackmailers who have stolen five ledgers from his safe. While at Procane's estate St. Ives meets the man's lovely companion, Janet Whistler (Jacqueline Bisset). At the laundromat where the money exchange is to take place, St. Ives finds a dead man, petty thief Jack Boykins (Jerry Brutsche), and is arrested by police detectives Deal (Harry Guardino) and Oller (Harris Yulin). At the police station St. Ives' old pal, Detective Charlie Bount (Dana Elcar), vouches for him and he is set free. After placing the money from the pickup in the safe at his seedy hotel, the writer is abducted by three thugs (Robert Englund, Jeff Goldblum, Mark Thomas) and taken to a deserted hotel where he is beaten. St. Ives, however, outsmarts the trio and is able to escape. Telling Procane what happened, he meets the man's psychiatrist, Dr. John Constable (Maximilian Schell). Through gangster Johnny Parisi (Michael J. Travanti) and lunchroom counterman Hesh (Dick O'Neill), St. Ives learns that cheap hood Finley Cummings (Val Bisoglio) has tried to peddle Procane's ledgers. From Cummings St. Ives learns that they were stolen by small time crook Jimmy Peskoe (Dan Robinson) but when he goes to the man's hotel he finds Peskoe has been pushed out of a window. Again Deal and Oller arrive and try to arrest him but for the second time Bount clears St. Ives. At Union Station, St. Ives finally makes the exchange for the ledgers but after reading them he realizes that Procane is a gangster and that four pages are missing. Procane wants him to find the missing pages and at the same time he gets involved with a deal involving the exchange of four million dollars from Arab interests for the missing pages. Meanwhile, Officer Frann (Burr De Benning), who was on hand when Boykins' body was found, tells St. Ives that for $20,000 he will name the man's killer. St. Ives takes the proposition to Procane who agrees but at the payoff place St. Ives finds Frann stabbed and takes him to the hospital where the police officer dies. Back at his hotel, someone tries to shoot St. Ives but misses. Later at Procane's estate, St. Ives is informed by Janet that Procane is impotent and then she seduces the writer. St. Ives accompanies Procane to

**Maximilian Schell, Jacqueline Bisset and Charles Bronson in *St. Ives* (Warner Bros., 1976).**

a drive-in theatre where the money exchange is to take place and there the murderers of Boykins are killed. Back at Procane's mansion, St. Ives learns the identity of the real brains behind the murder and blackmail scheme. Procane is killed and St. Ives captures the murderer for the police.

A well-paced, fast-moving and colorful suspense thriller, *St. Ives* packed lots of action into its 94 minutes, including the title character being dropped down an elevator shaft at an abandoned hotel. St. Ives is a likable, if somewhat indolent character, who is a gambler who rarely wins—after getting the job with Procane he bets $500 on a football game and promptly loses. Abner Procane is first seen watching John Gilbert in *The Big Parade* (1925) at his mansion. Gangsters in Bronson films seem to like old movies; Rod Steiger in *Love and Bullets* (1979) watched Jeanette MacDonald–Nelson Eddy musicals. While the Los Angeles locales may have been seedy, Jacqueline Bisset as the femme fatale was a feast for the eyes. St. Ives describes her as "a lot of great lookin' bits and pieces." Unforgettable is the finale scene with Bisset, soaking wet, asking Detective Bount to help her out of her wet clothes before they go to the police station.

As to be expected, the public took to *St Ives* more than the critics. *Variety* called it "a dull and plodding film … [it] is careful to show that Bronson's character does not need pistols." Jack Kroll in *Newsweek* dubbed it "boring hack work by director J. Lee Thompson" and Candice Russell in the *Miami*

*Herald* opined, "This is a decidedly less involving drama than other recent excuses for Bronson mayhem ... [it] provides the legendary screen figure with a role of crime intermediary, a role too small and bland for Bronson's dimensions." She further stated, "Bronson has long been past direction or past acting, for that matter. Like Clint Eastwood, he functions as a virile and mechanistic superhuman, not prone to the feelings or predicaments of the common man. These stars don't have to act, they just have to exist as implacable, emotionless and bold." Jack Cocks wrote in *Time*, "Barry Beckerman's screenplay offers director J. Lee Thompson several good chances to take advantage of the flush, neon lowlife of L.A. Thompson sedulously ignores every opportunity and does not try to sort much sense out of the plot, either. He has all he can do to keep his actors from tripping over corpses." Regarding the star he said, "Charles Bronson makes a pleasing shamus out of St. Ives ... he eases through the part with gruff grace and a few hints of low-rent charm. In *Breakout*, last year's *Hard Times*, and now here, Bronson has turned in good, engaging work. It's getting nice to have him around."

## *The Sandpiper* (Metro-Goldwyn-Mayer, 1965) 116 minutes Color

*P:* Martin Ransohoff. *AP:* John Calley. *D:* Vincente Minnelli. *Sc:* Dalton Trumbo & Michael Wilson. *St:* Martin Ransohoff. *Adaptation:* Irene Kamp & Louis Kamp. *Ph:* Milton Krasner. *Ed:* David Bretherton. *Mus:* Johnny Mandel. *Song:* Johnny Mandel & Paul Francis Webster. *Costumes:* Irene Sharaff. *Titles:* Herb Rosenthal. *Big Sur Scene Coordinator:* Eduardo Tirella. *Wildlife Ph:* Richard Borden. *Asst Dir:* William McGarry. *AD:* George W. Davis & Urie McCleary. *Sets:* Henry Grace & Keogh Gleason.

CAST: Elizabeth Taylor (Laura Reynolds), Richard Burton (Edward Hewitt), Eva Marie Saint (Claire Hewitt), Charles Bronson (Cos Erickson), Robert Webber (Ward Hendricks), Morgan Mason (Danny Reynolds), Tom Drake (Walter Robinson), James Edwards (Larry Brant), Torin Thatcher (Judge Thompson), Doug Henderson (Phil Sutcliff), John Hart, Dusty Cadis (Troopers), Jan Arvan, Tom Curtis (Trustees), Mary Benoit (Trustee's Wife), Paul Genge (Architect), Rex Holman, Kelton Garwood, Jimmy Murphy, Mel Gallagher, Diane Sayer, Joan Connors, Peggy Adams Laird, Shirley Bonne (Celebrants), Ron Whelan (Poet), Peter O'Toole (Voice).

Free spirit artist Laura Reynolds (Elizabeth Taylor) lives with her young fatherless son Danny (Morgan Mason) in a beach house in the Big Sur region near Monterey in California. Due to lack of parental guidance the boy has had run-ins with the law and a judge (Torin Thatcher) orders he be placed in a private school or be taken away from his mother. Laura, who feels she can better educate her son at home, is not happy with the order but complies and finds the boy easily adapting to the school's routine. At first Laura does not get along with the school's principal, Edward Hewitt (Richard Burton), an Episcopal minister who is married and the father of two boys. The two, however, soon find they are passionately attracted to each other and begin an affair. When Laura poses nude for neighbor sculptor Cos Erickson (Charles Bronson), Hewitt becomes jealous and the two men have a fight on the beach. Tormented by his actions, Hewitt confesses his infidelity to his wife Claire (Eva Marie Saint) and he publicly admits his affair with Laura. When she finds out what Edward has done, Laura denounces him and they break up. The politicians who have been using Hewitt and the school to their advantage are upset by what has happened and he is forced to resign his position before deciding to return to the ministry.

Like *Kid Galahad* three years earlier, Charles Bronson accepted a supporting role in *The Sandpiper* because it insured him of a massive screen audience, due to the popularity of stars Elizabeth Taylor and Richard Burton, thanks to their torrid love affair during the filming of *Cleopatra* (1963) and their subsequent stormy marriage. Cast against type as a beatnik-type sculptor, Charles Bronson again weathered a stormy script and troubled production to garner fine reviews and positive public notice. The film, the third of 11 Taylor–Burton vehicles, was one of their most successful, grossing $7 million domestically. Its exteriors were filmed at Big Sur with interiors lensed in Paris.

While *The Sandpiper* brought the public to the box office it failed to impress the critics. *Life* called it a "$5.3 million sleeping pill … one of the most tedious, inane and ludicrous films ever made." *Time* said, "*The Sandpiper*'s absurd situations are matched by dialogue that beauty (hers) and talent (his) cannot vanquish." Pauline Kael noted in *The New Yorker*, "The director, Vincente Minnelli, a man with a sophisticated, charming talent, who has in the past made movies about the Hollywood juggernaut, is here crushed under it." For the record, the Sandpiper is a small bird which nests on the ground and lays four color protected eggs. Perhaps it was *Newsweek* then that best summed it up by saying, "*The Sandpiper* lays just one egg, but it is the biggest one in years." In the *New York Herald-Tribune* Judith Crist complained *The Sandpiper* was a "two-hour travesty which may not be the most perfectly awful movie ever made but which is right down there fighting for the title. Perhaps it was made for connoisseurs of bad movies to delight in dialogue that reeks, characters that creak and a plot to make the ghost of Elinor Glyn green with envy."

The film did earn an Academy Award for its theme song, "The Shadow of Your Smile," and it also featured paintings by Elizabeth Duquette and redwood sculpture by Edmund Kara.

## *The Sea Wolf* (Turner Pictures, 1993) 93 minutes Color

*P:* Duke Fenady & W. Patterson Ferns. *EP:* Andrew J. Fenady & Bob Banner. *AP:* Eddie Saeta. *D:* Michael Anderson. *Sc:* Andrew J. Fenady, from the novel by Jack London. *Ph:* Glen MacPherson. *Ed:* Nick Rotundo. *Mus:* Charles Bernstein. *Prod Design:* Trevor Williams. *Costume Design:* Stephanie Nolan. *Asst Dir:* Lee Knippelberg, Morgan Beggs & Shirley Parsons. *Prod Executives:* Chuck Banner

& Stephanie Beeman. *Prod Mgr:* Grace Gilroy. *Makeup:* Jan Newman. *Hair Styles:* Kandace Loewen. *Location Mgr:* Christine Haebler. *Sc Supv:* Candice Field. *Prod Coordinators:* Jody Ann Ranney & Tim C. Hiltz. *Prod Sd Mixer:* Eric Batut. *Supv Sd Ed:* Jacqueline Cristianini. *Mus Ed:* Bruce Nyznik. *Transportation Coordinator:* Jake Callihoo. *Prod Accountant:* Lorraine Baird. *Camera Operator:* Stephen S. Campanelli. *First Asst Camera:* Chris Harris. *Gaffer:* Don Saari. *Sp Eff Coordinator:* Mike Vezina. *Property Master:* Grant Swain. *Costume Supv:* Bev Wowchuck. *Prod Associate:* Andrew Francis Fenady. *Casting:* Stuart Atkins Casting. *Casting Asst:* William Haines. *Extra Casting:* Annette McCaffrey. *Re-recording:* Sharpe Sound Studios. *Stunt Coordinators:* Stan Barrett & Ken Kirzinger. *Key Grip:* Dallas Brinson. *Set Decorator:* Dominique Fauquet-Lemaitre. *Still Photographer:* Chris Helcermanas-Benge. *Dir Trainee:* Michael A. Bafaro.

**CAST:** Charles Bronson (Captain Wolf Larsen), Christopher Reeve (Humphrey Van Weyden), Catherine Mary Stewart (Flaxen Brewster), Marc Singer (Johnson), Len Cariou (Dr. Prichard), Clive Revill (Cookie/Thomas C. Muckridge), Shane D. Kelly (Leach), Gary Chalk (Chandler), Tom McBeath (Latimer), Stan Barrett (Ofty Ofty), Dee Jay Jackson (Smoke), Eli Gabay (Dog Breath), Russell Roberts (French Frank), Bill Croft (Donovan), John Novak (Jameson Damisk), William Samples (Charles Furuseth), Peter Haworth (Reginald Brewster), Rachel Howard (Ann Treadwell), John Destrey, Gavin Buhr (Police Officers), A.J. Fenady (Bartender).

For his second telefeature of the 1990s, Charles Bronson again teamed with producer Andrew J. Fenady with whom he had previously worked in *Yes Virginia, There Is a Santa Claus* (1991). In this retelling of the famed Jack London novel, Bronson had a part which called for both intellectual prowess and physical action. For once he was given really solid lines as the character who believed John Milton in that "it is better to reign in hell than serve in heaven." During the course of the film Wolf Larsen reveals his beliefs that "life is the cheapest thing in the world" and "might is right and weakness is wrong." Yet the Larsen character is a multilayered one, a man who is highly intelligent and well read through years of self-education, one whose ambition led him from cabin boy to ship's captain and yet one so cruel that the character of Humphrey Van Weyden said, "I was to know and fear his voice like nothing else on Earth." Charles Bronson deftly handled this multifaceted character and his performance is a rich one, perhaps one of the finest of his career.

Set late in the last century, the film opens with snobbish writer-critic Humphrey Van Weyden (Christopher Reeve) returning from a Nob Hill party on a ferry boat and being the victim of pickpocket Reginald Brewster (Peter Haworth) and his pretty daughter Flaxen (Catherine Mary Stewart). Just as he is about to have the pair arrested the ferry is hit by another boat and sinks. Humphrey and Flaxen cling to wreckage of the ship until they are brought aboard a schooner, the *Ghost*, by its captain, Wolf Larsen (Charles Bronson). The first mate (Bill Croft) dies of a heart attack and the ship's physician, Dr. Prichard (Len Cariou), attends the badly wounded Flaxen.

Advertisement for *The Sea Wolf* (Turner Pictures, 1993).

Van Weyden offers Larsen one thousand dollars to return the boat to San Francisco, but Larsen takes sadistic delight in making Van Weyden the new cabin boy and he is badly mistreated by the cruel Cookie (Clive Revill). Befriended by seaman Johnson (Marc Singer), Van Weyden learns that Larsen is a self-taught, literate man and a cruel one who beats Johnson for complaining about conditions on the ship and forces him aloft for several days. Van Weyden, now called simply Hump, starts a journal of the voyage as Flaxen recovers and the doctor tells her it was Hump who saved her life. Larsen tells Hump the voyage is a seal hunting expedition and that he is at odds with his older brother, Death Larsen. He also tells him that some of the crew will mutiny and try to kill him, and then Larsen orders Johnson brought down. As Hump realizes Larsen suffers from periods of blindness, Johnson vows to kill the captain. Tired of being mistreated, Hump turns on Cookie and threatens to kill him. When Cookie tries to molest Flaxen, Hump nearly beats him to death. The ship reaches the hunting grounds in the Sea of Japan but Larsen finds his brother has been there first and killed all the seals. Johnson tries to kill Larsen with a knife but instead kills Dr. Prichard and is placed in irons. Larsen tells the crew he plans to hang Johnson and later he and first mate Chandler (Gary Chalk) are thrown overboard with only Larsen surviving. Later Larsen tests Hump by giving him a gun but Hump will not shoot the captain nor does he accept his offer to be the new first mate. Since he plans to attack and destroy his brother's boat and get the seals, Larsen eases up on the crew, gives Johnson a reprieve and passes out whiskey freely. He also tells the crew Cookie is a spy and they throw him overboard, with Cookie losing a leg when attacked by a shark. Realizing they cannot stay aboard the *Ghost*, Hump and Flaxen take a boat and plan to sail 600 miles to Japan. After drifting for many days and being caught in a terrible storm they come upon the *Ghost*, abandoned and sinking. Hump goes aboard for supplies and finds the now blind Larsen chained. Larsen tells him his brother fired on the Ghost and the crew jumped ship, leaving him to die. He locks Hump in his cabin, planning for them to die together when the ship sinks, but when he realizes Flaxen will not leave Hump he sets him free. Hump and Flaxen head for some nearby islands as Larsen goes down with his ship.

*The Sea Wolf* is a handsome looking telefeature with Charles Bernstein's music score being nominated for an Emmy Award. Director Michael Anderson kept the proceedings moving along at a good clip, being an old hand at adventure movies having directed *Around the World in 80 Days* (1956), *The Wreck of the Mary Deare* (1959), *The Quiller Memorandum* (1966), *Logan's Run* (1976) and the telefeature *The Martian Chronicles* (1979). The supporting cast also adds zest to the proceedings. Christopher Reeve, in one of the last films he made before the riding accident that left him paralyzed, is very good as the young snob who learns to become a man, and Catherine Mary Stewart is quite fetching as the lovely Flaxen, who falls in love with Humphrey Van Weyden. Len Cariou as Doc and Clive Revill as Cookie also add deft supporting performances. For authenticity, *The Sea Wolf* was filmed on a 120-foot, seven decades old schooner near Vancouver.

Like all of Charles Bronson's telefeatures, the film debuted on U.S. TV, this one on the TNT Network on April 18, 1993. It was then released to theatres abroad and on video domestically. The critics were mixed regarding the film. *The Washington Post* noted, "Bronson enjoys his intellectual sparring with the aristocratic Reeve as one man struggles to survive and the other hastens toward his demise." *TV Guide* complained "...with Bronson's zombified performance—he doesn't act like an old salt, he acts like a bored doorman—and a flat script, it would be called 'Sea Slug.'" On the other hand, Ray Loynd wrote in the *Los Angeles Times*, "Bronson, playing what's probably his first thinking man's heavy, seems right at home as the power-maddened Wolf Larsen...." He added the film "is essentially faithful to the novel." The *New York Times* opined, "The production is handsome but curiously lifeless, thanks in part to Mr. Bronson's insistent monotone." *Daily Variety* called the telefilm a "polished-looking production" but called it a "lumpish rendition" of the Jack London novel. Regarding the star, reviewer Tony Scott said, "Though struggling manfully with the complex role of Wolf, Bronson, stuck with some of London's original lines, not only can't find the pattern but acts ill at ease." The *Laser Disc Newsletter* (January 1993) called the movie "highly welcome" adding, "The film conveys a shipboard atmosphere effectively despite its limited production budget. Outdoor sequences are sharp."

The Charles Bronson telefilm was the ninth version of the 1904 Jack London novel, the first being a 655 foot Kalem production in 1907, directed by Herbert Brenon. In 1913 Hobart Bosworth produced a version of the novel and also starred as Wolf Larsen. Interestingly, Jack London appears as himself at the beginning of the film, which was released by W.W. Hodkinson. The next screen treatment came from George Medford Productions in 1920 with Noah Beery as Larsen in a release by Famous Players–Lasky. In 1926 PDC issued a fourth version of the London novel starring Ralph Ince and in 1930 the first sound film of the story came out from Fox, starring silent screen favorite Milton Sills as Wolf Larsen. Edward G. Robinson played Larsen in 1941's *The Sea Wolf* from Warner Bros., and in 1958 Allied Artists starred Barry Sullivan in still another rendition called *Wolf Larsen*. Chuck Connors had the title role in *Larsen: Wolf of the Seven Seas*, a 1975 Italian production from Cinetirrena–National Cinematografica.

## *Showdown at Boot Hill* (20th Century–Fox, 1958) 71 minutes B/W

*P:* Harold E. Knox. *D:* Gene Fowler Jr. *Sc:* Louis Vittes. *Ph:* John M. Nickolaus Jr. *Ed:* Frank Sullivan. *Mus:* Albert Harris. *AD:* John Mansbridge. *Asst Dir:* Nat Merman. *Sets:* Walter M. Scott & Maurice Mulcahy. *Sd:* David Dockendorf & Harry M. Leonard. *Makeup:* John Chambers. *Wardrobe:* Clark Ross. *Mus Ed:* Harry

Eisen. *Sc Supv:* Joan Eremin. *Property Master:* William Sittell. *Hair Stylist:* Eve Newing. *Transportation:* Joseph Padovich.

**CAST:** Charles Bronson (U.S. Deputy Marshal Luke Welsh), Robert Hutton (Sloane), John Carradine (Doc Weber), Carole Mathews (Jill), Fintan Meyler (Sally), Paul Maxey (The Judge), Thomas B. Henry (Con Maynor), William Stevens, Martin Smith (Cowhands), Joseph McGuinn (Mr. Creavy), George Douglas (Charles Maynor), Michael Mason (Les Patton), George Pembroke (Sheriff), Argentina Brunetti (Mrs. Bonventura), Ed Wright (Brent), Dan Simmons (Bartender), Barbara Woodell (Mrs. Maynor), Norman Leavitt (Photographer).

U.S. Deputy marshal and bounty hunter Luke Welsh (Charles Bronson) arrives in Mound City and finds Con Maynor (Thomas B. Henry) dining at the local hotel. Maynor is wanted for killing three men and Luke has a warrant for his arrest. He kills Maynor in a shootout but is unable to collect the $200 reward because the townspeople, who liked Maynor, refuse to identify him. When he has a picture taken of the corpse, snipers destroy the plates and the camera. Luke tries to get waitress Sally (Fintan Meyler), whose mother Jill (Carole Mathews) runs the local saloon, to identify Maynor but she refuses. Local cattleman Sloane (Robert Hutton), who was once aided by Maynor, wants revenge for the outlaw's death and sends word to the deceased's brother Charles (George Douglas) that his sibling has been killed. Sloane also wants Jill's lover, Les Patton (Michael Mason), to shoot Luke. The lawman, who is obsessed by his short stature, finds he has feelings for Sally who is withdrawn and ashamed of her mother, with whom she refuses to associate. When Luke takes Sally to the town dance he is asked to leave and when he goes to talk to Jill about her daughter he is goaded into a fight by Patton, who is injured in the fracas. Sloane incites the locals to go against Luke but Jill talks Sally into taking him to her house where he tells Sally he loves her. A crazed Patton barges in and tries to shoot Luke but instead wounds Jill, who dies within hours. The local doctor (John Carradine) tells Luke he could have prevented the tragedy 20 years before by asking Jill to marry him but he did not because he was too ashamed of being a cripple. At Maynor's funeral at Boot Hill, Luke confronts the dead man's brother who attacks him but Luke has thrown away his gun. When the brother is led away by the townspeople, Luke goes back to Sally.

A modest psychological Western, *Showdown at Boot Hill* is nonetheless an interesting programmer which spotlights Charles Bronson in his first starring sagebrush role. He is especially effective as the bounty hunter who the heroine says tries "to hide loneliness behind a gun." He is nicely complimented by Irish actress Fintan Meyler, in her screen debut, as the young woman who does not like men because of her mother's tainted past but who grows to trust and then love the lawman. Robert Hutton is fine as the vengeful rancher, John Carradine adds interest as the town's barber-doctor-undertaker who is lame from a stray bullet, and Carole Mathews nicely portrays

Advertisement for *Showdown at Boot Hill* (20th Century–Fox, 1958).

the hooker at the Crystal Palace. The supporting players also etch out interesting characterizations, especially corpulent Paul Maxey as the town's pseudo-judge, Michael Mason as the quick gun stud, George Pembroke's taciturn sheriff, Barbara Woodell as the wife who does not want her husband to take vengeance for the death of his outlaw brother, and Argentina Brunetti as the widowed storekeeper who promotes the romance between Luke and Sally. The script has some pungent dialogue, such as Luke telling the townspeople, after having shot Con Maynor, that they had "better have an inquest pretty quick. Weather like this he won't keep." There are a couple of well-played scenes showing Luke's growing affection for Sally, such as his buying a bottle of cream for her rough hands and Brunetti's presenting him with a beautiful nightgown for him to give to Sally as a present. The movie also opens with interesting credit panning shots as Luke arrives in Mound City and seeks out Con Maynor. The wanted man is played by Thomas Browne Henry, a one-time instructor of Bronson's at the Pasadena Playhouse and the man responsible for the actor getting his first screen role in 1951. Henry makes the most of his brief scenes as the slick killer.

*Variety* called the movie "a well-directed and well-acted film done with taste and imagination" while Phil Hardy in *The Western* (1983) wrote, "The best film of B director Fowler.... A superior B Western." Jay Robert Nash and Stanley Ralph Ross noted in *The Motion Picture Guide* (1985), "This interesting psychological Western is a well-scripted, nicely directed piece that goes well beyond its programmer budget." Regarding the star, they wrote, "Bronson gives one of his better performances as the tortured man.... Though Bronson (sans his famous Fu Manchu mustache) shows some real talent, it would take him ten more years and a new career in European film before he would become a star. Perhaps audiences of the 1950s were not yet ready for as untraditional a leading man as Bronson." The first film in which Bronson wore a mustache was *Villa Rides!* in 1968 and it became a near permanent fixture beginning with *La Passager de la Pluie (Rider on the Rain)* in 1970.

Charles Bronson had his first screen-starring role for producer Harold E. Knox in *Gang War*, issued theatrically two months before *Showdown at Boot Hill.* It too was a Regal Film in Regalscope, distributed by 20th Century–Fox, and directed by Gene Fowler Jr., written by Louis Vittes and photographed by John M. Nickolaus Jr.

## *Soleil Rouge (Red Sun)* (Corona Films/Oceania Films/Balcazar Films, 1971) 112 minutes Color

*P:* Ted Richmond. *EP:* Robert Dorfmann. *D:* Terence Young. *Sc:* Laird Koenig, Dennis Bart Petitclerc, William Roberts & Lawrence Roman. *St:* Laird Koenig. *Ph:* Henri Alekan. *Ed:* Johnny Dwyre. *Mus:* Maurice Jarre. *Second Unit Director:* Bernard Farrel. *Asst Dir:* Christian Raoux & Ricardo Huerta. *Second Unit Ph:* Raymond Picon-Borel. *AD:* Enrique Alarcon. *Set Decorator:* Rafael Salazar. *Sp Eff:* Karl Baumgartner. *Supv Ed:* Lou Lombardo. *Sd:* William R. Sivel & Maurice Laumain. *Costumes:* Tony Pulo. *Makeup:* Alberto De Rossi. *Prod Mgr:* Serge Lebeau & Julio Vallejo. *Continuity:* Joan Davis.

**CAST:** Charles Bronson (Link), Ursula Andress (Christina), Toshiro Mifune (Kuroda), Alain Delon (Gauche), Capucine (Pepita), Satoshi Nakamoura (Ambassador), Bart Barry (Sheriff), Monica Randall (Maria), Anthony Dawson (Hiatt), Hiroshi Tanaka (Warrior), Lee Burton, John Hamilton, George W. Lycan, Luc Merenda, Jose Nieto, Julio Pena, John Vermont.

In 1880 the Japanese ambassador (Satoshi Nakamoura) to the United States is on a train going east with a golden sword, a special gift from the Mikado to the country's president. Link (Charles Bronson) and Gauche (Alain Delon) and their men rob the train and Gauche steals the sword, killing one of its Samurai guards (Hiroshi Tanaka). In getting away with over a million dollars in government currency, Gauche also tries to kill Link but fails. The Japanese ambassador orders Link to lead the other Samurai guard, Kuroda (Toshiro Mifune), in his quest to retrieve the sword and kill Gauche. If the deed is not accomplished in a week then Kuroda will kill himself as a sign of disgrace. Link and Kuroda walk cross country but Link is always trying to lose the Japanese warrior, without success. Meanwhile Gauche buries

**Ursula Andress, Charles Bronson and Toshiro Mifune in *Soleil Rouge (Red Sun)* (Corona Films/Oceania Films/Balcazar Films, 1971).**

the gold in a secret place, killing all of those who know its whereabouts. As Link and Kuroda develop a wary respect for each other they see some of Gauche's men kill an old man at a remote ranch. They avenge his death and then leave on horses but Link still cannot convince Kuroda to let Gauche live long enough for him to find out the money's location. With Comanches on the prowl, the two head to San Lucas where Gauche's girlfriend, Christina (Ursula Andress), works in a brothel run by Link's lover Pepita (Capucine). Taking Christina prisoner, Link and Kuroda enjoy the pleasures of the brothel before killing some of Gauche's men who have come for the girl. Link lets Hiatt (Anthony Dawson) live and tells him to have Gauche meet them at an old mission, one day's ride away. On the way to the mission the girl gets away but is captured by Comanches who leave her to die in the sun. Link and Kuroda rescue her but when they arrive at the mission they are surrounded by Gauche's gang. The Comanches attack and all the men join in the fight which eventually ends up in a canebrake surrounding the mission. There the outlaws pick off the Comanches with Gauche being wounded. He mortally wounds Kuroda but is killed by Link, who promises the dying Samurai to return the sword to his country's ambassador. Link and Christina team up to find the hidden gold but Link also keeps his promise to Kuroda.

Based on an actual event in American history, *Red Sun* was financed by French, Italian and Spanish film companies. The film reunited Charles Bronson with executive producer Robert Dorfmann and director Terence Young from *De la Part des Copains*, Alain Delon from *Adieu l'Ami* and Ursula Andress from *4 for Texas*. Several members of the production team from *De la Part des Copains* also were involved in this feature as they were both partially financed by the French firm Les Films Corona. Besides a pleasing script containing the action and violence expected by Bronson fans, the movie boasted beautiful locales, good Eastmancolor photography by Henri Alekan and a stirring music score by Maurice Jarre. The film was Bronson's greatest international hit to date and in Japan it set an attendance record, playing in Tokyo for a record 35 weeks in its first run engagements. It was released in the United States in 1972 by National General Pictures but like most Bronson films of the time it did not have the success it attained abroad. In Italy it was called *Sole Rosso* and in Spain *Sol Rojo*.

Link, the role played by Charles Bronson in *Red Sun*, is one of his most interesting characters. When Kuroda tells Link one must live by ideas, the character responds, "You can't spend ideas." During the course of the film the outlaw goes from a loner only after riches to a man of feeling who learns there is more to life than money and self-pleasure. The screen charisma of both Charles Bronson and Toshiro Mifune, Japan's most popular film star, proved to be very appealing and the two actors from such diverse cultures worked well together making their characters both likable and heroic. Alain Delon had a relatively small role as the cold-blooded, left-handed gambler-killer

Gauche while Ursula Andress and Capucine were basically along for window dressing. A nicely played minor sequence had Kuroda developing a fondness for a young Mexican whore (Monica Randall) during his night at the brothel. While the plot of *Red Sun* was none too strong, it moved at such a good clip that audiences hardly noticed, although there were the usual grumblings among some critics.

While the *Independent Film Journal* did not care much for *Red Sun* the reviewer did note of its stars, "These two are virtual legends, Mifune in Japan, Bronson in Europe, and this film gives a pretty good idea why." Kevin Thomas in the *Los Angeles Times* thought, "This release is at its best in its humorous, affectionate treatment of the uneasy truce between Bronson and Mifune that develops into friendship...." The *New York Times* terms it "a very conventional western—a little above routine." Phil Hardy in *The Western* (1985) said, "This is a disaster of a would-be exotic international co-production of a Western," while Henry Herx and Tony Zaza in *The Family Guide to Movies on Video* (1988) noted, "Granted the fantasy plot, director Terence Young treats the derring-do with too little whimsical flair and too much prosaic gore."

It should be noted the success of *Red Sun* resulted in a spate of similar screen fare like Lee Van Cleef in *Stranger and the Gunfighter* (1973), *Kung Fu Brothers in the Wild West* (1973) and *The White, the Yellow and the Black* (1974) with Eli Wallach.

At the time of *Red Sun*'s release, Charles Bronson was enjoying great popularity in Japan not only due to his films but for his appearing in a TV commercial for a men's aftershave, Mandom. In 1971 he and Sean Connery received Hollywood's Foreign Press Association's Golden Globe Award as the most popular male film stars in the world. The same year the French voted Bronson the most attractive man in the world.

## *Someone Behind the Door* see *Quelqu'un Derrière la Porte*

## *The Stone Killer* (Columbia, 1973) 100 minutes Color

*P-D:* Michael Winner. *EP:* Dino De Laurentiis. *Sc:* Gerald Wilson, from the novel *A Complete State of Death* by John Gardner. *Ph:* Richard Moore. *Ed:* Frederick Wilson. *AD:* Ward Preston. *Mus:* Roy Budd. *Sd:* Thomas Thompson. *Prod Mgr:* Ralph Black. *Asst Dir:* Joe Ellis & Mel Efros. *Sets:* Norman Rockett. *Sd Ed:* Russ Hill. *Re-recordist:* Hugh Strain. *Stunt Coordinator:* Alan Gibbs. *Dubbing Ed:* Terence Rawlings. *Casting:* Joe Scully. *Camera Operators:* Hugh Ganger & Louis Barlia. *Continuity:* June Samson. *Makeup:* Philip Rhodes. *Costume Supv:* Seth Banks. *Unit Mgr:* Herb Wallerstein. *Asst to Producer:* Steve Cory.

**CAST:** Charles Bronson (Lieutenant Lou Torrey), Martin Balsam (Al

Vescari), Ralph Waite (Cracker Mathews), David Sheiner (Guido Lorenz), Norman Fell (Captain Les Daniels), Eddie Firestone (George Armitage), Walter Burke (J.D.), David Moody (Gustav "Gus" Lipper), Charles Tyner (Psychiatrist), Paul Koslo (Al Langley/Alfred Lawson), Stuart Margolin (Lawrence), John Ritter (Patrolman Hart), Byron Morrow (Los Angeles Police Chief), Jack Colvin (Lionel Henry Jumper), Frank Campanella (Calabriese), Alfred Ryder (Tony Champion), Gene Woodbury (Paul Long), Harry Basch (Mossman), Jan Arvan (Vechetti), Lisabeth Hush (Helen), Mary Cross (Waitress), Kelly Miles (Geraldine Wexton), Tom Falk (Police Sergeant), Robert Emhardt (Man from Seattle), Frenchie Guizon (Drug Pusher), Cristina Raines (Matthews' Daughter), Norman D. Paulson (Bartender), Sam Locanne (Soldier), Ed Madsen, Arthur Frank (New York City Detectives), Hank Howell (Garage Man), Ti Tatisha (Sales Girl), Hy Anzell (Cab Driver), Larry J. Elfex (Police Commissioner), Angelo Rossitto (Little Man), Chuck Roberson, Barry Cahill, William Daffano.

In Spanish Harlem, police detective Lou Torrey (Charles Bronson) is forced to kill a 17-year-old boy who had robbed a liquor store and shot a cop. There is such a public uproar, however, that Torrey accepts an invitation to go to work in Los Angeles for his friend, Captain Les Daniels (Norman Fell). One of his first assignments is the arrest of Armitage (Eddie Firestone), an old time Mafia shooter who is now a heroin addict wanted on a murder charge in Gotham. Torrey takes him back east only to see him gunned down at the airport. At the same time ex–GI Gus Lipper (David Moody) is under arrest on a minor charge but he is involved in an operation Mafia boss Al Vescari (Martin Balsam) wants kept quiet and he orders Lipper's murder. Involved in the proposed killing are jazz musician Al Langley (Paul Koslo) and Lionel Jumper (Jack Colvin). Al slips Lipper a gun and he gets the drop on his guard, Patrolman Hart (John Ritter), but is gunned down before he can make a getaway. Torrey, who has returned to Los Angeles, sees a connection between the two killings and he questions Jumper after the latter is picked up at the airport. Meanwhile Vescari is planning a "birthday party" for other "family" leaders whose ancestors murdered his kin in a blood feud 42 years before. He has hired Lawrence (Stuart Margolin) to train ex-servicemen to carry out a hit on other gangland bosses, Jumper, and the late Lipper, being part of the team. Torrey sends his partner, bumbling Mathews (Ralph Waite), to pick up Langley but the latter manages to get away. The police commissioner (Byron Morrow) orders the arrest of a black suspect, which causes unrest in the black community. Through an informant, Torrey locates Langley and is forced to chase him in a car through traffic, eventually killing him when his car crashes into Langley. Torrey then gets Jumper released on bond and trails him via helicopter to a remote spot in the Mojave Desert. It is there that Lawrence has been training his killers and when he gets a call from Jumper he orders him killed. Jumper is shot but Torrey arrives and before dying Jumper tells him of an impending gangland mass killing. Going back to New

**Charles Bronson and Ralph Waite in *The Stone Killer* (Columbia, 1973).**

York City, Torrey works with police captain Guido Lorenz (David Sheiner) on the case and they place a tail on underworld figures who have just arrived in town. They follow them to a hotel where the hit is carried out although the police arrive in time to stop the killers from escaping, with a shootout taking place in the building's parking garage.

*The Stone Killer* was Charles Bronson's third feature for producer Dino De Laurentiis and also his third with director Michael Winner. For once this Bronson feature was filmed entirely in the United States, with location shooting in New York City and Los Angeles. The picture was an even bigger success in the United States than *The Mechanic* and naturally it was a blockbuster overseas. A German source, *Lexikon de Internationalen Films*, claims it was an Italian-American co-production. In Italy the film was called *L'Assassino di Pietra* while in France it was released as *Le Cercle Noire.*

A complicated police thriller, *The Stone Killer* had a plot that was difficult to follow and a myriad of characters, all of them quite interesting. For action fans there was an exciting car-motorcycle chase sequence and well-staged shootouts at the desert training retreat and in the Gotham office building parking garage. The title refers to hired outside guns, such as those used by Lucky Luciano four decades before to wipe out Vescari's Sicilian ancestors.

The title also refers to the ex-soldiers he hires to knock off Luciano's modern-day counterparts. The film is a masculine one, containing very few female characters. Early in the film Torrey is chewed out by his sister (Lisabeth Hush) for not associating with his daughter and later he is propositioned by a pretty suspect (Kelly Miles) at a remote hippie commune. "Another time, another place, another cop," he tells her. Bronson's Lou Torrey is a stoic cop bent on strict law enforcement but not above bending the rules to get his way. He thinks nothing of slugging a suspect to get needed information as he does with a drug pusher (Frenchie Guizon) and later when he interrogates Jumper. When he is reprimanded for killing the young robbery suspect in self-defense he tells his superior, "The gun made him older." Lou Torrey is the type of law enforcer who goes straight from crime to justice, there is no in-between.

A top-notch production, *The Stone Killer*'s supporting cast is superb but the movie is weakened by an ambiguous ending. Martin Balsam is fine as the church-going Mafia don out to kill off his rivals and even an old "family" score. He is nicely abetted by henchmen Calabriese (Frank Campanella) and Tony Champion (Alfred Ryder), who dies in the desert shootout with the law. Norman Fell and David Sheiner are properly at a loss for words as Torrey's sympathetic superior officers while Byron Morrow is very good as the hard-headed L.A. police commissioner. Ralph Waite is fine as Torrey's quasi-partner, numbskull, racist Cracker Mathews, and Walter Burke is fun as a drug-pushing informant. Very good as sleazy gangland underlings are Paul Koslo, Eddie Firestone and Jack Colvin. John Ritter does well as an incompetent patrolman and Charles Tyner has a good scene as a psychiatrist who explains society's ills to a none-too-caring Torrey. Stuart Margolin has some nice lines as the stone killer's trainer: "I was fifteen when they hit Pearl Harbor and I've been at it ever since. Only now I'm for hire," he tells Vescari's henchman Tony Champion when asked about his mercenary lifestyle. Plotwise *The Stone Killer* has some harsh words for the FBI and law enforcement hierarchy in general.

*Films and Filming* said the movie was "a routine policer, distinguished only by [director Michael] Winner's usual unerring eye for character actors who tell it all in their faces, and by the steely presence of Mr. Bronson." *Variety* called it "a confused, meandering crime potboiler.... The story and director reach for so many bases that the end result is a lot of cinema razzle-dazzle without substance." Roy Frumkes wrote in *Films in Review*, "...Winner pins a tale on the level of the best of the heavyweights. There are seventy odd locations, used seldom more than twice in the film. Within each sequence he has placed seductive secondary emotional conflicts, whose primary purpose is to further the progression of the plot, succinctly filling film-time to overflowing with detail and interest." Regarding the star, he said, "Charles Bronson as the protagonist, performs with subdued animosity and compassion, degrees of tempered emotion called for by the role. In the last few years he has become a very capable leading man, able to sustain an entire film." The *New York Times* noted of the film, "It may come as close to inspired primitivism as we are likely to get in the movies these days." Lynn Minton in *Movie Guide For Puzzled Parents* (1984) said the film had "the usual mix of station humor, chases, tough interrogations, colorful locations and the obligatory killings" in its "convoluted and implausible plot." Henry Herx and Tony Zaza zeroed in on the social implications of the feature in *The Family Guide to Movies on Video* (1988) by noting "the film's core theme is the nearly interchangeable identities of police and criminal as they act out their respective vicious roles within a society pictured on the verge of collapse."

Charles Bronson would next work with producer Dino De Laurentiis and director Michael Winner on the biggest success of his career, *Death Wish* (1974).

## *Target Zero* (Warner Bros., 1955) 92 minutes B/W

*P:* David Weisbart. *D:* Harmon Jones. *Sc:* Sam Rolfe. *St:* James Warner Bellah. *P:* Edwin Du Pa. *Ed:* Clarence Kolster. *AD:* Leo K. Kuter. *Sets:* G.W. Bernstein. *Mus:* David Buttolph. *Sd:* Leslie G. Hewitt. *Asst Dir:* Oren Haglund.

**CAST:** Richard Conte (Lieutenant Tom Flagler), Peggie Castle (Ann Galloway), Charles Bronson (Sergeant Vince Gaspari), Richard Stapley (Sergeant David Kensemmit), L.Q. Jones (Private Felix Zimbalist), Chuck Connors (Private Moose), John Alderson (Corporal Devon Enouch), Terence De Marney (Private Harry Fontenoy), John Dennis (Private First Class George), Angela Loo (Sue), Abel Fernandez (Private Geronimo), Richard Park (Private Ma Koo Sung), Don Orbek (Private Stacey Zorbados), Strother Martin (Dan O'Hirons), Aaron Spelling (Strangler), George Chan (Priest), Joby Baker (Soldier), Leo K. Kuter (Colonel), Hal Sheiner (Marine Officer).

Caught behind enemy lines in Korea, a group of soldiers led by Lieutenant Tom Flagler (Richard Conte) and Sergeant Vince Gaspari (Charles Bronson) attempt to return to their destination, a ridge called Sullivan's Muscle. As they try to avoid enemy snipers along the way they pick up stranded United Nations biochemist Ann Galloway (Peggie Castle) and Yank-hating British sergeant David Kensemmit (Richard Stapley) and his two remaining men (John Alderson, Terence De Marney), who have escaped the enemy in a tank. After several skirmishes with the enemy, the ragtag group reaches its destination only to find the garrison has been wiped out. As the group holds the ridge, the fighting men begin to respect each other as Tom and Ann fall in love. Finally United Nations forces arrive on the scene and they are rescued.

Charles Bronson returned to a Korean War–themed picture with *Target Zero* but here he got the best billing yet of his career, third after stars Richard Conte and Peggie Castle, in deference to the bit he had done in his first Korean War effort, *Torpedo Alley* in 1953. While his role was large it was hardly taxing as a loyal and tough army sergeant. *Variety* did call attention to his

Advertisement for *Target Zero* (Warner Bros., 1955).

performance noting "Charles Bronson is good as a Yank sarge." Overall, though, critics did not take kindly to this low-budget war effort. The *Monthly Film Bulletin* wrote, "After a few tentative attempts at individual characterization, the film soon deteriorates into routine battle exploits culminating in one of the most cold-blooded massacres yet seen in an American war film." *The Green Sheet* said, "throughout the action much philosophical dialogue is exchanged by the soldiers." The *New York Times* complained the feature contained "an easy, wholesale slaughter of North Koreans as a climax."

Filmed at Fort Carson, Colorado, *Target Zero* got sad production publicity when two munitions experts were killed by exploding dynamite during the staging of a battle sequence.

*Target Zero* was not released in France until 1963, the same year as *Machine Gun Kelly* (1958). Both features helped the French in recognizing the screen persona which would make Bronson world famous by the end of the decade.

## *Telefon* (Metro-Goldwyn-Mayer, 1977) 103 minutes Color

*P:* James B. Harris. *D:* Don Siegel. *Sc:* Peter Hyams & Stirling Silliphant, from the novel by Walter Wager. *Ph:* Michael Butler. *Ed:* Douglas Stewart. *Mus:* Lalo Schifrin. *AD:* William F. O'Brien. *Prod Designer:* Ted Haworth. *Set Decorator:* Robert Benton. *Sd:* Alfred J. Overton, William McCaughey, Aaron Rochin & Michael J. Kohut. *Asst Dir:* David Hamburger & Luigi Alfano. *Asst Ed:* Hal G. Davis. *Sd Eff Ed:* John P. Riordan. *Mus Supv:* Harry V. Lojewski. *Mus Ed:* Joe Tuley. *Unit Prod Mgrs:* Louis A. Stroller, Jim Henderling, Bernard Hanson & Maurice Vaccarino. *Second Asst Dir:* Stephen Lim & Alan Brimfield. *Sc Supv:* Betsy Norton. *Dir Associate:* Carol Rydall. *Location Mgr:* Mary Eli Schwartz. *Unit Publicity:* Ernest Anderson. *Still Photographer:* Kenny Bell. *Finnish Liaison:* Ake Lindman. *Producer's Asst:* Dorothy Ringer. *Sp Eff Coordinator:* Joe Day. *Property Master:* Bill Dietz. *Stunt Coordinator:* Paul Baxley. *Camera Operators:* John Fleckenstein & Dick Colean. *Asst Cameramen:* Frank Tureen & Bob Guthrie. *Key Grip:* Gino Barragy. *Gaffer:* Michael Jones. *Miss Remick's Costumes:* Jane Robinson. *Men's Costumes:* Luther Bayless. *Women's Costumes:* Edna Taylor. *Makeup:* Philip Rhodes & Del Acevedo. *Hair Stylist:* Jean Burt Reilly. *Casting:* Rolifroni/ Sabba.

CAST: Charles Bronson (Major Grigori Borzov), Lee Remick (Barbara), Donald Pleasence (Nicolai Dalchimsky), Tyne Daly (Dorothy Putterman), Alan Badel (Colonel Malchenko), Patrick Magee (General Strelsky), Sheree North (Marie Wills), Frank Marth (Harley Sandburg), Helen Page Camp (Emma Stark), Roy Jenson (Doug Stark), Jacqueline Scott (Mrs. Hassler), Ed Bakey (Carl Hassler), John Mitchum (Harry Bascom), Iggie Wolfington (Father Stuart Diller), Kathleen O'Malley (Mrs. Maloney), Ake Lindman (Lieutenant Alexandrov), Ansa Konen (Mrs. Dalchimsky), Hank Brandt (William Enders), John Carter (Stroller), John Hambrick (TV Newsman), Henry Alfaro (TV Reporter), Glenda Wina (TV Anchor Woman), Jim Nolan (Appliance Store Clerk), Burton Gilliam (Gas Station Attendant), Regis J. Cordic (Doctor), George Petrie (Hotel Receptionist), Jeff David (Maitre d'), Carmen Zapata (Nurse), Carl Byrd (Navy Lieutenant), Lew Brown (Petty Officer), Peter Weiss (Radio Operator), Robert Phillips, Cliff Emmich (Highway Patrolmen), Alex Sharp (Martin Callender), Margaret Hall Baron (Airport Clerk), Al Dunlap (Taxi Driver), Sean Moloney (Hot Rod Kid), Ville Veikko Salminen (Russian Steward), Teppo Heiskanen, Mika Levio (Hockey Players), Marlene Hazlett, Thomas M. Runyon, Claudia Butler, Philippe Butler (Tourist Family), Stephanie Ann Rydall, Derek Rydall (The Wills Children).

The title of this film is from the Russian word for telephone and in *Telefon* Charles Bronson starred as a Soviet military man who comes to the United States to stop a Stalinist madman from possibly instigating a nuclear war. Even in the then new climate of detente, the movie's plot offended the

Soviet Union despite the fact that Bronson's character was presented as the movie's hero. For location shooting, the movie was lensed in Helsinki, Finland, because parts of the Finnish capital resemble Russian construction. The state building of Leningrad in Russia was designed by the same master architect who also designed many of Helsinki's buildings. When the film crew came to Helsinki they drew a great deal of national and international publicity. Bronson, whose films were very popular in Finland, received front page newspaper coverage as well as intensive radio and television stories. The Russian news agency, *Izvestia*, denounced *Telefon* and this made international news. The Russian publication complained about the film's $7 million budget and Charles Bronson's $1.5 million salary. Ironically, Bronson's international popularity also included many fans in the Soviet Union.

In Moscow, General Strelsky (Patrick Magee) and Colonel Malchenko (Alan Badel) lead a raid on the apartment of KGB employee Nicolai Dalchimsky (Donald Pleasence) but they find he has vanished. Coming to the United States, Dalchimsky telephones garage owner Harry Bascom (John Mitchum) in Denver, Colorado, and giving him a coded message he causes the man to drive to a local military installation, kill a sentry and plow into a building, causing a major explosion and fire. Meanwhile at CIA headquarters worker Dorothy Putterman (Tyne Daly) informs her boss, Harley Sandburg (Frank Marth), that there has been a recent rash of deaths among hard-line Stalinists in the Soviet Union. They also are informed that Bascom was an imposter. In Florida helicopter charter pilot Carl Hassler (Ed Bakey) gets a call from Dalchimsky and tries to fly into a government communications area but is shot down by a missile. In Leningrad, Major Grigori Borzov (Charles Bronson) is called to the headquarters of General Strelsky and there Colonel Malchenko informs him of a secret operation, Code Name Telefon, in which Soviets were placed in the United States and through drug-assisted hypnosis were to be used to sabotage strategic military installations. With the coming of the thaw in the Cold War the operation was dropped but the mad Dalchimsky has stolen the list of agents' names and must be stopped. With 51 agents still in America, Borzov is assigned to find and kill Dalchimsky before he sets off a nuclear war. Arriving in Calgary, Canada, Borzov, now calling himself Greg Taylor, meets Soviet operative Barbara (Lee Remick) and when they learn a priest (Iggie Wolfington) has blown up a telephone communications center in Los Angeles they fly there and Barbara carries out Borzov's orders to kill the priest. Next Dalchimsky contacts housewife Marie Wills (Sheree North) in New Mexico and she blows up another installation before committing suicide. Borzov realizes that Dalchimsky is using the letters of his own name to pick the locales to make his calls and they trace him to Houston, Texas, and businessman Martin Callender (Alex Sharp). Barbara, who is really a double agent, calls the CIA and Sandburg tells her to kill Borzov once his mission is completed. Callender is killed by Borzov after

**Charles Bronson in *Telefon* (Metro-Goldwyn-Mayer, 1977).**

being involved in a car crash in the garage of his office building and the two agents then follow Dalchimsky to Haldersville, Texas, where he plans to program roadhouse owner Doug Stark (Roy Jenson). Borzov and Barbara arrive first, however, and Borzov eliminates Stark before finally killing Dalchimsky in a telephone booth as he is trying to make more calls. Borzov and Barbara, who are in love, defect from their respective organizations telling them more phone calls will be made if they are ever bothered.

Early on in the film when the Russian general finds out that the Stalinist had escaped he says, "God help us." "God?," replies his started associate. *Telefon* is none too flattering to the Soviet KGB or military intelligence and it also takes some swipes at the rivalry between the FBI and the CIA. The latter's chief is shown to be little better than a cold-blooded murderer and Tyne Daly's role as the subordinate who is infatuated with him is basically superfluous. Charles Bronson is justly heroic as the Soviet agent and the film contains enough action to satisfy his legion of fans. Lee Remick is attractive as the somewhat addled double agent and Donald Pleasence mugs as the mad-as-a-hatter Stalinist. A large supporting cast does well, particularly

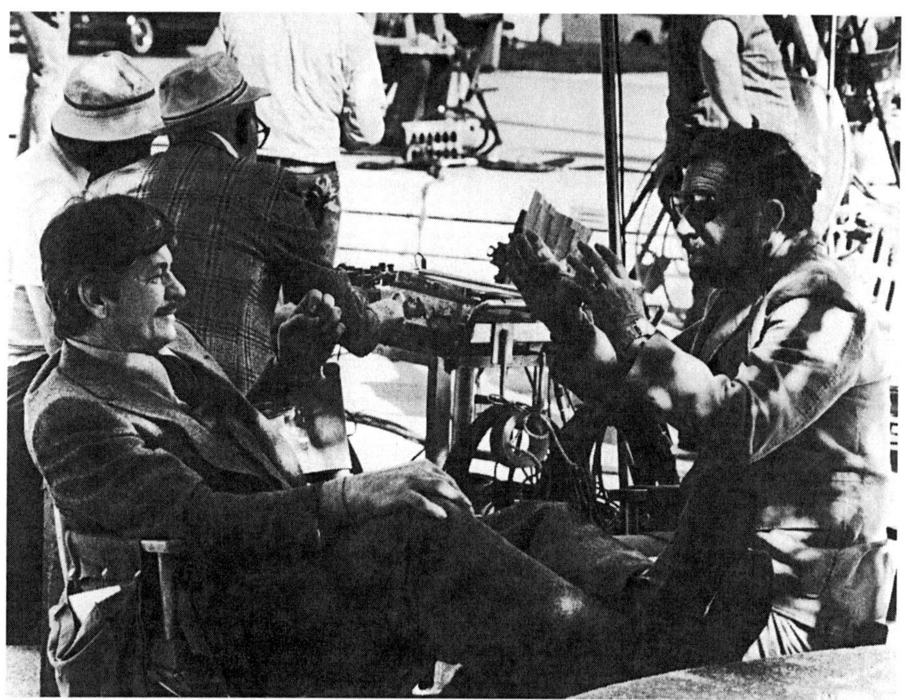

**Charles Bronson and director Don Siegel on the set of *Telefon* (Metro-Goldwyn-Mayer, 1977).**

Sheree North, John Mitchum and Roy Jenson as the automatons used for sabotage and Jacqueline Scott and Helen Page Camp as the wives of two of the saboteurs. Besides the Helsinki locations, the movie jumps around the U.S. from Colorado to Florida to Texas.

*Newsweek* called *Telefon* "good fun" while *Variety* thought it "pleasant escapism." Vincent Canby in the *New York Times* noted, "Mr. Bronson is a movie actor of the old school. He doesn't seem to act (though that is what he's doing) as much as he inhabits a film with his particular, massive presence, giving the film much-needed ballast. Without him, *Telefon* would fly up to the ceiling and just hang there." Lynn Minton wrote in *Movie Guide for Puzzled Parents* (1984), "Imaginative plotting, not bloodshed (there's very little), creates the suspense in this crackerjack thriller...." In *The Complete Guide to Videocassette Movies* (1987), Steven H. Scheuer said the film was an "engrossing spy story" adding "Bronson and Remick ... make an unusual but oddly workable romantic couple." Henry Herx and Tony Zaza wrote in *The Family Guide to Movies on Video* (1988), "Mediocre thriller made more bearable by a lavish production, Don Siegel's smooth direction and Lee Remick's personable performance.... Some graphic violence."

*Telefon* marked Charles Bronson's return to a popular vehicle following the unsuccessful *The White Buffalo* in 1977. It also was the third teaming of director Don Siegel and Bronson, although it was their first and only feature film together. Previously they had worked on television in a pilot for *The Lineup* and an episode of "The Legend of Jesse James," which was produced by Siegel, known best for films like *The Big Steal* (1949), *Invasion of the Body Snatchers* (1956), *Flaming Star* (1960), *Coogan's Bluff* (1968), *The Beguiled* (1970), *Dirty Harry* (1971), *The Shootist* (1976) and *Escape from Alcatraz* (1979).

## *Ten North Frederick* (20th Century–Fox, 1958) 102 minutes B/W

*P:* Charles Brackett. *D-Sc:* Philip Dunne, from the novel by John O'Hara. *Ph:* Joe MacDonald. *Ed:* David Bretherton. *AD:* Lyle Wheeler & Addison Hehr. *Sets:* Walter M. Scott & Eli Benneche. *Mus:* Leigh Harline. *Mus Dir:* Lionel Newman. *Sp Eff:* L.B. Abbott. *Costumes:* Charles Le Maire. *Makeup:* Ben Nye. *Hair Styles:* Helen Turpin. *Sd:* Alfred Bruzlin. *Orchestrator:* Edward B. Powell. *Asst Dir:* Hal Herman.

**CAST:** Gary Cooper (Joe Chapin), Diane Varsi (Ann Chapin), Suzy Parker (Kate Drummond), Geraldine Fitzgerald (Edith Chapin), Tom Tully (Slattery), Ray Stricklyn (Joby Chapin), Philip Ober (Lloyd Williams), John Emery (Paul Donaldson), Stuart Whitman (Charley Bongiorno), Linda Watkins (Peg Slattery), Barbara Nichols (Stella), Joe McGuinn (Dr. English), Jess Kirkpatrick (Arthur McHenry), Nolan Leary (Harry Jackson), Beverly Jo Morrow (Waitress), Buck Class (Bill), Rachel Stephens (Salesgirl), Bob Adler (Farmer), Linc Foster (Peter), John Harding (Robert Hooker), Dudley Manlove (Ted Wallace), Mack Williams (General Coates), Vernon Rich (Board Chairman), Mary Carroll (Nurse), George Davis (Waiter), Joey Faye (Taxi Driver), Fred Essler (Hoffman), Irene Seidner (Wife), Melinda Byron (Hope), Sean Meaney (Saxophone Player), John Indrisano, Michael Pataki, Michael Morelli (Men), Charles Bronson (Man in Background).

Businessman Joe Chapin (Gary Cooper) is married to an ambitious wife, Edith Chapin (Geraldine Fitzgerald), who wants him to be president of the United States. He contributes to a political party in return for the promise of being nominated for the post of the state's lieutenant governor. The Chapins' daughter Ann (Diane Varsi) gets involved with a musician (Philip Ober) whom she marries. When she is confronted by her mother the girl has a miscarriage and Joe buys off his son-in-law as Ann walks out on her parents. When his political cronies turn on Joe and make his daughter's situation known, Edith tells him she has a lover. Heading for New York City Joe meets Ann's college roommate Kate Drummond (Suzy Parker) and the two have an affair. Realizing he is too old for her, Joe leaves Kate. As he develops a terminal illness his son Joby (Ray Stricklyn) helps him to reconcile with Ann.

Charles Bronson's participation in this glossy but empty melodrama is merely a footnote in his filmography. He makes a fleeting appearance in the background of a crowd scene, apparently as a favor to star Gary Cooper with whom he was visiting.

## *10 to Midnight* (Cannon Group, 1983), 102 minutes Color

*P:* Pancho Kohner & Lance Hool. *EP:* Menahem Golan & Yoram Globus. *D:* J. Lee Thompson. *Sc:* William Roberts. *Ph:* Adam Greenburg. *Ed:* Peter Lee-Thompson. *Mus:* Robert O. Ragland. *AD:* Jim Frieburger. *Executive in Charge of Prod:* Christopher Pearce. *Unit Prod Mgr:* John Zane. *Asst Dir:* Barbara Michaels & Terry Buchinsky. *Prod Mgr:* Robert Ortwin. *Casting:* John Crowther. *Asst Ed:* Richard Mark & Debra Whitcomb. *Mus Ed:* Michael Linn. *Sp Eff Ed:* Mike Le Maire. *Policy Ed:* Michael Sloan. *ADR Editor:* Michael Redbourn. *Post Prod Supv:* K.V. Hozing. *Prod Sd Mixer:* Craig Felburg. *Re-recording Mixers:* Jay M. Harding, Paul Sharp & Gregory M. Watkins. *First Camera Asst:* Ted Hauser. *Second Camera Asst:* Ronny Dana & Diane Schneider. *Key Grip:* Dylan Shepard. *Boom Operator:* Hal Schwartz. *Gaffer:* Avraham Leidman. *Set Decorator:* Cecilia Rodarte. *Still Photography:* Dave King & Alan Levine. *Stunt Coordinator:* Ernie Orsatti. *Sc Supv:* Karin Cooper. *Costume Supv:* Poppy Cannon. *Women's Costumes:* Del Ady-Jones. *Men's Costumes:* Robert Dale. *Hairstylist:* Laurence Loverde. *Makeup:* Alan Marshall. *Property:* Randy Gunter. *Best Boy:* Scott Butterfield. *Transportation Coordinator:* Frank Ballou. *Transportation Captain:* Ron White. *Prod Coordinators:* Connie Sanchez & E. Ann Overman. *Prod Asst:* Paul Ford & Lyle Lytell. *Prod Accountant:* Elliott J. Miller. *Extra Casting:* Dennis Hansen. *Aerial Sequence:* Mischa Haussermann. *Police Technical Advisor:* William Hool.

**CAST:** Charles Bronson (Lieutenant Leo Kessler), Lisa Eilbacher (Laurie Kessler), Andrew Stevens (Detective Paul McAnn), Gene Davis (Warren Stacy), Geoffrey Lewis (Dave Dante), Wilford Brimley (Captain Malone), Robert F. Lyons (Nathan Zager), Bert Williams (F.L. Johnson), Ola Ray (Ola), Kelly Preston (Doreen), Cosie Costa (Dudley), Paul McCallum (Lab Technician), Jeana Tomasino (Karen Smalley), June Gilbert (Betty Johnson), Arthur Hansel (Judge Mellen), Sam Chew Jr. (Minister), Katrina Parish (Tina), Shawn Schepps (Peg), Barbara Pilavin (Mrs. Byrd), Beau Billingslea (Desk Sergeant), James Keane (Jerry), Jerome Thor (Medical Examiner), Breck Costin (Tim Bailey), Carmen Filip (Hotel Clerk), Jeane Manson (Margo), Lynette Harrison (Ticket Girl), Neal Fleming (Young Man), John Garwood (Millikan), Shay Duffin (Nestor), Daniel Ades (Ben Linker), Cynthia Reams (Hooker), Kyle Edward Cranston (Party Intern), Beth Reinglass, Monica Ekblad (Office Girls), Patti Trippo (Party Girl).

Charles Bronson's follow-up to the hugely successful *Death Wish II* (1982) again paired him with the production team of Menahem Golan and Yoram Globus and City Films. The resulting feature, *10 to Midnight*, was advertised originally as an international action thriller but instead it was a brutal, erotic police thriller. "I'm not a nice person. I'm a mean, selfish son-of-a-bitch," Bronson's character Leo Kessler tells a newsman trying to get information on a murder investigation. Like its predecessor, the movie was ultra violent and

Poster for *10 to Midnight* (Cannon Group, 1983).

very conservative in its outlook regarding law enforcement, criminals and the court system. As a result the media lambasted the feature with the same furor dealt *Death Wish II* but again the public paid little attention to the critics and *10 to Midnight* proved to be another Bronson box-office winner.

Los Angeles police Lieutenant Leo Kessler (Charles Bronson) is on the trail of a killer-rapist who disposes of his young female victims with a knife. The killer is office worker Warren Stacy (Gene Davis) who kills his victims while in the nude, thus avoiding getting blood stains on his clothing. Since co-worker Betty Johnson (June Gilbert) rebuffed his advances Warren makes plans to kill her. He goes to a theatre to watch a movie and makes a pass at two girls (Katrina Parish, Shawn Schepps) and then leaves through a restroom window. He goes to a secluded area by a lake where Betty is having sex with her boyfriend in a van. Warren kills the young man and then chases down Betty and kills her before returning to the theatre. Kessler and his new partner, Detective Paul McAnn (Andrew Stevens), are assigned to the case and Kessler realizes the murdered girl was a friend of his daughter Laurie (Lisa Eilbacher), a student nurse from whom he has been somewhat estranged since the death of his wife several years before. At Betty's funeral Kessler sees Laurie and introduces her to Paul. Later Laurie remembers that Betty had been afraid of Warren and gives the information to Paul since her father is too busy to see her. Warren finds out Betty kept a diary and he goes to her apartment to find it but ends up killing her roommate Karen (Jeana Tomasino), another of his co-workers. Kessler and Paul question Warren in his apartment before learning of Karen's murder. Kessler suspects Warren and he is pulled in for questioning but has an alibi due to the girls at the theatre. Having seen Laurie at Betty's funeral, Warren begins making obscene telephone calls to her and when she tells her father he has her telephone tapped. Warren is brought in on the obscene phone charge and knowing he killed Betty and Karen, Kessler plants evidence to get him convicted. Warren is arrested but his slick lawyer, Dave Dante (Geoffrey Lewis), tells him he may have to plead insanity. Paul, however, finds out Kessler planted the evidence and the latter admits this to the court, thus setting Warren free. Kessler resigns but he begins to stalk Warren while Laurie blames Paul for her father losing his job. Kessler plants photos of the murdered girl at Warren's work site, thus causing him to be fired. Knowing Kessler is tailing him, Warren picks up a hooker (Cynthia Reams) and takes her to a sleazy motel where he kills her. He then heads to the student dormitory where Laurie lives and there he kills her three roommates before chasing her into the street. By then Kessler and Paul have arrived as has a police helicopter. Kessler gets the drop on Warren who tells him he will plead insanity and eventually be free again. When Warren tells Kessler he will be back, the ex-policeman shoots him in the head.

*10 to Midnight* is a film which takes a dim view of the judicial system and those who coddle criminals. In it Bronson has lines like, "I remember when legal meant lawful—now it means some kind of loophole" and "Forget what's legal and do what's right." This narrow, but publicly popular, perception no doubt is what made it so unpopular with critics and endeared it to audiences. At one point Kessler tells his young partner that 20 years before he would not have tampered with evidence but after seeing so many criminals go free he felt he had no other choice but to do all he could to get Warren Stacy off the streets.

Ironically, *10 to Midnight* is one of Charles Bronson's most entertaining 1980s features, especially if one can overlook a nudist killer. Despite a plethora of nudity, violence and blood, the film is not without humor. At one point Kessler takes his daughter and partner to lunch at a hospital cafeteria and his daughter asks him why he ordered quiche. "I hate quiche," he responds. "I thought it was pie."

As expected, the critics were not kind to *10 to Midnight*. Richard F. Shepard in the *New York Times* opined, "If *10 to Midnight* ... is not among the worst of its kind, then it is because its kind is among the worst of any kind." He added, "It is also a propaganda piece that argues against laws that let brutal slayers escape with insanity pleas." *Variety* noted, "William Roberts' screenplay, while it sags in the middle, is damnably clever at dropping in its vicious vigilante theme without being didactic, and J. Lee Thompson's direction ... creates the full horror of blades thrusting into naked bellies without the viewer ever actually seeing it happen." *LA Weekly* called the film "a clinched bloodbath full of gratuitous violence against women with a law-and-order sermon attached to it." Regarding the star, the same reviewer, however, wrote, "Charles Bronson has one of the most unique presences in film; he's neither articulate like Bogart nor obsessive like de Niro, but he projects more authentically than either the true solitude of survival." The reviewer noted of Bronson, "The famous impassive manner, deep with intimacy with the triumph over poverty and suffering, is like a karate expert's list, alive but full of deadened nerves, powerful with ignored pain. Bronson virtually radiates what has been, for him, the high price of staying in the world at all. A pity movies sell this quality short—or don't pay him to reveal more of it." Linda Gross in the *Los Angeles Times* said *10 to Midnight* "is a slickly made, suspenseful and scary movie, it also is inflammatory and extremely dangerous." Eric Braun in the *British Films* magazine wrote, "The film to me represents one more horror for the headman's axe." Regarding the star he opined, "Never has Bronson's limitations as an actor been more apparent; a puffy scowl in [sic] all he can muster to cover every emotion." Al Clark in *The Film Yearbook 1984* (1983) called it a "thoroughly unpleasant movie."

*10 to Midnight*, while fictional, had its basis in two real cases: the Richard Speck murders of eight student nurses in Chicago in 1966 and a British case called "The Towpath Murders." The latter had a Scotland Yard investigator fired from his job for planting evidence to convict a Thames River killer. The man was let go only to commit three more homicides before finally being convicted.

*10 to Midnight* grossed nearly $6 million in its first ten days of domestic release, playing 595 theatres.

Next Charles Bronson would team again with director J. Lee Thompson and producer Pancho Kohner for the even more violent *The Evil That Men Do* (1984).

## *Tennessee Champ* (Metro-Goldwyn-Mayer, 1954) 73 minutes Color

*P:* Sol Baer Fielding. *D:* Fred M. Wilcox. *Sc:* Art Cohn. *St:* Eustace Cockrell. *Ph:* George Folsey. *Ed:* Ben Lewis. *AD:* Cedric Gibbons & Daniel B. Cathcart. *Mus:* Conrad Salinger. *Asst Dir:* Marvin Stuart. *Sd:* Douglas Shearer. *Color Consultant:* Alvord Eiseman.

**CAST:** Shelley Winters (Sarah Wurble), Keenan Wynn (Willy Wurble), Dewey Martin (Daniel Norson), Earl Holliman (Happy Jackfield), Dave O'Brien (Lucky MacWade), Charles Buchinsky (Sixty Jubel), Yvette Dugay (Blossom), Frank Richards (J.B. Backett), Jack Kruschen (Andrews), Alvin J. Gordon (Sam), Johnny [John] Indrisano, Charles Sullivan, Harold Tommy Hart, Mike Pat Donovan (Referees), Paul Hoffman, Bruno Ve Sota, John Damler (Poker Players), Fred Welch, John Logan, Rube Schaffer (Pursuers), Louis Mason (Hotel Clerk), Court Shepherd (Boxer), Paul Bryar (Radio Announcer), Howard Wright (Mr. Robinson), Dan White (Minister), William Lewin, Brad Hatton, Tom Daly, David Bair, Dick [Richard] Simmons, Dick Haynes, Hope Miller (Reporters), Dave White (Handler), Than Wyenn, Mickey McCardle (Ushers), Billy McClean (Vender), Al Hill (Customer), Harry Cody, Margaret Bert, Don Anderson (Committee).

*Tennessee Champ* gave Charles Bronson a nifty screen name, Sixty Jubel, and a part which called for him to appear at the beginning and climax of this comedy-drama. *Variety* said he was one of the cast members which "do their share towards helping the amusement." Unfortunately the feature was issued by MGM as a lower dual-bill item and its overseas exposure was just as sparse. While it attained British release in 1954 and was shown in Sweden in 1955, the feature was not released elsewhere in Europe.

Forced to fight a bully, Daniel Norson (Dewey Martin) thinks he has killed his adversary (Charles Buchinsky) and jumps into the Mississippi River in order to escape revenge from the bully's gang. He is fished out of the waters by Willy Wurble (Keenan Wynn), a boxing manager, who takes the religious-minded Daniel to Natchez where they meet Willy's wife Sarah (Shelley Winters) and his punch-drunk fighter Happy Jackfield (Earl Holliman). When he cannot find an opponent for Happy, Willy talks Daniel into fighting him and the young man knocks out the veteran fighter. Willy then wants to train Daniel to be a boxer but the young man objects on religious grounds.

Willy finally convinces Daniel that he can fight and preach to the boxing audiences and that he can make money to finish a church his deceased father started. Daniel agrees and he goes on a winning streak of 15 fights. Willy, however, wants a big payday and agrees to have Daniel take a dive in his next ring encounter but the young man refuses saying it is against the will of the Lord. As a result Willy has to pay off the hoodlums with whom he made the deal, leaving him and Daniel broke. Angry at first, Willy realizes that honesty is the best policy and he works with the Unity Gospel Tabernacle to match Daniel with the Biloxi Block Buster, Sixty Jubel, the bully Daniel thought he had killed. After a brutal match, Daniel defeats Jubel and retires from boxing to take over the ministry of his father's church. By now Sarah is proud of Willy for having helped Daniel and for becoming an honest man.

While top billing in *Tennessee Champ* went to Shelley Winters as the loyal wife, most of the footage was centered around sleazy fight manager Keenan Wynn and the religious boxer played by Dewey Martin. Charles Bronson, however, is quite good as Sixty Jubel and definitely looks the part of a boxer. Ironically 21 years later, at the age of 54, Bronson would again play a prizefighter in one of his most successful films, *Hard Times* (1975).

What little critical attention *Tennessee Champ* received was mixed. *Variety* felt it was "an above-average programmer.... The chuckles are constant in the fast 72 minutes, the trouping is nifty and the Anso color adds visual values...." *Harrison's Reports* thought it "A better-than-average program comedy drama, which offers an entertaining mixture of religion and prizefighting.... The fight sequences are well staged. The direction is very good, and the color photography is sharp and clear." *The Monthly Film Bulletin*, however, felt the feature "an undistinguished piece of work." *Library Journal* said, "It is a boxing picture with an angle that is different." *Catholic World* called the feature "an inexpensive minor item, one of those unexpectedly enjoyable films which turn up just when you least expect them." *National Parent-Teacher* noted, "An uneven, off-beat melodrama in the American 'warmhearted rogue' tradition popularized by Damon Runyon."

## *This Property Is Condemned* (Paramount, 1966) 110 minutes Color

*P:* John Houseman. *D:* Sydney Pollack. *Sc:* Francis Ford Coppola, Fred Coe & Edith Sommer, from the play by Tennessee Williams. *Ph:* James Wong Howe. *Ed:* Adrienne Fazan. *Mus:* Kenyon Hopkins. *Song:* Jay Livingston & Ray Evans. *AD:* Hal Pereira, Stephen Grimes & Phil Jeffries. *Sets:* William Kiernan. *Sd:* Harry Lindgren & James E. Murphy. *Prod Executive:* Milton Feldman. *Prod Mgr:* Clarence Eurist. *Costumes:* Edith Head & Ann Landers. *Makeup:* Wally Westmore. *Asst Dir:* Eddie Saeta.

**CAST:** Natalie Wood (Alva Starr), Robert Redford (Owen Legate), Charles Bronson (J.J. Nichols), Kate Reid (Hazel

Starr), Mary Badham (Willie Starr), Alan Baxter (Knopke), Robert Blake (Sidney), John Harding (Johnson), Dabney Coleman (Salesman), Ray Hemphill (Jimmy Bell), Brett Pearson (Charlie Steinkamp), Jon Provost (Tom), Quentin Sondergaard (Hank), Mike Steen (Max), Bruce Watson (Lindsay Tate), Bob Random (Tiny), Nick Stuart (Train Conductor).

Tennessee Williams' tepid one-act play "This Property Is Condemned" was used as the basis for this turgid, steamy melodrama on which some 16 writers labored, although only three, including Francis Ford Coppola, are credited. As usual, Charles Bronson is better than the picture, as noted by *Variety*: "Charles Bronson is excellent as the earthy boarder." Otherwise the production was a vehicle for Natalie Wood and in it "Miss Wood turns in her best acting since the memorable *Splendor in the Grass*" (*Independent Film Journal*). Co-starred was Robert Redford, fresh from his Broadway success in *Barefoot in the Park*, and Kate Reid excelled in the supporting role of Natalie Wood's vicious mother. The good cast, however, cannot save a basically mundane melodrama and only Bay St. Louis, Mississippi, locations and James Wong Howe's photography capture the heat, despair and decay of the story.

The movie is told in flashback as young Willie Starr (Mary Badham), halfway between childhood and being an adult at 13, tells the story of her older sister Alva (Natalie Wood) to her friend Tom (Jon Provost). Several years before, in the early 1930s, Willie and Alva's mother Hazel (Kate Reid) ran a boardinghouse for railway workers in their small Mississippi town. Hazel's lover is one of the boarders, J.J. Nichols (Charles Bronson), while nearly all of the men at the home are attracted to the beautiful and flirty Alva. Hazel wants Alva to marry money and tries to get her involved with successful, but lonely, Mr. Johnson (John Harding). Alva, however, falls for good-looking Owen Legate (Robert Redford), a railroad executive who has come to town to lay off several of the line's workers, a cutback due to the Depression. Five workers manhandle Owen and he plans to leave town with Alva but Hazel makes him think her daughter is engaged to Johnson and he leaves without her. In retaliation, Alva swims nude at a party and teases Nichols who she runs off with and marries. After spending one night with her new husband, Alva goes to New Orleans to find Owen and they renew their love affair. Hazel, however, arrives to tell Owen that Alva is married and he deserts her again. Alva then drifts into prostitution and succumbs to tuberculosis. As the story ends, Willie only has fanciful memories of her deceased sister.

*Variety* liked the film: "This is a handsomely-mounted, well acted Depression era drama about the effect of railroad retrenchment on a group of boarding-house people ... the production is adult without being sensational, touching without being maudlin." The *New York Times*, on the other hand, claimed "the folks here are corn-pone stereotypes in a story situation of equal synthetics...." F. Maurice Speed in *Film Review 1966–68* (1967) called it a "Fascinating glimpse of a strange world." *Time* noted, "The movie as a whole is too bright and vulgar to be dull, but expensive talent has been squandered on every chore except the crucial one of keeping a small, evanescent tragedy in focus."

Some publicity was engendered for the film by the casting of early sound film star Nick Stuart, who was living in the area where the movie was shot, in the role of a train conductor.

Veteran songwriters Jay Livingston and Ray Evans composed "Wish Me a Rainbow" for the feature which also used such vintage songs as "Just One More Chance" and "Sing You Sinners" for 1930s flavor.

## *This Rugged Land* (Columbia, 1965) 72 minutes B/W

*P:* William Sackheim. *D:* Arthur Hiller. *Sc:* Frank Nugent. *Ph:* Joseph Biroc. *Ed:* Jack Ruggiero. *AD:* Walter Holscher. *Sets:* James W. Crowe. *Mus:* Johnny Green. *Asst Dir:* Herb Wallerstein. *Mus Supv:* Irving Friedman. *Prod Supv:* Seymour Friedman. *Makeup:* Ben Lane. *Prod Asst:* John Coote. *Post Prod:* Lawrence Werner. *Creator:* Kathleen Hite. A Wilrich Production.

**CAST:** Richard Egan (Jim Redigo), Terry Moore (Connie Garrett), Charles Bronson (Paul Moreno), Anne Seymour (Lucia Garrett), Ryan O'Neal (Tal Garrett), Denver Pyle (Tom Rawlings), Oliver McGowan (Wells), Vic Perrin (Matt), Paul Tripp (Thayer Wilson).

The release of this television movie in England in 1965 predates Charles Bronson's international stardom by a few years but it does coincide with another Bronson TV program being shown in British theatres the year before, *Guns of Diablo* (1964). Both got new life, however, around 1970 in Europe when the demand for Bronson product was so great these two telefeatures were dusted off and billed as "new" productions. *This Rugged Land* is really the initial episode of the NBC-TV series *Empire*, which debuted September 25, 1962, and was entitled "The Day the Empire Stood Still." Charles Bronson guest starred as Paul Moreno and the character proved so popular that he became a regular on the series beginning in 1963 for 11 more episodes. In 1994 Mntex Entertainment released this Screen Gems production on video as *Mean Justice*.

Having just completed a big oil lease deal, Garrett Ranch manager Jim Redigo (Richard Egan) returns to the modern day sprawling spread to find that ranch hand Paul Moreno (Charles Bronson) has been accused of the assault and murder of the daughter of ranch foreman Tom Rawlings (Denver Pyle), who wants revenge for his girl's death. Redigo questions Moreno, whose attentions had been spurned by the girl on the night of her murder, and Moreno claims he went south with two men who promised him a new job, only he was beaten and robbed. Feeling that Moreno deserves a fair trial,

Redigo agrees to hire slick lawyer Thayer Wilson (Paul Tripp), much to the chagrin of his boss, Lucia Garrett (Anne Seymour) and her son Tal (Ryan O'Neal), although her daughter Connie (Terry Moore) also feels Moreno has a right to a fair hearing. During the trial Wilson points out that the murdered girl would hardly have picked up Moreno after having rejected him earlier and that Paul was penniless when he was found 60 miles from the crime scene. The jury finds Moreno innocent and Rawlings quits his job while Paul stays on at the Garrett ranch despite being hated by the other workers, most of whom quit. Redigo cannot replace the workers and tries to run the ranch with a small crew but the Garrett operation begins to incur heavy losses. Redigo himself plans to quit when a cattle disease goes through the ranch's vast herd and he and Moreno go to town for serum. There Rawlings confronts Moreno and beats him up as Paul refuses to defend himself. Redigo stops the fight and tells Rawlings Moreno will not fight because he is innocent. Redigo and Moreno return to try and save the cattle when the ranch workers come back to their jobs and Rawlings reconciles with Moreno as the cattle herd and the ranch are saved.

A sprawling modern-day western, *This Rugged Land* is somewhat dated today in looks but holds some entertainment value, mainly for Charles Bronson's convincing performance as the falsely accused Moreno. Ironically the movie makes no effort to uncover the real killer. Hampered by an overly loud music score and lots of stock shots, this telefeature was hardly good theatrical material but at the time of its re-release in the early 1970s it proved popular in Europe where the demand for Bronson features was beginning to snowball.

When the telefeature was issued in England in 1965 the *Monthly Film Bulletin* called it "a solidly competent low-budget Western" adding "Richard Egan and Charles Bronson are convincingly tough...." Reviewing the film when it was the debut episode of *Empire* in 1962, *Variety* noted, "Frank Nugent's script for the premiere could have been adapted to any number of Old West teleseries without a too drastic overhauling. Guest actor Charles Bronson gave the only notable performance...."

Although *Empire* ran only one season, Richard Egan continued the character of Jim Redigo in the short-lived 30 minute NBC-TV series *Redigo* in 1963; Charles Bronson did not appear in that series.

## *A Thunder of Drums* (Metro-Goldwyn-Mayer, 1961) 97 minutes Color

*P:* Robert J. Enders. *AP:* Stanley Bass. *D:* Joseph M. Newman. *Sc:* James Warner Bellah. *Ph:* William Spencer. *Ed:* Ferris Webster. *AD:* George W. Davis & Gabriel Scognamillo. *Mus:* Harry Sukman. *Songs:* Duane Eddy. *Sets:* Harry Grace & Jack Mills. *Asst Dir:* Hal Polaire. *Sd:* Franklin Milton. *Makeup:*

William Tuttle. *Color Consultant:* Charles K. Hagedon. *Hair Styles:* Mary Keats. *Women's Costumes:* Kitty Mager.

**CAST:** Richard Boone (Captain Stephen Maddocks), George Hamilton (Lieutenant Curtis McQuade), Luana Patten (Tracey Hamilton), Arthur O'Connell (Sergeant Rodermill), Charles Bronson (Trooper Hanna), Richard Chamberlain (Lieutenant Porter), Duane Eddy (Trooper Eddy), James Douglas (Lieutenant Gresham), Tammy Marihugh (Laurie), Carole Welles (Camden Yates), Slim Pickens (Trooper Erschick), Clem Harvey (Trooper Denton), Casey Tibbs (Trooper Baker), Irene Tedrow (Mrs. Scarborough), Marjorie Bennett (Mrs. Yates), J. Edward McKinley (Captain Scarborough).

Lieutenant Curtis McQuade (George Hamilton) is assigned to an army post at Fort Canby, Arizona. He is the son of a general who once had the post's commander, Captain Stephen Maddocks (Richard Boone), under his command. Maddocks, who resented the general for breaking him when he made a mistake in battle, thinks McQuade is an army brat and sets out to make a soldier of him. The young lieutenant finds garrison life dull with its routine daily activities, arid terrain and few women. He finds that most of the men, like Trooper Hanna (Charles Bronson), are Civil War veterans who live for drinking, fighting and the few women they can find. Considering himself a cavalier with women McQuade romances pretty Tracey Hamilton (Luana Patten) although he knows she is the fiancée of another soldier and this causes a fight with Hanna. When Indians attack a settlement and murder the men and rape and kill the women, Maddocks sends out a patrol under the command of the officer (James Douglas) whose girl McQuade has been romancing. Under pressure the man makes a fatal error and his men are massacred. This forces McQuade to see the error of his ways and as a result Maddocks lets him lead the next patrol in order to redeem himself.

Filmed on location in Arizona, *A Thunder of Drums* was intended as a screen vehicle for Richard Boone, the star of TV's popular *Have Gun—Will Travel* series. The resulting movie, however, put Boone's part into a subordinate role to that of the young, brash lieutenant portrayed by George Hamilton. The film gave Charles Bronson fifth billing in a fairly interesting role and *Variety* noted, "Arthur O'Connell and Charles Bronson contribute valuable, colorful character work. Most of the other characters are two-dimensional." The movie was written by veteran western writer James Warner Bellah who would also co-script Bronson's next feature, *X-15* (1962). Regarding Bellah's screenplay, Phil Hardy wrote in *The Western* (1983), "Sadly, Bellah's script compares unfavorably with his stories that provided the basis for (John) Ford's loose trilogy about the Cavalry, *Fort Apache* (1948), *She Wore a Yellow Ribbon* (1949) and *Rio Grande* (1950), even though it covers some of the same ground."

The *New York Times* said of *A Thunder of Drums*: "The impact of an otherwise professional Western is weakened, as emphasis shifts from the Apache menace of a lonely Southwestern Army outpost to the human palpitations within.... But, as has happened before, cavalry and Indians and the passions, both grand and base, don't mix too well." In *Film Review 1962–63*, F. Maurice Speed wrote, "MGM's *A Thunder of Drums* was a most interesting Western in that in spirit and treatment it lay somewhere between the new and the old school and gave what one imagined might be a pretty authentic picture of the monotonous and dangerous life of the American Cavalryman in Redskin country." *Time* called the film "the best western so far in 1961" but added "The picture cannot always pass a close inspection. The boy's character is often unclear, the screenplay sometimes cluttered, the dialogue occasionally cute."

*A Thunder of Drums* marked the screen debut of Richard Chamberlain, who Charles Bronson would work with in an episode of *Dr. Kildare* in 1963. He had also worked with top-billed Richard Boone in several segments of *Have Gun—Will Travel*. Also in the film, as another trooper, was popular guitarist Duane Eddy who composed two songs used in the feature, "Ballad of Camden Yates" and "Water from a Bad Well."

## *Torpedo Alley* (Allied Artists, 1953) 83 minutes B/W

*P:* Lindsey Parsons. *D:* Lew Landers. *Sc:* Sam Roeca & Warren Douglas. *Ph:* William Sickner. *Ed:* W. Doug Hayes.

**CAST:** Mark Stevens (Bingham), Dorothy Malone (Susan Peabody), Charles Winninger (Peabody), Bill Williams (Graham), Douglas Kennedy (Gates), James Millican (Heywood), Bill Henry (Instructor), James Seay (Skipper), Robert Rose (Anniston), Carleton Young (Psychiatrist), Ralph Sanford (Hedley), Charles Buchinsky (Sailor).

Near the end of World War II, Navy pilot Bingham (Mark Stevens) survives the crash of his plane in the Pacific Ocean but his two crewmen are killed. After being rescued by the crew of a submarine Bingham has guilt feelings about the incident. Liking submarine duty he signs on for such service after failing to make a go of it as a civilian. He is stationed at the Navy base at New London, Connecticut, and there he is attracted to nurse Susan Peabody (Dorothy Malone), the daughter of a veteran warrant office (Charles Winninger). Troubles arise, however, when the girl's boyfriend, Officer Gates (Douglas Kennedy), becomes jealous. It was Gates who commanded the submarine which rescued Bingham in the Pacific. As time passes, and the Korean conflict emerges, Bingham learns to accept his past and accept new responsibilities, including a life with Susan.

Veteran Monogram–Allied Artists producer Lindsey Parsons packed quite a bit of background training at the New London Navy submarine training center into this programmer, this type of action helping to nullify the feature's leaden love triangle subplot. The acting by the leads was uniformly good and director Lew Landers was an old hand at this type of dual-bill fodder. *Variety* felt this salute to the submarine service had "sufficient interest to assure it an okay playoff in the program situations."

*Torpedo Alley* is one of the most obscure of Charles Bronson's screen credits. In it he had only a passing bit as a sailor.

## *Twinky (Lola)* (World Film Services/Eurofilm, 1969) 98 minutes Color

*P:* Clive Sharp. *EP:* John Heyman & Bino Cicogna. *AP:* Norman Thaddeus Vane & Ralph Serpe. *D:* Richard Donner. *Sc:* Norman Thaddeus Vane. *Ph:* Walter Lassally. *Ed:* Norman Wanstall. *Mus:* John Scott. *Songs:* Jim Dale. *AD:* Michael Wild. *Asst Dir:* Richard Dalton. *Prod Mgr:* Geoffrey Haine. *Sd:* David Price. *Continuity:* Jane Buck. *Hairdresser:* Biddy Crystal. *Sd Ed:* Garth Craven & Derek Holding. *Wardrobe:* Elsa Fennel. *Camera Operator:* Vernon Layton. *Dubbing:* Doug Turner. *Asst Ed:* Jeff McBride & David Hitchcock. *Makeup:* Alan Brown. *Prod Accountant:* Martin Cahill. *Titles:* Chambers & Partners. Songs sung by Jim Dale.

**CAST:** Charles Bronson (Scott Wardman), Susan George (Sybil "Twinky" Londonderry), Orson Bean (Hal), Honor Blackman (Mrs. Londonderry), Michael Craig (Mr. Londonderry), Paul Ford (Mr. Wardman), Jack Hawkins (Judge Millington-Draper), Trevor Howard (Grandfather Londonderry), Lionel Jeffries (Barrister Creighton), Robert Morley (Judge Roxburgh), Kay Medford (Mrs. Wardman), Barney Martin (Walter, the Hotel Doorman), Peggy Atkinson (Mrs. Finchley), Eric Chitty (Client), Cathy Jose (Felicity), Anthony Kemp (Twinky's Brother), Polly Williams (Twinky's Sister), Norman Vaughan, Jimmy Tarbuck (Comedians), Leslie Schofield, Derek Steen (Policemen), Elspeth March (Secretary), Gordon Waller (Marty), Reg Lever (Old Man), Tony Arpino (New York Judge), Eric Barker (Marriage Clerk), John Rae (Hotel Receptionist), John Wright (Hotel Waiter); Sue Lloyd, Mark Robbins, Anne Shepard, Debbie Slater, Ruth Masters, Ann Way, Stephen White, Sheila Dunion, Nina Monique, Jack Somack, Doy Young, Marcia Carton, Annette Montgomery, Judith Furse, Melanie Marlene Islya.

Bino Cicogna was the executive producer of *Once Upon a Time in the West* (1969) and he retained that capacity in Charles Bronson's next feature film, *Twinky*, which was lensed at Twickenham Studios in London and in New York City. The film reunited Bronson with director Richard Donner with whom he had worked earlier in *X-15* in 1962. *Twinky* is known under a number of titles, that one being its original British release title in 1969. When American International Pictures acquired the film for U.S. distribution, the title was changed to *Lola* (to coincide with *Lolita* [1962] since both had the plot of a very young girl in love with an older man) with the girl's name Lola being dubbed on the soundtrack. Other titles for the feature were *Child Bride* and *The Statutory Affair*, and it plays on U.S. television as *London Affair*. Despite the notoriety, the film retained a PG rating. The feature got good reviews and was very popular with audiences in Great Britain and Europe (it was not shown in West Germany until 1974) but AIP apparently did not understand how to market this funny, bittersweet romantic comedy and it got few stateside playdates, joining *Adieu l'Ami* and *Once Upon a Time in the West* as another Bronson film not given decent release in his homeland.

British pop singer Jim Dale wrote the title song plus "The Lonely Years" and "Go Where the Sun Goes," all of which he sang on the film's soundtrack.

Certainly *Twinky* was a major change of pace for Charles Bronson. Clean shaven for the last time until he did *The Valachi Papers* in 1972, the actor played a character a decade younger than his real age and he carried off the low-key comedy in fine form. He also nicely captured on film the dilemma of a man in love with a girl young enough to be his daughter and the joys and frustrations of such a union. The film was a hectic comedy and Bronson's low-key performance nicely balanced the energetic one of Susan George in the title role. There was quite a bit of amusing throwaway dialogue in the feature such as the best friend (Orson Bean) of the newlywed Bronson telling him that if he ever divorced his young bride he would not pay alimony but child support. After the lovers have their first quarrel, Bronson tells George, "This is not an affair, it's a massacre of the innocent."

The plot has 16-year-old schoolgirl Twinky (Susan George) having an affair with 38-year-old porno novelist, American Scott Wardman (Charles Bronson). The affair becomes known to her parents (Michael Craig, Honor Blackman) after they find her diary and Scott is afraid he will be deported or go to jail. The two break up but Scott goes after Twinky and they end up flying to Scotland to get married. As a result they make newspaper headlines and become grist for comics. While Twinky's swinging grandfather (Trevor Howard) likes Scott, her father says he is ugly, middle-aged, filthy-minded and an American. The newlyweds decide to move to New York City where they are greeted by his surprised parents (Paul Ford, Kay Medford) and his lawyer pal Hal (Orson Bean) who constantly gives Scott bad advice. Twinky is forced to enroll in school and when she gets involved in a riot Scott comes to her rescue, ends up slugging a cop, and is sentenced to a month in jail. Tired of living with Scott's crying mother, Twinky hoodwinks a lecherous landlord into letting her rent a posh apartment for $100 a month and then throws a big party on the day Scott gets out of jail after getting his sentence commuted. When the hotel doorman (Barney Martin) will not let him enter, Scott calls Twinky and they are reunited. As time passes Scott finds he cannot write because of his young wife's constant need of attention and after awhile he can no longer get monetary advances for his work and tries to write television commercials, but unsuccessfully. He and Twinky fight and he tells her they should be divorced.The girl disappears and Scott finds her in the basement hiding. The next morning he finds she has gone. Twinky has returned to England hoping to find a new life.

With its frantic comedy pacing, emphasis on quick cuts and a bittersweet ending, *Twinky* is not an ordinary romantic farce. While its plot is somewhat jumbled, it is an amusing feature which moves quickly and is more than mildly entertaining. Both Charles Bronson and Susan George do well in the leads and Orson Bean makes the most of his co-starring role as the bumbling lawyer. Paul Ford and Kay Medford are amusing as Bronson's parents, as is Honor Blackman as George's feather-headed mother. Trevor Howard is especially good as the girl's lecherous grandfather who likes nothing better than for Twinky to bring a group of her female classmates to his country home for fun and games. However, Robert Morley and Jack Hawkins are wasted in throwaway roles as British judges as is Lionel Jeffries as a barrister who tries to explain statutory rape laws to Twinky over the telephone with a righteous-minded client in the room. Barney Martin does well by his role of the protective hotel doorman.

Critics were mixed in reviewing *Twinky*. *Variety* thought Bronson "surprising but effective casting" as the writer and Peter Buckley in *Films and Filming* said the two leads "make a little something special out of *Twinky*—an unpretentious, bittersweet, simple film that is finished off with style, that might make you cry, is guaranteed to make you laugh, and is sure to charm you." On the other hand, Henry Herx and Tony Zaza wrote in *The Family Guide to Movies on Video* (1988) that Bronson was "terribly miscast" adding "the story has some interest but ultimately fails on the dramatic levels of coherence and acting."

## *U.S.S. Teakettle (You're in the Navy Now)* (20th Century–Fox, 1951) 93 minutes B/W

*P:* Fred Kohlmar. *D:* Henry Hathaway. *Sc:* Richard Murphy. *St:* John W. Hazard. *Ph:* Joe MacDonald. *Ed:* James B. Clark. *Mus:* Cyril Mockridge. *Mus Dir:* Lionel Newman. *Orchestrations:* Edward Powell. *AD:* Lyle Wheeler & J. Russell Spencer. *Sets:* Thomas Little & Fred I. Rode. *Photography Sp Eff:* Ray Kellogg & Fred Sersen. *Sd:* W.D. Flick & Roger Heman. *Makeup:* Ben Nye. *Wardrobe Dir:* Charles Le Maire. *Technical Advisor:* Joseph Warren Lomax.

**CAST:** Gary Cooper (Lieutenant John Harkness), Jane Greer (Ellie Harkness), Millard Mitchell (Larrabee), Eddie Albert (Lieutenant Bill Barron), John McIntire (Commander Reynolds), Ray Collins (Admiral Tennant), Harry Von Zell (Captain Elliot), Jack Webb (Ensign Anthony Barbo), Richard Erdman (Ensign Chuck Dorrance), Harvey Lembeck (Norelli), Henry Slate (Chief Engineer Ryan), Ed Begley (Commander), Fay Roope (Battleship Admiral), Charles Tannen (Houlihan), Charles Buchinski (Wascylewski), Jack Warden (Morse), Lee Marvin, Ken Harvey, Jerry Hausner, Charles Smith (Crew Members), Bernard Kates (Tug Boat Sailor), James Cornell (New Sailor), Glen Gordon, Laurence Hugo (Shore Patrolmen), Damian O'Flynn (Doctor), Biff McGuire (Sailor Messenger), Norman McKay (Admiral's Aide), Elsa Peterson (Admiral's wife), Joel Fluellen (Mess Boy), John McGuire (Naval Commander), Herman Canton (Naval Captain), Rory Mallinson (Lieutenant Commander), William Leicester (C.P.O.), Ted Stanhope (Naval Officer).

After eight months as a student at the Pasadena Playhouse, Charles Bronson was tapped for the role of Polish-American sailor Wascylewski in *U.S.S. Teakettle*. One of his instructors, Thomas Browne Henry, was being considered for a part in the film and it was he who recommended Bronson to agent Gus Demling who arranged for the actor to audition for director Henry Hathaway. While not a flashy part, the role offered the 29-year-old actor (billed on screen here as Charles Buchinski) with a more than satisfactory screen debut.

Because he studied engineering in college years before, Lieutenant John Harkness (Gary Cooper) is assigned to command Patrol Craft 1168 which is using a steam turbine instead of a diesel engine as an experiment. Having little naval experience, Harkness finds out most of his crew is in the same boat except for Larrabee (Millard Mitchell), the Chief Boatswain's Mate. Numerous problems take place as the new boilers are being installed and once that is accomplished the ship, on its first mission, runs into an aircraft carrier. Harkness then learns that his ship will take part in a two day Admiral's Board official test. The valves on the engine freeze during the test and the ship goes out of control though the skipper and his crew manage to avert trouble. While waiting for the Board's report, Harkness goes to the office of his commanding officer, Captain Elliot (Harry Von Zell) planning to vent his anger over the situation. Instead he and his crew are given a commendation for their work. As Harkness later reads the commendation to his crew he sees a diesel engine being brought aboard PC 1168.

Initially released early in 1951 to good reviews, *U.S.S. Teakettle* (the name the crew dubbed their old tub, PC 1168) met with tepid results at the box office. Hurriedly 20th Century–Fox pulled the feature and retitled it *You're in the Navy Now*, thus giving it a new lease on life and one which made it financially successful. Bosley Crowther in the *New York Times* felt the movie "was the best comedy of the year" and he also included Charles Buchinsky as one of the cast members who "deserve particular mention here." *Variety* said it was "rib-tickling filmfare ... Humor springs from natural setup for laughs, and there are no dull moments...." The reviewer added, "Charles Buchinski and Jack Warden are among the motley crew making up the ship's complement, and each expertly furthers the laugh aims." In the *Hollywood Professionals, Vol. 1* (1973), Kingsley Canham, in studying director Henry Hathaway's career, felt the film "was light in tone and was more suited to the style of comedy in the Thirties with its decisive moral code and division of uncomplicated characters as well as a mistrust of specialized development."

The film had an excellent cast and Lee Marvin, whose career would cross paths with Charles Bronson's on several occasions in the next three decades, also made his film debut as a crew member. Sadly, second-billed Jane Greer was only on screen briefly as Harkness' wife, the secretary of the base commander. An interesting subplot found her unhappy at her husband's being assigned to command PC 1168 while he was somewhat jealous of her success in the WAVES. Also in the cast was Jack Warden who would later appear with Bronson in *The White Buffalo* (1977).

## *The Valachi Papers* (Columbia, 1972) 125 minutes Color

*P:* Dino De Laurentiis. *EP:* Nino E. Krisman. *D:* Terence Young. *Sc:* Stephen Geller, from the book by Peter Maas. *Ph:* Aldo Tonti. *Ed:* Johnny Dwyre. *Mus:* Riz Ortolani. *Prod Design:* Mario Garbuglia. *Sp Eff:* Eros Baciucchi. *Costume Design:* Ann Roth & Giorgio Desideri. *Set Decorators:* John Godfrey & Ferdinando Ruffo. *Asst Dir:* Christian Raoux, Gianni Cozzi, Giorgio Gentili & Kekiza Branka Soldo. *Camera Operators:* Cesare Allione & Luciano Tonti. *Prod Asst.:* Carlo Bartolini & Clo D'Olban. *Prod Mgr:* Fred C. Caruso & Felice D'Alisera. *Makeup:* Giannetto De Rossi. *Continuity:* Kay Mander. *Sd Mixer:* Roy Mangano. *Hair Styles:* Mirella De Rossi Sforza.

**CAST:** Charles Bronson (Joseph "Joe" Valachi), Lino Ventura (Vito Genovese), Walter Chiari (Dominick "The Gap" Petrilli), Joseph Wiseman (Salvatore Maranzano), Jill Ireland (Maria Reina Valachi), Gerald S. O'Loughlin (Agent Ryan), Amedeo Nazzari (Gaetano Reina), Angelo Infanti (Charles "Lucky" Luciano), Fausto Tozzi (Albert Anastasia), Guido Leontini (Anthony Strollo/ Tony Bender), Mario Pilar (Salerno), Fred Valleca (Johnny Beck), Giacomino De Michelis (Little Augie), Arny Freeman (Atlanta Penitentiary Warden), Sylvester Lamont (Fort Monmouth Commander), Franco Borelli (Buster from Chicago), Allesandro Sperli (Giuseppe "Joe the Boss" Masseria), John Alarimo (Ferrigno), Pupella Maggio (Rossana Reina), Sabine Sun (Jane), Isabella Marcal (Mary Lou), Maria Baxa (Donna Petrillo), Imelde Marani (Donna's Friend), Jason McCallum (Donald Valachi), Anthony Dawson, Gianni Medici (Federal Investigators), Frank Cio (Frank), Steve Belouise (Vinnie), Don Koll (State Trooper), Robert Trout (TV Newscaster).

Italian producer Dino De Laurentiis acquired the rights to Peter Maas' best-seller *The Valachi Papers*, which detailed the exposure of organized crime in America from the 1920s to the 1960s. De Laurentiis wanted Charles Bronson for the lead role, that of Joseph "Joe" Valachi, the Mafia soldier who testified for Senate hearings in 1963. Bronson turned down the part until DeLaurentiis offered him one million dollars plus two percent of the film's profit, in addition to a lucrative expense account and a three picture contract. Further enticement came with the fact the character of Joe Valachi ages in the film from 25 to 60. Bronson accepted the part and production began in 1972 in New York City but after two weeks alleged sabotage by the underworld forced the crew to finish the film at De Laurentiis' Cinecitta studio in Rome. A co-production of Euro France Films and De Laurentiis Intermarco, the feature was released in the United States in October 1972 where it was immediately compared to the box office blockbuster *The Godfather*, released earlier that year. The comparison was not complimentary but nonetheless *The Valachi Papers* grossed nearly $10 million in the United States alone, further solidifying Charles Bronson's homeland popularity. In reality *The*

*Valachi Papers* is a far more accurate exposé of organized crime than the fanciful *The Godfather*, in its tale of actual happenings in the inner workings of the Cosa Nostra. As would be expected, the film was a major success worldwide. In France it was called *Cosa Nostra: Le Dossier Valachi*, while in Italy it was released as *Joe Valachi: I Segreti di Cosa Nostra* and in the Spanish version it was *El Segreto de Cosa Nostra.*

Beginning the mid–1950s, the film starts with longtime Mafia soldier Joe Valachi (Charles Bronson) being sent to prison for 15 years after being busted on a narcotics charge. When old "family" friend Salerno (Mario Pilar) tries to kill him, Joe demands solitary. Refusing to cooperate with the authorities in exposing underworld activities he is put back in the prison population and mistakenly kills a man he thinks is out to get him. Learning that Mafia don Vito Genovese (Lino Ventura) has a contract out for his life Joe sees his boss and realizes he is marked by the "kiss of death." In order to protect himself and his family, Joe agrees to cooperate with FBI Agent Ryan (Gerald O'Loughlin) in exposing the rackets. He begins in 1929 when he is sent to Sing Sing for petty theft and there meets Tony Bender (Guido Leontini), a minion of Cosa Costra kingpin Salvatore Maranzano (Joseph Wiseman). Upon release Joe pulls a silk heist and barely escapes being arrested by hiding in Maranzano's restaurant. The latter hires him to kill a rival and when the hit is carried out he wins Maranzano's favor by having suggested to Bender that enemies Vito Genovese and Lucky Luciano (Angelo Infanti), who were meeting with the murdered man, also be rubbed out. As a result Joe is invited to join the Cosa Nostra and promises to forfeit his life if he betrays the organization. He is assigned as a driver to Gaetano Reina (Amedeo Nazzari), a lieutenant to Maranzano. As the war with the rival Guiseppe Masseria (Allesandro Sperli) mob continues in New York City, Reina is killed. At his funeral Genovese and Luciano ask for peace with Maranzano and to prove their good intentions they have Masseria killed. Maranzano then becomes the head of a supposed united Mafia in Gotham with the city divided among five families, each of whom have their own territories. Joe becomes Maranzano's driver but Tony Bender betrays his boss who is murdered by Bugsy Siegel's men dressed as cops after they were hired by Genovese and Luciano. Joe takes sanctuary in the Reina home and falls in love with pretty Maria Reina (Jill Ireland). When his old pal Gap (Walter Chiari) comes for him, Joe realizes he is back in the organization and Genovese asks Luciano to finance the two men in the slot machine business. Since Joe wants to marry Maria, Genovese intercedes on his behalf with her mother (Pupella Maggio). Returning the favor, Joe and Gap kill a man who turns out to be the husband of a showgirl, Donna (Maria Baxa), who Genovese wants. In 1932 Joe and Maria get married and he makes $2,500 a week off the slot machine business. Luciano is sent to prison on a trumped-up charge of operating brothels and Genovese goes to Italy to avoid arrest. During World War II Joe works as a loan shark and buys a restaurant and he and Gap are assigned by interim boss Albert Anastasia

(Fausto Tozzi) to watch out for Donna, but Gap becomes her lover. In 1946 Genovese returns to New York City and wants the organization to rid itself of outsiders and go into the narcotics business. He also has Anastasia murdered. Finding out about Gap and Donna, Genovese sends Bender to kill Gap, who takes refuge in Joe's restaurant. There Bender and his men cut off Gap's genitals. Gap begs Joe to kill him which he does reluctantly. Maria wants Joe to get out of the organization but he refuses saying "they make me feel like I belong; before I was nothin'." After the police raid a Cosa Nostra meeting, the FBI harasses Valachi, wanting information on Genovese. Needing money, Joe joins Bender on a drug grab but it goes wrong and he barely escapes. The law plants drugs in Genovese's apartment and he is arrested, blaming Joe and Tony Bender. Joe is arrested and sentenced to fifteen years in prison. After telling all to Ryan he agrees to testify before a Senate committee. Afterward, realizing he will never see his family again, he tries to commit suicide but is saved by Ryan. When told Genovese has put out a $100,000 contract on his life, Joe vows to live to spite his former boss. Both Valachi and Genovese die in prison in 1971, Valachi of natural causes six months after Don Vito Genovese.

Peter Maas' 1969 novel translated well to the screen as basically a series of vignettes from Valachi's past as he recounts his Mafia activities. Obedience to the "family" always clouds his life. Sans mustache, Charles Bronson is very effective as Joe Valachi and he easily handles the aging process from young man to tired informant. The rest of the cast is quite good, in particular Lino Ventura as the slick Vito Genovese, and Walter Chiari as Petrilli. The scene where Petrilli is emasculated in Valachi's restaurant is harrowing. The many crimes depicted in the film give a realistic picture of underworld conniving and add to its authenticity. The movie, however, is not without humor. Especially good is the scene where the refined Genovese intercedes for the rough hewn Valachi for the hand of Maria Reina, with her mother. While Genovese tries to carry out the bargain the oafish Valachi cracks nuts.

Although the public flocked to *The Valachi Papers*, the critics were not generally kind. Richard Schickel wrote in *Life*, "This is a compendium of movie-gangster types doing movie-gangster things in carefully researched period settings and costumes. Such meticulousness does not extend to the more important matters of moral intelligence, human curiosity or even acting, writing and direction. It's almost as if the moviemakers hoped stupidity could be the unifying force in an otherwise unshaped and unfelt film." *Newsweek* said, "Aside from an excessive taste for the mechanics of murder, with enough red across the screen to fill your average bloodmobile, there isn't the slightest indication that anyone connected with the film has seen any movies since 1940.... Charles Bronson as Valachi is caught in the cross-fire of a cliché-ridden script and [Terence] Young's direction...." Thomas Meehan wrote in *Saturday Review*, "...*The Valachi Papers* is one of the most godawful pictures I've seen in a long time. All but an insult to the Mafia, it is ineptly acted by an embalmed-looking cast headed by Charles Bronson, ludicrously written by Stephen Geller and flatly directed by Terence Young in an episodic, semi-documentary style that was already out of date when it was used in B-movies like *Kansas City Confidential* in the 1950s." *Variety* called the film "a hard-hitting, violence-ridden documented melodrama" and noted, "Terence Young, who directed, hits a shock note ... which climaxes numerous scenes of brutality...." *Gossip* called the movie "a pretty brutal look at the one 'organization' nobody even dares to talk about!"

*The Valachi Papers* was Charles Bronson's third and last feature with director Terence Young, following *De la Part des Copains* (1971) and *Soleil Rouge* (1971). As noted earlier, Bronson signed a three picture deal with Dino De Laurentiis and they went on to make *The Stone Killer* (1973), *Valdez il Mezzosangue* (1974) and Bronson's most successful feature *Death Wish* (1974). In 1977 they reteamed for the last time with *The White Buffalo.*

## *Valdez il Mezzosangue (Chino)* (De Laurentiis Intermaco/ Coral Producciones/Universal France, 1973) 95 minutes Color

*P-D:* John Sturges. *EP:* Alfredo De Laurentiis. *AP:* Duilio Coletti. *Sc:* Clair Huffaker, from the novel by Lee Hoffman. *Ph:* Armando Nannuzzi. *Ed:* Peter Zinner & Vanio Amici. *Mus:* Guido De Angelis & Maurizio De Angelis. *AD:* Mario Garbuglia. *Sets:* Boris Juraga. *Prod Mgr:* Peter Cocco & Vincente Sempere. *Sc Supv:* John Franco. *Makeup:* Gianetto de Rossi. *Camera Operator:* Guiseppe Beraldini. *Asst Camera Operator:* Jose A. Villara Rodriguez. *Asst Dir:* Tony Tarruella & Roberto Bodegas. *Asst Ed:* Georgio Di Venzio. *Costume Designer:* Osana Guardini. *Prod Asst:* Javier Cordello Martin & Marguerite Theouee. *Horse Trainers:* Mickey Gilbert & Rudy Ugland. *Still Photographer:* Alfonso Avincola.

**CAST:** Charles Bronson (Chino Valdez), Jill Ireland (Catherine Maral), Marcel Bozzufi (Maral), Vincent Van Patten (Jaimie Wagner), Fausto Tozzi (Cruz), Ettore Manni (Sheriff), Adolfo Thous (Coyote), Melissa Chimenti (Indian Girl), Florencio Amarilla (Little Bear), Diana Lorys, Corrado Gaida (Tribe Members).

This feature was the first of a three film contract Charles Bronson signed with Italian producer Dino De Laurentiis, his having made *The Valachi Papers* (1972) as a solo deal. The movie was shot in Spain but was a Spanish (Coral Film), French (Universal France) and Italian (De Laurentiis Intermaco) co-production with Bronson choosing John Sturges as the director. Credits for the production vary. While John Sturges was listed as producer-director when the film was released in the U.S., foreign credits list Duilio Coletti of Coral Film as the producer. Clair Huffaker gets solo writing credit on U.S. prints while abroad he is billed after Dino Maiuri and Massimo De Rita. To muddy the waters further, Dutch and West German prints bill producer Duilio Coletti as the film's director, not John Sturges. Even more in question is why the feature, while another huge box office success in Europe in 1973–74, did not see U.S. release until 1976, when it was issued here as *Chino* by Intercontinental

**Poster for *Valdez il Mezzosangue* (De Laurentiis Intermaco/Coral Producciones/Universal France, 1973), released in the U.S. as *Chino*.**

Releasing Company. It was also called *Chino* when released in France in 1974 and *The Valdez Horses* in England. Interestingly Paramount planned to release the film in the U.S. as *The Wild Horses* but never did so. With the box office successes of *The Valachi Papers*, *The Mechanic* and *The Stone Killer* in his homeland, it is difficult to understand Paramount's decision. Certainly the Bronson name alone would have caused the film to make money, as it did in 1976. Another point of interest is that the film was to have reteamed Bronson with Lino Ventura, who portrayed Vito Genovese in *The Valachi Papers*, but he withdrew due to smallness of the part and was replaced by Marcel Bozzufi, a popular Italian actor known for crime thrillers. Looking radiant, Jill Ireland co-starred for the first time since *Quelqu'un Derrière la Porte* in 1971, despite supporting roles in *The Mechanic* (1972) and *The Valachi Papers* (1972).

Young Jaimie Wagner (Vincent Van Patten) drifts into the remote ranch of half-breed Chino Valdez (Charles Bronson) and stays on as a hired hand, helping Chino run the ranch and break horses. Driving a herd into town, they see Catherine Maral (Jill Ireland), the sister of wealthy land owner Maral (Marcel Bozzufi). After a fight with a half-dozen wranglers, Chino is ordered out of town by the sheriff (Ettore Manni). His prize mare gives birth to a colt but Chino has to shoot her because she got mangled in barbed wire strung up by Maral. He goes to Maral's ranch and has a confrontation with him learning that Maral is really his landlord since the man's land grant extends over his property. Catherine comes to Chino's ranch to buy one of his horses and the two have an argument, but she returns and they become lovers. Maral orders Chino to never see his half-sister again and he and Jaimie go to the camp of friendly Apaches for Chino to meditate. While there Jaimie spends the night with a young Indian girl (Melissa Chimenti). The two return to town and watch a Christmas procession and Chino asks Catherine to marry him. Four of Maral's men attack Chino but the sheriff breaks up the fight and throws all five men in jail. Christmas Eve Chino returns home with the news he plans to marry Catherine. Maral forbids the marriage and tells Catherine to give up Chino or he will kill him. She reluctantly agrees. When Chino comes to the church Maral's men beat him up and then take him to his ranch where they beat him with a whip. Maral orders Chino off the land, kills his colt and threatens to kill his stud horse. Recovering, Chino kills four of Maral's men who try to shoot the stud and then stampedes his horse herd. Chino announces to Jaimie that he is going away and the pair go their separate ways.

A leisurely paced, low-key Western, *Valdez il Mezzosangue* gave Charles Bronson an excellent role, that of an outcast who makes a place for himself in life only to be rejected by society and forced from his land. The roles of Chino and Jaimie counterbalance each other: one is just beginning life while the other must give up all he has worked and cares for, including the woman he loves. Attractively photographed and nicely directed, the movie is a PG-rated entertainment which eschews violence except for a few minor brawls and the finale shootout. Jill Ireland, Vincent Van Patten and Marcel Bozzufi all handle their co-starring roles in fine fashion, but as expected, Charles Bronson dominates the film as Chino, a man who aspires only for dignity and acceptance.

The French publication *La Saison Cinématographique* 1974 noted, "*Chino* is a return to the sources of the traditional western: the landscape, the horses and the men here recapture their place and their importance." Steven H. Scheuer in *The Complete Guide to Videocassette Movies* (1987) said, "This rawhide Western is not one of Charles Bronson's better known assignments, but it's more enticing than a lot of his urban brass-knuckles adventures.... Bronson's a bit more sympathetic than usual as the beleaguered rancher; we're drawn into his quest for peace on the prairie."

Jill Ireland's role in the film is called Catherine in U.S. prints but Louise in all others. Marcel Bozzufi dubbed Charles Bronson for the French release prints of *Machine Gun Kelly* (1958) when that film was shown there in 1963.

Although the picture was one of the least known of Charles Bronson's 1970s features, today it is probably one of his most often viewed. *Chino* is one of the most widely available of Bronson videos, sometimes packaged with such previously obscure items as *De la Part des Copains* and *Quelqu'un Derrière la Porte.*

## *Vera Cruz* (United Artists, 1954) 94 minutes Color

*P:* James Hill. *D:* Robert Aldrich. *Sc:* Roland Kibbee & James R. Webb. *St:* Borden Chase. *Ph:* Ernest Laszlo. *Ed:* Alan Crosland Jr. *Mus:* Hugo Friedhofer. *AD:* Al Ybarra. *Sp Eff Ph:* Russell Sherman. *Conductor:* Raul Lavista. *Costumes:* Norma. *Song:* Hugo Friedhofer & Sammy Cahn.

**CAST:** Gary Cooper (Ben Trane), Burt Lancaster (Joe Erin), Denise Darcel (Countess Marie Duvarre), Sarita Montiel (Nina), Cesar Romero (Marquis de Labordere), George Macready (Emperor Maximilian), Ernest Borgnine (Donnegan), Morris Ankrum (General Ramirez), Charles Buchinsky (Pittsburgh),

James McCallion (Little Bit), Jack Lambert (Charlie), Henry Brandon (Danette), Jack Elam (Tex), James Seay (Abilene), Archie Savage (Ballard), Charles Horvath (Reno), Juan Garcia (Pedro).

Charles Bronson last used his surname Buchinsky in this lavish western filmed in Mexico, a fictional story set in the post–Civil War period when Benito Juarez and his rebel followers deposed the French controlled Emperor Maximilian. Bronson's character of Pittsburgh is a thuggish gang member who plays the harmonica, a precursor to the part he would play (albeit on the other side of the law) in *C'era una Volta il West (Once Upon a Time in the West)* 15 years later. Pittsburgh appears throughout the film but has little to do other than act loutish and look mean. Two brief scenes, however, highlight the character. In one he tries to rape Mexican girl Nina (Sarita Montiel) who fends him off with a low kick before he is dispatched with a right to the jaw by fellow outlaw Ballard (Archie Savage). The second scene takes place at a fiesta in Las Palmas with Pittsburgh playing harmonica with a Mexican band. When the band stops its song Pittsburgh pulls his gun and orders them to continue saying, "I've never played with a band before."

Defeated Confederate Ben Trane (Gary Cooper) travels to Mexico hoping to make enough money to restore his plantation which has been depleted by the Civil War. By chance he trades horses with Joe Erin (Burt Lancaster) and the two are pursued by government troops but escape with Trane joining Erin's gang, which includes thugs Donnegan (Ernest Borgnine) and Pittsburgh (Charles Buchinsky), to fight as mercenaries for whichever side will pay them the most. They are offered a commission by Marquis de Larbordere (Cesar Romero), who represents the government, but are surrounded by rebel General Ramirez (Morris Ankrum) and his men. Using local children as a ruse, Joe manages to force the rebels to leave peacefully and he and Ben and the gang go with the Marquis to Mexico City where Emperor Maximilian (George Macready) offers them $50,000 to accompany the beautiful Countess Marie Duvarre (Denise Darcel) and her caravan to Vera Cruz. They agree and along the way Ben and Joe find out the Countess is carrying three million dollars in gold in her coach, money to be used to bring troops from Europe to save Maximilian's throne. She joins the two fortune hunters in a scheme to steal the gold for themselves but along the way the caravan is attacked by rebel soldiers and pretty Nina (Sarita Montiel), a rebel spy, joins the group. The Marquis, the Countess' lover and leader of the caravan, realizes her treachery and in Las Palmas he steals the gold just as Joe and the Countess plan to betray Ben once they reach Vera Cruz. As the Marquis escapes with the gold in a supply wagon he also takes the Countess with him as Ben and Joe join forces with Ramirez to retrieve the money for a payment of $100,000. The Marquis and his men take the gold to a nearby fortress which the rebels attack. During the battle Ben and Joe get control of a repeating cannon and turn the tide in the rebel's favor. The Marquis is shot trying to escape as Joe turns on the

Countess and plans to take the gold for himself. Ben, however, stops him in a shootout, leaving the gold to Nina and the Juarez rebels.

Ernest Laszlo's on-location photography in Mexico is a high point of *Vera Cruz*, especially the scenes where the caravan snakes around a giant pyramid. Overall the film moves at a fairly nice pace although the plot appears to be a forerunner of the multiple double-crosses in *The Sting* (1973). The feature was produced by Harold Hecht and Burt Lancaster's Hecht–Lancaster Productions with Lancaster and top-billed Gary Cooper nicely handling their roles of the soldiers of fortune who innately distrust each other while more than once being called on to save the other's life. Denise Darcel and Sarita Montiel (who is introduced in the feature) adequately handle the love interests while Cesar Romero successfully gets screen attention as the Marquis. George Macready does well as the crafty emperor and Ernest Borgnine, Jack Elam, Henry Brandon and Jack Lambert vie with Charles Bronson for screen time as villainous gang members. Borgnine probably comes off best in this department as his character at least is given a death scene while Bronson's Pittsburgh apparently survives the final shootout.

*Vera Cruz* marked Bronson's second feature with Hecht–Lancaster Productions and director Robert Aldrich, having appeared with the same grouping earlier in the year in *Apache*. He would work with Sarita Montiel three years later in *Run of the Arrow*.

Costing $3 million, *Vera Cruz* grossed $4.565 million domestically, but it met with mixed critical reception. The *New York Times* opined, "Sadism is rampant in this atrocious adventure, apparently designed mainly to show how wicked and vicious men can be" while *Films and Filming* felt it was "one of the most exhilarating adventure stories ever filmed."

An interesting footnote to *Vera Cruz* is that it originally contained a theme song, following the trend started two years before when Tex Ritter sang in Gary Cooper's *High Noon*. Here Tony Martin sang the song "Vera Cruz" penned by Hugo Friedhofer and Sammy Cahn. For some unknown reason it was deleted just before the film was issued although Martin's recording of the song was issued commercially by RCA Victor Records (20–5946) coupled with Cole Porter's "All of You" from *Silk Stockings*.

## *Villa Rides!* (Paramount, 1968) 125 minutes Color

*P:* Ted Richmond. *D:* Buzz Kulik. *Sc:* Robert Towne & Sam Peckinpah, from the book *Pancho Villa* by William Douglas Lansford. *Ph:* Jack Hilyard. *Ed:* David Bretherton. *Mus:* Maurice Jarre. *Makeup:* Richard Mills. *Sp Eff:* Milt Rice. *AD:* Jose Alguero. *Sets:* Roman Calatayud. *Prod Design:* Ted Haworth. *Asst Dir:* Antonio Fuentes. *Prod Supv:* Robert Goodstein. *Asst Prod Supv:* Jose Maria Ochoa. *Hairstyles:* Carmen Sanchez. *Stunt Gaffer:* Chuck Hayward. *Camera:* Ricardo Navarrete. *Camera Asst:* Fernando Perrote & Ron Drinkwater. *Prod Mgr:* Roberto G. Maroto. *Chief Grip:* Mariano Denia.

**CAST:** Yul Brynner (Pancho Villa),

Robert Mitchum (Lee Arnold), Charles Bronson (Fierro), Maria Grazia Buccella (Fina), Roberto Viharo (Urbina), Frank Wolff (Ramirez), Herbert Lom (General Huerta), Alexander Knox (President Madero), Diana Lorys (Emilita), Robert Carricart (Don Luis), Fernando Rey (Fuentes), Regina de Julian (Lupita), Andres Monreal (Herrera), Antonio Padilla Ruiz (Juan), John Ireland (Man in Barber Shop), Jill Ireland (Girl in Restaurant), Jose Maria Prada.

American gunrunner Lee Arnold (Robert Mitchum) smuggles guns to General Ramirez (Frank Wolff) in Mexico in 1912, the weapons being used against the revolutionary government and Pancho Villa (Yul Brynner). While waiting for repairs on his airplane, Arnold see Ramirez' men savagely attack a small village loyal to Villa. Fierro (Charles Bronson), a bloodthirsty aide to Villa, recaptures the village with his men and executes the insurrectionists. Arnold too is sentenced to die but is reprieved after he agrees to use his plane to aid Villa. With Arnold's airborne aid, Villa and his army take an enemy troop train and then a town which his ally, General Huerta (Herbert Lom), has forbidden him to bother. Upset with Villa, Huerta, who plans to take over the revolutionary government from President Madero (Alexander Knox), orders Villa to attack Conejos, a mission he believes to be suicidal. With heavy losses, Villa's men capture the town with the aid of Arnold's air bombs. Villa has Ramirez killed but Huerta arrests him for disloyalty. Arnold escapes and makes it across the border to El Paso but later Villa and his men locate him in Texas and ask his aid again, since they have escaped from jail in order to overthrow the now-hated Huerta, who has become Mexico's dictator after murdering Madero. The alliance between Villa and Arnold is made as they plan to raise an army to fight Emiliano Zapata for Mexico City.

Given special billing in *Villa Rides*, Charles Bronson portrayed the sadistic Pancho Villa henchman Fierro in this loosely fact-based historical actioner dealing with only a brief interlude in the exciting career of the famous Mexican bandit-hero, portrayed by Yul Brynner, in his fifth film role in which he had a full head of hair. Filmed in Spain, *Villa Rides!* was Bronson's last Hollywood-financed feature (except for *You Can't Win 'Em All*, which was lensed in Turkey) until *Chato's Land*, which was also done in Spain, in 1972. In the interim he would attain international movie stardom. As to be expected from a script by Robert Towne (*Bonnie and Clyde*) and Sam Peckinpah, *Villa Rides!* was heavy on violence and Arthur Knight complained in *Saturday Review*, "the film's historicity is merely a pretext, an excuse to douse the screen with one bloodbath after another."

Released in the early summer of 1968, Paramount feared the film's violence might not set well following the assassinations of Dr. Martin Luther King and Robert Kennedy, but the movie did respectable business both here and abroad. It was issued in portions of Europe in 1969. Critical reaction to the movie was mixed. *Variety* noted, "Script fails to establish clearly the precise political framework, while over-developing some lesser details. This, plus overlength, adds up to dramatic tedium." The same reviewer commented, "Bronson delights a trifle too much in murder...." *Box Office* said the feature "should please action fans.... Producer Ted Richmond spared no expense or research to achieve authenticity for the 1912 background of Mexico." A.H. Weiller in the *New York Times* insisted "... *Villa Rides!* is simply a sprawling Western and not history." F. Maurice Speed wrote in *Film Review 1969–70* (1969) that the feature was "brilliantly photographed, often bloodily violent." Henry Herx and Tony Zaza opined in *The Family Guide to Movies on Video* (1988) that it was "a dismissible, violent Western ... (Director Buzz) Kulik ignores the historical complexity of the period and emphasizes its violence, with men being lined up and slaughtered, ad nauseam." In *The Paramount Story* (1985), John Douglas Eames noted the movie and its battles "were filmed in rousing style, but too many irrelevant scenes ... and too much footage given to a 1912 pioneer airman and gun-runner played by Robert Mitchum made the movie seem over-full of action, yet at the same time dull...." Phil Hardy wrote in *The Western* (1983) "this brutal essay about the Mexican Revolution is transformed by director Kulik into an anodyne, if

**Advertisement for *Villa Rides!* (Paramount, 1968).**

violent, adventure film, the dedication to Pancho Villa amongst the credits notwithstanding.... Kulik resolves the complex issues the script raises in 'heroic action' too often for the characters to remain credible, historical inaccuracies aside."

The film marked the first of many features with both Charles Bronson and his future wife Jill Ireland in the cast. In *Villa Rides!* they did not share screen time, however. Jill Ireland's brief cameo cast her as a Southwestern gal in a bordertown restaurant whose physical charms convince Robert Mitchum's character to stay on and fight with Villa.

## *When Hell Broke Loose* (Paramount, 1958) 78 minutes B/W

*P:* Oscar Brodney & Sol Doglin. *D:* Kenneth G. Crane. *Sc:* Oscar Brodney, from the *Reader's Digest* article by Ib Melchoir. *Ph:* Hal McAlpin. *Ed:* Asa Clark. *Mus:* Albert Glasser. *Asst Dir:* Hal Klein. *Sd:* Jack Goodrich. *Sets:* G.W. Bernstein. *Sp Eff:* Jess Davidson. *Makeup:* Gustaf Norin. *Wardrobe:* Byron Munson. *Technical Advisor:* Ib Melchoir.

**CAST:** Charles Bronson (Steve Boland), Violet Rensing (Ilsa), Richard Jaeckel (Karl), Arvid Nelson (Ludwig), Robert Easton (Jonesie), Dennis McCarthy (Captain Melton), Bob Stevenson (Captain Grayson), Eddie Foy III (Brooklyn), Kathy Carlyle (Ruby), Ann Wakefield (Myra), John Morley (Chaplain), Ed Penny (Bertie).

In order to escape going to jail, bookie Steve Boland (Charles Bronson) joins the army during World War II and ends up in detention before finally being shipped to Germany toward the war's end where he meets beautiful Ilsa (Violet Rensing). The two fall in love and she ends up reforming Steve. A gang of Nazis called Werewolves plan to assassinate General Dwight D. Eisenhower and Ilsa learns that her brother Karl (Richard Jaeckel) is a member of the group. Ilsa helps Steve and his commanding officer, Captain Melton (Dennis McCarthy) find the Werewolves' headquarters but they are discovered by Karl and a fight ensues with Ilsa being mortally wounded. In retaliation for Ilsa's death Steve singlehandedly guns down several of the Nazis before being aided by the military police.

Following his two starring features for Regal Film/20th Century–Fox in 1958, Charles Bronson headlined another programmer that year for Dolworth Productions, which was released by Paramount. *When Hell Broke Loose* was definitely inferior to the Regal films but it did provide him with another starring feature film role. "The plot is slight, and a capable cast can do little with the feeble script," the *Monthly Film Bulletin* reviewer wrote. *Variety* concurred with, "The cast try to give some vitality to their shapeless characterizations." The *Hollywood Reporter* noted, "Bronson's morose and rugged screen personality still is effective, but he needs a change of pace if his screen career is to prosper." John Douglas Eames said in *The Paramount Story* (1985), "According to the movies, a favorite Nazi ploy during the war was infiltrating

**Violet Rensing and Charles Bronson in *When Hell Broke Loose* (Paramount, 1958).**

Allied lines with English-speaking German soldiers in American uniforms. *When Hell Broke Loose* was among the films which made use of this gambit, thus giving its otherwise unremarkable drama an exciting lift."

Director Kenneth G. Crane, who *Variety* also credits as the film's editor, is best known as an editor but he directed the U.S. scenes for the Japanese horror films *Half-Human* (1955) and *The Manster* (1962) as well as Jim Davis in *The Monster from Green Hell* (1958).

## *The White Buffalo* (United Artists, 1977) 97 minutes Color

*P:* Pancho Kohner. *EP:* Dino De Laurentiis. *D:* J. Lee Thompson. *Sc:* Richard Sale, from his novel. *Ph:* Paul Lohmann. *Ed:* Michael F. Anderson. *Mus:* John Barry. *Asst Dir:* Jack Aldworth & Pat Kehoe. *Prod Design:* Tambi Larsen. *Sets:* James I. Berkey. *Sp Eff:* Richard M. Parker & Ron Downey. *Buffalo Sp Eff:* Carlo Rambaldi. *Sd:* Harlan Riggs. *Prod Mgr:* Hal Klein. *Unit Design:* Dan Perri. *Property Master:* Greg Elson. *Casting:* Joyce Selznick & Associates. *Set Coordinator:* Dennis Fill. *Costumer:* Eric Seeling. *Post Production Asst:* Ann Morrissey. *Camera Operator:* Ed Noons. *Second Unit Camera Operator:* Ron Vidor. *Location Mgr:* R. Anthony Brown. *Asst Property Master:* Craig Rache. *Producer's Secretary:* Nanette Rosen. *Transportation Coordinator:* Jerry Molen. *Sd Ed:* Dan Carlin. *Executive Coordinator:* Gordon Fletcher. *Sp Eff Ed:* Ross Taylor. *Prod Auditor:* Ruth West. *Sc*

*Supv:* Virginia Cook. *Gaffer:* Michael Malett. *Property Grip:* Tom Prophett. *Stunt Coordinator:* Ben Dobbins. *Still Man:* Kenneth Bishop. *Asst Film Ed:* Michael Copeland & Terence Anderson. *Producer's Associate:* George Van Noy. *Unit Publicist:* Ernie Anderson. *Hair Stylist:* Shirley Bladgett. *Ramrod:* Rudy Ugland Jr.

**CAST:** Charles Bronson (Wild Bill Hickok /James Otis), Jack Warden (Charlie Zane), Will Sampson (Crazy Horse), Kim Novak (Poker Jenny/Mrs. Schermerhorn), Clint Walker (Whistling Jack Kileen), Stuart Whitman (Winifred Coxy), Slim Pickens (Abel Pinkney), John Carradine (Amos Briggs), Cara Williams (Cassie Ollinger), Shay Duffin (Tim Brady), Douglas V. Fowley (Amos Bixby/Narrator), Cliff Pellow (Pete Holt), Ed Lauter (Captain Tom Custer), Martin Kove (Jack McCall), Scott Walker (Gyp Hook-Hand), Ed Bakey (Ben Corbett), Richard Gilliland (Corporal Kileen), David Roy Chandler (Kid Jelly), Philip Montgomery (Wes Pugh), Linda Moon Redfern (Black Shawl), Chief Tug Smith (Old Worm), Douglas Hume (Aaron Pratt), Cliff Carnell (Johnny Varner), Ron Thompson (Frozen Dog Pimp), Eve Brent (Frieda), Joe Roman (Silky Smith), Bert Williams (Paddy Welsh), Dan Vadis (Tall Man), Christopher Cary (Short Man), Larry Martindale (Man in Cheyenne Bar), Scott Bryson, Will Walker, Gregg White (Frozen Dog Miners), Hal Southern, Harold Hensley (Men in Bar).

Filmed on location in Canon City, Colorado, with interiors at the Metro-Goldwyn-Mayer lot, *The White Buffalo* marked Charles Bronson's return to the Western and with the possible exception of *Death Hunt* (1981), it would be his final genre outing to date. The decade of the 1970s was not kind to Westerns and with the exception of John Wayne's final film, *The Shootist* (1976) there were few memorable outings. In fact, *Heaven's Gate* (1980), would not only kill off MGM but it almost did in the Western genre. Unfortunately *The White Buffalo* did not help matters. Despite its $3 million budget the film's title monster was about the most ridiculous looking thing to hit the big screen since *The Giant Claw* (1957). Further the film was hampered by a muddled plot, murky photography and hard-to-understand dialogue and soundtrack. To make matters worse United Artists released the feature to a number of drive-ins where nearly all of the film was unwatchable due to the dark photography. *Variety* called the film a "turkey" and it was probably the least seen stateside of Bronson's 1970s features. When it made its network television debut on NBC-TV on July 31, 1982, it was retitled *Hunt to Kill.*

In September 1874, Wild Bill Hickok (Charles Bronson) returns to the West under the alias James Otis. Despite the new name and dark glasses to protect his sensitive eyes, Hickok is easily recognized by train conductor Bixby (Douglas V. Fowley). Hickok tells Bixby he has come back to face a nightmare, that of being charged by a white buffalo. Bixby tells him the last white buffalo was killed months before. Meanwhile a monstrous white buffalo rampages through an Indian village and kills the little daughter of Crazy Horse (Will Sampson). Because of his sorrow, Crazy Horse is called Worm by his tribe and told he must bear that name until he avenges his child's death. When Hickok's train stops at Cheyenne, Captain Tom Custer (Ed Lauter), who hates him, plans to kill Hickok but in a shootout it is the latter who kills

Poster for *The White Buffalo* (United Artists, 1977).

five soldiers, including Corporal Kileen (Richard Gilliland). Heading for the gold strike in the Black Hills, Hickok rides a stage driven by Abel Pinkney (Slim Pickens) and on board are gambler Coxy (Stuart Whitman) and his lady friend Cassie (Cara Williams). When Coxy tries to stab Hickok he is pushed off the stage and shot by Crazy Horse, who fires at the coach, killing Cassie. Further on Abel and Hickok find the bodies of two miners killed by the Indian and they take the corpses to Cheyenne to be buried by undertaker Briggs (John Carradine). There Hickok is reunited with his old love, Poker Jenny (Kim Novak), and in the local saloon he meets old friend Charlie Zane (Jack Warden), a one-time buffalo hunter. Also in the saloon is Whistling Jack Kileen (Clint Walker) who wants revenge on Hickok for killing his soldier brother. Another shootout takes place with Kileen's man Kid Jelly (David Roy Chandler) being shot as Hickok and Zane make their escape. The two leave on horseback for Deadwood but are surrounded by a band of Crow Indians. Crazy Horse arrives and together the three fight off the invaders. That night the white buffalo invades their camp and kills a mare and when he chases the beast Hickok is pinned down by Jack Kileen and his men. Crazy Horse, however, kills Kileen and Hickok invites him to his camp, much to the chagrin of Indian-hater Zane. Both Hickok and Crazy Horse vow to kill the white buffalo and later Hickok finds the spot in his dreams where he has been charged by the beast. When the buffalo does charge Hickok's gun jams but Crazy Horse jumps atop the bovine and stabs it repeatedly before being thrown off. When the bison charges again Hickok takes Crazy Horse's pistol and shoots it and together the two men kill the beast. When Hickok stops Zane from killing Crazy Horse the two men part enemies. Hickok and Crazy Horse, however, part company as friends but not allies.

Despite its many drawbacks, *The White Buffalo* is not without viewing enjoyment. The scenes showing mountains of bleached white buffalo bones are indeed harrowing as is the cruelty by both whites and Indians, as well as the title beast. Charles Bronson gives a very interesting performance as Wild Bill Hickok who tells Zane that what he hates "even more than dyin' is bein' afraid." The film is also populated with some delightful performances, especially Jack Warden as the hardened Charlie Zane, Stuart Whitman as the slimy gambler, Cara Williams as a loud mouthed slut, Clint Walker as the murderous Whistling Jack Kileen, Slim Pickens' very vocal stage driver and John Carradine as the undertaker who tells Pickens to lay corpses in the snow "to keep 'em fresh." The Colorado locales are quite scenic and Kim Novak made a welcome return to the big screen in the role of Poker Jenny, a one-time hooker turned respectable. Will Sampson is properly stoic as Crazy Horse.

*Variety* complained, "Production features arch scripting by Richard Sale (from his novel), stilted acting by the cast and forced direction by J. Lee Thompson.... The buffalo trackdown is actually more of a cheap writing hook, on which to hang a lot of dubious sociological gab between the players, than an outdoor adventure story." Phil Hardy in *The Western* (1983) called it, "A silly Western variant on the *Moby Dick* story.... The beast of the title represents one of the most unconvincing special effects of the decade." In *The Complete Guide to Videocassette Movies* (1987), Steven H. Scheurer wrote, "Dino De Laurentiis' abominable-animal movie has a ludicrous plot, ridiculous characters and astounding dialogue.... A white elephant."

While *The White Buffalo* marked Charles Bronson's final association with Dino De Laurentiis, it marked the second of several features with director J. Lee Thompson and producer Pancho Kohner, the son of his agent, Paul Kohner.

## *The Wild West* (Trans America Film Distributors, 1977) 100 minutes B/W & Color

*P:* Laurence Joachim & Barbara Holden. *Sc:* Max Wernberg. *Ed:* Tom Fucci. *Titles:* Ramon Ferro. *Narrator:* Ray Owens.

**CAST:** Charles Bronson, Clint Eastwood, Steve McQueen, John Wayne, Ernest Borgnine, William Boyd, Raymond Burr, Lee Van Cleef, Broderick Crawford, John Derek, Angie Dickinson, Bill Elliott, Henry Fonda, Glenn Ford, William Holden, Rita Hayworth, Ben Johnson, Lash LaRue, Fred MacMurray, Joel McCrea, Tim McCoy, Ken Maynard, Robert Mitchum, Maureen O'Hara, Gregory Peck, Roy Rogers, Leonard Nimoy, Mickey Rooney, Randolph Scott, Barbara Stanwyck, Robert Vaughn.

"The most fabulous cast of stars and action scenes are spotlighted in this Western spectacular," read the advertising copy for this feature film compilation which tells the story of the West with footage from various feature films. This is one of the most obscure of Charles Bronson's films and despite first billing (the top four stars are billed alphabetically above the title in its advertising) he appears for only 35 seconds in uncredited footage from *Showdown at Boot Hill* (1958). No titles of the movies used in the film are mentioned and the feature appears to have received little distribution although it was copyrighted.

In 1977 Filmways Australasian Distributors advertised *The Wild West* for showings in Australia, New Zealand and the Pacific Islands and a decade later it was issued stateside on video by Twin Tower Enterprises.

## *X-15* (United Artists, 1962) 107 minutes Color

*P:* Henry Sanicola & Tony Lazzarino. *EP:* Howard W. Koch. *D:* Richard Donner. *Sc:* Tony Lazzarino & James Warner Bellah. *St:* Tony Lazzarino. *Ph:* Carl Guthrie. *Ed:* Stanley Rabjohn. *Mus:* Nathan Scott. *AD:* Roland M. Brooks. *Sd:* Victor Appel & Don Jones. *Sets:* Kenneth Schwartz. *Sp Eff:* Paul Pollard. *Asst Dir:* Russ Haverick & Jay Sandrich. *Photographic Eff:* Howard Anderson. *Wardrobe:* Wesley V. Jeffries. *Makeup:* Beans Pondell.

**CAST:** David McLean (Matt Powell), Charles Bronson (Lieutenant Colonel Lee Brandon), Ralph Taeger (Major Ernest Wilde), Brad Dexter (Major Anthony Rinaldi), Kenneth Tobey (Colonel Craig Brewster), James Gregory (Tom Deparma), Mary Tyler Moore (Pamela Stewart), Patricia Owens (Margaret Brandon),

Lisabeth Hush (Diane Wilde), Stanley Livingston (Mike Brandon), Lauren Gilbert (Colonel Jessup), Phil Dean (Major McCully), Chuck Stanford (Lieutenant Commander Joe Lacrosse), Patty McDonald (Susan Brandon), Mike McKane (B-52 Pilot), Robert Dornnam (Test Engineer), Frank Watkins (Security Policeman), Barbara Kelly (Secretary), Darlene Hendricks (Nurse), Ric Applewhite, Pat Renella (Engineers), Jerry Lawrence, Richard Norris (Operators), Ed Fleming, Lee Giroux, Grant Holcomb, Lee Irwin (Themselves), James Stewart (Narrator).

Filmed in Panavision and Technicolor, *X-15* was narrated by James Stewart and told the story of the development of the X-15 fighter plane at Edwards Air Force Base in California. An intermingling of documentary and melodrama, the film attempted not only to show how the Air Force developed the X-15 but also the lives of those involved with the project, including a test pilot portrayed by Charles Bronson. He got reviews for the feature which reunited him with executive producer Howard W. Koch, with whom he worked earlier in *Big House, U.S.A.* (1955). The feature also marked the directorial debut of Richard Donner, with whom Bronson would work again in *Twinky* (1969).

Against the background of the work behind putting together the X-15, a rocketship designed to fly 4,000 miles per hour into the fringes of outer space, the movie told the story of the test pilots involved in the project. Beginning with an aborted space flight, the film detailed how working under the pressure of the project affected civilian pilot Matt Powell (David McLean), Lieutenant Colonel Lee Brandon (Charles Bronson), whose wife Margaret (Patricia Owens) wants another child, and the also happily married Major Anthony Rinaldi (Brad Dexter). With the support of his family Brandon is able to endure the job pressures and winds up setting a world's flight record only to give his life to save that of fellow aviator Powell. Brandon's family grieves for his loss but at the same time realizes he was a hero who gave his life for his country.

*Newsweek* said, "*X-15* is a dramatization of the U.S. rocket-plane program and, except for a moving tragedy near the end, the only fiction is in a series of misfirings. But as a re-creation of the lean poetry of flight, *X-15* is a thrilling, illuminating show." Howard Thompson in the *New York Times* called the film, "A surprisingly appealing and sensible low-budget picture—a semi-documentary with some harmless fictional embroidery." In referring to the cast he noted "the always reliable Charles Bronson." *Variety* complained the feature was "Much too technically involved for the layman—at times it resembles a training film more than a popular entertainment." Regarding the cast the same reviewer noted, "Charles Bronson and James Gregory seem to fare best." The *New York Herald-Tribune* felt the scene in which Bronson has a heart-to-heart talk with his young son (Stanley Livingston, later on TV's *My Three Sons*) "impressive." In retrospect, *Movies on TV* (1977) by Steven H. Scheuer stated, "Stilted semi-documentary.... This one is Grade B fare with all the clichés, including the patient wives who wait for their husbands while

**Charles Bronson in *X-15* (United Artists, 1962).**

they serve science." *Leonard Maltin's 1996 Movie & Video Guide* (1995) called the film a "Mild narrative" adding "Unusual role for Bronson, even then."

## *Yes Virginia, There Is a Santa Claus* (ABC-TV/Quinta Communications/Paradigm Entertainment, 1991) 95 minutes Color

*P:* Duke Fenady & Nick Anderson. *EP:* Andrew J. Fenady, Bob Banner, Gary L. Pudney & Silvio Muraglia. *D:* Charles Jarrott. *Sc:* Val De Crowl & Andrew J.

Fenady. *Ph:* John S. Bartley. *Ed:* Dann Cahn. *Mus:* Charles Bernstein. *Prod Design:* Richard Hudolin. *Executive in Charge of Prod:* David S. Harding. *Asst Dir:* Vladimir Stefoff, Kathy A. Gilroy & Cynthia Clayton. *Prod Mgr:* Grace Gilroy. *Camera Operator:* Ron Pridy. *Set Decorator:* Barry Kemp. *Prop Master:* Grant R. Swain. *Casting Asst—Canada:* William Haines. *Location Mgrs:* Christian Haebler & Hagan Beggs. *Vocal Casting:* Catherine Daly. *Costume Design:* Patricia Smith & Maureen Hiscox. *Prod Asst:* Maria Plosz. *Asst to Producers:* Andrew Francis Fenady. *Titles:* Howard A. Anderson Co. *Cost Supv:* Jennifer Grossman. *Costumes:* Kevin Knight. *Sd Mixer:* Ralph Parker. *Boom Operator:* Darren Brisker. *Asst AD:* Sheila Haley. *Transportation Coordinator:* Jake Callihoo. *Asst Ed:* Brossy Reiner. *Stunt Coordinators:* Stan Barrett & John Scott. *Stunts:* Guy Bews, Jacob Rupp, John Dobb, Tony Morelli & Brent Woolsey. *Makeup:* Jan Newman. *Hairstyles:* Janet Silva. *Sc Supv:* Susan Weber. *Prod Coordinator—Canada:* E. Robert Sheehy. *Asst Prod Coordinator:* Kandis Armstrong. *Prod Accountant:* Lorraine Baird. *Asst Accountant:* Jackie Wechselbarger. *First Asst Cameraman:* Martin McInally. *Gaffer:* Ronald Williams. *Best Boy:* David Tiekell. *Key Grip:* Andrew Mulkani. *Asst Dir Trainee:* Michael Bafaro. *Still Photographer:* Chris Helcermanas-Benge.

CAST: Charles Bronson (Francis P. "Frank" Church), Richard Thomas (James O'Hanlon), Edward Asner (Frank P. Mitchell), Katherine Isobel (Virginia O'Hanlon), Tamsin Kelsey (Evie O'Hanlon), Colleen Winton (Andrea Borland), Massimo Bonetti (Dominic Donelli), Peter Breck (Mr. Chambers), John Novak (Barrington), Shawn MacDonald (Teddy Murray), Gary Chalk (Goss), Lillian Carlson (Mrs. Goldstein), Virginia Bagnato (Maria Donelli), John Kirkconnell (Sean O'Hanlon), Kerry Sandomirsky (Celeste), William Samples (Mr. Schuller), Tom Heaton (O'Hara), Tom McBeath (Senior Officer Flynn), Hagan Beggs (Bartender), Frank C. Turner (Produce Keeper), Anthony Holland (Misery), Crystaleen Obray (Julie), Sarah Perkins (Susan), Dwight McFee, Gary Davey (Officers), Paul Batten (Otho), Andrew J. Fenady (Reporter).

Charles Bronson's first television movie since *Act of Vengeance* in 1986, *Yes Virginia, There Is a Santa Claus*, was based on the famous *New York Sun* editorial written by Frank Church in 1897. While the story was based on fact, many of the characters and situations were fictionalized. For Bronson the film provided a major change of pace, casting him as a reformer reporter-editorial writer who fights with words instead of his fists, although he is allowed one scene where he flattens a smart-mouthed rival. Bronson's character in the film had lost his wife and baby daughter the year before to pneumonia, and in real life the actor's wife, Jill Ireland, had died after a long bout with cancer in 1990. Now 70, but looking much younger, the actor conveyed the emotions of a man who cannot cope with the loss of loved ones. Not only is the film an inspiring Christmas feature but it also contains one of Charles Bronson's best performances.

Set in New York City before the turn of the century, the film relates how Irishman James O'Hanlon (Richard Thomas) and his friend, Italian Dominic Donelli (Massimo Bonetti), are fired from their jobs as dock workers after being harassed by bully Goss (Gary Chalk). At the same time *New York Sun* writer Frank Church (Charles Bronson) mourns the deaths of his wife and

Advertisement for *Yes Virginia, There Is a Santa Claus* (ABC-TV, 1991).

baby and turns to alcohol, losing interest in his work. When he fails to finish a story on social reform, co-worker Andrea Borland (Colleen Winton) takes the story, finishes it for Church and gives it to managing editor Frank P. Mitchell (Edward Asner). Although he is supposed to be working on a Tammany Hall exposé, Church chides Andrea and tells her their profession is fleeting and that stories are only good for a single day and are then forgotten. O'Hanlon helps in capturing a thief and his eight-year-old daughter Virginia (Katherine Isobel) asks him if there is really a Santa Claus. He tells her to ask the *New York Sun* because if it is printed there is must be the truth. The little girl writes a letter to the *Sun* asking if there is really a Santa Claus. Church's nasty rival Barrington (John Novak) continually pokes fun at him and his drinking but when he makes a disparaging remark about Andrea, Church knocks him out. That evening Church attempts to kill himself but is interrupted by Mitchell who tells him he has a special assignment. Donelli gets a job cleaning up a bar while O'Hanlon gets day work delivering ice. When Goss and his nephews attempt to beat up Donelli in the bar, O'Hanlon happens on the scene and the two men beat the bullies. That morning Mitchell gives Church the assignment of answering Virginia's letter. Unsure of how to go about writing this editorial, Church wanders the streets and sees first hand the spirit of Christmas. When the editorial is published it is a great success and O'Hanlon, who starts out Christmas Eve unhappy at having no presents for his three children, ends up being offered a job as a rookie cop and gets a reward for his earlier capture of the thief. The O'Hanlon family have a happy Christmas as they read Church's reply to Virginia's letter.

In addition to Charles Bronson's outstanding work as Frank Church, the film also has good work by Richard Thomas and Tamsin Kelsey as the little girl's parents and Katherine Isobel is quite appealing as Virginia. Colleen Winton does a good job as the young reporter who is attracted to Church and wants to help him. Edward Asner has a few good scenes as the *New York Sun*'s managing editor. The movie nicely recaptures the era in which it is set, due to Richard Hudolin's production design and set decorator Barry Kemp. Charles Jarrott's direction keeps the film moving nicely despite commercial breaks.

Roberta Bernstein wrote in *Variety*, "The pace is refreshingly unhurried. But while this provides ample time for rich characterizations, the clichéd script results merely in stick figures and stilted dialogue.... The warm and happy ending is appropriate both to the season and the movie's consistently amiable if bland tone." Regarding the star she said, "Bronson's economic gestures convey great pain and warmth." *TV Guide* said Bronson "is cast against type" and reviewing the telefeature on its second run in 1993, the same publication called it "TV-movie hokum." Linda Renaud in *The Hollywood Reporter* said "you will be charmed by this wonderfully sentimental telefilm.... For a telefilm, the production values are exceptional. Many of the exteriors in this exquisite period piece were shot in Vancouver's Gastown." She added,

"Bronson, in a rare television appearance and cast totally against type, is thoroughly convincing as the distraught newspaperman."

The telefeature has become a holiday perennial, one of a number of holiday movies always shown on television at Christmastime.

On Christmas Eve in 1974, ABC-TV telecast an animated cartoon special also called *Yes Virginia, There Is a Santa Claus*. Narrated by Jim Backus, it told the same story as the 1991 telefeature.

## *You Can't Win 'Em All* (Columbia, 1970) 99 minutes Color

*P:* Gene Corman. *AP:* Harold Buck. *D:* Peter Collinson. *Sc:* Leo V. Gordon. *Ph:* Kenneth Higgins. *Ed:* Ray Poulton. *Mus:* Bert Kaempfert. *Sd:* Barrie Copeland. *Sd Recording:* Arthur Vincent. *Prod Mgr:* Derek Parr. *Second Unit Dir:* Skeets Kelly. *Asst Dir:* Scott Wodehouse. *Second Unit Photography:* Frank Kingston. *AD:* Seamus Flannery. *Mus Dir:* Muir Mathieson.

**CAST:** Tony Curtis (Adam Dyer), Charles Bronson (Josh Corey), Michele Mercier (Aila), Fikret Hakan (Colonel Elci), Gregoire Aslan (Osman Bey), Salih Guney (Captain Enver), Patrick Magee (General), Tony Bonner (Reese), John Acheson (Davis), John Alderson (U.S. Major), Horst Jansen (Woller), Leo Gordon (Bolek), Reed De Ruen (U.S. Chief Petty Officer), Paul Stassino (Gunner Major), Suna Keskin (Cafe Girl), Yuksel Gozen (Papadopoulos), Jenia Halil (Madam).

Leo Gordon (1922—) has appeared in character roles in films since the early 1950s and over the years he has also scripted such features as *Black Patch* (1957), *Hot Rod Girl* (1958), *Crybaby Killer* (1958), *Attack of the Giant Leeches* (1959), *Tower of London* (1962), *The Terror* (1963; additional scenes) and *Tobruk* (1967). He wrote this exotic adventure romp for producer Gene Corman's S.R.O. Company with filming on location in Turkey in the summer of 1969. Gordon also played the role of a mercenary soldier in the feature. While Tony Curtis got top billing it was second-billed Charles Bronson who garnered most of the publicity in the course of the movie's production. He also managed to garner some good reviews as noted by Margaret Tarratt in *Films and Filming* who said, "Charles Bronson as the engaging, amoral scoundrel takes most of the honors in a rather dull film." Originally Howard Hawks was to direct the film, which was also called *Dubious Patriots* and *Soldiers of Fortune*, but he was replaced by Peter Collinson. Bronson previously worked with producer Gene Corman on the latter's brother's (Roger Corman) film, *Machine Gun Kelly* (1958).

The comic-adventure tells the story of vagabond Mediterranean adventurers Adam Dyer (Tony Curtis) and Josh Corey (Charles Bronson), who both wind up in Turkey in 1922 and get involved in its civil war. Adam wants to recover one of his family's ships which the Germans pressed into service during the World War and he meets up with Josh and his mercenary gang which included Bolek (Leo Gordon). The local governor, Osman Bey (Gregoire Aslan), hires them to escort his three daughters and their companion Aila

**Michele Mercier, Charles Bronson and Tony Curtis in *You Can't Win 'Em All* (Columbia, 1970).**

(Michele Mercier) to Smyrna, along with a gold shipment intended to aid the Ottoman Empire's Sultan. Going along with them is Colonel Elci (Fikret Hakan) who secretly plans to steal the gold for himself. When Adam finds out the gold is actually lead, Aila, who is being romanced by both adventurers, tells him they are also bringing along a casket of jewels. The three then plan to take the gems for themselves but Colonel Elci also finds out about them and when he tries to steal the jewels he is killed by Aila. Josh and the girl then run off with the gems to Smyrna with Adam following but the town has been taken over by revolutionaries and the trio is arrested. Although they have lost the jewels, Adam and Josh win their freedom by turning over a valuable copy of the Koran, which was also in the caravan, to the local rebel leader. While they escape with their lives, neither of the two men win Aila.

Like most Charles Bronson starrers of the time, *You Can't Win 'Em All* got quick and mild playoffs in the United States. It opened in Dallas, Texas, in July 1970. Overseas, however, it did fine at the box office when issued in West

Germany, Sweden and Denmark in 1970 and the next year in Great Britain and France. It has, however, become a perennial on late night U.S. television.

*Variety* called it "dull derring-do" but added, "Bronson's mercenaries provide some action relief from the talky, convoluted double-crossing of assorted guerilla intrigue." The *Monthly Film Bulletin* referred to the feature as "all muddle and flurry" while Henry Herx and Tony Zaza wrote in *The Family Guide to Movies on Video* (1988) that it was a "tired, formula adventure." The authors did note "the real star of this turkey is a beautiful old steam-engine, lovingly photographed against picturesque Turkish locations." On the other hand, F. Maurice Speed opined in *Film Review 1971–1972* (1971) that the film was "A quite satisfying slice of good old Hollywood hokum: done in a spectacular and amusing way."

## *You're in the Navy Now* see *U.S.S. Teakettle*

# The Television Appearances

***Act of Vengeance*** (Home Box Office [HBO], April 20, 1986)—see Filmography under *Act of Vengeance* (1986).

## *Adventure in Java* (NBC-TV, July 8, 1954) 30 minutes B/W

**CAST:** Tim Holt, Charles Buchinsky.

This was a pilot for a projected television series produced by MCA and filmed on the Republic Pictures lot. Former cowboy star Tim Holt and Charles Bronson were teamed as two rugged adventurers for hire whose exploits take them to various exotic locales. Although the pilot did not sell as a series it was telecast on NBC-TV.

In a revamped version the format became the syndicated television series *Soldiers of Fortune* starring John Russell and Chick Chandler which ran from 1955 to 1956 for 52 episodes. In 1997 Brad Johnson starred in a new syndicated version called *Soldier of Fortune, Inc.*

## *Adventures in Paradise* "Survival" (ABC-TV, December 31, 1961) 60 minutes B/W

*P:* Art Wallace. *D:* David Orrick McDearmon. *Sc:* Fred Freiberger. *Creator:* James A. Michener. *Ph:* Lloyd Ahern. *Ed:* Gerald Wilson. *Mus:* Lionel Newman.

**CAST:** Gardner McKay (Captain Adam Troy), Guy Stockwell (Chris Parker), Lani Kai (Kelly), Charles Bronson (Dan Morton), Pippa Scott (Judith Mills), Russell Johnson (Herbert Bowman), Werner Klemperer.

Chris Parker (Guy Stockwell), first mate of Captain Adam Troy's (Gardner McKay) boat the *Tiki*, gets a job as skipper of wealthy Dan Morton's (Charles Bronson) yacht. Everyone on board is having a good time until trouble ensues.

James A. Michener created this series for ABC-TV which dealt with the adventures of a schooner captain in the South Pacific. The show ran from 1959 to 1962 on ABC-TV and was made by Martin Manulis Productions, Marjay Productions and 20th Century–Fox Television.

## *Alcoa Presents* "The Last Round" (ABC-TV, January 10, 1961) 30 minutes B/W

*P:* Collier Young. *AP-Creator:* Merwin Gerard. *D:* John Newland. *Sc:* Don W. Mankiewicz. *Executive Writer:* Larry Marcus. *Ph:* Dale Deverman. *Ed:* Henry Berman. *Mus:* Harry Lubin. *AD:* George W. Davis & Addison Hehr. *Asst Dir:* Donald C. Klune. *Sc Consultant:* Ivan Kappler. *Set Decorators:* Henry Grace & Jack Mills. *Mus Ed:* Gilbert Merchant. *Recording Supv:* Franklin Milton. *Sc Supv:* Jane Ficker.

**CAST:** John Newland (Host), Charles Bronson (Yank Dawson), Felix Deebank (Chipper "Whitey" White), Ronald Long (Alfie Jones), Wally Cassell (Collins), Gordon Richards (Doctor), John Indrisano, Peter Fontaine, Stewart Taylor.

On the eve of a fight in 1944 wartime London, faded American boxer Yank Dawson (Charles Bronson) thinks he sees the ghost of a former champion and loses the match.

*Alcoa Presents* was a supernatural anthology series which ran on ABC-TV from 1959 to 1961 for 94 episodes. It was syndicated in 1962 as *One Step Beyond.*

## *Alfred Hitchcock Presents* (CBS-TV, 1955–1962) 30 minutes B/W

### "And So Died Riabouchinska" (February 12, 1956)

*P:* Alfred Hitchcock. *D:* Robert Stevenson. *Sc:* Mel Dinelli. *St:* Ray Bradbury. *Ph:* Reggie Lanning. *Ed:* Edward Wilson.

**CAST:** Claude Rains (Fabian), Charles Bronson (Detective Krovitch), Bill [William] Haade (Stagehand), Claire Carleton, Lowell Gilmore, Charles Cantor, Harry Tyler, Iris Adrian, Virginia Gregg.

In the first of three appearances on *Alfred Hitchcock Presents*, Charles Bronson played a police detective assigned to solve a murder in a threatre. He questions several suspects, including ventriloquist Fabian (Claude Rains).

### "There Was an Old Woman" (March 18, 1956)

*P:* Alfred Hitchcock. *D:* Robert Stevenson. *Sc:* Marion Cockrell. *St:* Gerry & Harold Hackaday. *Ph:* Reggie Lanning. *Ed:* Edward Williams. *Supv Ed:* Stanley Wilson. *AD:* Martin Obzina.

**CAST:** Estelle Winwood (Monica Laughton), Charles Bronson (Frank Bramwell), Norma Crane (Lorna Bramwell), Dabbs Greer (Milkman), Emerson Treacy (Druggist).

A young couple (Charles Bronson, Norma Crane) befriend an eccentric old woman (Estelle Winwood) in order to steal her money but she turns the tables on them.

### "The Woman Who Wanted to Live" (February 6, 1962)

**CAST:** Charles Bronson (Ray Bardon), Lola Albright (Lisa), Ray Montgomery (Attendant), Craig Curtis (Rook), Ben Bryant (Fat Boy), Robert Rudelson (Cuke).

After killing a man, an escaped convict (Charles Bronson) forces a woman (Lola Albright) to drive him to a hideout.

## *All-Star Party for Clint Eastwood* (CBS-TV, December 15, 1986) 120 minutes Color

*P:* Paul W. Keyes. *D:* Dick McDonough. *Mus:* Nick Perito.

**CAST:** Lucille Ball (Host), Clint Eastwood (Guest of Honor), Charles Bronson, Sammy Davis Jr., Roberta Flack, Cary Grant, Merv Griffin, Monty Hall, Bob Hope, Marsha Mason, Don Rickles, James Stewart.

Charles Bronson appeared in this TV special tribute to Clint Eastwood.

## *All-Star Tribute to Elizabeth Taylor* (ABC-TV, March 9, 1989) 60 minutes Color

*P-D:* Marty Pasetta. *Sc:* Stephen Pouliot, Ken Welch & Mitzie Welch. *Mus:* Lenny Stack.

**CAST:** Elizabeth Taylor (Guest of Honor), Charles Bronson (Host), June Allyson, Beau Bridges, Carol Burnett, Bob Hope, Roddy McDowall, Vera Miles, Margaret O'Brien, Mickey Rooney, Robert Stack, Stevie Wonder, Kenny Rogers, Dudley Moore, Ann Miller.

A special on Elizabeth Taylor's career in which she received the second annual America's Hope Award. Charles Bronson hosted the variety event which was taped February 23, 1989, in the Bob Hope Cultural Center at Palm Springs, California.

## *All-Star Tribute to John Wayne* (ABC-TV, November 26, 1976) 60 minutes Color

*P:* Paul W. Keyes. *D:* Dick McDonough. *Sc:* Paul W. Keyes & Marc London. *Mus:* Nelson Riddle.

**CAST:** John Wayne (Guest of Honor), Frank Sinatra (Host), Charles Bronson, John Byner, Glen Campbell, Sammy Davis Jr., Angie Dickinson, Monty Hall, Bob Hope, Ron Howard, Lee Marvin, Maureen O'Hara, James Stewart, Claire Trevor, Henry Winkler, Dan Rowan, Dick Martin.

A variety special honoring screen legend John Wayne, produced in association with Variety Clubs International. Charles Bronson appeared giving a testimonial to John Wayne.

## *The Aquanauts* "The Cave Divers" (CBS-TV, December 7, 1960) 60 minutes B/W

*P:* Ivan Tors. *Mus:* Andre Previn.

**CAST:** Keith Larsen (Drake Andrews), Jeremy Slate (Larry Lohr), Paula Raymond (Judy O'Brien), Charles Bronson (Hector Morrison), Robert Knapp (Joe Tydell).

When a geologist dies while prospecting for uranium, his daughter (Paula Raymond) asks Southern California salvage divers Drake Andrews (Keith Larsen) and Larry Lohr (Jeremy Slate) to continue his work.

## *Biff Baker, U.S.A.* (CBS-TV) 30 minutes B/W

### "Koblen" (November 5, 1952)

*D:* Richard Irving. *Sc:* Frank Burt. *St:* Fenton Earnshaw. *Ph:* Ellsworth Fredericks. *Ed Supv:* Richard Currier. *Ed:* Michael R. McAdams. *Sd:* William Lynch. *AD:* Martin Obzina.

**CAST:** Alan Hale Jr. (Biff Baker), Randy Stuart (Louise Baker), Walter Reed, Henry Brandon, Maurice Doner, Charles Buchinsky, Marta Mitrovich, Leonids Ossetynsky, Lou Nova, Leonard George, Harold Dreynforth, Albert Taylor.

In the series' debut episode, Charles Bronson had a supporting role in this tale of American businessman Biff Baker (Alan Hale Jr.) and his wife Louise (Randy Stuart) going to Czechoslovakia on business and being asked by the U.S. Army Intelligence to bring back secret information via microfilm.

## "Alpine Assignment" (November 12, 1952)

*D:* Richard Irving. *Sc:* Jerome Gary & Fenton W. Earnshaw. *Ph:* Ellsworth Fredericks. *AD:* Martin Obinza. *Supv Ed:* Richard Currier. *Ed:* Michael R. McAdam. *Sd:* William Lynch.

**CAST:** Alan Hale Jr. (Biff Baker), Randy Stuart (Louise Baker), Lee Marvin (Michler/Captain Hollis), Leon Askin (Reicher), Robert Warwick (Commander), Charles Buchinsky (Wilhelm), Bill Boyett, Keith Richards (Soldiers), Terry Frost (Johnson).

While vacationing at an Austrian resort near the Iron Curtain, American businessman Biff Baker (Alan Hale Jr.) and his wife Louise (Randy Stuart) become involved with Soviet agents operating a phony *Voice of America* radio station. Charles Bronson, in his second appearance in the series in as many weeks, played one of the Reds, who is gunned down by a military intelligence officer, played by Lee Marvin.

*Biff Baker, U.S.A.* dealt with the title character and his spouse being involved in various cases of espionage in Europe. It was produced by Revue Studios for the American Tobacco Company.

# *The Big Valley* "Earthquake" (ABC-TV, November 10, 1965)

60 minutes Color

*P:* Jules Levy, Arthur Gardner & Arnold Laven. *AP:* Lou Morheim. *D:* Paul Henreid. *Sc:* Oliver Crawford. *Ph:* Wilfred M. Cline. *Ed:* Anthony Woolner. *Mus:* George Duning. *Mus Supv:* Alfred Perry. *Mus Ed:* Harry King. *Set Design:* Jack De Shield. *Prod Supv:* Norman S. Powell. *Editorial Supv:* Bernard Barton. *Sd:* Don Rush. *Prod Mgr:* Don Torpin. *Supv AD:* Bill Rose. *Asst Dir:* Marty Moss. *Set Decorator:* Pierre Ludum. *Sc Supv:* Joseph Mazzuca. *Wardrobe:* Robert B. Harris. *Makeup:* Sidney Perrell. *Sd Eff:* Madine Rogue. *Hairstylist:* Scott Rackin. *Miss Stanwyck's Costumes:* Jack Muhs. *Casting:* Robert Walker. *Prod Asst:* Marilyn Carpenter & Marilyn Fibelkorn. *Series Creators:* A.I. Bezzederis & Louis F. Edelman.

**CAST:** Barbara Stanwyck (Victoria Barkley), Richard Long (Jarrod Barkley), Peter Breck (Nick Barkley), Lee Majors (Heath Barkley), Linda Evans (Audra Barkley), Charles Bronson (Tate), Alizia Gur (Naomi), Audrey Dalton (Ann Snyder), Wesley Lau (Roy Snyder), Robert E. Williams (Joel), William Fawcett (Jeb Wilson), John Craven (Doctor), Robert Karnes (Padre), Mort Mills (Sheriff).

Following an earthquake, ranch owner Victoria Barkley (Barbara Stanwyck) is trapped in the wine cellar of a church with saddle bum Tate (Charles Bronson), who has a grudge against the Barkleys for firing him due to drinking, and pregnant Indian girl Naomi (Alizia Gur). The trio find an old gold mine but during an aftershock Tate is killed by falling rocks and the girl dies in childbirth. Victoria's children (Richard Long, Peter Breck, Lee Majors,

Linda Evans) rescue her and the baby is taken by the wife (Audrey Dalton) of its father (Wesley Lau), a local trader.

Set in the San Joaquin Valley of California in 1898, *The Big Valley* ran for 112 episodes on ABC-TV from 1965 to 1969. "Earthquake" was the series' ninth telecast.

## *The Bob Newhart Show* (NBC-TV, April 11, 1962) 60 minutes Color

*P:* Roland Kibbee. *D:* Coby Ruskin. *Announcer:* Dan Sorkin.

**CAST:** Bob Newhart, Charles Bronson, Anita Gordon.

In this weekly comedy-variety program, guest star Charles Bronson joined Bob Newhart in a comedy sketch kidding television watchers and ways to help them.

## *Bonanza* "The Underdog" (NBC-TV, December 13, 1964) 60 minutes Color

*P:* Don Dorforth. *AP:* James W. Lane. *D:* William F. Claxton. *Sc:* Donn Mullally. *Ph:* William F. Whitley. *Ed:* Marvin Coil. *Mus:* David Rose. *Mus Supv:* William Lava. *Song:* Jay Livingston & Ray Evans. *Prod Executive:* Robert Stillman. *St Consultant:* Frank Cleaver. *Prod Supv:* Kent McCray. *Color Consultant:* Frank P. Pancona Jr. *AD:* Hal Pereira & Earl Hedrick. *Set Decorators:* Sam Comer & Grace Gregory. *Makeup:* Wally Westmore. *Sd:* Lyle Figland & Joe Moss. *Casting:* William Mayberry. *Hair Stylist Supv:* Nellie Manley. *Asst Dir:* Ralph E. Black.

**CAST:** Lorne Greene (Ben Cartwright), Dan Blocker (Hoss Cartwright), Michael Landon (Little Joe Cartwright), Charles Bronson (Harry Starr), Tom Reese (Lee Burton), Ray Teal (Sheriff Roy Coffee), Bill Clark (Warren), Robert Hoy (Klawson), Henry Wills (Stokey), Mimi Walters (Marie), Bruno Ve Sota (Bartender).

The Cartwrights (Lorne Greene, Dan Blocker, Michael Landon) give a helping hand to half-breed Harry Starr (Charles Bronson), putting him in charge of tending one of the Ponderosa line shacks, but he turns out to be the leader of a gang of horse rustlers.

One of the most popular of television westerns, *Bonanza* was telecast by NBC-TV from 1959 to 1973 and it was the first of its genre to be televised in color.

## *Breach of Faith: A Family of Cops II* (CBS-TV, February 2, 1997)—

see Filmography under *Breach of Faith: A Family of Cops II* (1997).

## *Cain's Hundred* "Dead Load" (NBC-TV, November 21, 1961) 60 minutes B/W

*P:* Charles Russell. *EP-Creator:* Paul Monash. *Mus:* Jerry Goldsmith.

**CAST:** [Peter] Mark Richman (Nicholas "Nick" Cain), Charles Bronson (Hank Conrad), Harold J. Stone (Dave Braddock), Robert Stevenson (Tommy Jackson), Allen Jaffe (Eddie), Mary Munday (Irma Farrell).

One-time gangland lawyer and now a federal agent, Nick Cain (Mark Richman) tries to get the goods on a waterfront extortionist (Harold J. Stone) but witnesses clam up following the brutal beating of a dockworker (Robert Stevenson).

This police drama ran on NBC-TV from 1961 to 1962.

## *Catastrophe! No Safe Place* (Syndicated, 1980–81) 180 minutes Color

*P:* Sherman Grinberg. *D:* Dan Gingold.

**CAST:** Charles Bronson, Jill Ireland (Narrators).

Made by Alan Landsburg Productions, this three-part syndicated television special delved into various natural calamities. Charles Bronson and Jill Ireland narrated.

Survivors of three major disasters tell of their adventures and footage is shown of the dirigible Hindenburg explosion, the bursting of the Teton Dam and the Mount St. Helen's volcano eruption.

It was released on video in a 48 minute version by Star Classics in 1989.

## *Cavalcade Theatre* "A Chain of Hearts" (ABC-TV, November 1, 1955) 30 minutes B/W

*Sc:* Frederic Brady.

**CAST:** Charles Bronson (John Staniszewski), Joyce McCluskey (Dolly Staniszewski).

The true story of a Polish sailor (Charles Bronson) and his attempts to become an American citizen after World War II.

Originally called *Cavalcade of America* on radio and later television, the DuPont-sponsored anthology series based on actual events was also known as *Dupont Cavalcade* and later as *Dupont Theatre*. The series ran from 1952 to 1957, the first season on NBC-TV and the rest on ABC-TV.

## *Colt .45* "Young Gun" (ABC-TV, December 13, 1957) 30 minutes B/W

*P:* Joseph Hoffman. *EP:* William T. Orr. *D:* Walter Grauman. *Sc:* Daniel Ullman, Joel M. Rapp & Daniel Driskill. *St:* Joel M. Ryan & Daniel Driskill. *Ph:* Frank Phillips. *Supv Ed:* James Moore. *Ed:* Fred M. Bohanan. *AD:* Art Loel. *Prod Mgr:* Oren W. Haglund. *Sd:* Frank Hansen. *Set Decorator:* Frank M. Miller. *Makeup Artist:* Gordon Bau. *Asst Dir:* Claude E. Archer.

**CAST:** Wayde Preston (Christopher Colt), Peter Brown (Jimmy Benedict), Charles Bronson (Danny Gordon), Lurene Tuttle (Frances Benedict), Hugh Sanders (Sheriff Powers), Jacylnne Greene (Julie), James Anderson (Jeff Lanier), Mervyn Vye (Sheriff Willoughby), Roy Barcroft (Customer), Nesdon Booth (Bartender).

In the 1880s undercover agent Christopher Colt (Wayde Preston), who masquerades as a Colt .45 salesman, tries to save a 16-year-old boy (Peter Brown) from a gunfight with the outlaw (Charles Bronson) who killed his father in a bank holdup.

*Colt .45* ran on ABC-TV from 1957 to 1960 for a total of 67 episodes. Donald May took over the lead role as Christopher Colt's cousin during the series' third and final season.

## *Combat!* "Heritage" (ABC-TV, April 13, 1965) 60 minutes B/W

*P:* Andy White. *EP:* Selig J. Seligman. *AP:* Michael Caffey. *D:* John Peyser. *Sc:* Barry Trivers. *Creator:* Robert Pirosh. *Ph:* Emmett Bergholz. *Ed:* Jim Faris. *Mus:* Leonard Rosenman. *Post Prod Executive:* James Moore. *St Consultant:* Richard P. McDonagh. *AD:* George W. Davis & Phil Barber. *Asst Dir:* Harker Wade. *Set Decorators:* Henry Grace & Francisco Lombardo. *Sp Eff:* A.D. Flowers. *Sp Eff Ed:* Finn Ulback. *Mus Supv:* Richard Lapham. *Mus Orchestrations:* John Fresco. *Sd:* Franklin Milton & Bill Edmondson. *Casting:* Marvin Paige.

**CAST:** Rick Jason (Lieutenant Gil Hanley), Vic Morrow (Sergeant Chip Saunders), Charles Bronson (Corporal Velasquez), Jack Hogan (Kirby), Conlan Carter (Doc), Dick Peabody (Littlejohn), Robert Fortier (Captain Jampel), Kort Falkenberg (German Sergeant), Michael Stroka (Scope Man), Gunther Weishoff, Alf George (German Soldiers).

On a mission to destroy a German post, a demolition expert (Charles Bronson) balks at orders when he finds out the locale, a chateau's underground vault, houses priceless art treasures.

*Combat!* was the story of K Company, a U.S. Army platoon in World War II, fighting in Western Europe. The series was telecast by ABC-TV from 1962 to 1967 for 152 episodes.

## *The Court of Last Resort* "The Steve Hrdlika Case" (NBC-TV, January 24, 1958) 30 minutes B/W

*P:* Elliott Lewis & Jules Goldstone.

**CAST:** Lyle Bettger (Sam Larsen), Paul Birch (Erle Stanley Gardner), Charles Meredith (Dr. LeMoyne Snyder), Robert H. Harris (Raymond Schindler), Carleton Young ( Harry Steeger), John Launer (Marshall Houts), John Maxwell (Alex Gregory), Robert Anderson (Park Street Jr.), Charles Bronson (Steve Hrdlika), Francis X. Bushman (Priest), Norma Moore (Wilma Neal), Herbert Lytton (Victim).

The members of The Court of Last Resort look into the case of convicted murderer Steve Hrdlika (Charles Bronson) who has only a week to live before his scheduled execution.

Erle Stanley Gardner, the creator of *Perry Mason*, helped establish *The Court of Last Resort* in 1948. It was made up of a panel of legal and medical experts who tried to reverse convictions of those wrongfully sent to jail for crimes they did not commit. This NBC-TV series was based on actual cases from the files of the group and consisted of 26 half-hour episodes. The series was retelecast by ABC-TV during 1959–60 and in 1996 was offered to video distributors and European broadcasters by Buttle Broadcasting.

## *Crusader* (CBS-TV, 1955–56) 30 minutes B/W

### "A Boxing Match" (October 21, 1955)

*P:* Richard Lewis. *D:* Herschel Daugherty. *Sc:* David Chandler. *Ph:* Herb Kirkpatrick. *Supv Ed:* Richard G. Wray. *Ed:* Edward W. Williams. *Mus Supv:* Stanley Wilson. *AD:* John Meehan. *Set Decorator:* James S. Redd. *Sd:* Roy Meadows. *Asst Dir:* Richard Birnie. *Wardrobe:* Vincent Dee. *Makeup:* Leo Lotito Jr.

**CAST:** Brian Keith (Matt Anders), Charles Bronson (Mike Brod), Joan Elan (Lisa Gaela), Ben Wright (Bratesque), Joe Mell (Joe Maxl), Richard Karan (Negli), Lomax Study (Kurt), Bert Hans (Ed), Ed Reimers (Narrator), Norman Bishop, Kenneth Albon, John Indrisano.

Revue Studios produced *Crusader*, a 52-episode adventure series centered around globe-trotting writer Matt Anders, played by Brian Keith. Charles Bronson made two guest appearances on the program, both times playing boxer Mike Brod, and fight footage from both episodes was later interpolated into Bronson's episode "Fight" on *M Squad* (NBC-TV, April 18, 1958), also produced by Richard Lewis.

"A Boxing Match" told of Rumanian boxing champion Mike Brod

(Charles Bronson) escaping to West Berlin where he is befriended by freelance magazine writer Matt Anders (Brian Keith). Bratesque (Ben Wright), the attaché from Brod's former homeland, offers him a deal: if he will throw a fight to a regime-supported boxer his fiancée Lisa (Joan Elan) will be allowed to join him.

### "Freezeout" (February 17, 1956)

*P:* Richard Lewis. *D:* Justus Andiss. *Sc:* David Chandler. *Ph:* Herbert J. Kirkpatrick. *Supv Ed:* Richard G. Wray. *Ed:* Edward Haire. *Mus Supv:* Stanley Wilson. *AD:* John Meehan. *Asst Dir:* James Hogan. *Set Decorator:* Perry Murdock. *Sd:* William Brady. *Wardrobe:* Vincent Dee. *Makeup:* Leo Lotito Jr.

**CAST:** Brian Keith (Matt Anders), Charles Bronson (Mike Brod), Diane Brewster (Charlene Hayes), Joe Mell (Joe Maxl), Paul Dubov (Ted Frost), David Sharpe (Johnny Adams), Frankie Van (Referee), Raymond Railey (Boxing Commissioner), Billy Nelson, Stuart Taylor, Gil Perkins, Eddie Saenz.

European boxer Mike Brod (Charles Bronson) and his manager Joe Maxl (Joe Mell) come to the United States where writer Matt Anders (Brian Keith) again helps Brod when crooks try to take over his management in order to fix a fight so he will lose and they will make a big profit.

## *Dinah!* (Syndicated, 1974–80) 90 minutes Color

**CAST:** Dinah Shore (Host).

Charles Bronson and Jill Ireland made a guest appearance on this weekday variety-talk show, hosted by songstress Dinah Shore. The exact date of their appearance is not known.

In some markets the taped episodes were shown in a 60-minute format and during its final season the show was called *Dinah and Friends.*

## *The Doctor* (NBC-TV, 1952–53) 30 minutes B/W

### "The Guest" (October 26, 1952)

*P:* Marion Parsonet.

**CAST:** Warner Anderson (The Doctor), Beulah Bondi, Charles Buchinski.

Charles Bronson made his dramatic television debut in this medical anthology series which centered around emotional distress and its effect on illness. In this episode Bronson, billed as Charles Buchinski, played a young man who had just committed a robbery. He forces his way into the home of an old lady (Beulah Bondi) who has become an invalid due to a heart attack brought on by the loss of her son in Korea.

### "Take the Odds" (January 18, 1953)

*P:* Martin Parsonet. *D-SC:* Robert Aldrich.

**CAST:** Warner Anderson (The Doctor), Charles Buchinski, Ann Summers, Michael Mann.

Charles Bronson's second appearance on *The Doctor* had Warner Anderson narrating the story of a fading boxer whose son tries to protect him from the ridicule of others.

*The Doctor*, which was sponsored by Proctor and Gamble, was filmed in New York City on a three day per episode shooting schedule. A total of 44 episodes were telecast by NBC-TV from August 24, 1952, to June 28, 1953, in the 10 P.M., EST, time slot. The series was later syndicated as *The Visitor*.

## *Dr. Kildare* "Who Ever Heard of a Two-Headed Doll?" (NBC-TV, September 26, 1963) 60 minutes B/W

*P:* David Victor. *D:* Don Medford. *Sc:* Jerry McNally.

**CAST:** Richard Chamberlain (Dr. James Kildare), Raymond Massey (Dr. Leonard Gillespie), Jean Inness (Nurse Fain), Jud Taylor (Gerson), Charles Bronson (Harry Gregg), Janice Rule (Lila Gregg), Richard Anderson (Dr. Norman Phelps), Steven Bell (Dr. Quint Lowry), David Whorf (Dr. Oscar Bittner), Charity Grace (Mrs. Zwicker).

Dr. Kildare (Richard Chamberlain) learns an old friend, Harry Gregg (Charles Bronson), is terminally ill with leukemia and he must tell the man and his wife (Janice Rule).

This episode was the series' third-season opener and in it Dr. Kildare was promoted to resident physician. The series ran for 132 episodes in a one hour format on NBC-TV from 1961 to 1965 and in its final season it was shown for one half hour each Monday and Tuesday evening for an additional 58 segments in 1965–66.

## *Donato and Daughter* (CBS-TV, September 21, 1993)—see Filmography under *Donato and Daughter* (1993).

## *Dundee and the Culhane* "The Cat in the Bag Brief"
(CBS-TV, September 20, 1967) 60 minutes Color

*P:* Sam H. Rolfe & David Victor. *Mus:* David Rose.
**CAST:** John Mills (Dundee), Sean Garrison (The Culhane), Charles Bronson, Donnelly Rhodes, Frank Silvera, Benson Fong.

An English barrister (John Mills) and his assistant (Sean Garrison) try to establish law and order in the West in the 1870s. In this episode gang leader (Charles Bronson) tries to hang one of Dundee's clients.

This western series ran for 13 episodes on CBS-TV on Wednesday from 10 to 11 P.M., EST.

## *Empire* (NBC-TV, 1962–63) 60 minutes Color
*P:* Frank Pierson. *EP:* William Sackheim. *Mus:* Johnny Green.

"Empire" was a modern day western centered around the huge New Mexico ranch of the Garret family. Richard Egan starred as Jim Redigo, the foreman of the spread, and co-starred were Terry Moore as Constance Garret, Ryan O'Neal as Tal Garret and Anne Seymour as their mother, Lucia Garret. Charles Bronson guest starred as Paul Moreno on the initial series episode, "The Day the Empire Stood Still," and so popular was his character that when the show was revamped in midseason with Terry Moore being dropped from the cast, Bronson returned as Moreno with second billing after Richard Egan. Beginning with "Seven Days on Rough Street," the series' 22nd episode, he remained with *Empire* through the remainder of the series' 32 episodes. In 1963 the series was again revamped, this time being cut to a half hour and retitled *Redigo*. Only star Richard Egan remained and the new outing was telecast from September through December, 1963, on NBC-TV. ABC-TV reran the original *Empire* episodes in prime time on Sundays from March to September, 1964.

### "The Day the Empire Stood Still" (September 25, 1962)—see Filmography under *This Rugged Land* (1965).

### "Seven Days on Rough Street" (February 26, 1963)

*P:* Frank Pierson. *EP:* William Sackheim. *D:* Bernard McEveety. *Sc:* Ken Trevey. *Creator:* Kathleen Hite. *St Executive:* Anthony Wilson. *Ph:* Charles S. Weldon. *Ed:* Harry Gerstad. *Mus:* Johnny Green. *AD:* Robert Peterson. *Set Decorator:* Sidney Clifford. *Makeup:* Ben Lane. *Mus Supv:* Irving Friedman. *Mus*

*Ed:* Igor Kantor. *Sd Eff Ed:* Jack Kirshner. *Prod Supv:* Seymour Friedman. *Post Prod Supv:* Lawrence Werner. *Asst Dir:* William P. Owens.

**CAST:** Richard Egan (Jim Redigo), Charles Bronson (Paul Moreno), Ryan O'Neal (Tal Garret), Frank Sutton (Young Floyd), John Davis Chandler (Arlen), Clegg Hoyt (Beanie), Suzi Carnell (Twila), Jack Searl (Phipps), Victor French (Bodie), Rue McClanahan (B Girl), Jerry Douglas (Leroy), Paul Sorenson (Policeman), Don Easton (Young Sailor), Mark Tapscott (Soldier).

Charles Bronson joined the permanent cast of *Empire* with this episode. In it his character of ranch worker Paul Moreno bets young Tal Garret (Ryan O'Neal) that he cannot survive one week in the rough town of Delgado. Tal takes the bet and is forced to learn to survive despite being put in jail and beaten by thugs.

## "A House in Order" (March 5, 1963)

**CAST:** Richard Egan (Jim Redigo), Charles Bronson (Paul Moreno), Ryan O'Neal (Tal Garret), Anne Seymour (Lucia Garret), Warren Vanders (Chuck Davis), Virginia Gregg (Mrs. Austin), James Callahan (Redford), Russell Thorson (Austin), Oliver McGowan (Harvey Welk), Don Harvey, James Doohan, Jason Johnson.

Lucia Garret (Anne Seymour), owner of the sprawling Garret ranch, finds out she has a fatal illness and longs for a better relationship between her son Tal (Ryan O'Neal) and foreman Jim Redigo (Richard Egan).

## "Down There, the World" (March 12, 1963)

**CAST:** Richard Egan (Jim Redigo), Charles Bronson (Paul Moreno), Ryan O'Neal (Tal Garret), Warren Vanders (Chuck Davis), Joanna Barnes (Neva Bradford), John Vivyan (Shelley Hanson), Dayton Lummis (Thomas Fenton Giler), Oliver McGowan (Harvey Welk), Philip Ober (Walter Kenner), Bern Hoffman (George Neimeyer), William Quinn (Lupak), Herb Armstrong, Ken Drake, Paul Fierro.

Jim Redigo (Richard Egan) must deal with the ranch's mining operations being shut down when the local processing plant is taken over by a woman (Joanna Barnes) who wants the Garret mines for herself.

## "Burnout" (March 19, 1963)

**CAST:** Richard Egan (Jim Redigo), Charles Bronson (Paul Moreno), Ryan O'Neal (Tal Garret), Karen Steele (Kate Callahan), John Milford (Ranger Tom Barton), Joseph Gallison (Kelly Haines), Gunnar Hellstrom (Chris Norden), Burt Douglas (Jack Pittman), Byron Morrow (Lloyd Halstead), Nancy Hadley (Ruth Barton).

A forest ranger (John Milford) uncovers the fact the Garret logging operation is violating government rules.

### "Hidden Asset" (March 26, 1963)

**CAST:** Richard Egan (Jim Redigo), Charles Bronson (Paul Moreno), Ryan O'Neal (Tal Garret), Warren Vanders (Chuck Davis), Lon Chaney (Bart Howe), William Windom (Lawrence Rowan), John Mathews (Matt Christopher), Joseph Hoover (Johnny Howe), Barbara Bain, Willard Sage.

Moreno (Charles Bronson) and Tal (Ryan O'Neal) oppose Redigo (Richard Egan) when he proposes cutting the payroll in order to get a needed bank loan.

### "Arrow in the Sky" (April 9, 1963)

**CAST:** Richard Egan (Jim Redigo), Charles Bronson (Paul Moreno), Ryan O'Neal (Tal Garret), Telly Savalas (Tibor), Ilka Windish (Eva), Russell Johnson (Bill Carey), Michael Davis, Don Diamond.

Thinking his wife is at the Garret Ranch, a former Hungarian freedom fighter (Telly Savalas) illegally crosses the Mexican border and asks Moreno (Charles Bronson) for work.

### "Nobody Dies on Saturday" (April 16, 1963)

**CAST:** Richard Egan (Jim Redigo), Charles Bronson (Paul Moreno), Ryan O'Neal (Tal Garret), Warren Vanders (Chuck Davis), Don Gordon (Quinn Serrato), William Schallert (Sully Mason), Dean Stanton (Nick Crider), Jean Inness, Willard Sage, Jon Lormer, Jim Galante, Hugh Lawrence.

Stabbing a guard during a breakout, a prisoner and his pals come looking for Jim Redigo (Richard Egan), the man's former boss who is responsible for sending him to jail. Also called "Breakout."

### "65 Miles Is a Long, Long Way" (April 23, 1963)

**CAST:** Richard Egan (Jim Redigo), Charles Bronson (Paul Moreno), Ryan O'Neal (Tal Garret), Warren Vanders (Chuck Davis), Claude Akins (Horvath), Jena Ingstrom (Mrs. Sangster), Woodrow Parfrey (Gates), Ann Carroll (Helen), Hank Patterson, Robert J. Stevenson.

Because a woman landowner charges too much to cross her right-of-way, Jim Redigo (Richard Egan) and two other cattlemen have to take a long route to get their cattle to market.

### "Duel for Eight Wheels" (April 30, 1963)

**CAST:** Richard Egan (Jim Redigo), Charles Bronson (Paul Moreno), Ryan O'Neal (Tal Garret), Warren Vanders (Chuck Davis), Inger Stevens (Ellen Thompson), Lawrence Dobkin (Dr. Kane), Noah Keen (Dr. Phelps), Lauren Gilbert (Dr. Crymer), Don Wilbanks (Corley), Gil Rankin.

Jim Redigo (Richard Egan) is confined to a wheelchair after being attacked by a wild stallion.

### "Between Friday and Monday" (May 7, 1963)

**CAST:** Richard Egan (Jim Redigo), Charles Bronson (Paul Moreno), Ryan O'Neal (Tal Garret), Warren Vanders (Chuck Davis), Joan Hackett (Dolores Lanza), William Mims (Perry Wilmot), Dort Clark (Panhandler) Naomi Stevens (Mrs. Quintero), Maida Severn (Spinster), Harvey Johnson (Desk Clerk), Peggy Adams.

A young woman (Joan Hackett), about to enter a convent, is stuck in a small town amid cowboys on a wild spree.

### "The Convention" (May 14, 1963)

**CAST:** Richard Egan (Jim Redigo), Charles Bronson (Paul Moreno), Ryan O'Neal (Tal Garret), Diane Brewster (Caroline), Rudy Bond (Sam Callison), Anne Helm (Joanie), Alan Hale, L.Q. Jones, Jean Willes, William Brimley, Doye O'Dell, Robert Anderson.

Jim Redigo (Richard Egan) tells Moreno (Charles Bronson) and Tal (Ryan O'Neal) he will go with them to a convention if they forgo women and gambling.

## *A Family of Cops* (CBS-TV, November 26, 1995)—see Filmography under *A Family of Cops* (1995).

## *Family of Cops III* (CBS-TV, January 12, 1999)—see Filmography under *A Family of Cops III* (1999).

## *The FBI* "The Animal" (ABC-TV, April 17, 1966) 60 minutes Color

*P:* Charles Larson. *EP:* Quinn Martin. *AP:* Norman Jolley. *D:* Christian Nyby. *Sc:* Mark Rogers. *Ph:* William W. Spencer. *Ed:* Mariston Fay. *Mus:* Bronislaw Kaper.

*AD:* Richard V. Haman. *Prod Mgr:* Howard Alston. *EP's Asst:* Arthur Fellows. *P's Asst:* John Conwell. *Asst Dir:* Phil Cook. *Asst Ed:* Ray Daniels. *Post Prod Supv:* John Elizade. *Sp Eff Ed:* William Phillips. *Mus Ed:* Ted Roberts. *Set Decorator:* Hoyle Barrett. *Chief Electrician:* Glen Bird. *Mus Conductor:* Dominic Frontiere. *Editorial Consultant:* Carl Barth. *Sd Mixer:* Frank Stahl. *St Consultant:* Robert Leslie Bellem. *Makeup:* Dan Greenway.

**CAST:** Efrem Zimbalist Jr. (Inspector Lewis Erskine), Charles Bronson (Earl Clayton), Tim McIntire (Lambert Hayes), Philip Abbott (Arthur Ward), Stephen Brooks (Special Agent Jim Rhodes), Mimsy Farmer (Jody Connors), Crehan Denton (Vince "Doc" Lafavre), Harry Lauter (Jud Connors), Ted Gehring (Roy Joe Spencer), Norma Connelly (Norma Spencer), Barry Russo (Myron Pierce), James Noah (Ed Brocton), James Doohan (Claude Bell), Doris Singleton (Renata Walker), Barry Basch (Albertson), Robert Bice (Sheriff Wiley), Valentine De Vargas (Agent Henry Galva).

Headed for death row, killer Earl Clayton (Charles Bronson) leads four other convicts in escaping from the Las Casas County Jail. FBI agents Lewis Erskine (Efrem Zimbalist Jr.) and Jim Rhodes (Stephen Brooks) get on the trail leading to Clayton and fellow escapee Lambert Hayes (Tim McIntire) who have taken hostages at a mountain hunting lodge.

Filmed at San Bernardino National Forest, this was the 29th segment of the 234 episodes *The FBI* series which ran on ABC-TV from 1965 to 1974. The programs were based on actual cases from Federal Bureau of Investigation files. It is interesting to note that well-known pulp fiction writer Robert Leslie Bellem was the story consultant for this episode.

## *Four Star Playhouse* "The Witness" (CBS-TV, October 22, 1953) 30 minutes B/W

*P:* Dick Powell. *EP:* Don W. Sharpe. *AP:* Warren Lewis. *D:* Robert Aldrich. *Sc:* Seeley Lester & Merwin Gerard. *Ph:* George F. Diskant. *Ed:* Samuel E. Beetley. *AD:* Duncan Cramer. *Prod Supv:* Lloyd Richards. *Editorial Supv:* Bernard Burton. *Asst Dir:* Bruce Fowler Jr. *Makeup:* Karl Herlinger.

**CAST:** Dick Powell (Mike Donegan), James Millican (District Attorney), Charles Buchinsky (Frank Dana), Marion Carr (Alice Blair), Strother Martin (Tom Blair), Robert Sherman (Philip Radecker), Walter Sande (Peterson), Charles Evans (Judge), Nick Dennis (Nick the Waiter).

Slick attorney Mike Donegan (Dick Powell) defends Frank Dana (Charles Buchinsky) who is accused of robbery and murder. Donegan must find the young woman who can provide Dana with an alibi.

*Four Star Playhouse* was telecast on CBS-TV from 1952 to 1956 and was later syndicated by Official Films.

## *The Fugitive* "The One That Got Away" (ABC-TV, January 10, 1967) 60 minutes Color

*P:* William Schiller, John Meredyth Lucas & George Eckstein. *EP:* Quinn Martin. *D:* Leo Penn. *Sc:* Philip Saltzman & Harry Kronman. *Creator:* Roy Huggins. *Ph:* Robert Hoffman. *Mus:* Pete Rugolo. *Prod Mgr:* Fred Ahern. *AD:* John D. Vance & James Hulsey.

CAST: David Janssen (Dr. Richard Kimble), Barry Morse (Lieutenant Philip Gerard), William Conrad (Narrator), Charles Bronson (Ralph Schuyler), Anne Francis (Felice Greer), Charles Drake (Oliver Greer), David Renard (Guillermo), Vince Howard (Brooks), Harlan Warde (Mitchell), Pepe Callahan (Calderon), David Fresco (Hodges), Thordis Brandt (Girl Friend), Rico Alaniz (Perez).

Fugitive Dr. Richard Kimble (David Janssen), using the name Bill March, takes a job as a deckhand on a yacht belonging to wealthy Oliver Greer (Charles Drake) and his wife (Anne Francis). Greer is an international embezzler who reportedly is planning to use the yacht to get back into the country. Posing as its captain is government agent Ralph Schuyler (Charles Bronson). Finding out Kimble is using an alias, Schuyler takes his fingerprints and then pursues him when he learns Kimble is a wanted man.

"The One That Got Away" was the 107th of the 120 episodes of *The Fugitive* which ABC-TV telecast from 1963 to 1967. The series was also the basis for the 1993 feature film *The Fugitive* starring Harrison Ford and Tommy Lee Jones.

## *General Electric Theatre* (CBS-TV, 1953–62) 30 minutes B/W

CAST: Ronald Reagan (Host).

### "Prosper's Old Mother" (November 20, 1955)

*D:* Sidney Lanfield. *Sc:* William Bowers. *St:* Bret Harte. *Ph:* John Russell. *Ed:* Michael McAdam.

CAST: Ethel Barrymore (Mother), Ronald Reagan (Prosper), Joyce Holden (Janet), Edgar Buchanan (Colonel Starbottle), Norman Leavitt (Slim), Charles Bronson (Pike), Dabbs Greer (Tom), John Doucette (Bartender), Charles Halton.

Going to San Francisco to find a mother, orphaned miner Prosper (Ronald Reagan) brings back a hard-drinking eccentric (Ethel Barrymore) and her daughter (Joyce Holden) to his remote mining camp. Charles Bronson played one of the miners.

### "Memory in White" (January 9, 1961)

*Sc-St:* Budd Schulberg. *Mus:* Charles Bernstein.

**CAST:** Sammy Davis Jr. (Pancho Villa III), Charles Bronson (Soldier Condon), Bert Freed (Eddie Gibbs), Art Aragon (Nick Dorso), Joe Besser (Ootzie).

Now a gym handyman, ex-boxer Pancho Villa III (Sammy Davis Jr.) dreams of being a ring announcer and feels he needs a white suit to get the job.

Charles Bronson, in his second appearance in this series, was nominated for an Emmy Award for Outstanding Performance in a Supporting Role by an Actor or Actress in a Single Program for his performance as boxer Soldier Condon.

## *Good Morning America* (ABC-TV, February 3, 1989) 90 minutes Color

Charles Bronson was interviewed on this early morning talk-entertainment-news program about his latest film, *Kinjite: Forbidden Subjects*.

## *Gunsmoke* (CBS-TV, 1955–1975) 30/60 minutes B/W & Color

### "The Killer" (May 26, 1956)

*P:* Charles Marquis Warren. *AP:* Norman Macdonnell. *D:* Robert Stevenson. *Sc:* John Dunkel. *St:* John Meston. *Ph:* Fleet Southcott. *Ed:* Leslie Vidor. *Supv Ed:* Fred W. Berger. *AD:* Nicolai Remisoff. *Sd:* Roderick Sound, Inc. *Sc Supv:* Mary Chaffee. *Property Mgr:* Mike Gordon. *Asst Dir:* Glen Cook. *Sp Eff:* Jack Rabin & Lou De Witt. *Makeup:* Glen Alden. *Hair Stylist:* Fay Whiffing. *Wardrobe:* John E. Downing Jr. *Casting:* Lynn Stalmaster & Associates.

**CAST:** James Arness (Matt Dillon), Dennis Weaver (Chester Goode), Milburn Stone (Doc Adams), Amanda Blake (Kitty Russell), Charles Bronson (Crego), Dave Chapman (Jesse Hill), Dabbs Greer (Mr. Joneas), James Nusser (Saddle Tramp).

In his first *Gunsmoke* appearance Charles Bronson gives an outstanding performance as the cowardly killer Crego, who murders a man (James Nusser) on the trail for talking too much. Then he arrives in Dodge City where he tries to goad a cowboy (Dave Chapman) into a fight but is thwarted by U.S. Marshal Matt Dillon (James Arness). When Crego bothers saloon hostess Miss Kitty (Amanda Blake), Matt forces him to back down but Crego then brutally murders a farmer and the cowboy he first intended to kill. Finally Matt forces Crego into a showdown in which the bad man is mortally wounded.

### "The Long Rifle" (November 1, 1958)

*P:* Norman Macdonnell. *D:* Richard Whorf. *Sc:* John Meston. *Ph:* Fleet Southcott. *Ed:* Al Joseph. *Supv Ed:* Fred W. Berger. *Asst Dir:* Nathan Barragar. *Sd:* Roderick Sound. *Prod Mgr:* Glenn Cook. *Sets:* Paul Sylos. *Property Master:* Ted Cooper. *Makeup:* Glen Alden. *Hair Stylist:* Pat Whiffing. *Wardrobe:* Robert Odell. *Sc Supv:* Mary Chaffee. *Set Decorator:* Raymond Bolt Jr. *Optical Eff:* Jack Rabin & Louis DeWitt. *Casting:* Stalmaster-Lister Company.

**CAST:** James Arness (Matt Dillon), Dennis Weaver (Chester Goode), Milburn Stone (Doc Adams), Amanda Blake (Kitty Russell), Charles Bronson (Ben Tiple), Paul Engel (Andy Spangler), Lew Gallo (Joe Spangler), Tom Greenway (Will Gibbs), George Selk [Budd Buster] (Moss Grimmick).

In his second guest appearance on *Gunsmoke*, Charles Bronson played farmer Ben Tiple who is accused of murdering a man (Tom Greenway) who had been trying to goad him into a fight.

*Gunsmoke* was a thirty minute black-and-white series on CBS-TV from 1955 to 1961. From 1961 to 1975 it ran for one hour and in the mid–1960s it became a color program.

## *Happy Birthday, Hollywood* (ABC-TV, May 18, 1987) 180 minutes Color

*P:* Alexander H. Cohen. *D:* Jeff Margolis. *Sc:* Hildy Parks. *Mus:* Elliot Lawrence. *Announcer:* Charlie O'Donnell.

Charles Bronson was one of more than 150 stars who appeared in this three hour gala celebrating the one hundredth birthday of Hollywood. The special included production numbers and clips from classic films.

## *Have Gun—Will Travel* (CBS-TV, 1957–1963) 30 minutes B/W

### "The Outlaw" (September 21, 1957)

*P:* Julian Claman. *D:* Andrew V. McLaglen. *Sc:* Sam Rolfe. *Creators:* Sam Rolfe & Herb Meadow. *Ph:* William Margulies. *Ed:* Leslie Vidor. *Supv Ed:* Fred W. Berger. *AD:* James W. Sullivan. *Asst Dir:* Howard Joslin. *Prod Mgr:* William Wood. *Property Master:* Mike Gordon. *Hair Stylist:* Madeline Danks. *Wardrobe:* Joseph Dimmitt. *Sd:* Roderick Sound, Inc. *Casting:* Lynn Stalmaster & Associates.

**CAST:** Richard Boone (Paladin), Charles Bronson (Manfred Holt), Grant Withers (Sheriff Jake Ludlow), Peggy Stewart (Sarah Holt), Steve Mitchell (Gage), Barry Cahill (Alec Talltree), Kam Tong (Hey Boy), Warren Parker (Ned Alcorn).

San Francisco gunfighter Paladin (Richard Boone) is hired to bring in wanted killer Manfred Holt (Charles Bronson). He journeys to Black Mountain where he finds the local sheriff (Grant Withers) with his posse planning to kill Holt and not bring him in for trial. Holt eludes the law but is captured by Paladin who takes a liking to him and agrees to let Holt see his wife (Peggy Stewart) and newborn son before being returned to prison. Along the trail Holt saves Paladin's life when he falls into a gulch. Later at Holt's shack, Paladin leads the lawman and his posse on a wild goose chase so Manfred can see his family. When it is time to leave Holt draws on Paladin and is killed.

Charles Bronson, sporting a beard, turned in a good characterization as good bad-man Holt.

Charles Bronson and Peggy Stewart again played a married couple in the 1959 unsold television pilot, "The Attorney," starring Cameron Mitchell and Patricia Barry, which was produced by Metro-Goldwyn-Mayer. Charles Bronson was the episode's guest star.

## "The Gentleman" (September 27, 1958)

**CAST:** Richard Boone (Paladin), Kam Tong (Hey Boy), Charles Bronson (Chris Sorenson), Grace Raynor (Maria De Castro), Edmund Johnson, Harry Carey Jr., Junius Matthews, Marion Collier.

In the second of five guest appearances on *Have Gun—Will Travel*, Charles Bronson played a rough edged rancher who hires Paladin (Richard Boone) to teach him gentlemanly ways so he can court and win pretty Maria De Castro (Grace Raynor), who owns a neighboring ranch. The two men, however, soon learn the woman's foreman (Edmund Johnson) wants her ranch for himself.

## "A Proof of Love" (October 14, 1961)

*P:* Frank R. Pierson. *D:* Richard Boone. *Sc:* Peggy & Lou Shaw. *Ph:* Frank Phillips. *Ed:* Samuel Gold. *AD:* Richard Haman. *Casting:* Peggy Rea. *Sets:* Fay Babcock. *Property Master:* Arthur Friedrich. *Makeup:* Donald Roberson. *Sc Supv:* Richard Chaffee. *Costumes:* Joseph Dimmitt. *Prod Sd Mixer:* Frederick A. Kessler. *Asst Dir:* Gary Nelson. Title song sung by Johnny Western.

**CAST:** Richard Boone (Paladin), Charles Bronson (Henry Grey), Chana Eden (Callie), George Kennedy (Rud Saxon), Shirley O'Hara (Mrs. Grey), Jack Marshall (Banjo Player), Robert Cole (Dancer/Choreographer), Kam Tong (Hey Boy).

Charles Bronson's third *Have Gun—Will Travel* appearance was a serio-comedy episode which cast him as bumpkin farmer Henry Grey who hires Paladin (Richard Boone) to teach him to shoot so he can retrieve his Greek mail-order bride Callie (Chana Eden) who has run off with neighbor Rud Saxon (George Kennedy). While Saxon agrees to pay Grey for his expenses so he can have Callie, Paladin convinces Grey, with the help of whiskey, to fight for his wife.

Star Richard Boone directed this amusing series segment which contains some nice underplayed comedy by Charles Bronson and an exuberant performance by Chana Eden as the fun-loving Callie.

## "Ben Jalisco" (November 18, 1961)

*P:* Frank R. Pierson. *AP:* Albert Ruben & Howard Joslin. *D:* Andrew V. McLaglen. *Sc:* Harry Julian Fink. *Ph:* Frank Phillips. *Ed:* Samuel Gold. *AD:* Richard Haman. *Asst Dir:* Gary Nelson. *Casting:* Peggy Rea. *Sets:* Fay Babcock. *Property Master:* Arthur Friedrich. *Makeup:* Donald Roberson. *Sc Supv:* Richard Chaffee. *Costumes:* Joseph Dimmitt. *Prod Sd Mixer:* Frederick A. Kessler. Title song sung by Johnny Western.

**CAST:** Richard Boone (Paladin), Charles Bronson (Ben Jalisco), Coleen Gray (Lucy Jalisco), John Litel (Sheriff John Armsteader), Lane Chandler (John Tay), Rick Silver (Will Tay), Kam Tong (Hey Boy), Chuck Roberson (Carly).

Six years before, Paladin (Richard Boone) had been assisted by Lucy Jalisco (Coleen Gray) in bringing in her husband, gunman Ben Jalisco (Charles Bronson). Ben has escaped from prison and fearing he will kill his wife, Paladin tries to save her. Ben kills the lawman (John Litel) guarding Lucy but is shot in the leg by Paladin. Ben threatens to kill Lucy unless Paladin takes them across the Mexican border but in a shootout Jalisco is killed by the gunfighter.

For his fourth *Have Gun—Will Travel* episode Charles Bronson imbues the character of Ben Jalisco with animal-like qualities, explaining his predisposition for killing. The segment was shot on location at Lone Pine and at Paramount studios.

## "Brotherhood" (January 5, 1963)

*P:* Robert Sparks. *AP:* Don Ingalls. *D:* Andrew V. McLaglen. *Sc:* Herb Meadow & Albert Ruben. *Ph:* Frank Phillips. *Ed:* Everett Sutherland. *Prod Mgr:* Howard Joslin. *Asst Dir:* Gary Nelson. *Casting:* Peggy Rea. *Costumes:* Joseph Dimmitt. *Mus:* Lucien Moraweck. *Conductor:* Lud Gluskin. *Sets:* Claude Carpenter. *Property master:* Arthur Friedrich. *makeup:* Donald Roberson. *Sc Supv:* Richard Chaffee. *Prod Sd Mixer:* Frederick A. Kessler. Title song sun by Johnny Western.

**CAST:** Richard Boone (Paladin),

Charles Bronson (Sheriff Jim Redrock), Myron Healey (Stennis), Michael Keep (Abe Redrock), Shug Fisher (Kroll), Mark Mellinger (Alfred E. Mossman), Dawn Littlesky (Mrs. Redrock), Warren Joslin (Driver), Kam Tong (Hey Boy).

Two Indian brothers both hire Paladin to bring in the other. Jim Redrock (Charles Bronson) is the sheriff of Latigo while his brother Abe (Michael Keep) is a renegade wanted by the law. Paladin captures Abe and brings him back to jail but the townspeople, led by racist businessman Stennis (Myron Healey) and his cohort Kroll (Shug Fisher), force Jim to turn his brother over to them. Having a change of heart, Jim joins Paladin in rescuing Abe from the mob and cements his authority as the area lawman.

Charles Bronson's fifth and final *Have Gun—Will Travel* episode cast him as a Native American willing to bow to the will of his white brothers in order to gain social status.

## *Hennesey* (CBS-TV, 1959–62) 30 minutes B/W

### "Hennesey at La Gunn" (October 17, 1960)

*P:* Jackie Cooper & Don McGuire.

**CAST:** Jackie Cooper (Lieutenant Charles J. "Chick" Hennesey), Abby Dalton (Martha Hale), Roscoe Karns (Captain Walter Shafer), Henry Kulky (Max Bronski), Charles Bronson (Ogrodowski), Diane Strom (Helen).

Naval intelligence officer Ogrodowski (Charles Bronson) is assigned to find out who is stealing drugs from the base hospital and he asks the aid of medical officer Hennesey (Jackie Cooper).

### "The Nogoodnik" (April 17, 1961)

**CAST:** Jackie Cooper (Lieutenant Charles J. "Chick" Hennesey), Abby Dalton (Martha Hale), Roscoe Karns (Captain Walter Shafer), Henry Kulky (Max Bronski), Charles Bronson (Seaman Pierce).

After being accused of stealing from the ship's supplies, a seaman (Charles Bronson) is wounded trying to escape from the brig.

## *Here's Hollywood* (NBC-TV, August 8, 1962) 30 minutes B/W

*P:* Jess Oppenheimer & Pier Oppenheimer.

**CAST:** Dean Miller, Joanne Jordan (Hosts), Charles Bronson.

Charles Bronson was interviewed in a fifteen-minute segment of this late afternoon weekday program from Hollywood.

## *Hey, Jeannie!* "Jeannie, the Policewoman" (CBS-TV, March 2, 1957) 30 minutes B/W

*P:* Charles Isaacs.

**CAST:** Jeannie Carson (Jeannie MacLennan), Allen Jenkins (Al Murray), Janet Dulo (Liz Murray), Charles Bronson (Rocky), Emlen Davies (Lieutenant O'Flaherty), Darlene Fields (Marge).

Transplanted Scottish lass Jeannie MacLennon (Jeannie Carson), who resides with cab driver Al (Allen Jenkins) and his sister Liz (Janet Dulo), joins the Gotham police force and is sworn to secrecy on her first case.

This comedy series ran for one season, 1956-57, on CBS-TV and had prime-time reruns on ABC-TV during the summer of 1960 as *The Jeannie Carson Show.*

## *The Islanders* "The Generous Politician" (ABC-TV, January 15, 1961) 60 minutes B/W

*P:* Richard L. Bare. *Mus:* Sonny Burke.

**CAST:** William Reynolds (Sandy Wade), James Philbrook (Zack Malloy), Diane Brewster (Wilhelmina "Steamboat Willie" Vandeaveer), Charles Bronson (Dutch Malkin), Philip Ahn (Governor Galli), J. Pat O'Malley (James J. Lacey), Benson Fong (O'Hara), Mickey Simpson (Hudson).

Pilot Zack Malloy (James Philbrook) is hired to fly medical supplies to Marula in the Spice Islands but finds out his cargo is really illegal whisky.

## *Jeanne Wolf* (PBS-TV, October 14, 1976) 30 minutes Color

**CAST:** Jeanne Wolf (Host).

In this interview series' third-season opener, Charles Bronson talked with hostess Jeanne Wolf on the set of *The White Buffalo* (1977). He discussed movie violence, film critics and the audiences who come to see his movies.

## *The Joe Palooka Story* (Syndicated, 1954) 30 minutes B/W

### "Two Rings for Eddie" (April 10, 1954)

*P:* Richard Bare. *AP:* Joe Kirkwood Jr. *D:* Arnold Laven. *Sc:* Monroe Manning. *Creator:* Ham Fisher. *Ph:* John MacBurnie. *Ed:* Everett Sutherland. *Sd:* Francis Scheid. *Technical Dir:* John Indrisano. *Prod Controller:* Martin

Eisenberg. *Set Design:* Al Price. *Prod Coordinator:* Leon Chooluck. *Set Dresser:* Joe Kish. *Joe Kirkwood Jr.'s Wardrobe:* MacIntosh. *Gowns:* Orbach's. *Sports Equipment:* Everlast.

**CAST:** Joe Kirkwood Jr. (Joe Palooka), Cathy Lewis (Ann Palooka), Maxie Rosenbloom (Clyde), Sid Tomack (Knobby Walsh), Charles Buchinsky (Eddie Crane), Mary Ellen Kay (Doris Willis), Ray Walker (Maxie), Lou Nova (Big Boy Metz).

Joe Palooka (Joe Kirkwood Jr.) has faith in promising welterweight Eddie Crane (Charles Buchinsky) whose girlfriend (Mary Ellen Kay) is opposed to his boxing career. When a bully (Lou Nova) wants a fight with Palooka he picks on Eddie so Joe will give him a title match.

### "Neutral Corner" (May 8, 1954)

**CAST:** Joe Kirkwood Jr. (Joe Palooka), Cathy Lewis (Ann Palooka), Maxie Rosenbloom (Clyde), Sid Tomack (Knobby Walsh), Charles Buchinsky (Eddie Crane).

Heavyweight boxing champion Joe Palooka (Joe Kirkwood Jr.) must tell his despondent protégé Eddie Crane (Charles Buchinsky) that he can never fight again after being badly injured in an automobile accident.

Charles Bronson made two guest appearances on the syndicated program *The Joe Palooka Story*, playing boxer Eddie Crane in both segments. Series star Joe Kirkwood Jr. was associate producer of this 26 episode series, from Guild Film Productions, based on the Ham Fisher cartoon strip. Kirkwood earlier played Joe Palooka in a series of feature films at Monogram from 1946 to 1951.

The dates given are for the episodes' original telecasts on WABD-TV, Channel 5, in New York City. Elsewhere they may have had different telecast dates.

## *Laramie* (NBC-TV, 1959–63) 60 minutes B/W

### "Street of Hate" (March 1, 1960)

**CAST:** John Smith (Slim Sherman), Robert Fuller (Jess Harper), Hoagy Carmichael (Jonesy), Charles Bronson (Frank Buckley), R.G. Armstrong (Jud), Harry Lauter (Harry), Kathleen Crowley, Barton MacLane, Dean Fredericks.

When a paroled murderer (Charles Bronson) arrives in the area, the townspeople become upset when Slim Sherman (John Smith) says he will be responsible for him.

### "Run of the Hunted" (April 4, 1961)

**CAST:** John Smith (Slim Sherman), Robert Fuller (Jess Harper), Charles Bronson (Cory Lake), Harry Lauter, R.G. Armstrong, Kevin Hagen, Leonard Geer, Harry Harvey Jr., Gregg Barton.

When Slim's (John Smith) friend Cory Lake (Charles Bronson) is committed to an insane asylum by his family, he suspects they are after the man's ranch.

*Laramie* was telecast by NBC-TV from 1959 to 1963 for a total of 124 one-hour episodes.

## *The Legend of Jesse James* "The Chase" (ABC-TV, March 7, 1966) 30 minutes B/W

*P:* Don Siegel. *Sc:* Carey Wilber. *Mus:* Joseph Hoover.

**CAST:** Chris Jones (Jesse James), Charles Bronson (Cheyney).

Sadist bounty hunter Cheyney (Charles Bronson) stalks Jesse James (Chris Jones), planning to make him suffer before killing him, in this two character drama.

This white-washed look at the exploits of Missouri outlaws Jesse and Frank James ran for 26 episodes on ABC-TV from 1965 to 1966.

## *The Lineup* "The Paisley Gang" (CBS-TV, October 1, 1954) 30 minutes B/W

*P:* Jaime Del Valle. *D:* Don Siegel.

**CAST:** Warner Anderson (Lieutenant Ben Guthrie), Tom Tully (Inspector Matt Grebb), Marshall Reed (Inspector Fred Asher), Charles Buchinsky.

Members of the San Francisco Police force are after a gang of young criminals who commit a series of armed robberies after breaking into a gun shop.

Running on CBS-TV from 1954 to 1960, this dramatic police series was told in a semidocumentary style. Charles Bronson guest starred on the series opener and was chosen for the role of one of the hoodlums by director Don Siegel. In 1958 producer Jaimie Del Valle and director Don Siegel did a feature version of *The Lineup* for Columbia Pictures.

## *The Loretta Young Show* "Wood Lot" (NBC-TV, March 26, 1961) 30 minutes B/W

*Mus:* Harry Lubin.
**CAST:** Loretta Young (Host), Charles Bronson (Eugene Walters), Ellen McRae (Mrs. Walters), Ted Stanhope, John Clarke.

A man (Charles Bronson) goes into a state of shock after seeing his wife (Ellen McRae) embracing another (Ted Stanhope).

*The Loretta Young Show*, originally entitled *Letter to Loretta*, was telecast by NBC-TV from 1953 to 1961. From 1960 to 1964 the same network reran the episodes weekdays as *The Loretta Young Threatre*.

## *Lux Video Theatre* "A Bell for Adano" (NBC-TV, February 10, 1955) 60 minutes B/W

*P:* Carl Kuhl. *D:* Richard Goode. *Sc:* Richard McDonagh, from the novel by John Hersey and the play by Paul Osborn. *Mus:* Rudolph [Rudy] Schrager. *Prod Supv:* Stanley Quinn. *Sets:* William Smith.
**CAST:** Edmond O'Brien (Major Jepelo), Charles Bronson (Sergeant Borth), Frank Puglia (Father Pensovecchio), Dan Tobin (Captain Purvis), Elliott Reid (Lieutenant Livingston), George Pieronne (Corporal Trapani), Tito Vuolo (Zito), Michael Vallon (Bellianca), Fortunio Bonanova (Gargano), Vincent Padula (Erbo), Joe Duval (Basilo), Paul Cesari (D'Arpa), Orente Seragnooli (Dresi), Felix Romano (Spinato), Ruth Gillis, Inez Palange (Women).

A small screen adaptation of the 1945 20th Century–Fox feature film, *A Bell for Adano*, this version gave Charles Bronson second billing as Sergeant Borth. The plot dealt with Allied soldiers in a small village in Sicily during World War II, with their commander (Edmond O'Brien) winning over the locals by replacing the village bell. *Variety* reported this version "kept the meat of the drama intact within the limiting confines of live television, so nothing was lost from the plot...."

The drama was hosted by James Mason with Ken Carpenter as the series' announcer. *Lux Video Theatre* ran on CBS-TV from 1950 to 1954 and on NBC-TV from 1954 to 1959. It was a one hour show during its first eight seasons and one-half hour during the 1958-59 final season.

## *M Squad* "Fight" (NBC-TV, April 18, 1958) 30 minutes B/W

*P:* John Larkin. *EP:* Richard Lewis. *D:* Don Taylor. *Sc:* Jack Laird & Wilton Schiller. *Ph:* Ray Rennahan. *Supv Ed:* Richard G. Wray. *Ed:* Patrick McCormack. *Mus:* Stanley Wilson. *Sd:* B.F. Ryan. *Set Decorator:* Glen L. Daniels.

*AD:* Don Meehan. *Asst Dir:* Ben Bishop. *Costume Supv:* Vincent Dee. *Makeup:* Jack Barron. *Hair Stylist:* Florence Bush.

**CAST:** Lee Marvin (Lieutenant Frank Ballinger), Paul Newlan (Captain Grey), Charles Bronson (Eddie Loder), Judith Ames (Greta Loder), Rusty Lane (Sam), John Harmon (Charlie Andalugia), Leonard Bell (Mel Harmon), David Sharpe (Jesse Verdugo).

When a threat is made on the life of promising middleweight boxing contender Eddie Loder (Charles Bronson), the case is given to plainclothes Chicago police detective Lieutenant Frank Ballinger (Lee Marvin). The investigator soon learns that Loder has enemies and that his wife (Judith Ames) plans to divorce him. After several attempts on the boxer's life, however, he begins to suspect someone close to the fighter may be the culprit.

*M Squad* was telecast for 117 episodes on NBC-TV from 1957 to 1960. Regarding Charles Bronson's work on the "Fight" segment of the show, Steven Whitney wrote in *Charles Bronson Superstar* (1975) "his [Bronson] interplay with [Lee] Marvin was one of the highlights of the television season."

The boxing sequences in "Fight" were taken from the two episodes of *Crusader* in which Charles Bronson guest starred. Both series were produced by Richard Lewis at Revue Studios.

## *The Man Behind the Badge* "The Case of the Invisible Mark" (Syndicated, 1955) 30 minutes B/W

**CAST:** Charles Bickford (Host/Narrator), William Demarest, Charles Bronson.

*The Man Behind the Badge* first ran as a live police anthology drama on CBS-TV from 1953 to 1954. For its second season the segments were filmed and "The Case of the Invisible Mark" was about a compassionate young parole officer who aids a parolee in his quest for success in a business career.

Although the episode's official telecast date was February 19, 1955, it varied according to the market in which it played. It was shown in Philadelphia on March 5, 1955, and in New York City on April 2, 1955.

## *Man with a Camera* (ABC-TV, 1958–60) 30 minutes B/W

Charles Bronson's first starring television series, *Man with a Camera*, was filmed by producers Warren Lewis and Don Sharpe for General Electric, which sponsored the 30 minute action show in order to promote a new type of flashbulb. In the show Bronson starred as World War II combat veteran and freelance photojournalist Mike Kovac. Lewis and Sharpe had

**Charles Bronson in *Man with a Camera* (ABC-TV, 1958–1960).**

obtained the rights to a book about such a character and had planned to make a movie but when those plans fell through they developed the TV series with Four Star and Desilu. A total of 29 half-hour black and white episodes were filmed, 15 first run during the 1958-59 TV season and 14 more for the 1959-60 season. Two episodes a week were shot at a budget of slightly under $25,000 per segment with star Charles Bronson being paid about $2,000 a week. When the series was in hiatus from February to October 1959, Bronson spent part of that time touring the country promoting the program. Moderately successful in the ratings and with audiences and critics, *Man with a Camera* was cancelled because a rival company developed a flashbulb which made General Electric's obsolete and they withdrew sponsorship.

The series debuted October 10, 1958, on ABC-TV and ran Friday at 9 P.M., EST, until January 23, 1959. It then was in reruns until March. The series resumed October 19, 1959, on the same network, showing at 10:30 P.M., EST, each Monday. It ran for 14 more episodes, its final telecast being February 8, 1960.

## "Second Avenue Assassin" (October 10, 1958)

*P:* A.E. Houghton Jr. *D:* Gerald Mayer. *Sc:* William Fay. *Ph:* Howard Schwartz. *Ed:* Jay Whittredge.

**CAST:** Charles Bronson (Mike Kovac), Ruta Lee (Dolly MacDermott), Tom Laughlin (Joey Savoyan), Leonard Bell (Jasper), Theodore Marcuse, Walter Barnes, John Becheram, Art Lewis, Don Kennedy.

Sent to get photos for a fight promotion story, Mike Kovac (Charles Bronson) learns that a dishonest fight promoter with mob connections is planning to fix a championship bout.

## "The Warning" (October 17, 1958)

*P:* A.E. Houghton Jr. *D:* Gerald Mayer. *Sc:* Richard Bluel.

**CAST:** Charles Bronson (Mike Kovac), Ludwig Stossel (Anton Kovac), Berry Kroeger (Glenn Markey), Robert Ellenstein (Lieutenant Abrams), Arthur Hanson (Winkler), Robert Carricart (Carver), William "Bill" Erwin (Sam Bartlett), Rush Williams.

Criminals threaten the life of Mike Kovac (Charles Bronson) after he mistakenly photographs them committing a murder.

## "Profile of a Killer" (October 24, 1958)

**CAST:** Charles Bronson (Mike Kovac), Tom Pittman, James Handler.

On an assignment taking photographs at a bank, Mike Kovac (Charles Bronson) is taken prisoner by a homicidal maniac and his partner.

## "Turntable" (November 7, 1958)

**CAST:** Charles Bronson (Mike Kovac), Ludwig Stossel (Anton Kovac), Logan Field (Senator Payson), Phyllis Avery, Dennis Patrick.

Mike Kovac (Charles Bronson) checks into the rumor that a composite photograph has been made to incriminate a politician by depicting him with two gamblers.

## "Close-Up on Violence" (November 14, 1958)

**CAST:** Charles Bronson (Mike Kovac), Angie Dickinson, Robert Armstrong.

Photojournalist Mike Kovac (Charles Bronson) becomes involved in a case of mistaken identity.

## "Double Negative" (November 21, 1958)

*P:* A.E. Houghton Jr. *D:* Gerald Mayer. *Sc:* James Edmiston.
**CAST:** Charles Bronson (Mike Kovac), Tracey Roberts, Frank Faylen, Karl Lukas, Stephen Ellsworth, Don Durant.

After taking a picture of a woman, Mike Kovac (Charles Bronson) later learns she has been reported murdered.

## "Another Barrier" (November 28, 1958)

*P:* A.E. Houghton Jr. *D:* Gerald Mayer. *Sc:* Stanley Niss.
**CAST:** Charles Bronson (Mike Kovac), Grant Williams (Sandy Dickson), Norma Crane (Liz Howell), Peter Walker, Morgan Jones, Jesse Kirkpatrick, David Whorf, Ann Morrison.

Mike Kovac (Charles Bronson) is assigned to do a photo-story of a test pilot flying an experimental plane.

## "Blind Spot" (December 5, 1958)

**CAST:** Charles Bronson (Mike Kovac), Mario Alcade (Al Alviello), Terry Alden (Terry Ross), Chana Eden.

Mike Kovac (Charles Bronson) becomes involved in intrigue in Lisbon when he goes there to investigate the murder of his wartime friend.

Advertisement for the *Man with a Camera* episode "Blind Spot," telecast December 5, 1958 on ABC-TV.

### "Two Strings of Pearls" (December 12, 1958)

*P:* A.E. Houghton Jr. *AP:* Jason H. Bernie. *D:* Gerald Mayer. *Sc:* Robert J.Shaw. *St Ed:* Richard Bluel. *Ph:* Robert B. Hauser. *Ed:* Elmo Veron. *AD:* Ralph Berger & Duncan Cramer. *Prod Supv:* W. Argyle Nelson. *Prod Mgr:* Lloyd Richards. *Set Decorator:* William L. Stevens. *Casting:* Harvey Clermont & Marvin Schnell. *St Associate:* William Koenig. *Sd Mixer:* Jack F. Lilly. *Asst Dir:* Tommy Thompson. *Wardrobe:* Frank Delmar. *Properties:* Bud Hollis. *Makeup:* George Lane. *Recordist:* Glen Glenn Sound. *Still Eff:* Ted Allan. *Photography Consultant:* Joseph Bennett.

**CAST:** Charles Bronson (Mike Kovac), Audrey Dalton (Sharon Rogers), King Calder (Jonathan Rogers), Alberto Morin (Mrs. Partolo), Bert Remsen (Barnes), Elizabeth Fraser (Ellie McMahon), Elaine Edwards (Mona Rogers), Warren Douglas (Tommy).

In Rome, Mike Kovac is pushed into a pool after taking a photo of a well-known American. He decides to investigate the man, who turns out to be an international con artist.

### "Six Faces of Satan" (December 19, 1958)

**CAST:** Charles Bronson (Mike Kovac), Ludwig Stossel (Anton Kovac), Linda Lawson (Carmen), Joe Di Reda, Dean Stanton, Arthur Batanides.

In search of good photo shoots, Mike Kovac (Charles Bronson) goes along with a police patrol.

### "Lady on the Loose" (December 26, 1958)

**CAST:** Charles Bronson (Mike Kovac), Ludwig Stossel (Anton Kovac), Judith Braun (Fredericka), Ivan Triesault, Henry Rowland.

Mike Kovac (Charles Bronson) becomes the escort of the daughter (Judith Braun) of an American millionaire and shows her around the Big Apple.

### "The Last Portrait" (January 2, 1959)

**CAST:** Charles Bronson (Mike Kovac), Virginia Field (Sarah Castle), Booth Colman, Russell Thorson.

After taking a photo of an Arab leader being murdered in a woman's (Virginia Field) apartment, Mike Kovac (Charles Bronson) finds himself being framed for the homicide.

### "Face of Murder" (January 9, 1959)

**CAST:** Charles Bronson (Mike Kovac), Phillip Pine (Edwin Bray), Jay Barney, Richard Wessell.

When he is granted an interview with a condemned murderer (Phillip Pine), Mike Kovac (Charles Bronson) gets caught in the middle of a prison break.

## "Mute Evidence" (January 16, 1959)

*P:* A.E. Houghton Jr. *AP:* Jason H. Bernie. *D:* Paul Landres. *Sc:* Dallas Gautois & James Edmiston. *St Ed:* Richard Bluel. *Ph:* Robert B. Hauser. *Ed:* Irving Berlin. *AD:* Ralph Berger & Duncan Cramer. *St Associate:* William Koenig. *Prod Supv:* W. Argyle Nelson. *Prod Mgr:* Lloyd Richards. *Casting:* Harvey Clermont & Marvin Schnell. *Asst Dir:* Tommy Thompson. *Set Decorator:* William L. Stevens. *Sd Mixer:* Jack F. Lilly. *Wardrobe:* Frank Delmar. *Properties:* Don D. Smith. *Makeup:* George Lane. *Recordist:* Glen Glenn Sound. *Sp Eff:* Ted Allan & Eugene Richee. *Photography Consultant:* Joseph Bennett. *Audiological Consultant:* Edgar L. Lowell.

**CAST:** Charles Bronson (Mike Kovac), Sue George (Susan Barnes), Simon Scott (Earl Grant), Judith Ames (Lila), Russ Conway (Sheriff), George Cesar (Bill the Hotel Clerk).

Accepting an invitation from a retired doctor to visit his farm, Mike Kovac (Charles Bronson), upon arrival, finds his host is missing and that his patient, a young mute girl (Sue George), is badly frightened.

## "The Big Squeeze" (January 23, 1959)

*P:* A.E. Houghton. Jr. *AP:* Jason H. Bernie. *D:* Harold Schuster. *Sc:* David P. Harmon. *St Ed:* Richard Bluel. *St Associate:* William Koenig. *Ph:* Robert B. Hauser. *Ed:* Irving Berlin. *AD:* Ralph Berger & Duncan Cramer. *Casting:* Harvey Clermont & Marvin Schnell. *Prod Supv:* W. Argyle Nelson. *Prod Mgr:* Lloyd Richards. *Asst Dir:* Tommy Thompson. *Set Decorator:* William L. Stevens. *Sd Mixer:* Jack L. Lilly. *Wardrobe:* Frank Delmar. *Properties:* Don D. Smith. *Makeup:* George Lane. *Recordist:* Glen Glenn Sound. *Sp Eff:* Ted Allan & Eugene Richee. *Photography Consultant:* Joseph Bennett.

**CAST:** Charles Bronson (Mike Kovac), Ludwig Stossel (Anton Kovac), May Wynn (Lorraine Johnson), Steven Ritch (Johnny Ricco), Robert Osterloh (Big Joe Tennuto), Robert Cornthwaite (Lieutenant Fields), Steve Graves (Sid).

After a gangster (Steven Ritch) is murdered, Mike Kovac (Charles Bronson) becomes acquainted with his girlfriend (May Wynn), who wants him to find the killer.

## "The Killer" (October 19, 1959)

*D:* Paul Landres. *Sc:* E. Jack Neuman. *Ph:* Paul Ivano. *Ed:* Irving Berlin.

**CAST:** Charles Bronson (Mike Kovac), James Flavin (Lieutenant Donovan), Lawrence Dobkin (Detective James Angelo), Harlan Warde (Detective John Butler), I. Stanford Jolley, Lee Roberts, Bek Nelson, James Parnell.

At a small town airport, Mike Kovac (Charles Bronson) is shot by a woman and another attempt is made on his life after he is hospitalized.

### "Eye Witness" (October 26, 1959)

**CAST:** Charles Bronson (Mike Kovac), James Flavin (Lieutenant Donovan), Joseph Hamilton (Timothy), Marian Collier, Douglas Dick, Casey Walters.

The defense lawyer in a murder case requests that Mike Kovac (Charles Bronson) investigate the photographic evidence against his client.

### "The Man Below" (November 2, 1959)

**CAST:** Charles Bronson (Mike Kovac), Dave Lewis (Carl Baines), Patricia Donahue (Helen), Rusty Lane.

Mike Kovac (Charles Bronson) looks into the possibility of insurance fraud when a company suspects a deceased policyholder may still be alive.

### "Black Light" (November 9, 1959)

**CAST:** Charles Bronson (Mike Kovac), James Flavin (Lieutenant Donovan), Hugh Sanders (Inspector Randolph), Michael Harris (Lieutenant Monta).

Suspecting that some of his officers are receiving payoffs, a police inspector (Hugh Sanders) asks Mike Kovac (Charles Bronson) to get photographic proof.

### "The Positive Negative" (November 16, 1959)

**CAST:** Charles Bronson (Mike Kovac), James Flavin (Lieutenant Donovan), Anne Neyland (Ellen), Anthony Caruso, Susan Cummings, Richard Gaines.

A pretty nightclub photographer (Anne Neyland) asks the help of Mike Kovac (Charles Bronson) when gangsters try to steal the negative of a picture she took of a rich man.

### "Missing" (November 23, 1959)

**CAST:** Charles Bronson (Mike Kovac), Cece Whitney (Jill Kern), Steve Brodie (Ed Kern), Wendell Holmes.

When a San Diego cop (Steve Brodie) asks Mike Kovac (Charles Bronson) to help find his missing wife, the cameraman learns she has been kidnapped.

## "Live Target" (December 7, 1959)

*AP:* Jason H. Bernie. *D:* Paul Landres. *Sc:* Barry Trivers. *St Ed:* William Koenig. *Ph:* Paul Ivano. *Ed:* Sherman A. Rose. *Prod Supv:* W. Argyle Nelson. *Prod Mgr:* J. Walter Daniels. *Ad:* Ralph Berger & Howard Hollander. *Casting:* Harvey Clermont. *Asst Dir:* Vernon Keays. *Set Decorator:* George R. Nelson. *Technical Advisor:* Ralph Murphy. *Mus:* Leon Klatzkin. *Wardrobe:* Stan Kuffel. *Properties:* Ralph Hansen. *Makeup:* Robert Cowan. *Sd Mixer:* William Brady. *Recordist:* Glen Glenn Sound.

**CAST:** Charles Bronson (Mike Kovac), James Lydon (Eddie Wilson), Toni Gerry (Bess Wilson), Robert Carson (Martin Denny), Fred Essler (Mr. Korman), Gavin McLeod (Johnny Patch), George Keymas (Santos), Tracy Stafford (Susie Wilson).

Mike Kovac (Charles Bronson) is hired by the district attorney's office to help protect a witness (James Lydon) threatened by gangsters and ends up trying to save the man and his family from a hired assassin (Gavin McLeod).

## "Girl in the Dark" (December 14, 1959)

**CAST:** Charles Bronson (Mike Kovac), James Flavin (Lieutenant Donovan), Gregory Morton.

A rich man hires Mike Kovac (Charles Bronson) to get photographic evidence against a blackmailer.

## "The Bride" (December 21, 1959)

**CAST:** Charles Bronson (Mike Kovac), George Conrad, Nick Paul.

While doing a photo shoot, Mike Kovac (Charles Bronson) uncovers a marriage racket and sets out to break up the operation.

## "The Picture War" (January 4, 1960)

**CAST:** Charles Bronson (Mike Kovac), James Flavin (Lieutenant Donovan), Jeanne Bates (Mrs. Mason), John Seven, Don Dillaway, Dolores Donlon.

After several accidents befall witnesses in a murder case, Mike Kovac (Charles Bronson) tries to catch a killer.

## "Touch Off" (January 11, 1960)

**CAST:** Charles Bronson (Mike Kovac), James Flavin (Lieutenant Donovan), Stacy Harris (Billy), Sebastian Cabot (Hartwell), Sylvia Lewis, Nancy Valentine.

In order to get the goods on an arson gang, Mike Kovac (Charles Bronson) infiltrates the group to take the pictures necessary to bring them to justice.

### "Hot Ice Cream" (January 25, 1960)

**CAST:** Charles Bronson (Mike Kovac), Yvonne Craig (Jo Stokes), Lawrence Tierney (Charlie Stokes), Paul Bryar, Roscoe Ates.

When a murder takes place at her father's (Lawrence Tierney) amusement park, a young woman photographer (Yvonne Craig) joins forces with Mike Kovac (Charles Bronson) to find the killer.

### "Fragment of Murder" (February 1, 1960)

**CAST:** Charles Bronson (Mike Kovac), James Flavin (Lieutenant Donovan), Jesse White (Frankie Billings), Doris Singleton (Cara), Gordon Wynn, Don Rhodes, Larry Blake, Shari Lee Bernath.

Mike Kovac (Charles Bronson) is hired by a gangster to prove that the latter's friend did not commit a crime for which he was accused.

### "Kangaroo Court" (February 8, 1960)

*AP:* Jason H. Bernie. *D:* Gilbert L. Kay. *Sc:* Wilton Schiller. *St Ed:* William Koenig. *Ph:* Charles S. Burke. *Ed:* Sherman A. Rose. *Mus:* Leon Klatzkin. *AD:* Ralph Berger & Howard Hollander. *Prod Supv:* W. Argyle Nelson. *Prod Mgr:* J. Walter Daniels. *Casting:* Harvey Clermont. *Asst Dir:* Vernon Keays. *Technical Advisor:* Ralph Murphy. *Properties:* Ralph Hansen. *Set Decorator:* George R. Nelson. *Makeup:* Mel Berns. *Sd Mixer:* William Brady. *Recordist:* Glen Glenn Sound.

**CAST:** Charles Bronson (Mike Kovac), Don Gordon (Colonel), John Dennis (Sanders), William Lally (Turity), Richard Benedict (Crane), George Wallace (Hank Fletcher), Danielle Aubry (Annette), John Goddard (Lurie), Maurice Marsac (Parrot), Ralph Gary (Corelli), Arthur Space (Colonel Boyor).

Mike Kovac (Charles Bronson) goes to France on the request of the Army in order to prevent the kidnapping of a film star (George Wallace) by a gang headed by "The Colonel" (Don Gordon), a World War II deserter.

During part of the first 15 episodes of *Man with a Camera*, Ludwig Stossel was a series regular as Mike Kovac's father. During some of the last 14 segments of the series, James Flavin portrayed Kovac's policeman pal, Lieutenant Donovan.

## *Medic* (NBC-TV, 1954–1956) 30 minutes B/W

### "My Brother Joe" (October 25, 1954)

*P:* Frank La Tourette. *EP:* Worthington E. Miner. *D:* Bernard Girard. *Creator-Sc:* James E. Moser. *Ph:* Lester Shorr. *Ed:* Robert Siedel. *Mus:* Victor Young. *Prod Mgr:* Lonnie D'Orsa. *Asst Dir:* Bert Cherwin & Bernard Kowalski. *AD:*

Danny Hill. *Sd:* Walter Appel. *Sd Ed:* James Nelson. *Mus Ed:* Aubrey Granville. *Sc Supv:* Elizabeth Fancher. *Set Dresser:* Victor Taylor. *Head Grip:* Martin Kasnek. *Chief Electrician:* Robert E. Jones. *Lighting Foreman:* Joe Barnes. *Property Master:* Arden Cripe. *Sp Eff:* Louis De Witt & Jack Rabin.

**CAST:** Richard Boone (Dr. Konrad Styner/Narrator), Charles Bronson (Dr. John Bircher), Paul Hahn (Dr. Ortega), Jack Dimond (Stanley Lockwood), Tom Greenway (William Lockwood), Lorna Thayer (Lorraine Lockwood), Dr. Theodore Kurze, Dr. Max Pierce, Dr. Forrest Lionel Johnson, Dr. Alan Wintner Rosenberg, Catherine McCabe, R.N.

A ten-year-old boy is badly injured in an automobile accident and a medical team fights unsuccessfully to save his life. Charles Bronson, billed under that name for the first time in a television program, played the sympathetic head of the medical team, giving a low key and very effective performance.

### "Who Search for Truth" (February 27, 1956)

**CAST:** Richard Boone (Dr. Konrad Styner/Narrator), Ainslie Pryor (Dr. William Beaumont), Claudia Bryar (Deborah), Charles Bronson (Alexis St. Martin), Marshall Bradford (Major Kenzie).

The life story of Dr. William Beaumont (Ainslie Pryor), who was the first to detail the digestive process and who pioneered research in digestive disorders.

*Medic* was telecast on NBC-TV from 1954 to 1956 and is considered to be one of the first realism series. It was filmed in actual hospitals using real doctors and nurses in its cast and its stories were taken from Los Angeles County Medical Association cases.

The series theme song, "Blue Star," was composed by Edward Heyman and Victor Young.

## *The Millionaire* "The Story of Jerry Bell" (CBS-TV, February 27, 1957) 30 minutes B/W

*P:* Don Fedderson. *EP:* Fred Henry. *D:* Alfred E. Green. *Mus:* Jerry Adelson.

**CAST:** Marvin Miller (Michael Anthony), Charles Bronson (Jerry Bell), Georgann Johnson (Myra), Louise Lorimer (Mrs. Bell), Harvey Stephens (Doctor), Paul Frees (Voice of John Beresford Tipton).

Falling in love with a blind girl (Georgann Johnson), a man (Charles Bronson) is given a million dollars by an anonymous millionaire. He now has the money to get the girl an operation which will restore her sight but he fears she may then no longer love him.

*The Millionaire* ran on CBS-TV from 1955–60 for 188 episodes. This outing with Charles Bronson was the 83rd episode in the series.

## *The New Breed* "The Valley of the Three Charlies" (ABC-TV, December 5, 1961) 60 minutes B/W

*P-D:* Allen H. Miner. *EP:* Quinn Martin. *AP:* Arthur Fellows. *Creator:* Hank Searls. *Sc:* Jesse Lasky Jr. & Pat Silver. *Ph:* Meredith Nicholson. *Ed:* Jerry Young. *Mus:* Dominic Frontiere. *AD:* Frank T. Smith. *Asst Dir:* Maxwell O. Henry & Sam Stragis. *Prod Mgr:* Fred Ahern. *Second Camera:* Jack McCosky. *Sd Ed:* Chuck Overhulser. *Photographic Sp Eff:* Howard Anderson Co. *Asst Ed:* John Post. *Sc Supv:* Helen Gailey. *Set Decorator:* Sandy Grace. *Dialogue Dir:* Milton Stark. *Costume Supv:* Bob Wolfe. *Chief Electrician:* Vaughn Ashen. *Property Master:* Irving Sindler. *Casting:* Stalmaster–Lister. *Makeup:* Walter Schenk. *Technical Supv:* Gordon Sawyer. *Prod Mixer:* John Kean. *Re-recording:* Buddy Myers. *Mus Supv:* John Elizade.

**CAST:** Leslie Nielsen (Lieutenant Price Adams), John Beradino (Sergeant Vince Cavelli), John Clarke (Patrolman Joe Huddleston), Greg Roman (Patrolman Pete Garcia), Byron Morrow (Captain Keith Gregory), Keenan Wynn (Griffo Ronson), Charles Bronson (Jerry Bergason), Mike Kellin (Moss Moran), Anita Sands (Sue Daniel), William Fawcett (Old Charley), Michael Mikler (Buck), Paul Wexler (Dakota Charlie), Orville Sherman (Charlie Nellis), Ted Bergen (Salesman), Art Gilmore (Narrator).

A trio (Keenan Wynn, Charles Bronson, Mike Kellin) of criminals reunite after 20 years to dig up a half million dollars they hid from a robbery. The leader (Keenan Wynn) kills an old man (William Fawcett) who finds them with the money and they take his riding companion, a young girl (Anita Sands), hostage. Lieutenant Price (Leslie Nielsen) and members of the Los Angeles Police Department's Metro Squad are called into the case, eventually trapping the criminals and their hostage in a remote cabin in the Malibu Mountains.

Made by QM Productions in association with Selmer Productions and filmed at the Samuel Goldwyn Studios, *The New Breed* was telecast on ABC-TV from 1961 to 1962.

## *Night of 100 Stars II* (ABC-TV, March 10, 1985) 180 minutes Color

*EP:* Alexander H. Cohen. *P:* Hildy Parks & Martha Mason. *D:* Clark Jones. *Sc:* Hildy Parks. *Mus Dir:* Elliot Lawrence. *Sp Mus & Lyrics:* Buz Kohan. *Choreography:* Albert Stephenson.

Taped February 17, 1985, at Radio City Music Hall in New York City, this special was edited down from seven hours of entertainment with over

300 stars. Like its 1982 predecessor, *Night of 100 Stars* in 1982, it was a celebrity benefit for the Actors' Fund of America. In one sequence, a rendition of the song "One," Charles Bronson appeared with James Stewart and New York City Mayor Ed Koch as part of a 32-man chorus line which was aided by The Rockettes.

## *100 Years of the Hollywood Western* (NBC-TV, November 25, 1994) 120 minutes Color

**CAST:** Charles Bronson, James Coburn, James Garner, Gene Hackman, Robert Mitchum, Kurt Russell, Jane Seymour (Hosts).

Charles Bronson was one of the hosts for this tribute to the western film.

## *Pepsi-Cola Playhouse* "The Woman in the Mine" (ABC-TV, June 12, 1955) 30 minutes B/W

*D:* Stuart Gilmore. *Sc-St:* John McGreevey. *Ph:* John MacBurnie. *AD:* Martin Obzina. *Ed:* Daniel A. Nathan. *Mus:* Stanley Wilson.

**CAST:** Beverly Garland (Claire Walkowsky), Charles Bronson (Joe Krossen), Claude Akins (Pete Nemecek), John Alderson.

A miner (Claude Akins) asks his best friend (Charles Bronson) to be the best man at his wedding. When his fiancée (Beverly Garland) arrives from the East she immediately falls in love with the friend. The two rob the company payroll and then take refuge in the mine.

Hosted by Polly Bergen, *Pepsi-Cola Playhouse* was telecast on ABC-TV from 1953 to 1955. It was syndicated as *Polly Bergen Playhouse*.

## *Playhouse 90* (CBS-TV, 1956-60) 90 minutes B/W

### "Rank and File" (May 28, 1959)

*D:* Franklin Schaffner. *Sc:* Rod Serling.

**CAST:** Van Heflin (William Kilcoyne), Luther Adler (Irving Werner), Charles Bronson (Kovaric), Harry Townes (Gabe Brewster), Carl Benton Reid (Senator Henders), Bruce Gordon (Russo), Cameron Prud'homme (Farrell), Addison Richards (Parker), Whitney Blake, Wright King, Tom Palmer, Danny Richards Jr.

While testifying before a Senate hearing, labor leader William Kilcoyne (Van Heflin) tells how he rose in the ranks from factory worker to the top position of power using any means he could, including destroying his friends. *Variety* commented, "Charles Bronson creates a tremendously compelling character out of the 'friend' not fooled, but ultimately destroyed, by Heflin's greedy heroics."

### "The Cruel Day" (March 7, 1960)

*D:* Franklin Schaffner. *Sc:* Reginald Rose. *Mus:* Jerry Goldsmith. *AD:* Craig Smith.

**CAST:** Van Heflin (Captain), Cliff Robertson (Lieutenant), Phyllis Thaxter (Nicole), Raymond Massey (Father Ricquoi), Peter Lorre (Cafe Owner), Charles Bronson (Sergeant), Nehemiah Persoff (Prisoner's Father), Thane Rama, Mike Oscard.

Assigned to a remote Algerian outpost, a French army captain (Van Heflin) tries to bring peace to the area but his plans are constantly thwarted by an ambitious lieutenant (Cliff Robertson). The latter wants to torture a confession from a prisoner captured following the massacre of a local family by rebels.

Charles Bronson was cast as the outpost's sergeant in this live drama. It was his second appearance on the series and it reteamed him with star Van Heflin and director Franklin Schaffner.

## *Public Defender* "Cornered" (March 24, 1955) 30 minutes B/W

*P:* Hal Roach Jr. *AP-D:* Harve Foster. *Sc:* William P. Rousseau. *Ph:* Jack MacKenzie. *Supv Ed:* Otho Lovering. *Ed:* Bud Small. *AD:* William Farrari. *Asst Dir:* Bob Shannon. *Prod Mgr:* E.H. Goldstein. *Photographic Eff:* Jack R. Glass. *Set Decorator:* Ben Lane. *Sd:* Jack Goodrich. *Wardrobe:* John E. Downing Jr. *Makeup:* Nick Wehr. *St Ed:* Henry F. Goldberg. *Technical Advisor:* Edward W. Ross Jr. *Creators:* Mort Mills & Sam Shayon.

**CAST:** Reed Hadley (Bart Matthews), Charles Bronson (Knobby Bullaid), Kenneth Tobey (Sergeant Jack Angel), Frankie Darro (Jake South), Jack Kruschen (Roxey Williams), Tom E. Jackson (Lieutenant Vaughn), Stanley Clements (Duke Shannon), Lillian Buyeff (Miss Janis), George Neise (Jim Parker), Jan Shepard (Judy Parker), Jerry Hausner (Clerk), Jean Willes (Fight Patron).

After being convicted of an assault charge, boxer Knobby Bullaid (Charles Bronson) breaks parole but contacts Public Defender Bart Matthews (Reed Hadley), wanting to give himself up. Seeing Matthews with policeman friend Sergeant Jack Angel (Kenneth Tobey), Knobby thinks he has been double-crossed and tries to get away, taking a married couple (George Neise, Jan Shepard) hostage.

*Public Defender* took its plots from real-life cases of people who could not afford legal aid and were given it without cost. The series ran on CBS-TV from 1954 to 1955 for 69 episodes.

***Raid on Entebbe*** (NBC-TV, January 9, 1977)—see Filmography under *Raid on Entebbe* (1977).

## *Rawhide* "Duel at Daybreak" (CBS-TV, November 16, 1965) 60 minutes B/W

*P:* Ben Brady. *EP:* Robert E. Thompson. *AP:* Robert Stillman. *D:* Sutton Roley. *Sc:* Bob Bloomfield & Herman Miller. *St:* Bob Bloomfield. *Ph:* Neal Beckner. *Ed:* Everett Sutherland. *Mus:* Dmitri Tiomkin. *Song:* Dmitri Tiomkin & Ned Washington, sung by Frankie Laine. *AD:* John B. Goodman. *St Ed:* Herman Miller. *Unit Prod Mgr:* Harry Templeton. *Set Decorator:* Donald E. Webb. *Asst Dir:* Jack Cunningham. *MusEd:* Gene Feldman. *Sd Eff:* Jack A. Findlay. *Casting:* James Lister.

**CAST:** Clint Eastwood (Rowdy Yates), John Ireland (Jed Colby), Charles Bronson (Del Lingman), Jill Haworth (Vicki Woodruff), Larry Gates (Mason Woodruff), Brendon Boone (Roman Bedford), Paul Brinegar (Wishbone), Steve Raines (Jim Quince), Raymond St. Jacques (Simon Blake), Joe Di Reda (Woodruff Cowboy).

Trail herder Rowdy Yates (Clint Eastwood) contracts with ranch owner Mason Woodruff (Larry Gates) to deliver the man's cattle to market. Woodruff's foreman Del Lingman (Charles Bronson) becomes jealous of Yates' trail hand Roman Bedford (Brendon Boone) over the affections of his boss' pretty daughter Vicki (Jill Haworth). Lingman tries to goad Bedford into a fight and the cowboy challenges him to a duel.

*Rawhide* was telecast by CBS-TV from 1959 to 1966 and this was the 213th episode of the series.

## *Richard Diamond, Private Detective* "The Pete Rocco Case" (CBS-TV, September 9, 1957) 30 minutes B/W

*P-Sc:* Richard Carr. *D:* Bernard Kowalski. *Creator:* Blake Edwards. *Ph:* Charles E. Burke. *Ed:* Samuel E. Beetley. *Mus Supv:* Frank DeVol. *St Ed:* Coles Trapnel. *Prod Executive:* Frank Baur. *Supv Ed:* Bernard Burton. *Supv AD:* Bill Ross. *Asst Dir:* Jack Sonntag. *Set Decorator:* Budd S. Friend. *Makeup Artist:* Karl Herlinger.

**CAST:** David Janssen (Richard Diamond), Regis Toomey (Lieutenant Dennis McGough), Charles Bronson (Dan Rocco), Bill Erwin (Sergeant Riker), Richard Devon (Pete Rocco), Marga Ann Deighton (Mrs. Rocco), Marvin Press (Elmer Nacy), Anne Neyland (Waitress).

New York City private investigator and former policeman Richard Diamond (David Janssen) learns that Pete Rocco (Richard Devon), who he helped send to prison, has escaped and holds a grudge against him. Rocco's brother Dan (Charles Bronson) and mother (Marga Ann Deighton) hire Diamond to find Pete and put him back behind bars.

Four Star Productions made this detective series which was telecast by CBS-TV from 1957 to 1959 and NBC-TV from 1959 to 1960. Charles Bronson and Richard Devon, who played brothers in this episode, the tenth of 51 filmed segments, would reteam the next year in the film *Machine Gun Kelly*. When the series was syndicated in 1960 as *Calling Mr. D*, "The Pete Rocco Case" was retitled "Prison Break."

## *Riverboat* "Zig Zag" (NBC-TV, December 26, 1960) 60 minutes B/W

*P:* Boris D. Kaplan. *D:* Sidney Lanfield. *Sc:* David Lang. *Ph:* Neal Beckner. *Supv Ed:* David J. O'Connell. *Ed:* George Nicholson. *Mus:* Gerald Fried. *Mus Supv:* Stanley Wilson. *AD:* George Patrick. *Sd:* John W. Rixey. *Asst Dir:* Ben Bishop. *Set Decorators:* John McCarthy & James W. Walters. *Costume Supv:* Vincent Dee. *Makeup:* Leo Lotito Jr. *Hair Stylist:* Florence Bush.

**CAST:** Darren McGavin (Captain Grey Holden), Noah Beery (Bill Blake), Dick Wessel (Carney), Charles Bronson (Crowley), Stella Stevens (Lisa Walters), William Fawcett (Pinky Walters), Tom Fadden (Lear), John Milford (Egan), Ray Teal (Sheriff Clay), Don O'Kelly (Convict), Phil Tully (Bartender).

Charles Bronson guest starred as Crowley, the leader of a quartet of escaped convicts, who hold up in a shack belonging to Pinky Walters (William Fawcett) and his pretty daughter Lisa (Stella Stevens). One of the men (Tom Fadden) is blind and dying and he wants to be with his son before the end. Since the man claims to have hidden $100,000, Crowley has his two cohorts (John Milford, Don O'Kelly) abduct the dying man's physician son but the duo mistakenly capture riverboat pilot Bill Blake (Noah Beery), who in a drunken state was in the doctor's office trying to pull a co-worker's (Dick Wessel) tooth.

Produced by Revue Studios, *Riverboat* was telecast on NBC-TV from 1959 to 1961. The series launched the career of Burt Reynolds, who co-starred for part of the first season as pilot Ben Frazer.

## *The Roy Rogers Show* "Knockout" CBS-TV, December 28, 1952 30 minutes B/W

*P:* Jack C. Lacey. *D:* Robert G. Walker. *Sc:* Dwight Cummins. *Ph:* Joe Novak. *Ed:* J.B. Wittenridge. *Mus:* Frank Worth. *Song:* Dale Evans. *Asst Dir:* Nathan Barranger. *St Ed:* Tom Hargis. *Set Continuity:* Len Martinson. *Makeup:* David Newell. *Hair Stylist:* Mildred Burns. *Properties:* Tom Coleman. *Sd:* Fred Lau. *Management:* Arthur [Art] Rush & Larry Kent.

**CAST:** Roy Rogers (Himself), Dale Evans (Herself), Pat Brady (Himself), Sarah Padden (Grandma Conley), Leonard Penn (Sheriff Jim Wiley), Charles Buchinski (Willie "Killer" Conley), Roy Brent (Bill Tolan), Wally West (Mack Fuller), Frank Jenks (Art Guley), Russ Scott.

An elderly woman (Sarah Padden) enlists the aid of Roy Rogers and Dale Evans (Themselves) in locating her boxer grandson (Charles Buchinski) who has become involved with three crooks (Roy Brent, Wally West, Frank Jenks) trying to find stolen bank loot buried on Rogers' ranch.

This was the first of several television programs which cast Charles Bronson as a boxer.

***The Sea Wolf*** (Turner Network Television [TNT], April 18, 1993)— see Filmography under *The Sea Wolf* (1993).

## *Sinatra 75: The Best Is Yet to Come* (CBS-TV, December 16, 1990) 120 minutes Color

*P:* George Schlatter & Tina Sinatra. *D:* Jeff Margolis. *Sc:* Buz Kohan.

**CAST:** Frank Sinatra, Tony Bennett, Charles Bronson, George Burns, Rosemary Clooney, Harry Connick Jr., Tony Danza, Ella Fitzgerald, Helen Forrest, Eydie Gorme, Jack Jones, Quincy Jones, Gene Kelly, Steve Lawrence, Peggy Lee, Sophia Loren, Shirley MacLaine, The Manhattan Transfer, Roger Moore, Paul Newman, Helen O'Connell, Tom Selleck, Jo Stafford, Barbra Streisand, Robert Wagner, Bruce Willis.

A two hour special celebrating Frank Sinatra's 75th birthday. Charles Bronson was one of the celebrities appearing on the program.

## *Stage 7* (CBS-TV, 1954-55) 30 minutes B/W

### "Debt of Honor" (February 20, 1955)

*P:* Warren Lewis. *D:* Lewis Foster. *Sc:* Frederic Brady. *St:* Cornell Woolrich. *Ph:* George Diskant. *Ed Supv:* Bernard Burton.

**CAST:** Edmond O'Brien (Captain Sturges), Charles Bronson, Laura Elliott, Wendy Winkleman, Steve Pendleton.

A policeman (Edmond O'Brien) shields an escaped killer (Charles Bronson) in his home because the man once saved the life of his small daughter (Wendy Winkleman).

For the second time in the same month, February 1955, Charles Bronson co-starred with Edmond O'Brien in a TV series drama, having previously done "A Bell for Adano" on *Lux Video Theatre* ten days earlier. In this outing, Edmond O'Brien's character has to decide between loyalty and the law while Charles Bronson "is correctly tempered to the menacing mood" (*Variety*).

### "The Time of Day" (May 29, 1955)

*P:* Warren Lewis. *D:* Arnold Laven. *Sc:* Laszlo Gorog. *St:* Peggy Chantler. *Ph:* Nick Musuraca. *Ed Supv:* Bernard Burton. *Ed:* Roland Gross. *AD:* Charles H. Clarke.

**CAST:** Peggy Ann Garner (Miranda), Charles Bronson (Jerry), Irene Hervey (Fran), Grandon Rhodes (Wilson), Leo Curley (Gilby), Robert Osterloh (Detective).

A young man (Charles Bronson) goes to jail for stealing a watch and when he gets out he meets and falls in love with a young socialite (Peggy Ann Garner). When she gives him a watch as a gift the police think he has stolen it.

Made by Four Star Productions, *Stage 7* was a half-hour anthology series which ran on CBS-TV for 24 episodes from 1954-55.

## *Studio 57* "Outpost" (ABC-TV, January 3, 1957) 30 minutes B/W

*P:* William C. Pine & William H. Thomas. *D:* Byron Haskin. *Sc:* Paul Monash & Martin Berkeley. *Ph:* William A. Sickner. *Ed:* Bill Mosher. *AD:* John Lloyd. *Mus Supv:* Stanley Wilson.

**CAST:** Lex Barker, Charles Bronson, Rita Lynn, Douglas Fowley, Jack Lambert, Jim Nolan, Adam Kennedy, Douglas Spencer, Kim Dibbs, George Keymas, Jonathan Hole, George Robotham, Boyd "Red" Morgan, John War Eagle.

A new trooper (Charles Bronson) arrives at a frontier cavalry outpost where its commander (Lex Barker) finds out the man is on the trail of a deserter who has killed his pal and stolen company money. When the deserter escapes, after killing a cavalry recruit, the commander and his men pursue him into hostile Indian country.

A pilot for a TV series that did not sell, this Pine–Thomas Productions western was telecast as an episode of *Studio 57*.

## *Sugarfoot* (ABC-TV, 1957–60) 60 minutes B/W

### "Man Wanted" (February 18, 1958)

*P:* Carroll Case. *EP:* William T. Orr. *D:* Franklin Adreon. *Sc:* Sig Herzig. *Ph:* Harold Stine. *Supv Ed:* James Moore. *Ed:* Carl Pingitore. *AD:* Perry Ferguson. *Prod Mgr:* Oren W. Haglund. *Sd:* Eugene F. Westfall. *Set Decorator:* Ben Bone. *Makeup Supv:* Gordon Bau. *Asst Dir:* Claude E. Archer.

**CAST:** Will Hutchins (Tom Brewster), Charles Bronson (Sandy Randall), Anna-Lisa (Ellie Peterson), Pernell Roberts (Deuce Braden), Mort Mills (Smiley), Mickey Simpson (Marblehead), Paul Keast (Sheriff Carson), Fred Essler (Amos Lampton), Frank Kreig (Jesse), Kermit Maynard (Townsman).

Traveling law student Tom "Sugarfoot" Brewster (Will Hutchins) unwittingly gets involved in romance when his pal, rancher Sandy Randall (Charles Bronson), writes for a mail-order bride and sends Tom's photograph instead of his own. More trouble develops when the young woman (Anna-Lisa) arrives as does her jealous ex-boyfriend (Pernell Roberts) who is planning to rob the local bank.

### "The Bullet and the Cross" (May 27, 1958)

*P:* Harry Tatelman. *EP:* William T. Orr. *D:* Lee Sholem. *Sc:* Peter R. Brooke. *Ph:* Harold Stine. *Supv Ed:* James Moore. *Ed:* Carl Pingitore. *AD:* Perry Ferguson. *Prod Mgr:* Oren W. Haglund. *Sd:* Samuel F. Goode. *Set Decorator:* Ben Bone. *Makeup Supv:* Gordon Bau. *Asst Dir:* Rusty Meek.

**CAST:** Will Hutchins (Tom Brewster), Charles Bronson (Cliff Raven), Stuart Randall (Sheriff Olson), Robert Wark (Deputy Jeff Williams), Mickey Simpson (Ramsey).

Tom Brewster (Will Hutchins) is trapped in a mine cave-in with half-breed schoolteacher Cliff Raven (Charles Bronson) who is on the run from the law after being falsely accused of murdering his fiancée.

Charles Bronson guest starred in two episodes of this Warner Bros.–produced western series which ran for four seasons on ABC-TV but never on a weekly basis. For its first two seasons the series ran alternately with *Cheyenne* (ABC-TV, 1955–63) starring Clint Walker; from 1959 to 1960 it alternated with *Bronco* (ABC-TV, 1958–62) starring Ty Hardin; and during its last season it was part of the *Cheyenne* trio of rotating series.

## *Suspicion* "Doomsday" (NBC-TV, December 16, 1957) 60 minutes B/W

*P:* Richard Lewis. *D:* Bernard Girard. *Sc:* Sy Bartlett. *Ph:* Bud Thackery. *Supv Ed:* Richard G. Wray. *Ed:* Bill Mosher. *AD:* John Lloyd. *Sd:* Melvin Metcalfe Sr. *Set Decorator:* James S. Redd. *Asst Dir:* Willard Sheldon. *Costume Supv:* Vincent Dee. *Makeup:* Jack Barron. *Hair Stylist:* Florence Bush.

**CAST:** Dan Duryea (McDillard), Robert Middleton (Banton), Charles Bronson (Cal), Edward Binns (Slavins), Robert Cornthwaite (Fitzgerald), Paul Birch (Big George), William Phipps (Vavick), Bing Russell (Mechanic), Ken Hooker (Cab Driver), Mike Ragan [Holly Bane] (Angy), Howard Wendell (Mr. Tucker), Naomi Perry (Bank Teller), Robert Whitney, Lomax Study, Edward Colmans, Martin Balk, Gregg Barton, George Dorstader, George Byrnes, Ray Gordon.

Using clever disguises, a master criminal (Dan Duryea) has not only avoided arrest, but only a close cohort (Robert Middleton) knows his true identity. Planning a $300,000 bank payroll heist, he poses as an insurance inspector and rehearses his partners so the robbery will be carried out successfully, only to be foiled by an unavoidable incident.

This Revue Studios–produced melodrama cast Charles Bronson as Cal, a level-headed criminal involved in the theft. The role has much suspense as he and another criminal (Mike Ragan) pose as street workers drilling in front of a bank as a prelude to the stickup. *Suspicion* was telecast by NBC-TV from 1957 to 1959.

## *Tales of Wells Fargo* "Butch Cassidy" (NBC-TV, October 13, 1958) 30 minutes B/W

*P:* Nat Holt & Earl Lyon.

**CAST:** Dale Robertson (Jim Hardie), Charles Bronson (Butch Cassidy), Jim [James] Coburn (Idaho), Barbara Pepper (Boxcar Annie), Murvyn Vye (Virgie).

When Wells Fargo undercover agent Jim Hardie (Dale Robertson) investigates a train robbery, his pal, former outlaw Butch Cassidy (Charles Bronson), insists on helping him so he will not fall into a trap.

*Tales of Wells Fargo* ran as a half-hour program on NBC-TV from 1957 to 1961 and as a one hour show in its last season on the network from 1961 to 1962.

## *Today* (NBC-TV, October 31, 1985) 120 minutes Color

In a ten minute interview with Jane Pauley, Charles Bronson discusses his new film, *Death Wish 3*, and denies any connection between the production and the New York City subway vigilante case involving Bernhard Goetz.

## *The Travels of Jaimie McPheeters* (ABC-TV, 1963-64) 60 minutes B/W

Based on Robert Lewis Taylor's Pulitzer Prize–winning novel, *The Travels of Jaimie McPheeters* was telecast on ABC-TV from September 15, 1963, to March 15, 1964, for a total of 26 one hour episodes. The program was aired in the 7:30 to 8:30 P.M., EST, time period. Charles Bronson joined the program in progress, taking the role of Linc Murdock in the tenth episode. Since the series' previous wagon master, played by Michael Whitney, had been killed saving the title character, Murdock's character took over the part after being introduced into the series' plotline. As with his previous work in

*Empire*, Bronson was brought in to boost the series' ratings and while he handled his part well the show lasted but one season. Each week the series found the denizens of a wagon train going to California in 1849 involved in various adventures and regular characters included Jaimie McPheeters (Kurt Russell), a 12-year-old boy, his reprobate father, Dr. Sardius McPheeters (Dan O'Herlihy), crooked partners John Murrell (James Westerfield) and Shep Boaggott (Sandy Kenyon), and pretty orphan Jenny (Donna Anderson). The Osmond Brothers played the sons of a religious couple, the Kissels (Mark Allen, Meg Wyllie). Another passenger was aristocratic Henry T. Coe (Hedley Mattingly) and his servant Othello (Vernet Allen III).

## "The Day of the Killer" (November 17, 1963)

**CAST:** Dan O'Herlihy (Dr. Sardius McPheeters), Kurt Russell (Jaimie McPheeters), Charles Bronson (Linc Murdock), Martin Landau.

Arriving at a river ford, members of the Beaver company wagon train come upon two dead men and frightened Linc Murdock (Charles Bronson), who is carrying a gun. By the end of this episode, the tenth in the series, Bronson's character of Linc Murdock had signed on as the company's new wagon master.

## "The Day of the Homeless" (December 8, 1963)

**CAST:** Dan O'Herlihy (Dr. Sardius McPheeters), Kurt Russell (Jaimie McPheeters), Charles Bronson (Linc Murdock), John Williams (Stephen Runcilman), Antoinette Bower (Nellie), Slim Pickens (Bly), Jimmy Baird (Bains), Milton Parsons (Orval Rheem).

With his father (Dan O'Herlihy) and Linc (Charles Bronson) gone off to a nearby town, Jaimie (Kurt Russell) meets an orphan boy (Jimmy Baird) and the men who are after him.

## "The Day of the Misfits" (December 15, 1963)

**CAST:** Dan O'Herlihy (Dr. Sardius McPheeters), Kurt Russell (Jaimie McPheeters), Charles Bronson (Linc Murdock), Henry Hull (Abel Menifee), Mariette Hartley (Hagar), Lee Van Cleef (Raoul Volta), John Van Dreelan (Dr. Armin Weeler), Mort Thompson (Jakins).

Seeking a midwife, two men arrive at the Beaver party camp and kidnap Doc McPheeters (Dan O'Herlihy).

## "The Day of the Toll Takers" (January 5, 1964)

**CAST:** Dan O'Herlihy (Dr. Sardius McPheeters), Kurt Russell (Jaimie McPheeters), Charles Bronson (Linc Murdock), Leif Erickson (Devlin), Mary Anderson (Hannah Devlin), Michael Petit (Tubal), Nick Georgiade (Cairo), Bern Hoffman (Piggot).

When the wagon train arrives at a river ford, Linc (Charles Bronson) learns that there is only one barge and the owner plans to charge an exorbitant toll.

## "The Day of the Wizard" (January 12, 1964)

**CAST:** Dan O'Herlihy (Dr. Sardius McPheeters), Kurt Russell (Jaimie McPheeters), Charles Bronson (Linc Murdock), Burgess Meredith (Sarcen), Joan Tompkins (Martha Pollux), Vitina Marcus (Irina), Crehan Denton (Colonel Ewen Pollux).

A traveling oracle (Burgess Meredith) arrives in camp and predicts that Jaimie (Kurt Russell) will murder his father (Dan O'Herlihy).

## "The Day of the Search" (January 19, 1964)

**CAST:** Dan O'Herlihy (Dr. Sardius McPheeters), Kurt Russell (Jaimie McPheeters), Charles Bronson (Linc Murdock), Keenan Wynn (Sam Parks), Charles McGraw (Dan Carver), David McCallum, Karl Swenson, Susan Seaforth.

Jaimie (Kurt Russell) comes upon three men: one behind a rock, a second man with a gun under a fallen tree, and the third a dead man.

## "The Day of the Haunted Trail" (January 26, 1964)

**CAST:** Dan O'Herlihy (Dr. Sardius McPheeters), Kurt Russell (Jaimie McPheeters), Charles Bronson (Linc Murdock), Royal Dano (James Weston), John Harmon (Huddlestone), Paul Baxley (Tracey), Abel Fernandez (Joseph), Mark Allen (Kissel), Meg Wyllie (Mrs. Kissel).

Unable to find a mountain pass and without water, the wagon train passengers are further plagued by the ten foot ghost of a monk.

## "The Day of the Tin Trumpet" (February 2, 1964)

**CAST:** Dan O'Herlihy (Dr. Sardius McPheeters), Kurt Russell (Jaimie McPheeters), Charles Bronson (Linc Murdock), Wallace Ford (Buffalo Pete), Antoinette Bower (Nellie), Arch Johnson (Lize Coggett), Rodolfo Acosta (Joe Oswego), Meg Wyllie (Mrs. Kissel), Doodles Weaver.

Three new passengers join the wagon train: a loud-mouth drunk, a man who has murdered a marshal and a wounded half breed.

## "The Day of the Lame Duck" (February 9, 1964)

**CAST:** Dan O'Herlihy (Dr. Sardius McPheeters), Kurt Russell (Jaimie McPheeters), Charles Bronson (Linc Murdock), Ruta Lee (Zoe Pigalle), Joe Mantell (Piggy Trewblood), Paul Langton (Beaufroy).

Jaimie (Kurt Russell) meets a former politician who plans to commit suicide.

## "The Day of the 12 Candles" (February 23, 1964)

**CAST:** Dan O'Herlihy (Dr. Sardius McPheeters), Kurt Russell (Jaimie McPheeters), Charles Bronson (Linc Murdock), Joan Freeman (Sarah Oliver), Paul Carr (Russ Oliver), Frank De Kova (Arapaho Chief), John Harmon (Wagontrainer), Richard Garland (Captain), Meg Wyllie (Mrs. Kissel), Mark Allen (Kissel).

Finding a murdered Indian woman, Jaimie (Kurt Russell) brings the woman's baby back to the Beaver company.

## "The Day of the Pretenders" (March 1, 1964)

**CAST:** Dan O'Herlihy (Dr. Sardius McPheeters), Kurt Russell (Jaimie McPheeters), Charles Bronson (Linc Murdock), Carl Esmond (Baron Pyrrhos), Steven Geray (Anton Berg), Michael Petit (Paul), James Griffith, Nick Georgiade.

A cultured man and his nephew join the wagon train but it is soon discovered there are men after them.

## "The Day of Reckoning" (March 15, 1964)

**CAST:** Kurt Russell (Jaimie McPheeters), Charles Bronson (Linc Murdock), Susan Oliver (Maria Macklin), John Fielder (Ives), Jan Merlin (Rance Macklin), Douglas Fowley (Knudson), Rayford Barnes (Dan Macklin), Ron Hagerthy (Carey Macklin).

Linc (Charles Bronson) and Jaimie (Kurt Russell) ride into a nearby town for supplies and there Linc sees his old love Maria (Susan Oliver), now the unhappy wife of town boss Rance Macklin (Jan Merlin), who hates Linc for causing him to lose an arm in a gun fight over the woman.

The final episode of the series, "The Day of the Reckoning," was expanded into a color feature film for European release. In it Russ Conway took over the role of Doc McPheeters. See Filmography under *Guns of Diablo* (1964).

Ironically, after *The Travels of Jaimie McPheeters* left the air it was replaced by reruns of Charles Bronson's previous series, *Empire.*

## *Treasury Men in Action* (ABC-TV) 30 minutes B/W

### "The Case of the Escaped Convict" (December 9, 1954)

**CAST:** Walter Graeza (The Chief), Charles Bronson, Aaron Spelling, Joyce McCluskey, Tom McKee.

Agents of the United States Customs and Treasury Department are on the trail of an escaped convict who is out for revenge. Also called "The Case of the Desperate Man."

### "The Case of the Deadly Dilemma" (March 24, 1955)

*P:* Robert Sloane. *EP:* Everett Rosenthall. *D:* Leigh Jason. *Sc:* Leonard Heideman. *Ph:* Lester Shorr. *Ed:* Irving Berlin. *Asst Dir:* Gilbert L. Kay. *Mus:* Melvyn Lenard. *Sets:* Ray Boltz. *Makeup:* Curly Batson. *Sp Eff:* Louis De Witt & Jack Rabin. *Wardrobe:* Jack Masters. *AD:* C. Daniel Hall.

**CAST:** Walter Graeza (The Chief), Charles Bronson (Frank Ames), Lewis Charles (Herb Carey), Clark Howat (Agent Dalton), Ralph Moody (Seth Ogden), Lillian Buyeff (Molly Ogden), Julian Upton (Chester Palmer), John Beradino (George Troy).

In his second of three appearances in this series, Charles Bronson played undercover Treasury Department agent Frank Ames, who has infiltrated Herb Carey's (Lewis Charles) gang, hoping to uncover his counterfeiting operation. First assigned as a numbers collector, Ames is tested by Carey who wants him to murder an elderly man (Ralph Moody) for his insurance, at the instigation of the man's much younger wife (Lillian Buyeff). Ames keeps stalling Carey in hopes of getting the goods on him and his gang, which includes cohort Chester Palmer (Julian Upton) and driver George Troy (John Beradino). Ames is finally able to lead his bosses to the whereabouts of Troy, eventually cracking the counterfeiting operation. When Carey tries to force Ames into killing the old man, the agent bests him in a scuffle, but the blow to the head Carey gave the old man leads to his demise.

### "The Case of the Shot in the Dark" (June 9, 1955)

**CAST:** Walter Graeza (The Chief), Charles Bronson.

A United States Customs Department official is shot and killed by a drug pusher who is smuggling heroin across the border from Mexico into the United States. This was Charles Bronson's third and final appearance in the series.

Running on ABC-TV from 1950 to 1955, *Treasury Men in Action* was based on actual cases from Treasury Department and U.S. Customs files. The program was filmed at American National Studios in Hollywood and later syndicated as *Federal Men*.

## *The Twilight Zone* "Two" (CBS-TV, September 15, 1961)

30 minutes B/W

*P:* Buck Houghton. *EP-Creator:* Rod Serling. *D-Sc:* Montgomery Pittman. *Ph:* George T. Clemens. *Ed:* Bill Mosher. *Mus:* Van Cleave. *AD:* George W. Davis & Phil Barber. *Prod Mgr:* Ralph W. Nelson. *Sd:* Franklin Milton & Bill Edmondson. *Set Decorator:* H. Web Arrowsmith. *Asst Dir:* E. Darrell Hallenbeck. *Casting:* Stalmaster–Lister. *Optical Eff:* Pacific Title.

**CAST:** Rod Serling (Host), Elizabeth Montgomery (The Woman), Charles Bronson (The Man).

Five years after the end of mankind's final war, two adversaries, a man (Charles Bronson) and a woman (Elizabeth Montgomery), meet in a deserted city.

Filmed at Metro-Goldwyn-Mayer Studios, "Two" was the first episode in *The Twilight Zone*'s third season. The science fiction anthology series ran on CBS-TV from 1959 to 1962 in a half-hour format before going to a full hour in 1963. In its final season in 1963-64 the show reverted back to a half-hour. Charles Aidman hosted a revival of the show on CBS-TV from 1985–87.

## *United States Marshal* "Pursuit" (Syndicated, May 26, 1959)

30 minutes B/W

*P:* John H. Auer. *EP-Creator:* Mort Briskin. *D:* Earl Bellamy. *Mus:* Ray Ellis.

**CAST:** John Bromfield (Marshal Frank Morgan), James Griffith (Deputy Tom Ferguson), Charles Bronson (The Apache Kid).

A United States marshal (John Bromfield) pursues an Apache Indian (Charles Bronson) who robbed a Cochise County, Arizona, bank.

Called *The Sheriff of Cochise* when it was syndicated from 1956 to 1958, this modern day western series had a total run of 156 episodes from 1956 to 1960. It was later retitled *Man from Cochise* and this episode is also called "The Apache Kid." The series was produced by Desilu/National Telefilm Association.

## *The Untouchables* "The Death Tree" (ABC-TV, February 15, 1962) 60 minutes B/W

*P:* Quinn Martin. *D:* Vincent McEveety. *Mus:* Harry Kronman. *Narrator:* Walter Winchell.

**CAST:** Robert Stack (Eliot Ness), Charles Bronson (Yonish Kolesku), Barbara Luna (Margot Bartok), Theodore Marcuse (Alex), Edward Asner (Felo Bartok), Richard Bakalyan (Benno), Paul Picerni (Lee Hobson), Nick Georgiade (Enrico Rossi), Abel Fernandez (William Youngfellow).

Treasury Department agent Eliot Ness (Robert Stack) and his officers are after a gang of gypsies involved in a bootlegging operation.

This quasi-documentary police drama about 1930s Chicago ran on ABC-TV from 1959 to 1963 and during its second season it was the eighth-ranked program in the Nielsen ratings.

## *Vacation Playhouse* "Luke and the Tenderfoot" (CBS-TV, August 13, 1965) 60 minutes B/W

*P-Sc:* Steve Fisher. *D:* Herman Hoffman.

**CAST:** Edgar Buchanan (Luke Herkimer), Carleton Carpenter (Pete Queen), Charles Bronson (John Wesley Hardin), Richard Jaeckel (The Man).

A dishonest wagon peddler (Edgar Buchanan) and his young friend (Carleton Carpenter) travel through the West meeting various characters, including outlaw John Wesley Hardin (Charles Bronson).

"Luke and the Tenderfoot" was a two-part unsold TV pilot which was shown on the summer series *Vacation Playhouse*. The first episode of this comedy aired August 6, 1965, and guest starred Michael Landon. It was directed by Montgomery Pittman.

## *The Virginian* (NBC-TV, 1962–70) 90 minutes Color

### "Nobility of Kings" (November 10, 1965)

**CAST:** Lee J. Cobb (Judge Henry Garth), James Drury (The Virginian), Doug McClure (Trampas), Randy Boone (Randy), Charles Bronson (Ben Justin), Lois Nettleton (Mary Justin), George Kennedy (Tom "Bear" Suchette), Vito Scotti (Gilley).

Loner Ben Justin (Charles Bronson) buys an angus bull to increase his herd but has troubles with neighboring ranchers as well as coming to grips with his own past. This segment of *The Virginian* was refashioned into a feature film for the European market. See Filmography under *Bull of the West* (1971).

### "The Reckoning" (September 13, 1967)

*P:* Cy Chermak, Winston Miller & Joel Rogosin. *EP:* Norman Macdonnell. *D:* Charles S. Dubin. *Sc:* Ed Waters. *Ph:* Alric Eden. *Mus:* Hal Mooney.

**CAST:** Charles Bickford (John Grainger), James Drury (The Virginian), Doug McClure (Trampas), Charles Bronson (Harge Talbot), Miriam Colon (Eva Talbot), Sara Lane (Elizabeth Grainger), Don Quine (Stacy Grainger).

Harge Talbot (Charles Bronson) and his men kidnap the niece (Sara Lane) of a big rancher (Charles Bickford) in order to lure the man's foreman (James Drury) who Harge thinks was responsible for sending him to jail years before. As Harge's wife (Miriam Colon) is about to have a baby, the girl helps her.

Like Charles Bronson's other appearance on *The Virginian* this episode was re-edited with another segment to produce a feature for European theatres. See Filmography under *The Meanest Men in the West* (1976).

## *Warner Bros. Presents* (ABC-TV, 1955–57) 60 minutes B/W

"Explosion!" (March 27, 1956)—see Filmography under *Explosion!* (1957).

### "Deep Freeze" (May 8, 1956)

*P-St:* Ellis St. Joseph. *D:* Jack Gage. *Sc:* Jack Patrick. *Ph:* Harold Stine. *Ed:* Robert Watts. *Mus:* David Buttolph.

**CAST:** Gerald Mohr (Dave), Charles Bronson (Vic), Jon Shepodd (Carl), Allison Hayes (Thela).

In his second appearance on this anthology series hosted by Gig Young, Charles Bronson played one of three scientists installing weather-recording devices in a remote region of the South Pole. A mysterious electronic force cuts off their radio contact with the outside world and the three men (Bronson, Gerald Mohr, Jon Shepodd) witness the arrival of a beautiful, scantily-clad alien (Allison Hayes) in a spacecraft. The alien not only places a spell over the trio but also has the power to resurrect the dead. Eventually she and her flying saucer are destroyed when she attempts to return home, leaving no trace of her earthly visit.

This strange small screen mixture of *The Thing* (1951), *The Man from Planet X* (1951) and *Devil Girl from Mars* (1954) is a forgotten science fiction thriller from the mid–1950s, enhanced by good work by Gerald Mohr, Charles Bronson and Jon Sheppod as the men faced with a seductive alien, portrayed by Allison Hayes, who had the lead in *The Attack of the 50 Foot Woman* (1958). *Variety* called it "interesting but bewildering."

## *Yancy Derringer* "Hell or High Water" (CBS-TV, February 19, 1959) 30 minutes B/W

*P:* Richard Sale & Mary Loos. *EP:* Don Sharpe & Warren Lewis. *AP:* A.E. Houghton Jr. *Mus:* Leon Klatzen.

**CAST:** Jock Mahoney (Yancy Derringer), X. Brands (Pahoo-Ka-Ta-Wah), Charles Bronson (Rogue Donovan), Patricia Cutts.

When a Mississippi River flood threatens a plantation, two crooks (Charles Bronson, Patricia Cutts) devise a scheme to obtain the land.

Jock Mahoney starred as a New Orleans troubleshooter in this series which ran for one season, 1958-59, on CBS-TV.

## *Yes Virginia, There Is a Santa Claus* (ABC-TV, December 8, 1991)—see Filmography under *Yes Virginia, There Is a Santa Claus* (1991).

## *You Don't Say* (NBC-TV, August 31–September 4, 1964) 30 minutes B/W

**CAST:** Tom Kennedy (Host).

Charles Bronson was one of the celebrity guests on five segments of this game show in which two teams, consisting of a contestant and a celebrity on each, try to guess the names of noted people.

The series ran weekdays on NBC-TV from 1963 to 1969 and during the first four months of 1964 there was a prime-time version each Tuesday night from 8:30 to 9:00 P.M., EST. The series also had a brief run in 1975, again with Tom Kennedy as host, and during the 1978-79 season Jim Peck hosted a syndicated version.

## *Your First Impression* (NBC-TV, January 8, 1964) 30 minutes B/W

Charles Bronson made a guest appearance on this daytime game show which identified a mystery guest.

# Chronologies (Film and Television)

Films are in order of release. Television appearances are in order of air date.

## FILMS

*U.S.S. Teakettle (You're in the Navy Now)* 1951
*The People Against O'Hara* 1951
*The Mob* 1951
*Red Skies of Montana* 1952
*My Six Convicts* 1952
*The Marrying Kind* 1952
*Pat and Mike* 1952
*Diplomatic Courier* 1952
*Bloodhounds of Broadway* 1952
*Torpedo Alley* 1953
*The Clown* 1953
*House of Wax* 1953
*Miss Sadie Thompson* 1953
*Crime Wave* 1954
*Riding Shotgun* 1954
*Tennessee Champ* 1954
*Apache* 1954
*Drum Beat* 1954
*Vera Cruz* 1954
*Big House U.S.A.* 1955
*Target Zero* 1955
*Jubal* 1956
*Explosion!* 1957
*Run of the Arrow* 1957
*Ten North Frederick* 1958
*Gang War* 1958
*Showdown at Boot Hill* 1958
*Machine Gun Kelly* 1958
*When Hell Broke Loose* 1958
*Never So Few* 1959
*The Magnificent Seven* 1960
*Master of the World* 1961
*A Thunder of Drums* 1961
*X-15* 1962
*Kid Galahad* 1962
*The Great Escape* 1963
*4 for Texas* 1963
*Guns of Diablo* 1964
*This Rugged Land* 1965
*The Sandpiper* 1965
*Battle of the Bulge* 1965
*This Property Is Condemned* 1966
*The Dirty Dozen* 1967
*Guns for San Sebastian* 1968
*Adieu l'Ami Villa Rides!* 1968
*C'Era una Volta il West (Once Upon a Time in the West)* 1969

*Twinky (Lola)* 1969
*Le Passager de la Pluie (Rider on the Rain)* 1969
*You Can't Win 'Em All* 1970
*Città Violenta (The Family)* 1970
*Bull of the West* 1971
*De la Part des Copains (Cold Sweat)* 1971
*Quelqu'un Derrière la Porte (Someone Behind the Door)* 1971
*Soleil Rouge (Red Sun)* 1971
*Chato's Land* 1972
*The Mechanic* 1972
*The Valachi Papers* 1972
*Valdez il Mezzosangue (Chino)* 1973
*The Stone Killer* 1973
*Mr. Majestyk* 1974
*Death Wish* 1974
*Breakout* 1975
*Hard Times* 1975
*Breakheart Pass* 1976
*St. Ives* 1976
*From Noon Till Three* 1976
*The Meanest Men in the West* 1976
*Raid on Entebbe* 1977
*The White Buffalo* 1977
*The Wild West* 1977
*Telefon* 1977
*Love and Bullets* 1979
*Caboblanco* 1980
*Borderline* 1980
*Death Hunt* 1981
*Real Heroes* 1981
*Death Wish II* 1982
*10 to Midnight* 1983
*The Evil That Men Do* 1984
*Death Wish 3* 1985
*Act of Vengeance* 1986
*Murphy's Law* 1986
*Assassination* 1987
*Death Wish 4: The Crackdown* 1987
*Messenger of Death* 1988
*Kinjite: Forbidden Subjects* 1989
*The Indian Runner* 1991
*Yes Virginia, There Is a Santa Claus* 1991
*The Sea Wolf* 1993
*Donato and Daughter (Dead to Rights)* 1993
*Death Wish V: The Face of Death* 1994
*A Family of Cops* 1995
*Breach of Faith: A Family of Cops II* 1997
*Family of Cops III* 1999

# Television Appearances

*The Doctor*, "The Guest" October 26, 1952
*Biff Baker, U.S.A.*, "Koblen" November 5, 1952; "Alpine Assignment" November 12, 1952
*The Roy Rogers Show*, "Knockout" December 28, 1952
*The Doctor*, "Take the Odds" January 18, 1953
*Four Star Playhouse*, "The Witness" October 22, 1953
*The Joe Palooka Story*, "Two Rings for Eddie" April 10, 1954; "Neutral Corner" May 8, 1954
*Adventure in Java*, July 8, 1954
*The Lineup*, "The Paisley Gang" October 1, 1954
*Medic*, "My Brother Joe" October 25, 1954
*Treasury Men in Action*, "The Case of the Escaped Convict" December 9, 1954

*Lux Video Theatre*, "A Bell for Adano" February 10, 1955
*Stage 7*, "Debt of Honor" February 20, 1955
*Public Defender*, "Cornered" March 24, 1955
*Treasury Men in Action*, "The Case of the Deadly Dilemma" March 24, 1955
*The Man Behind the Badge*, "The Case of the Invisible Mark" April 2, 1955 (N.Y.C.)
*Stage 7*, "The Time of Day" May 29, 1955
*Treasury Men in Action*, "The Case of the Shot in the Dark" June 9, 1955
*Pepsi-Cola Playhouse*, "The Woman in the Mine" June 12, 1955
*Crusader*, "A Boxing Match" October 21, 1955
*Cavalcade Theatre*, "A Chain of Hearts" November 1, 1955
*G.E. Theatre*, "Prosper's Old Mother" November 20, 1955
*Alfred Hitchcock Presents*, "And So Died Riabouchinska" February 12, 1956
*Crusader*, "Freezeout" February 17, 1956
*Medic*, "Who Search for Truth" February 27, 1956
*Alfred Hitchcock Presents*, "There Was an Old Woman" March 18, 1956
*Warner Bros. Presents*, "Explosion!" March 27, 1956; "Deep Freeze" May 8, 1956
*Gunsmoke*, "The Killer" May 26, 1956
*Studio 57*, "Outpost" January 3, 1957
*The Millionaire*, "The Story of Jerry Bell" February 27, 1957
*Hey, Jeannie!*, "Jeannie, the Police Woman" March 2, 1957
*Richard Diamond, Private Detective*, "The Pete Rocco Case" September 9, 1957
*Have Gun—Will Travel*, "The Outlaw" September 21, 1957
*Colt .45*, "Young Gun" December 13, 1957
*Suspicion*, "Doomsday" December 16, 1957
*The Court of Last Resort*, "The Steve Hrdlika Case" January 24, 1958
*Sugarfoot*, "Man Wanted" February 18, 1958
*M Squad*, "Fight" April 18, 1958
*Sugarfoot*, "The Bullet and the Cross" May 27, 1958
*Have Gun—Will Travel*, "The Gentleman" September 27, 1958
*Man with a Camera*, "Second Avenue Assassin" October 10, 1958
*Tales of Wells Fargo*, "Butch Cassidy" October 13, 1958
*Man with a Camera*, "The Warning" October 17, 1958; "Profile of a Killer" October 24, 1958
*Gunsmoke*, "The Long Rifle" November 1, 1958
*Man with a Camera*, "Turntable" November 7, 1958; "Close-Up on Violence" November 14, 1958; "Double Negative" November 21, 1958; "Another Barrier" November 28, 1958; "Blind Spot" December 5, 1958; "Two Strings of Pearls" December 12, 1958; "Six Faces of Satan" December 19, 1958; "Lady on the Loose" December 26, 1958; "Last Portrait"

January 2, 1959; "Face of Murder" January 9, 1959; "Mute Evidence" January 16, 1959; "The Big Squeeze" January 23, 1959

*Yancy Derringer*, "Hell or High Water" February 19, 1959

*United States Marshal*, "Pursuit" May 26, 1959

*Playhouse 90*, "Rank and File" May 28, 1959

*Man with a Camera*, "The Killer" October 19, 1959; "Eye Witness" October 26, 1959; "The Man Below" November 2, 1959; "Black Light" November 9, 1959; "The Positive Negative" November 16, 1959; "Missing" November 23, 1959; "Light Target" December 7, 1959; "Girl in the Dark" December 14, 1959; "The Bride" December 21, 1959; "The Picture War" January 4, 1960; "Touch Off" January 11, 1960; "Hot Ice Cream" January 25, 1960; "Fragment of Murder" February 1, 1960; "Kangaroo Court" February 8, 1960

*Laramie*, "Street of Hate" March 1, 1960

*Playhouse 90*, "The Cruel Day" March 7, 1960

*Hennesey*, "Hennesey at La Gunn" October 17, 1960

*The Aquanauts*, "The Cave Divers" December 7, 1960

*Riverboat*, "Zig Zag" December 26, 1960

*G.E. Theatre*, "Memory in White" January 9, 1961

*Alcoa Presents*, "The Last Round" January 10, 1961

*The Islanders*, "The Generous Politician" January 15, 1961

*The Loretta Young Show*, "Wood Lot" March 26, 1961

*Laramie*, "Run of the Hunted" April 4, 1961

*Hennesey*, "The Nogoodnik" April 17, 1961

*The Twilight Zone*, "Two" September 15, 1961

*Have Gun—Will Travel*, "A Proof of Love" October 14, 1961; "Ben Jalisco" November 18, 1961

*Cain's Hundred*, "Dead Load" November 21, 1961

*The New Breed*, "The Valley of the Three Charlies" December 5, 1961

*Adventures in Paradise*, "Survival" December 31, 1961

*Alfred Hitchcock Presents*, "The Woman Who Wanted to Live" February 6, 1962

*The Untouchables*, "The Death Tree" February 15, 1962

*The Bob Newhart Show*, April 11, 1962

*Here's Hollywood*, August 8, 1962

*Empire*, "The Day the Empire Stood Still" September 25, 1962

*Have Gun—Will Travel*, "Brotherhood" January 5, 1963

*Empire*, "Seven Days on Rough Street" February 26, 1963; "A House in Order" March 5, 1963; "Down There, the World" March 12, 1963; "Burnout" March 19, 1963; "Hidden Asset" March 26, 1963; "Arrow in the Sky" April 9, 1963; "Nobody Dies on Saturday" April 16, 1963; "65 Miles Is a Long, Long

Way" April 23, 1963; "Duel for Eight Wheels" April 30, 1963; "Between Friday and Monday" May 7, 1963; "The Convention" May 14, 1963

*Dr. Kildare*, "Who Ever Heard of a Two-Headed Doll?" September 26, 1963

*The Travels of Jaimie McPheeters*, "The Day of the Killer" November 17, 1963; "The Day of the Homeless" December 8, 1963; "The Day of the Misfits" December 15, 1963; "The Day of the Toll Takers" January 5, 1964;

*Your First Impression* January 8, 1964

*The Travels of Jaimie McPheeters*, "The Day of the Wizard" January 12, 1964; "The Day of the Search" January 19, 1964; "The Day of the Haunted Trail" January 26, 1964; "The Day of the Tin Trumpet" February 2, 1964; "The Day of the Lame Duck" February 9, 1964; "The Day of the 12 Candles" February 23, 1964; "The Day of the Pretenders" March 1, 1964; "The Day of Reckoning" March 15, 1964

*You Don't Say,* August 31–September 4, 1964

*Bonanza*, "The Underdog" December 13, 1964

*Combat!* "Heritage" April 13, 1965

*Vacation Playhouse*, "Luke and the Tenderfoot" August 13, 1965

*The Big Valley*, "Earthquake" November 10, 1965

*The Virginian*, "Nobility of Kings" November 10, 1965

*Rawhide*, "Duel at Daybreak" November 16, 1965

*The Legend of Jesse James*, "The Chase" March 7, 1966

*The FBI*, "The Animal" April 17, 1966

*The Fugitive,* "The One That Got Away" January 10, 1967

*The Virginian*, "The Reckoning" September 13, 1967

*Dundee and the Culhane*, "The Cat in the Bag Brief" September 20, 1967

*Dinah!*, 1970s

*Jeanne Wolf*, October 14, 1976

*All-Star Tribute to John Wayne*, November 26, 1976

*Raid on Entebbe*, January 9, 1977

*Catastrophe! No Safe Place*, 1980–81

*Night of 100 Stars II*, March 10, 1985

*Today*, October 31, 1985

*Act of Vengeance*, April 20, 1986

*All-Star Party for Clint Eastwood*, December 15, 1986

*Happy Birthday, Hollywood*, May 18, 1987

*Good Morning America*, February 3, 1989

*All-Star Tribute to Elizabeth Taylor*, March 9, 1989

*Sinatra 75: The Best Is Yet to Come*, December 16, 1990

*Yes Virginia, There Is a Santa Claus*, December 8, 1991

*The Sea Wolf*, April 18, 1993

*Donato and Daughter*, September 21, 1993

*100 Years of the Hollywood Western*, November 25, 1994

*A Family of Cops*, November 26, 1995

*Breach of Faith: A Family of Cops II*, February 2, 1997

*Family of Cops III* January 12, 1999

# Video Releases

## Feature Films

Films are listed in alphabetical order followed by the video companies which have released them. Some titles may be out of print.

*Act of Vengeance* (1986) HBO Home Video, MCA/Cineplex Odeon

*Adieu l'Ami* (1968) ETC (as *Farewell Friend*); Critics Choice Video, Mntex, Monterey Home Video, MPI Home Video, Video Treasures (all as *Honor Among Thieves*)

*Apache* (1954) Playhouse Video

*Assassination* (1987) Media Home Entertainment, Video Treasures

*Battle of the Bulge* (1965) Warner Home Video

*Borderline* (1980) Avid, CBS/Fox Video

*Breakheart Pass* (1976) CBS/Fox Video, MGM/UA Home Entertainment

*Breakout* (1975) Columbia/Tristar Home Video, Goodtimes Entertainment, RCA/Columbia Home Video

*Bull of the West* (1971) Mntex (as *Hot Lead*); Front Row Entertainment (as *Hot Lead*, with *Guns of Diablo*)

*Caboblanco* (1980) Media Home Entertainment

*C'Era una Volta il West* (1969) Paramount Home Video (as *Once Upon a Time in the West*)

*Chato's Land* (1972) MGM/UA Home Video, Mntex, Video Treasures

*Città Violenta* (1970) ETC (as *Violent City*); JTC, MPI Home Video (both as *The Family*)

*The Clown* (1953) MGM/UA Home Video

*Death Hunt* (1981) CBS/Fox Video, Fox Video

*Death Wish* (1974) Paramount Home Video, MGM/UA Home Video

*Death Wish II* (1982) Warner Home Video, Goodtimes Entertainment

*Death Wish 3* (1985) MGM/UA Home Video

*Death Wish 4: The Crackdown* (1987) Media Home Entertainment, Video Treasures

*Death Wish V: The Face of Death* (1994) Vidmark Entertainment, C/FP Video
*De la Part des Copains* (1970) Mntex, Moore Video, United American Video, Video Gems; Front Row Entertainment (with *Chino* and *Someone Behind the Door*), Quality Video (with *Chino*); United American Video (in *Tough Guys*, a four feature film package); all as *Cold Sweat*
*Diplomatic Courier* (1952) 20th Century–Fox
*The Dirty Dozen* (1967) MGM/UA Home Video
*Donato and Daughter* (1993) Vidmark Entertainment (as *Dead to Rights*)
*Drum Beat* (1954) United Home Video
*The Evil That Men Do* (1984) Columbia/Tristar Home Video, Goodtimes Entertainment, RCA/Columbia Home Video
*A Family of Cops* (1995) Vidmark Entertainment
*4 for Texas* (1963) Warner Home Video, Facets Multimedia
*From Noon Till Three* (1976) MGM/UA Home Entertainment
*The Great Escape* (1963) MGM/UA Home Video
*Guns of Diablo* (1964) Ace Video, MNTEX, Video Treasures; Front Row Entertainment (with *Hot Lead*)
*Hard Times* (1975) RCA/Columbia Home Video, Goodtimes Entertainment
*House of Wax* (1953) Warner Home Video
*The Indian Runner* (1991) Columbia/Tristar Home Video, MGM/UA Home Entertainment
*Jubal* (1956) RCA/Columbia Home Video
*Kid Galahad* (1962) MGM/UA Home Video
*Kinjite: Forbidden Subjects* (1989) Cannon Video, MGM/UA Home Entertainment
*Love and Bullets* (1979) Avid, Key Video
*Machine Gun Kelly* (1958) RCA/Columbia Home Video
*The Magnificent Seven* (1960) MGM/UA Home Video
*The Marrying Kind* (1952) Columbia Home Video
*Master of the World* (1961) Orion Home Video, Warner Home Video
*The Meanest Men in the West* (1976) MCA/Universal Home Video
*The Mechanic* (1972) CBS/Fox Video
*Messenger of Death* (1988) Media Home Entertainment, Video Treasures
*Miss Sadie Thompson* (1954) RCA/Columbia Home Video
*Mr. Majestyk* (1974) MGM/UA Home Video
*Murphy's Law* (1986) Media Home Entertainment, Video Treasures
*Never So Few* (1959) MGM/UA Home Entertainment
*La Passager de la Pluie* (1969) Facets

Multimedia, Monterey Home Video, Star Classics; all as *Rider on the Rain*

*Pat and Mike* (1952) MGM/UA Home Video

*Quelqu'un Derrière la Porte* (1971) Star Classics, Unicorn Video, Video Treasures; Front Row Entertainment (with *Chino* and *Cold Sweat*); Simitar Entertainment, United American Video (both with *Chino* and *Cold Sweat*); all as *Someone Behind the Door*

*Raid on Entebbe* (1977) HBO Home Video

*Run of the Arrow* (1957) United Home Video

*St. Ives* (1976) Warner Home Video

*The Sandpiper* (1965) MGM/UA Home Video

*The Sea Wolf* (1993) Turner Home Entertainment

*Showdown at Boot Hill* (1958) Republic Pictures Home Video, Spotlite Video

*Soleil Rouge* (1971) Video Gems, United Home Video (both as *Red Sun*)

*The Stone Killer* (1973) RCA/Columbia Home Video

*Telefon* (1977) MGM/UA Home Video

*10 to Midnight* (1983) MGM/UA Home Video

*This Property Is Condemned* (1966) Paramount Home Video

*This Rugged Land* (1965) Mntex (as *Blind Justice*)

*Twinky* (1969) Facets Multimedia, Moore Video, United American Video; all as *Lola*

*The Valachi Papers* (1972) Video Communications Inc. (VCI), ETC

*Valdez il Mezzosangue* (1973) Front Row Entertainment, Mntex, MPI Home Video, Moore Video, Video Treasures; quality Video (with *Cold Sweat*); Simitar Entertainment, United American Video (both with *Cold Sweat* and *Someone Beyond the Door*); all as *Chino*

*Vera Cruz* (1954) Key Video

*Villa Rides!* (1968) Kartes Video Communications

*When Hell Broke Loose* (1958) Paramount Home Video

*The White Buffalo* (1977) MGM/UA Home Entertainment

*The Wild West* (1977) Starvision, Twin Tower Enterprises

# Television Shows

Listed are Charles Bronson's television shows available on video. Given is the series, episode title and company releasing the video. Telefeatures are not included since they are listed in the movie video listing. Some titles may be out of print.

*Alcoa Presents* "The Last Round" Panda Productions

*Biff Baker, U.S.A.* "Alpine Assignment" Moviecraft

*The Big Valley* "Earthquake" Vid America
*Bonanza* "The Underdog" Republic Home Video
*Catastrophe! No Safe Place* Star Classics
*Combat!* "Heritage" Goodtimes Entertainment
*The Court of Last Resort* "The Steve Hrdlika Case" Buttle Broadcasting
*Empire* "The Day the Empire Stood Still" Mntex (as *Mean Justice*)
*Four Star Playhouse* "The Witness" Facets Multimedia, Rhino Home Video; Discount Video, Foothill Video, Nostalgia Family Video (as *Ford Star Theatre*)
*The Fugitive* "The One That Got Away" Nu Ventures Video
*Have Gun—Will Travel* "Ben Jalisco," "Brotherhood," "The Outlaw" Columbia House
*The Joe Palooka Story* "Two Rings for Eddie" Kid Klassics
*Medic* "My Brother Joe" Panda Productions, Videoplex
*Public Defender* "Cornered" MPI Home Video
*The Roy Rogers Show* "Knockout" Video West
*The Travels of Jaimie McPheeters* "The Day of Reckoning" Ace Video, Front Row Video, Mntex, Video Treasures (as *Guns of Diablo*)
*Treasury Men in Action* "The Case of the Deadly Dilemma" Rhino Home Video (as *Federal Men*)
*The Twilight Zone* "Two" CBS/Fox Video, Facets Multimedia, Fox Video
*The Virginian* "A Nobility of Kings" Front Row Entertainment, Mntex (reworked as *Hot Lead*); "The Reckoning" MCA/Universal Home Video (reworked as *The Meanest Men in the West*)

# Bibliography

Andrews, Emma. *The Films of Charles Bronson*. London: Barnden Castell Williams, 1975.

Brooks, Tim, and Marsh, Earle. *The Complete Directory of Prime Time Network Shows 1946–Present* (4th edition). New York: Ballantine, 1988.

Carter, E. Graydon. "Yeah, Bronson Would Love to Walk Away from a Fight or Two." *TV Guide*, April 19, 1986.

"Charles Bronson, The New King of the Movies." *New York Daily News Sunday Magazine*, February 11, 1973.

*The Death Wish Page*. geocities.com/Hollywood/Set/5040. 1999.

Downing, David. *Charles Bronson*. London: W.H. Allen, 1982.

Harbinson, W.A. *Bronson!* London: W.H. Allen, 1975.

Herx, Henry, and Zaza, Tony. *The Family Guide to Movies on Video*. New York: Crossroads, 1988.

Hoppe, Andreas. *Charles Bronson Homepage*. lavender.fortunecity.com/mitchum/513/. 1999.

Hunter, Allen. *Chambers Films Facts*. Edinburgh: Chambers, 1993.

Ireland, Jill. *Life Lines*. New York: Warner, 1989.

_____. *Life Wish*. New York: Little, Brown, 1987.

Lentz, Harris M., III. *Television Westerns Episode Guide: All United States Series, 1949–1996*. Jefferson, N.C.: McFarland, 1997.

_____. *Western and Frontier Film and Television Credits: 1903–1995*. Jefferson, N.C.: McFarland, 1996.

Menton, Lynn. *Movie Guide for Puzzled Parents*. New York: Delta, 1984.

Murphy, Mary. "Yes, Virginia, There Is a Charles Bronson." *TV Guide*, December 7, 1991.

Pitts, Michael R. "Charles Bronson: A Filmography." *Classic Images*, no. 85 (July 1982); no. 86 (August 1982).

Royce, Bill. "Charles Bronson—The World's Number One Box Office Star ... at 50?" *Rona Barrett's Hollywood*, March 1973.

Scheuer, Steven H. *The Complete Guide to Videocassette Movies*. New York: Henry Holt, 1987.

Setbon, Philippe. *Bronson*. Paris: Editions PAC, 1977, 1983.

Steinberg, Cobbett. *TV Facts*. New York: Facts on File, 1985.

Terrace, Vincent. *The Complete Encyclopedia of Television Programs 1947–1976*. South Brunswick, N.J.: A.S. Barnes & Co., 1976.

_____. *Television Specials: 3,201 Entertainment Spectaculars, 1939 through 1993*. Jefferson, N.C.: McFarland, 1995.

*TV Guide*. 1952–1999.
*Variety*. 1951–1997.
Vermilye, Jerry. *The Films of Charles Bronson*. Secaucus, N.J.: Citadel, 1980.
*The Video Source Book*. Detroit: Gale Research, 1996.
Whitney, Steven. *Charles Bronson Superstar*. New York: Dell, 1975.

# Index